Fodor's 95
Arizona

D1343024

PRAISE FOR FODOR'S GUIDES

"Fodor's guides . . . are an admirable blend of the cultural and the practical."
—The Washington Post

"Researched by people chosen because they lived or have lived in the country, well-written, and with good historical sections . . . Obligatory reading for millions of tourists."
—The Independent, *London*

"Usable, sophisticated restaurant coverage, with an emphasis on good value."
—Andy Birsh, Gourmet restaurant columnist, quoted by Gannett News Service

"Packed with dependable information."
—Atlanta Journal Constitution

"Fodor's always delivers high quality . . . thoughtfully presented . . . thorough."
—Houston Post

"Valuable because of their comprehensiveness."
—Minneapolis Star-Tribune

Fodor's Travel Publications, Inc.
New York • Toronto • London • Sydney • Auckland

Fodor's Arizona

Editor: Marcy Pritchard
Editorial Contributors: Suzanne Carmichael, Echo Garrett, William Hafford, Mark Hein, Edie Jarolim, Laura M. Kidder, Bevin McLaughlin, Trudy Thompson Rice, Nancy van Itallie
Creative Director: Fabrizio LaRocca
Cartographers: David Lindroth, Mapping Specialists
Illustrator: Karl Tanner
Cover Photograph: Peter Guttman

Design: Vignelli Associates

Special Sales

Contents

Maps

Foreword

Many people have assisted in preparing this guide. Special thanks go to Marjorie Magnusson of the Arizona Office of Tourism, whose helpfulness is matched only by her cheerfulness, and to Jean E. McNight of the Tucson Convention & Visitors Bureau. Thanks also to Frank Miller of the Sedona Chamber of Commerce and L. Greer Price, Information Specialist at Grand Canyon National Park.

While every care has been taken to ensure the accuracy of the information in this guide, the passage of time will always bring change, and consequently the publisher cannot accept responsibility for errors that may occur.

All prices and opening times quoted here are based on information supplied to us at press time. Hours and admission fees may change, however, and the prudent traveler will avoid inconvenience by calling ahead.

Fodor's wants to hear about your travel experiences, both pleasant and unpleasant. When a hotel or restaurant fails to live up to its billing, let us know and we will investigate the complaint and revise our entries where the facts warrant it.

Send your letters to the editors of Fodor's Travel Publications, 201 E. 50th Street, New York, NY 10022.

Highlights'95 and Fodor's Choice

Highlights '95

Record cold temperatures on the East Coast, earthquakes in California, negative publicity about Florida, and a resurgence of interest in western films all combined to help Arizona tourism skyrocket in 1994. The boom is projected to continue through 1995 and beyond.

As a result, the state has had to cope with some of the side effects of success. One of the nation's most popular national parks, the **Grand Canyon** welcomes almost 5 million visitors annually; each day some 6,500 cars attempt to fit into 2,000 parking spaces at the South Rim. To deal with the overcrowding, which has led to pollution as well as inconvenience, Interior Secretary Bruce Babbitt has proposed closing the park to private vehicles and setting up buses and light-rail networks in satellite "gateway villages." Others have suggested requiring permits for visits. These long-term proposals won't be enacted anytime soon, but a reservation system for cars will likely be in place by the summer of 1995.

In the meantime, other natural attractions in Arizona are being readied for tourists. In 1967, some of the world's finest live limestone caves were discovered near Benson in southeast Arizona; more than 2 miles long, the system contains an unusually large variety of multicolored formations. To ensure that workers don't damage the fragile underground environment, efforts to prepare **Kartchner Caverns** to open as Arizona's next state park are proceeding slowly. Though slated to debut by 1995, the park is more likely to open in 1996.

By the fall of 1995, repeat visitors should find a new face on an old sight. As part of the nationwide Main Street Foundation urban-renewal project, historic downtown **Flagstaff** is being restored. Such structures as the 1888 Babbitt building, owned by the prominent Arizona family, are being returned to their former grandeur, and historical details such as gaslamp-style streetlights and brick tiles are being installed. Public rest rooms and a new $1.2-million underground parking facility will help visitors enjoy their visit to the past with the comfort of modern amenities.

Sports are a draw for visitors and residents alike, and football festivities loom large in Arizona's future. January 1, 1996, will mark the 25th anniversary of college football's Fiesta Bowl at Tempe's Sun Devil Stadium, and November and December 1995 will see celebrations throughout the state—everything from televised parades and battles of the bands to black-tie balls. Also at Sun Devil Stadium, the National Football League's **Super Bowl XXX** will inspire lots of hoopla before the January 28, 1996, game.

Fodor's Choice

No two people will agree on what makes a perfect vacation, but it's fun and helpful to know what others think. We hope you'll have a chance to experience some of Fodor's Choices in Arizona. For detailed information about each entry, refer to the appropriate chapter.

Activities

A mule ride or hike to the bottom of the Grand Canyon

A raft trip on the Colorado, white water or quiet water, Grand Canyon

The East Rim Tour, along the Grand Canyon's South Rim

Lake Powell excursion to Rainbow Bridge, The Northeast

Picnic in Monument Valley, The Northeast

Hiking tour to Betatakin Ruin, Navajo National Monument, The Northeast

Hiking into Canyon de Chelly National Monument, The Northeast

Looking through the telescope at Lowell Observatory, North-Central Arizona

Hiking along the rim of a volcano at Sunset Crater National Monument, North-Central Arizona

A Jeep ride through the red rocks of Sedona, North-Central Arizona

An early morning walk through the Desert Botanical Gardens, Phoenix

Climbing Squaw Peak at sunset, Phoenix

Casa Grande Ruins National Monument, Central Arizona

San Xavier del Bac Mission, Tucson

Arizona–Sonora Desert Museum, Tucson

The Copper Queen Mine, Bisbee, Southern Arizona

Scenic Drives

The 210-mile drive from the South Rim to the North Rim, Grand Canyon

The dirt-road drive to Point Sublime, North Rim, Grand Canyon

West Rim Drive, South Rim, Grand Canyon

Petrified Forest National Monument—U.S. 163 from Kayenta to the Goosenecks of the San Juan River, The Northeast

AZ 264 across the Hopi Mesas, The Northeast

Flagstaff to Sedona via Oak Creek Canyon, North-Central Arizona

Sedona to Jerome, North-Central Arizona

Phoenix to Prescott and Wickenburg, Phoenix and Central Arizona

Along I–10 east of Benson through Texas Canyon, Southern Arizona

Tucson to Kitt Peak, Tucson and Southern Arizona

Shopping

Cameron Trading Post, Grand Canyon

Desert View Trading Post, South Rim, Grand Canyon

Hubbell Trading Post, The Northeast

Navajo Arts and Crafts Enterprises in Cameron and Window Rock, The Northeast

Coconino Center for the Arts, Flagstaff, North-Central Arizona

Tlaquepaque Mall, Sedona, North-Central Arizona

The Mercado and Arizona Center, Phoenix

The Heard Museum gift shop, Phoenix

Main Street, Scottsdale, Central Arizona

Fourth Avenue, Tucson

San Xavier Plaza, Tucson

Tubac, Southern Arizona

Dining

Vincent's on Camelback, Phoenix (*$$$$*)

El Tovar Dining Room, South Rim, Grand Canyon (*$$$–$$$$*)

La Hacienda, Scottsdale, Central Arizona (*$$$–$$$$*)

Janos, Tucson (*$$$–$$$$*)

Compass Room, Phoenix (*$$$*)

Heartline Café, Sedona, North-Central Arizona (*$$–$$$*)

Brix Grill & Wine Bar, Flagstaff (*$$*)

Grand Canyon Lodge Dining Room, North Rim, Grand Canyon (*$$*)

Rustler's Rooste, Phoenix and Central Arizona (*$$*)

Café Poca Cosa, Tucson (*$–$$*)

Adrian's, Phoenix (*$*)

Jack's Original Bar-B-Q, Tucson (*$*)

Lodging

Enchantment Resort, Sedona, North-Central Arizona (*$$$$*)

Sheraton Tucson El Conquistador, Tucson (*$$$$*)

Arizona Inn, Tucson (*$$$–$$$$*)

Briar Patch Inn, Sedona (*$$$–$$$$*)

The Buttes, Phoenix and Central Arizona (*$$$–$$$$*)

The Pointe Hilton on South Mountain, Phoenix (*$$$–$$$$*)

El Tovar Hotel, South Rim, Grand Canyon (*$$$–$$$$*)

Goulding's Lodging at Monument Valley, The Northeast (*$$$*)

Wahweap Lodge at Lake Powell, The Northeast (*$$$*)

Best Western Executive Park, Phoenix (*$$*)

Cameron Trading Post at Cameron, Grand Canyon (*$$*)

Grand Canyon Lodge, North Rim, Grand Canyon (*$$*)

Sky Ranch Lodge, Sedona, North-Central Arizona (*$–$$*)

Casa Tierra Bed & Breakfast, Tucson (*$–$$*)

Inn at Four Ten, Flagstaff (*$–$$*)

Motel 6 Scottsdale, Central Arizona (*$*)

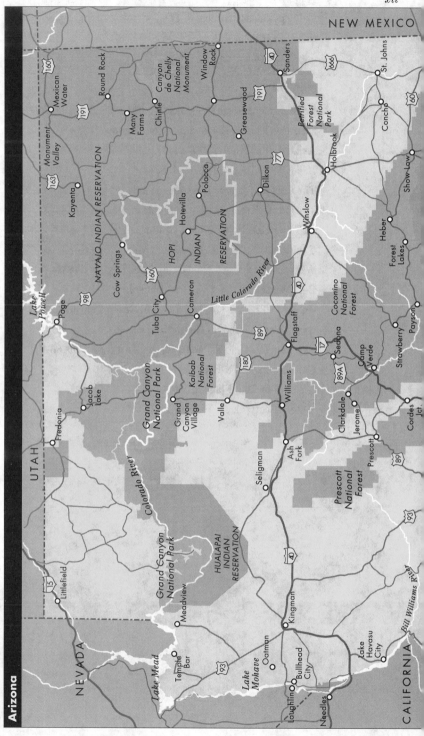

Arizona

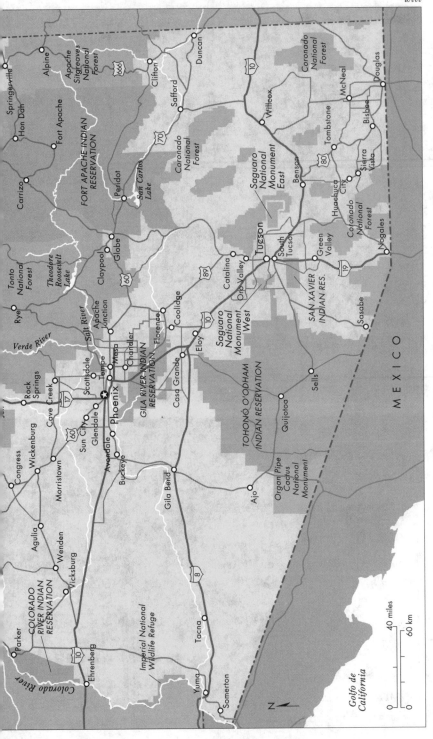

The United States

World Time Zones

Numbers below vertical bands relate each zone to Greenwich Mean Time (0 hrs.).
Local times frequently differ from these general indications,
as indicated by light-face numbers on map.

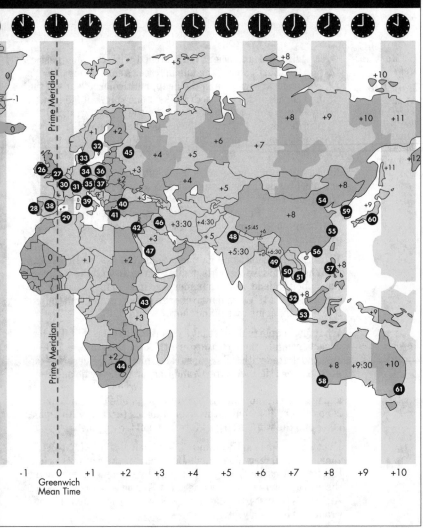

Introduction

By Mark Hein

Mark Hein is an editor and a writer in the features department of the Arizona Republic.

Arizona is an ancient land, etched with the long past of the Earth and of the human race. Aeons of our planet's story are written in the deep, multicolored walls of the Grand Canyon and the cathedral-like stone spires of Monument Valley. Ages of human history echo in the hidden grandeur of Canyon de Chelly, the "sky villages" perched atop Hopi reservation mesas, and the prehistoric ruins of Montezuma Castle and Casa Grande.

At the same time, Arizona is a lively hub of modern life, a quickening center in the emerging web of communications and trade, travel and recreation, that links western North America with the Pacific Rim. Phoenix, the state's capital and the Southwest's metropolitan center, is America's ninth-largest and fastest-growing city.

Visitors to Arizona usually wonder about the desert: How hot is it? What should we wear? Is it safe? These are intelligent questions about a land where summer daytime temperatures often exceed 100°F (38°C), major rivers run underground, and the native flora are spiny cactus and thorny scrub.

What few people realize is that Arizona has two deserts. The low desert (roughly the southwestern third of the state) is indeed arid and dotted with tall saguaro cacti, but the high desert—the northeastern tier, with the Grand Canyon and Navajo and Hopi lands—is a savannalike plain, thousands of feet above sea level and mantled in snow all winter. And the middle third of Arizona is not desert at all but rather mountainous terrain, with alpine lakes and the world's largest forest of ponderosa pines.

Even with—and partly because of—its low-desert climate, Arizona has an irresistible draw. Long one of the nation's prime tourist destinations, visited annually by millions from around the world, in the past two decades Arizona has been one of America's fastest-growing states, as tens of thousands of immigrants arrive each year.

That growth transformed Phoenix from a farming town of 60,000 people in 1940 to an urban center of 1 million by 1990; it also doubled and redoubled the population of Tucson, the "Old Pueblo" in the southern part of the state. Yet Arizona remains a place of boundless vistas, with more than 80% of its land in U.S. and state parks and preserves or Native American reservations. Whether they are in the deserts or the mountains, Arizona's small towns still have vast spaces between them.

Arizona has also retained much of its rich Native American and Spanish colonial heritage. More Native Americans live here than in any other state, and the Hopi village of Oraibi is the oldest continually inhabited community in North America. Mexican and Central American families continue to immigrate, many following routes opened by Spanish explorers a century before the Pilgrims landed; numerous Tucson families trace their lineage to Mexican pioneers who arrived in the days of the American Revolution.

Visitors can readily see some of the gifts modern Arizona has received from these ancient cultures: the Native American and Spanish names of most of its mountains and rivers, plants, and animals, even its streets; the pervasive influence of Hopi and Mexican architecture in homes and public buildings. Other aspects of this heritage appear only after some study: the canals that carry Arizona's mountain streams into the low desert, the legal system that gives husband and wife equal shares in their "community property."

One part of Arizona's cultural heritage that almost everyone gets to share is the relaxed pace and style of living: In almost everything, from clothing to art, from home decor to meals, the desert dwellers of each era have learned to prize the unhurried and the informal, to accept the calming lessons of the heat and the majestic landscape. Leave your tie and tails at home and, even if you're on business, plan to take time out: Lean back for a leisurely late lunch during the hottest part of the day; stretch out under a patio awning beside a pool or fountain during the long, cool evenings.

And wherever you take your siesta, cast your eye toward the horizon: You'll see deep skies and luminous, gold-edged sunsets; the towering silhouettes of buttes and mountain ranges, their rugged surfaces subtly alive with shifting shadows and pastel colors; a forest of widely spaced saguaros, standing like many-armed sentinels amid sketchy bushes of creosote and ocotillo, while birds and lizards dart from one spiny haven to the next; the long, green bowl of a mountain meadow, dusted with poppy clusters and blue lupine beds, edged in shimmering aspens. Arizonans and visitors alike never tire of watching the play of sun and shadows on some corner of this magnificent land.

1 Essential Information

Before You Go

Tourist Information

Even if you're not the type to plan your Arizona vacation down to the last cactus, golf ball, or canyon vista, why not do a bit of reading and research anyway? A descriptive passage, a colorful photo, or a historical reference might inspire an unexpected turn or a spontaneous twist in your itinerary. With knowledge gleaned and imagination triggered, you'll find that even pre-planned vacations can take on an aura of adventure.

The **Arizona Office of Tourism** (1100 W. Washington St., Phoenix 85007, tel. 602/542–8687 or 800/842–8257, fax 602/542–4068) can send a comprehensive tourist kit as well as information on the 14 tribal councils, a map of reservations, and a list of addresses and phone numbers.

The **Hopi Tribe Office of Public Relations** (Box 123, Kykotsmovi 86039, tel. 602/734–2441) and the **Navajoland Tourism Department** (Box 663, Window Rock 86515, tel. 602/871–6659 or 871–7371) can inform you of upcoming tribal activities.

Tours and Packages

Should you buy your travel arrangements to Arizona packaged or do it yourself? There are advantages either way. Buying packaged arrangements saves you money, particularly if you can find a program that includes exactly the features you want. You also get a pretty good idea of what your trip will cost from the outset. Generally, you have two options: escorted tours and independent packages. Each has its advantages.

Escorted tours are most often via motor coach, with a tour director in charge. They're ideal if you don't mind having limited free time and vacationing with strangers. Your baggage is handled, your time rigorously scheduled, and most meals planned. Escorted tours are therefore the most hassle-free way to see a destination and are generally the least expensive. Independent packages allow plenty of flexibility. They usually include airline travel and hotels, with certain options available, such as sightseeing, car rental, and excursions. Independent packages are usually more expensive than escorted tours, but your time is your own.

Travel agents are your best source of recommendations for both tours and packages. They will have the largest selection, and the cost to you is the same as buying direct. Whatever program you ultimately choose, be sure to find out exactly what is included: taxes, tips, transfers, meals, baggage handling, ground transportation, entertainment, excursions, sports, or recreation (and rental equipment if necessary). Ask about the hotel used, its location, the size of its rooms, the kind of beds, and its amenities, such as pool, room service, or programs for children, if they're important to you. Find out the operator's cancellation penalties. Nearly everyone charges them, and the only way to avoid them is to buy trip-cancellation insurance. Also ask about the single supplement, a surcharge assessed to solo travelers. Some operators do not make you pay it if you agree to be matched up with a roommate of the same sex, even if one is not found by departure time. Remember that a program that has features you won't use, whether for rental of sporting equipment or discounted museum admissions, may not be the most cost-efficient choice for you. Don't buy a Rolls-Royce, even at a reduced price, if all you want is a Chevy!

Fully Escorted Tours Escorted tours are usually sold in three categories: deluxe, first class, and tourist or budget class. The most important differences are the price, of course, and the level of accommodations. Some operators specialize in one category, while others offer a range.

Top operators include **Maupintour** (Box 807, Lawrence, KS 66044, tel. 800/255–4266 or 913/843–1211) and **Tauck Tours** (11 Wilton Rd., Westport, CT 06881, tel. 800/468–2825 or 203/226–6911) in the deluxe category; **Bixler Tours** (Box 37, Hiram, OH 44234, tel. 216/569–3222 or 800/325–5087), **Domenico Tours** (751 Broadway, Bayonne, NJ 07002, tel. 201/823–8687or 800/554–8687), **Gadabout Tours** (700 E. Tahquitz Way, Palm Springs, CA 92262, tel. 619/325–5556 or 800/952–5068), **Globus** (5301 S. Federal Circle, Littleton, CO 80123, tel. 303/797–2800 or 800/221–0090), **Go America Tours** (733 3rd Ave., 7th Floor, New York, NY 10017, tel. 212/370–5080), **Mayflower Tours** (1225 Warren Ave., Box 490, Downers Grove, IL 60515, tel. 708/960–3430 or 800/323–7604), **Parker Tours** (218-14 Northern Blvd., Bayside, NY 11361, tel. 718/428–7800 or 800/833–9600), **Talmage Tours** (1223 Walnut St., Philadelphia, PA 19107, tel. 215/923–7100 or 800/825–6243), and **Trieloff Tours** (24301 El Toro Rd., Suite 140, Laguna Hills, CA 92653, tel. 800/248–6877 or 800/432–7125 in CA) in the first-class range; and Globus' sister operator, **Cosmos Tourama** (*see above*) in the budget category.

Most itineraries are jam-packed with sightseeing, so you see a lot in a short amount of time (usually one place per day). To judge the pace of the tour, review the itinerary carefully. If you are in a different hotel each night, you will be getting up early each day to head out, travel to your next destination, do some sightseeing, have dinner, and go to bed. Then, the next day, you'll start all over again. If you want some free time, make sure it's mentioned in the tour brochure; if you want to be escorted to every meal, confirm that any tour you consider does that. Also, when comparing programs, be sure to find out if the motor coach is air-conditioned and has a rest room on board. Make your selection based on price and stops on the itinerary.

Independent Packages Independent packages are offered by airlines, tour operators who may also run escorted programs (*see above*), and any number of other companies, from large, established firms to small, new ones.

Airlines offering packages to Arizona include **American Airlines Fly AAway Vacations** (tel. 800/321–2121), **Continental Airlines'**

Grand Destinations (tel. 800/634–5555), **Delta Dream Vacations** (tel. 800/872–7786), **TWA Getaway Vacations** (tel. 800/438–2929), **United Airlines' Vacation Planning Center** (tel. 800/328–6877), and **USAir Vacations** (tel. 800/428–4322). **Gogo Tours,** which you must book through a travel agent, also offers a variety of packages to the state.

These programs are available for a wide range of prices based on levels of luxury and options—in addition to hotel and airfare, sightseeing, car rental, transfers, admission to local attractions, and other extras. Note that when pricing different packages, it sometimes pays to purchase the same arrangements separately, as when a rock-bottom promotional airfare is being offered, for example.

Special-Interest Travel Special-interest programs may be fully escorted or independent. Some require a certain amount of expertise, but most are for the average traveler with an interest and are usually hosted by experts in the subject matter. When the program is escorted, it offers the advantages and disadvantages of all escorted programs. Because your fellow travelers are apt to be passionate or knowledgeable about the subject, they can prove as enjoyable a part of your travel experience as the destination itself. The price range is wide, but the cost is usually higher—sometimes a lot higher—than for ordinary escorted tours and packages, because of the expert guiding and special activities.

Biking **Backroads** (1516 5th St., Suite Q333, Berkeley, CA 94710-1740, tel. 800/243–8747 or 510/527–1555) and **Bike Arizona** (7454 E. Broadway #102, Tucson 85710, tel. 602/722–3228) have multiday bike tours that include hotels and meals.

Hiking **Trek America** (Box 470, Blairstown, NJ 07825, tel. 908/362–9198 or 800/221–0596) includes hiking, camping, and hotel stays on several tours that pass through the wide-open spaces of the state on its *Westerner* treks.

Horseback Riding **American Wilderness Experience** (Box 1486, Boulder, CO 80306, tel. 303/444–2622 or 800/444–0099) has eight-day riding trips from a comfortable base camp into Monument Valley.

Motorcycle Tours **Western States Motorcycle Tours** (543 Wilshire Dr., Phoenix 85003, tel. 602/943–9030) will help you play out all your *Easy Rider* fantasies.

Native American History **Earthwatch** (680 Mt. Auburn St., Watertown, MA 02272, tel. 617/926–8000) recruits volunteers to serve in its EarthCorps as short-term assistants to archaeologists researching early Hopi cultures. **Far Horizons Archaeological & Cultural Trips** (Box 91900, Albuquerque, NM 87199, tel. 505/822–9100 or 800/552–4575) has a tour through the history-rich Four Corners area of the Southwest, home to many Native American cultures.

Tips for British Travelers

Tourist Information Write or fax the **United States Travel and Tourism Administration** (Box 1EN, London W1A 1EN, tel. 0171/495–4466, fax 0171/409–0566) for a free USA pack.

Passports and Visas British citizens need a valid 10-year passport. A visa is not necessary unless (1) you are planning to stay more than 90 days; (2) your trip is for purposes other than vacation; (3) you have at some time been refused a visa, or admission, to the United States, or have been required to leave by the U.S. Immigration and Naturalization Service; or (4) you do not have a return or onward ticket. You will need to fill out the Visa Waiver Form 1–94W supplied by the airline.

To apply for a visa or for more information, call the U.S. Embassy's Visa Information Line (tel. 01891/200–290; calls cost 48 pence per minute or 36 pence per minute cheap rate).

Customs British visitors age 21 or over may import the following into the United States: 200 cigarettes or 50 cigars or 2 kilograms of tobacco; 1 U.S. liter of alcohol; gifts to the value of $100. Restricted items include meat products, seeds, plants, and fruits. Never carry illegal drugs.

Returning to the United Kingdom, you may import duty-free 200 cigarettes, 100 cigarillos, 50 cigars or 250 grams of tobacco; 1 liter of spirits or 2 liters of fortified or sparkling wine; 2 liters of still table wine; 60 milliliters of perfume; 250 milliliters of toilet water; plus £36 worth of other goods, including gifts and souvenirs.

Insurance Most tour operators, travel agents, and insurance agents sell specialized policies covering accidents, medical expenses, personal liability, trip cancellation, and loss or theft of personal property. Some policies include coverage for delayed departure and legal expenses, winter sports, or motoring abroad. You can also purchase an annual travel-insurance policy valid for every trip you make during the year in which it's purchased (usually only trips of less than 90 days). Before you leave, make sure you will be covered if you have a preexisting medical condition or are pregnant; your insurers may not pay for routine or continuing treatment, or may require a note from your doctor certifying your fitness to travel.

The **Association of British Insurers,** a trade association representing 450 insurance companies, advises extra medical coverage for visitors to the United States.

Tour Operators Companies offering packages to Arizona and the Southwest include **Bales Tours Ltd** (Bales House, Junction Rd., Dorking, Surrey RH4 3HB, tel. 01306/76881); **British Airways Holidays** (Atlantic House, Hazelwick Ave., Three Bridges, Crawley, West Sussex RH10 1NP, tel. 01293/611611); **Greyhound International Travel** (Sussex House, London Rd., East Grinstead, West Sussex RH19 1LD, tel. 01342/317317); **Jetsave Travel Ltd.** (Sussex House, London Rd., East Grinstead, West Sussex RH19

1LD, tel. 01342/312033); and **Kuoni Travel** (Kuoni House, Dorking, Surrey RH5 4AZ, tel. 01306/742222).

Airlines and Airfares Flying time from London to Phoenix, the major airport for Arizona, is approximately 13½ hours, but varies with the airline and the itinerary.

Car Rentals In the United States you must be 21, and sometimes 25, to rent a car; rates may be higher for those under 25. Extra costs cover child seats, which are compulsory for children under 5 (about $3 per day); additional drivers (around $1.50 per day); and the all-but-compulsory collision damage waiver (CDW). Make the arrangements from home to avoid inconvenience, save money, and guarantee yourself a vehicle. Major firms include **Alamo** (tel. 0800/272–200), **Budget** (tel. 0800/181–181), **EuroDollar** (tel. 01895/233–300), **Europcar** (tel. 0181/950–5050), and **Hertz** (tel. 0181/679–1799). *See* Car Rentals in Arriving and Departing, *below*.

Travelers with Disabilities Main information sources include the **Royal Association for Disability and Rehabilitation** (RADAR, 25 Mortimer St., London W1N 8AB, tel. 0171/637–5400), which publishes travel information for people with disabilities in Britain, and **Mobility International** (228 Borough High St., London SE1 1JX, tel. 0171/403–5688), the headquarters of an international membership organization that serves as a clearinghouse of travel information for people with disabilities.

When to Go

When you travel to Arizona depends on whether you prefer scorching desert or snowy slopes, elbow-to-elbow resorts or wide-open territory. In general, the best seasons are spring and autumn, when the temperatures are milder and the crowds have thinned out.

Winter is prime time in the central and southern parts of the state. The weather is sunny and mild, and the cities bustle with travelers escaping the cold. Conversely, northern Arizona—including the Grand Canyon—can be wintry, with snow, freezing rain, and subzero temperatures; the road to the Grand Canyon's North Rim is closed during this time.

Arizona's desert regions sizzle in summer, and travelers and their vehicles should be adequately prepared. Practically every restaurant and accommodation is air-conditioned, though, and you can get great deals on tony southern Arizona resorts you might not be able to afford in high season. Summer is also a delightful time to visit northern Arizona's high country, when temperatures are 18°F–20°F lower than they are down south.

Climate Phoenix averages 300 sunny days and 7 inches of precipitation annually. Tucson gets all of 11 inches of rain each year, and the high mountains see about 25 inches. The Grand Canyon is usually cool on the rim, and about 20°F warmer on the floor. During winter months, approximately 6–12 inches of snow fall on the North Rim, while the South Rim receives half that amount.

The following average daily maximum and minimum temperatures for two major cities in Arizona offer a representative range of temperatures in the state.

Tucson								
Jan.	64F	18C	May	89F	32C	Sept.	96F	36C
	37	3		57	14		68	20
Feb.	68F	20C	June	98F	37C	Oct.	84F	29C
	39	4		66	19		57	14
Mar.	73F	23C	July	101F	38C	Nov.	73F	23C
	44	7		73	23		44	7
Apr.	82F	28C	Aug.	96F	36C	Dec.	66F	19C
	51	11		71	22		39	4

Flagstaff								
Jan.	41F	5C	May	66F	19C	Sept.	71F	22C
	14	-10		33	1		41	5
Feb.	44F	7C	June	77F	25C	Oct.	62F	17C
	17	- 8		41	5		30	- 1
Mar.	48F	9C	July	80F	27C	Nov.	51F	11C
	23	- 5		50	10		21	- 6
Apr.	57F	14C	Aug.	78F	26C	Dec.	42F	6C
	28	- 2		48	9		15	- 9

Information Sources For current weather conditions and forecasts for cities in the United States and abroad, plus the local time and helpful travel tips, call the **Weather Channel Connection** (tel. 900/932–8437; 95¢ per minute) from a Touch-Tone phone.

Time

Arizona sets its clocks to mountain standard time—two hours earlier than eastern standard, one hour later than Pacific standard. From April to October, though, when other states switch to daylight saving time, Arizona does *not* change its clocks; during this portion of the year, the mountain standard hour in Arizona is the same as the Pacific daylight hour in California. To complicate matters, the vast Navajo reservation in the northeastern section of the state *does* observe daylight saving time, so that from April to October it's an hour later on the reservation than it is in the rest of the state. Finally, to add to the confusion, the Hopi reservation, whose borders fall within those of the Navajo reservation, stays on the same non-Navajo, nondaylight saving clock as the remainder of the state.

Festivals and Seasonal Events

Arizona's sunny days, sporty lifestyle, fiesta atmosphere, and rich Native American heritage are natural components of a multitude of spirited festivals, musical celebrations, and competitive sporting events. Following is a list of perennial favorites.

January **Fiesta Bowl Footbowl Classic,** Tempe. This nationally televised New Year's Day event kicks off the year with a match between two of the top college teams.
Phoenix Open Golf Tournament, Scottsdale. Big names play and attend this PGA tournament at the Tournament Players Club.

Northern Telecom Tucson Open, Tucson. The other top PGA event, this is co-hosted by Tucson National Golf & Conference Resort and Starr Pass Golf Club.

January–February

Hashknife Pony Express Ride, Holbrook. Each year a sheriff's posse transports the U.S. mail from Holbrook to Scottsdale over the Mogollon Rim.

Parada del Sol Rodeo and Parade, Scottsdale. This popular state attraction on Scottsdale Road features lots of dressed-up cowboys and cowgirls, plus horses and floats.

February

Quartzsite Pow Wow Gem and Mineral Show, Quartzsite. This gigantic flea market, held the first Wednesday through Sunday in February, attracts more than 100,000 buyers and sellers of rocks, minerals, gems, and related crafts and supplies.

O'odham Tash, Casa Grande. Indian tribes from around the country host parades, native dances, a rodeo, costume displays, and food stands.

Wickenburg Gold Rush Days, Wickenburg. History comes to life when this Old West town puts on a rodeo, dances, gold-panning demonstrations, a mineral show, and other activities.

La Fiesta de los Vaqueros, Tucson. The world's longest "non-mechanized" parade—horses pull the floats and carry the dignitaries—launches this four-day rodeo at the Tucson Rodeo Grounds.

Tucson Gem and Mineral Show. Rock hounds—amateur and professional—from all over the world come to buy, sell, and display their geological treasures at this huge downtown event, which includes lectures and competitive exhibits.

March

LPGA Samaritan Turquoise Classic, Phoenix. Top women players compete for the prestigious—and lucrative—award.

Pioneer Days, Tucson. Celebrating the era before Arizona became a state, this two-day festival features military reenactments as well as Western crafts displays.

Heard Museum Guild Indian Fair and Market, Phoenix. This prestigious juried show of Native American arts and crafts brings together participants from all over the Southwest; visitors can also enjoy Native American foods, music, and dance.

April

International Mariachi Conference, Tucson. The Tucson Convention Center is the setting for four days of mariachi music, plus cultural and educational exhibits, for mariachi music lovers.

Route 66 Fun Run Weekend, Seligman/Topock. The historic road between Chicago and Los Angeles is feted with classic car rallies, hot rod and antique-car shows, and various other events—including a 1950s hop.

Yaqui Easter, Tucson. Visitors are welcome to watch the dances and ceremonies performed by the Yaqui Indians in old Pasqua village on the Saturday nights preceding Palm Sunday and Easter Sunday.

La Vuelta de Bisbee, Bisbee. Arizona's largest bicycle race attracts top racers from around the country.

May **Bill Williams Mountain Men Parade and Rodeo,** Williams. The events of the mid-1800s are reenacted by the townspeople, who dress in period costume for the occasion.

Lake Havasu Western Outdoor News Striper Derby. This two-day fishing tournament, the largest in Arizona, has drawn teams from as far away as Michigan and Idaho.

May–June **Trappings of the American West Festival,** Flagstaff. The featured attraction at this two-week festival is cowboy art—everything from painting and sculpture to cowboy poetry readings.

June **Old West Day/Bucket of Blood Races,** Holbrook. Arts and crafts, western dress, and Native American song and dance are part of the festivities that surround the 10-kilometer fun run and 20-mile bike ride from Petrified Forest National Park to Holbrook.

All Indian Powwow and **Native American Arts Fair,** Flagstaff. On the weekend before July 4, tribes from all over the world hold dance performances and competitions, while an international array of crafts is displayed and sold.

July **Prescott Frontier Days and Rodeo,** Prescott. Billed as the world's oldest rodeo, this event sees big crowds and an equally big party on downtown Whiskey Row.

Loggers Festival, Payson. Loggers from the United States and Canada test their skills and strength.

August **Payson Rodeo,** Payson. Top cowboys from around the country compete in calf- and steer-roping contests.

Festival in the Pines, Flagstaff. Painters, potters, and other artists from around the United States vie with musicians, carnival rides, and food vendors for the crowd's attention.

September **Jazz on the Rocks Festival,** Sedona. Six or seven ensembles perform in a striking outdoor setting.

Navajo Nation Annual Tribal Fair, Window Rock. The world's largest Native American fair includes a rodeo, traditional Navajo music and dances, food booths, and an intertribal powwow.

October **Arizona State Fair,** Phoenix. This massive event, at the state fairgrounds, features entertainment, games, rides, exhibits, livestock, art shows, and more.

Tombstone Helldorado Days, Tombstone. The town relives the spirited Wyatt Earp era and the shoot-out at the OK Corral.

London Bridge Days, Lake Havasu City. A triathlon, parade, and a variety of contests are part of this week-long event.

November **Heard Museum Native American Art Show,** Phoenix. Exhibits feature fine tribal arts and crafts from across the state.

Havasu Classic Outboard World Championships, Lake Havasu City. Various classes of racing boats compete for prize money and trophies.

Thunderbird Balloon Classic & Air Show, Glendale. One hundred or more balloons participate in a colorful race.

December **Arizona Temple Christmas Lighting,** Tempe. More than 300,000 lights illuminate the walkways, reflection pool, trees, and plants at the Arizona Temple Gardens and Visitors Center.

Festival of Lights Boat Parade, Page. Lake Powell sparkles with the lights of dozens of boats gliding from Wahweap Lodge to Glen Canyon Dam and back.

Old Town Tempe Fall Festival of the Arts, Tempe. The downtown area closes to traffic for three days of art exhibits, food booths, musical performances, and other entertainment.

What to Pack

Clothing Casual clothing and resort wear fit in well with Arizona's climate and attractions. In some of the tonier restaurants in the larger cities, as well as in the dining rooms of the high-class resorts, most men wear jackets and nice slacks; few places require ties, however. Dressy casual wear is also appropriate for women, even in the nicest spots; take along a silky blouse and chunky silver jewelry and you'll fit in almost anywhere.

T-shirts, polo shirts, sundresses, and lightweight shorts, trousers, skirts, and blouses are just right for summer. Cotton fabrics and light colors will help keep you cool. Sun hats, swimsuits, sandals, and sunscreen are mandatory warm-weather items. In winter be sure to include a sweater and a warm jacket, particularly for high-country travel. Jeans and sneakers or sturdy walking shoes are important year-round.

Naturally, take along the appropriate gear for any sport you plan to pursue. Tennis, golf, ski, and horseback-riding equipment are readily available for rental.

Miscellaneous Pack a camera and film, sunglasses, and an extra pair of eyeglasses or contact lenses in your carry-on luggage. If you have a health problem that requires a prescription drug, pack enough to last the duration of the trip. Don't pack them in luggage that you plan to check, in case your bags go astray. Pack a list of the offices that supply refunds for lost or stolen traveler's checks.

Luggage Free airline baggage allowances depend on the airline, the
Regulations route, and the class of your ticket; ask in advance. In general, on domestic flights you are entitled to check two bags—neither exceeding 62 inches, or 158 centimeters (length + width + height), or weighing more than 70 pounds (32 kilograms). A third piece may be brought aboard; its total dimensions are generally limited to less than 45 inches (114 centimeters), so it will fit easily under the seat in front of you or in the overhead compartment. In the U.S., the Federal Aviation Administration (FAA) gives airlines broad latitude to limit carry-on allowances and tailor them to different aircraft and operational conditions. Charges for excess, oversize, or overweight pieces vary.

Safeguarding Before leaving home, itemize your bags' contents and their
Your Luggage worth in case they're lost. To minimize that risk, tag them inside and out with your name, address, and phone number. (If you use your home address, cover it so that potential thieves can't see it.) Put a copy of your itinerary inside each bag so that you can be tracked down. At check-in, make sure that the tag attached by baggage handlers bears the correct three-letter code for your destination. If your bags do not arrive with you, or if you detect

damage, file a written report with the airline before you leave the airport.

Insurance In the event of loss, damage, or theft on domestic flights, airlines' liability is $1,250 per passenger, excluding the valuable items such as jewelry, cameras, and more that are listed in the fine print on your ticket. Excess-valuation insurance can be bought directly from the airline at check-in. Your homeowner's policy may fill the gap; or firms such as **The Travelers Companies** (1 Tower Sq., Hartford, CT 06183, tel. 203/277–0111 or 800/243–3174) and **Wallach and Company, Inc.** (107 W. Federal St., Box 480, Middleburg, VA 22117, tel. 703/687–3166 or 800/237–6615), sell baggage insurance.

Getting Money from Home

Cash Machines Many automated-teller machines (ATMs) are tied to international networks such as **Cirrus** and **Plus.** You can use your bank card at ATMs to withdraw money from an account and get cash advances on a credit-card account if your card has been programmed with a personal identification number, or PIN. Check in advance on limits on withdrawals and cash advances within specified periods. On cash advances, you are charged interest from the day you receive the money from ATMs as well as from tellers. Transaction fees for ATM withdrawals outside your home turf may be higher than for withdrawals at home.

For specific Cirrus locations in the United States and Canada, call 800/424–7787. For U.S. Plus locations, call 800/843–7587 and press the area code and first three digits of the number you're calling from (or of the calling area where you want an ATM).

Note: There are remote parts of Arizona—most notably the Indian reservations and the North Rim of the Grand Canyon and surrounding Arizona Strip country—where you won't be able to find banks or ATMs. Plan accordingly.

Wiring Money You don't have to be a cardholder to send or receive a **MoneyGram from American Express** for up to $10,000. Go to a MoneyGram agent in retail and convenience stores and American Express travel offices, and pay up to $1,000 with a credit card and anything over that in cash. You are allowed a free long-distance call to give the transaction code to your intended recipient, who only needs to present identification and the transaction reference number to the nearest MoneyGram agent to pick up the cash. MoneyGram agents are in more than 70 countries (call 800/926–9400 for locations). Fees range from 3% to 10%, depending on the amount and how you pay.

You can also use **Western Union.** To wire money, take either cash or a cashier's check to the nearest office or call and use MasterCard or Visa. Money sent from the United States or Canada will be available for pick up at any of the 22,000 agent locations in 78 countries within minutes; call 800/325–6000 for the one nearest you.

Traveling with Cameras, Camcorders, and Laptops

Film and Cameras If your camera is new or if you haven't used it for a while, shoot and develop a few test rolls of film before you leave. Store film in a cool, dry place—never in the car's glove compartment or on the shelf under the rear window.

Airport security X-rays generally aren't harmful to film with an ISO rating of less than 400. To protect your film, carry it with you in a clear plastic bag and ask for a hand inspection. Such requests are honored at U.S. airports. Don't depend on a lead-lined bag to protect film in checked luggage—the airline may increase the radiation to see what's inside.

Camcorders Before your trip, put camcorders through their paces, invest in a skylight filter to protect the lens, and check all the batteries.

Videotape Videotape is not damaged by X-rays, but it may be harmed by the magnetic field of a walk-through metal detector, so ask for a hand check. Airport security personnel may ask you to turn on the camcorder to prove that it's what it appears to be, so make sure the battery is charged.

Laptops Security X-rays do not harm hard-disk or floppy-disk storage, but you may request a hand check, at which point you may be asked to turn on the computer to prove that it is what it appears to be. (Check your battery before departure.) Most airlines allow you to use your laptop aloft except during takeoff and landing (so as not to interfere with navigation equipment).

Traveling with Children

Many of the big resorts and dude ranches offer special activities just for children, and many offer baby-sitting services. Children of all ages are enthralled by the Wild West flavor around Tucson and the southeastern part of the state, with Tombstone ranking as a particular favorite. If you're driving some of the long desert stretches, take along plenty of games and snacks.

Publications *A Family Guide to Arizona,* by Catherine Dunes (Kids Touring
Local Guide Arizona, 4201 W. Villa Maria Dr., Glendale, AZ 85308, tel. 602/ 439–2324; $6.95), contains Arizona-related fun facts, games, puzzles, and palatable educational information.

Newsletter **Family Travel Times,** published 10 times a year by **Travel With Your Children** (TWYCH, 45 W. 18th St., 7th Floor Tower, New York, NY 10011, tel. 212/206–0688; annual subscription $55), covers destinations, types of vacations, and modes of travel. TWYCH also publishes *Cruising with Children* and *Skiing with Children*.

Books *Great Vacations with Your Kids,* by Dorothy Jordan and Marjorie Cohen (Penguin USA, 120 Woodbine St., Bergenfield, NJ 07621, tel. 800/253–6476; $13), and *Traveling with Children—And Enjoying It,* by Arlene K. Butler (Globe Pequot Press, Box 833, 6 Business Park Rd., Old Saybrook, CT 06475, tel. 800/243–0495 or 800/962–0973 in CT; $11.95 plus $3 shipping per book), both help you plan your trip with children, from toddlers to teens. From the same publisher are *Recommended Family Resorts in the United States, Canada, and the Caribbean*, by Jane Wilford with Janet Tice ($12.95), and *Recommended Family Inns of America* ($12.95).

Tour **Grandtravel** (6900 Wisconsin Ave., Suite 706, Chevy Chase, MD
Operators 20815, tel. 301/986–0790 or 800/247–7651) offers tours for people who are traveling with their grandchildren. The catalogue, as charmingly written and illustrated as a children's book, positively invites armchair traveling with lap-sitters aboard. **Rascals in Paradise** (650 5th St., Suite 505, San Francisco, CA 94107, tel. 415/978–9800 or 800/872–7225) specializes in adventurous, exotic and fun-filled vacations for families to carefully screened resorts and hotels around the world.

Getting On domestic flights, children under 2 not occupying a seat travel
There free, and older children currently travel on the "lowest applica
Airfares ble" adult fare.

Baggage The adult baggage allowance applies for children paying half or more of the adult fare.

Safety Seats The FAA recommends the use of safety seats aloft and details approved models in the free leaflet **"Child/Infant Safety Seats Recommended for Use in Aircraft"** (available from the FAA, APA–200, 800 Independence Ave. SW, Washington, DC 20591, tel. 202/267–3479; information hot line, tel. 800/322–7873). Airline policy varies. U.S. carriers allow FAA-approved models bearing a sticker declaring their FAA approval. Because these seats are strapped into regular passenger seats, airlines may require that a ticket be bought for an infant who would otherwise ride free.

Facilities Aloft Some airlines provide other services for children, such as children's meals and freestanding bassinets (only to those with seats at the bulkhead, where there's enough legroom). Make your request when reserving. The annual February/March issue of *Family Travel Times* details children's services on dozens of airlines ($10; *see above*). "Kids and Teens in Flight" (free from the U.S. Department of Transportation's Office of Consumer Affairs, R–25, Washington, DC 20590, tel. 202/366–2220) offers tips for children flying alone.

Lodging All **Holiday Inns** (tel. 800/465–4329) allow children age 12 or under to stay free when sharing a room with an adult, and some offer family plans, providing the same privileges for children 18 or under. In summer, the **Westin La Paloma Hotel** in Tucson (tel. 800/228–3000) has supervised activities for children ages 6–12, as well as junior tennis camps for kids 5–14 years old. From Thanksgiving through April, the **Tanque Verde Guest Ranch** (tel. 800/234–3833), also in Tucson, offers activities for children 4–11, including horseback-riding lessons, tennis, and nature walks in the daytime, and arts and crafts and games in the evening. In the Phoenix area, the **Pointe Hilton Resort** (tel. 800/ 934–1000) runs its Coyote Camp for children ages 4–12 year-round, including such activities as hiking, swimming, arts and crafts, and cooking. The **Phoenician Resort** (tel. 800/888–8234) in Scottsdale has a summer camp, with four week-long sessions for children 5–12, as well as junior golf and tennis clinics for kids up to 17; the **Hyatt Regency** (tel. 800/233–1234), also in Scottsdale, offers a full range of supervised daytime activities for kids 3–12 year-round; in addition, there are evening sessions each Friday and Saturday. All of the above resorts also have baby-sitting services.

Hints for Travelers with Disabilities

Most of the region's national parks and recreation areas have wheelchair-accessible visitor centers, rest rooms, campsites, and trails, and more are being added every year. For information on accessible facilities at specific parks and sites in northeastern Arizona, contact the **National Park Service, Southwest Regional Office** (tel. 505/988–6375); for sites in southwestern Arizona, contact the **Western Regional Office** (tel. 415/744–3929).

Organizations Several organizations provide travel information for people with disabilities, usually for a membership fee, and some publish newsletters and bulletins. Among them are the **Information Center for Individuals with Disabilities** (Fort Point Pl., 27–43 Wormwood St., Boston, MA 02210, tel. 617/727–5540 or 800/462–5015 in MA between 11 and 4, or leave message, TTY 617/345–9743); **Mobility International USA** (Box 10767, Eugene, OR 97440, tel. and TTY 503/343–1284, fax 503/343–6812), the U.S. branch of an international organization based in Britain (*see above*) that has affiliates in 30 countries; **MossRehab Hospital Travel Information Service** (tel. 215/456–9603, TTY 215/456–9602); the **Travel Industry and Disabled Exchange** (TIDE, 5435 Donna Ave., Tarzana, CA 91356, tel. 818/344–3640, fax 818/344–0078); and **Travelin' Talk** (Box 3534, Clarksville, TN 37043, tel. 615/552–6670, fax 615/552–1182).

Travel Agencies and Tour Operators Group tours for travelers with disabilities are regularly scheduled by the Arizona Recreation Center for the Handicapped (1550 W. Colter St., Phoenix 85015, tel. 602/230–2226). **Flying Wheels Travel** (143 W. Bridge St., Box 382, Owatonna, MN 55060, tel. 507/451–5005 or 800/535–6790) is a travel agency that specializes in domestic and worldwide cruises, tours, and independent travel itineraries for people with mobility problems. Adventurers should contact **Wilderness Inquiry** (1313 5th St. SE, Minneapolis, MN 55414, tel. and TTY 612/379–3838), which orchestrates action-packed trips like white-water rafting, sea kayaking, and dogsledding for people with disabilities. Tours are designed to bring people who have disabilities together with those who don't.

Publications Local Guides *Access Arizona: An Atlas & Travel Guide for Disabled & Mature Travelers to Major Outdoor Recreation Areas*, published by the **Arizona State Parks Department** (1300 W. Washington St., Phoenix 85007, tel. 602/542–6931), details the accessibility of national and state parks facilities to those with mobility impairments. The **Arizona Easter Seal Society** (903 N. 2nd St., Phoenix 85004, tel. 602/252–6061) publishes *Access Valley of the Sun*, covering Phoenix and environs; *Access Tucson & Green Valley*, focusing on the southeastern region; and *Access Northern Arizona*, encompassing Flagstaff and surrounding communities. Also consult the *Arizona Accommodations Directory*, published by the **Arizona Hotel and Motel Association** (2201 E. Camelback Rd., Suite 125-B, Phoenix 85016, tel. 602/553–8802).

General Information Several free publications are available from the Consumer Information Center (Pueblo, CO 81009): "New Horizons for the Air Traveler with a Disability" (include Dept. 608Y in the address), a U.S. Department of Transportation booklet describing changes resulting from the 1986 Air Carrier Access Act and from the 1990 Americans with Disabilities Act, and the Airport Operators Council's *Access Travel: Airports* (Dept. 5804), which describes facilities and services for people with disabilities at more than 500 airports worldwide.

Fodor's publishes *Great American Vacations for Travelers with Disabilities* (available in bookstores, or call 800/533–6478), detailing services and accessible attractions, restaurants, and hotels in Arizona and other U.S. destinations. The 500-page *Travelin' Talk Directory* (*see* Organizations, *above*; $35 check or money order with a money-back guarantee) lists names and addresses of people and organizations that offer help for travelers with disabilities. Twin Peaks Press (Box 129, Vancouver, WA 98666, tel. 206/694–2462 or 800/637–2256) publishes the *Directory of Travel Agencies for the Disabled* ($19.95 plus $2 for shipping), listing more than 370 agencies worldwide. The Sierra Club publishes *Easy Access to National Parks* ($16 plus $3 shipping; 730 Polk St., San Francisco, CA 94109, tel. 415/776–2211).

Getting Around *By Bus* **Greyhound** (tel. 800/752–4841; TTY 800/345–3109), which provides service to many destinations in Arizona, will carry a disabled person and a companion for the price of a single fare.

By Train **Amtrak** (National Railroad Passenger Corp., 60 Massachusetts Ave., NE, Washington, DC 20002, tel. 800/872–7245) advises that you request Redcap service, special seats, or wheelchair assistance when you make reservations. Also note that not all stations are equipped to provide these services. All passengers with disabilities are entitled to a 15% discount on the lowest fare, and there are special fares for children with disabilities as well. Contact Amtrak for a free brochure that outlines services for older travelers and people with disabilities.

By Car **Avis** (tel. 800/331–1212), **Hertz** (tel. 800/654–3131), and **National** (tel. 800/328–4567) can provide hand controls on some rental cars with advance notice.

Discounts The **National Park Service** (Box 37127, Washington, DC 20013–7127) provides a Golden Access Passport free to those who are legally blind or have a permanent disability; the passport covers the entry fee for the holder and anyone accompanying the holder in the same private vehicle and a 50% discount on camping and some other user fees. Apply for the passport in person at a national recreational facility that charges an entrance fee; proof of disability is required.

Hints for Older Travelers

The state's healthful environment and many retirement communities make it a popular destination for older travelers. As such, Arizona has a multitude of recreational, sports, and entertainment facilities geared especially to senior citizens' needs and interests. In addition, discounts are offered on public transportation, museum entrance fees, fishing and hunting licenses, cinemas, musical and theatrical performances, and a wide variety of other services. The minimum age limit varies between 55 and 65 years. If you fall into this age group, be sure to inquire about discounts before putting your money on the counter; savings can be substantial.

Organizations The **American Association of Retired Persons** (AARP, 601 E St. NW, Washington, DC 20049, tel. 202/434–2277) provides independent travelers who are members of the AARP (open to those age 50 or older; $8 per person or couple annually) with the Purchase Privilege Program, which offers discounts on lodging, car rentals, and sightseeing. AARP also arranges group tours, cruises, and apartment living through AARP Travel Experience from American Express (400 Pinnacle Way, Suite 450, Norcross, GA 30071, tel. 800/927–0111 or 800/745–4567), and the AARP Motoring Plan, which furnishes domestic trip-routing information and emergency road-service aid for an annual fee of $39.95 per person or couple ($59.95 for a premium version).

Two other organizations offer discounts on lodgings, car rentals, and other travel products, along with such nontravel perks as magazines and newsletters: the **National Council of Senior Citizens** (1331 F St. NW, Washington, DC 20004, tel. 202/347–8800; membership $12 annually) and **Mature Outlook** (6001 N. Clark St., Chicago, IL 60660, tel. 800/336–6330; $9.95 annually).

Note: For reduced rates, mention your senior-citizen identification card when booking hotel reservations, not when checking out. At restaurants, show your card before you're seated; discounts may be limited to certain menus, days, or hours. If you are renting a car, ask about promotional rates that might improve on your senior-citizen discount.

Educational The nonprofit Elderhostel (75 Federal St., 3rd Floor, Boston,
Travel MA 02110, tel. 617/426–7788) has offered inexpensive study programs for people 60 and older since 1975. Held at more than 1,800 educational institutions, courses cover everything from marine science to Greek myths and cowboy poetry. Participants generally attend lectures in the morning and spend the afternoon sightseeing or on field trips; they live in dorms on the host campuses. Fees for programs in the United States and Canada, which usually last one week, run about $300, not including transportation. With dozens of Arizona college and university

campuses participating, Elderhostel has a particularly extensive program in that state. Some scheduled classes include Native American Archaeology, Geology of the Grand Canyon,
Flora and Fauna of the Sonoran Desert, Astronomy, and Cowboys and the Old West; one program involves staying on the
Hopi reservation and learning about Hopi culture from members of the tribe.

Tour The following operators specialize in tours for older travelers: If
Operators you want to take your grandchildren, look into **Grandtravel** (*see*
Traveling with Children, *above*); **Saga International Holidays**
(222 Berkeley St., Boston, MA 02116, tel. 800/343–0273) caters
to those over age 60 who like to travel in groups. **SeniorTours**
(508 Irvington Rd., Drexel Hill, PA 19026, tel. 215/626–1977 or
800/227–1100) arranges motor-coach tours throughout the
United States and Nova Scotia, as well as Caribbean cruises.

Hints for Gay and Lesbian Travelers

Organizations The **International Gay Travel Association** (Box 4974, Key West,
FL 33041, tel. 305/292–0217, 800/999–7925, or 800/448–8550),
which has 700 members, will provide you with names of travel
agents and tour operators who specialize in gay travel. The **Gay
& Lesbian Visitors Center of New York Inc.** (135 West 20th St.,
3rd Floor, New York, NY 10011, tel. 212/463–9030 or 800/395–
2315; $100 annually) mails a monthly newsletter, valuable cou-
pons, and more to its members.

Tour The dominant travel agency in the market is **Above and Beyond**
Operators (3568 Sacramento St., San Francisco, CA 94118, tel. 415/922–
and Travel 2683 or 800/397–2681). Tour operator **Olympus Vacations** (8424
Agencies Santa Monica Blvd. #721, West Hollywood, CA 90069; tel. 310/
657–2220) offers all-gay-and-lesbian resort holidays. **Skylink
Women's Travel** (746 Ashland Ave., Santa Monica, CA 90405,
tel. 310/452–0506 or 800/225–5759) handles individual travel for
lesbians all over the world and conducts two international and
five domestic group trips annually.

Publications The premiere international travel magazine for gays and
lesbians is *Our World* (1104 North Nova Rd., Suite 251, Daytona
Beach, FL 32117, tel. 904/441–5367; $35 for 10 issues). **"Out &
About"** (tel. 203/789–8518 or 800/929–2268; $49 for 10 issues, full
refund if you aren't satisfied) is a 16-page monthly newsletter
with extensive information on resorts, hotels, and airlines that
are gay-friendly.

Further Reading

Essays and *Going Back to Bisbee*, by Richard Shelton, *Frog Mountain*
Fiction *Blues*, by Charles Bowden, and *The Mountains Next Day*, by
Janice Emily Bowers, are all fine personal accounts of life in
southern Arizona. The hipster fiction classic *The Monkey
Wrench Gang*, by Edward Abbey, details an ecoanarchist plot to
blow up Glen Canyon Dam. *Stolen Gods*, a thriller by Jake Page,
is set largely on Arizona's Hopi reservation and in Tucson.

Three novels by Tucson-based writers skillfully evoke the interplay between Native American culture and contemporary Southwest life: *Animal Dreams*, by Barbara Kingsolver, *Almanac of the Dead*, by Leslie Marmon Silko, and *Yes Is Better Than No*, by Byrd Baylor. Almost any of Zane Grey's Western adventures or Tony Hillerman's mysteries will put you in a Southwest mood.

General History *Arizona Cowboys*, by Dane Coolidge, is an illustrated account of the cowboys, Indians, settlers, and explorers of the early 1900s. Buried-treasure hunters will be inspired by *Lost Mines of the Great Southwest*, by John D. Mitchell, which is just enough of a nibble to start you sketching maps and planning strategy. First printed back in 1891, *Some Strange Corners of Our Country*, by Charles F. Lummis, takes readers on a century-old journey to the Grand Canyon, Montezuma Castle, the Petrified Forest, and other Arizonan "strange corners." *Roadside History of Arizona*, by Marshall Trimble, is a great book for the person not driving to read aloud while tooling around the state. *Ghost Towns of Arizona*, by James E. and Barbara H. Sherman, gives historical details on the abandoned mining towns that dot the state and provides maps to find them.

Native American History *The Anasazi: Prehistoric Peoples of the Four Corners Region*, by J. Richard Ambler, is an intriguing study of this area and its early inhabitants. *Hohokam Indians of the Tucson Basin*, by Linda Gregonis, offers an in-depth look at this prehistoric tribe. In *Hopi*, by Susanne Page and Jake Page, the daily, ceremonial, and spiritual life of the tribe are explored in detail. Study up on the history of Hopi silversmithing techniques in *Hopi Silver*, by Margaret Wright. The beautifully illustrated *Hopi Indian Kachina Dolls*, by Oscar T. Branson, details the different ceremonial roles of the colorful Native American figurines. Navajo homes, ceremonies, crafts, and tribal traditions are kept alive in *The Enduring Navajo*, by Laura Gilpin. Navajo legends and trends from early days to the present are collected in *The Book of the Navajo*, by Raymond F. Locke.

Natural History *A Guide to Exploring Oak Creek and the Sedona Area*, by Stewart Aitchison, provides natural-history driving tours of this very scenic district. In *100 Desert Wildflowers in Natural Color*, by Natt N. Dodge, you'll find a color photo and brief description of each of the flowers included. Also written by Natt N. Dodge, *Poisonous Dwellers of the Desert* gives precise information on both venomous and nonvenomous creatures of the Southwest. *Cacti of the Southwest*, by W. Hubert Earle, depicts some of the best-known species of the region with color photos and descriptive material. For comprehensive information on Grand Canyon geology, history, flora and fauna, plus hiking suggestions, pick up *A Field Guide to the Grand Canyon*, by Steve Whitney. *Common Edible and Useful Plants of the West*, by Muriel Sweet, gives the layperson descriptions of medicinal and other plants and shrubs, most of which were first discovered by Native Americans. *Roadside Geology of Arizona*, by Halka

Chronic, is a good resource for finding the causes of the striking natural formations you'll see throughout the state.

Crafts *The Traveler's Guide to American Crafts: West of the Mississippi*, by Suzanne Carmichael, gives browsers and buyers alike a useful overview of Arizona's traditional and contemporary handiwork.

General *Arizona Highways*, a monthly magazine, features exquisite col-
Interest or photography of this versatile state. Useful general travel information, fine pictures, and well-written historical essays all make *Arizona*, by Larry Cheek, a good pretrip resource.

Arriving and Departing

By Plane

Flights are either nonstop, direct, or connecting. A **nonstop** flight requires no change of plane and makes no stops. A **direct** flight stops at least once and can involve a change of plane, although the flight number remains the same; if the first leg is late, the second waits. This is not the case with a **connecting** flight, which involves a different plane and a different flight number.

Airports and Most major domestic airlines fly into Phoenix and Tucson from
Airlines all parts of the United States. Busy Phoenix Sky Harbor International, about 3 miles east of the city center, also serves as the hub for flights to other parts of the state. Tucson International Air Terminal is located about 8½ miles south of the central business area. Both facilities offer a number of transportation services into the city, from minivan shuttles to stretch limousines.

Air carriers to Arizona are **Aeromexico** (tel. 800/237–6639), **Alaska** (tel. 800/426–0333), **American** (tel. 800/433–7300), **America West** (tel. 800/235–9292), **Continental** (tel. 800/525–0280), **Delta** (tel. 800/221–1212), **Morris Air** (tel. 800/444–5660), **Northwest** (tel. 800/225–2525), **Reno Air** (tel. 800/736–6247), **Southwest** (tel. 800/435–9792), **TWA** (tel. 800/221–2000), **United** (tel. 800/241–6522), and **USAir** (tel. 800/428–4322).

Within the state, **America West Express/Mesa** (tel. 800/247–5692) and **Skywest** (tel. 800/453–9417) operate regularly scheduled flights from Phoenix to Flagstaff and Yuma; Skywest also flies from Phoenix to Page/Lake Powell. **Arizona Pacific** (tel. 800/225–0844), based in Prescott, has regularly scheduled routes between that city and the Grand Canyon.

Cutting Costs The Sunday travel section of most newspapers is a good place to find deals. When booking, particularly through an unfamiliar company, call the Better Business Bureau and your local or state Consumer Protection Bureau to find out whether any complaints have been registered against the company, pay with a credit card if you can, and consider trip-cancellation and default insurance.

Promotional Less expensive fares, called promotional or discount fares, are
Airfares round-trip and involve restrictions that vary according to the
route and season. You must usually buy the ticket—commonly
called an advance purchase excursion (APEX) when it's for international travel—in advance (seven, 14, or 21 days are standard), although some of the major airlines have added no-frills,
cheap flights to compete with new bargain airlines on certain
routes.

With the major airlines the cheaper fares generally require minimum and maximum stays (for instance, over a Saturday night
or at least seven and no more than 30 days). Airlines generally
allow some return date changes for a $25 to $50 fee, but most
low-fare tickets are nonrefundable. Only a death in the family
would prompt the airline to return any of your money if you can-
cel a nonrefundable ticket. However, you can apply an unused
nonrefundable ticket toward a new ticket, again with a small
fee. The lowest fare is subject to availability, and only a small
percentage of the plane's total seats will be sold at that price.
Contact the U.S. Department of Transportation's Office of Consumer Affairs (I–25, Washington, DC 20590, tel. 202/366–2220)
for a copy of "Fly-Rights: A Guide to Air Travel in the U.S." *The
Official Frequent Flyer Guidebook* by Randy Petersen (4715-C
Town Center Dr., Colorado Springs, CO 80916, tel. 719/597–
8899, 800/487–8893, or 800/485–8893; $14.99 plus $3 shipping)
yields valuable hints on getting the most for your air-travel dollars.

Consolidators Consolidators, which are also called bulk-fare operators or
"bucket shops," buy blocks of seats on scheduled flights that airlines anticipate they won't be able to sell. They pay wholesale
prices, add a markup, and resell the seats to travel agents or directly to the public at prices that still undercut the airline's promotional or discount fares (higher than a charter ticket but
lower than an APEX ticket, and usually without the advance-
purchase restriction). Moreover, some consolidators give you
your money back. Carefully read the fine print detailing penalties for changes and cancellations. If you doubt the reliability of
a company, call the airline once you've made your booking and
confirm that you do, indeed, have a reservation on the flight.

The biggest U.S. consolidator, C. L. Thomson Express, sells
only to travel agents. Well-established consolidators selling to
the public include **UniTravel** (Box 12485, St. Louis, MO 63132,
tel. 314/569–0900 or 800/325–2222); **Council Charter** (205 E.
42nd St., New York, NY 10017, tel. 212/661–0311 or 800/800–
8222), a division of the Council on International Educational Exchange and a longtime charter operator now functioning more as
a consolidator; and **Travac** (989 6th Ave., New York, NY 10018,
tel. 212/563–3303 or 800/872–8800), also a former charterer.

Discount Travel clubs offer members unsold space on airplanes, cruise
Travel Clubs ships, and package tours at as much as 50% below regular
prices. Membership may include a regular bulletin or access to a
toll-free hot line giving details of available trips departing from
three or four days to several months in the future. Most also of-

fer 50% discounts off hotel rack rates, but double-check with the hotel to make sure it isn't offering a better promotional rate independent of the club. Clubs include **Discount Travel International** (114 Forrest Ave., Suite 203, Narberth, PA 19072, tel. 215/668–7184; $45 annually, single or family), **Entertainment Travel Editions** (Box 1014, Trumbull, CT 06611, tel. 800/445–4137; price ranges $28–$48), **Great American Traveler** (Box 27965, Salt Lake City, UT 84127, tel. 800/548–2812; $29.95 annually), **Moment's Notice Discount Travel Club** (425 Madison Ave., New York, NY 10017, tel. 212/486–0503; $45 annually, single or family), **Privilege Card** (3391 Peachtree Rd. NE, Suite 110, Atlanta, GA 30326, tel. 404/262–0222 or 800/236–9732; domestic annual membership $49.95, international, $74.95), **Travelers Advantage** (CUC Travel Service, 49 Music Sq. W, Nashville, TN 37203, tel. 800/548–1116; $49 annually, single or family), and **Worldwide Discount Travel Club** (1674 Meridian Ave., Miami Beach, FL 33139, tel. 305/534–2082; $50 annually for family, $40 single).

Publication The newsletter "Travel Smart" (40 Beechdale Rd., Dobbs Ferry, NY 10522, tel. 800/327–3633; $44 a year) has a wealth of travel deals in each monthly issue.

Smoking Since February 1990, smoking has been banned on all domestic flights of less than six hours' duration; the ban also applies to domestic segments of international flights aboard U.S. and foreign carriers.

By Car

Major approaches from the east and west are I–40, I–10, I–8, and U.S. 60. Main north–south routes are I–17, I–10 (from Phoenix to Tucson), and U.S. 89. Other artery roads are U.S. 70 and U.S. 64 (U.S. 160 in Arizona) from the east.

Most highways into the state are good to excellent, with easy access, roadside facilities, rest stops, and scenic views. The speed limit is 65 miles per hour, but even though it may be tempting to let the speedometer needle fly in the wide-open desert, beware—police use sophisticated detection systems to nab violators.

Hazards to desert drivers include dust storms and flash floods. Dust storms usually occur mid-July to mid-September (the monsoon months), just before thunderstorms hit, causing extremely low visibility. If you're on the highway, pull as far off the road as possible, turn off your headlights, and wait for the storm to subside. Flash floods strike low-lying areas during both the monsoon and winter rainy seasons. Dry washes, which fill quickly with running water, are particularly dangerous and should not be crossed until you can see the bottom.

Vehicles and passengers should be well equipped for searing summer heat in the low desert. Always carry plenty of water, a good spare tire, a jack, and emergency supplies. If you get stranded, stay with your vehicle and wait for help to arrive.

At some point you will probably pass through one or more of the state's 23 Indian reservations. Roads and other areas within reservation boundaries are under the jurisdiction of reservation police and governed by separate rules and regulations. Observe all signs and respect residents' privacy.

For up-to-date information on highway conditions and road closings throughout the state, call 602/252–1010, ext. 7623.

Car Rentals

All major car-rental companies are represented in Arizona, including **Alamo** (tel. 800/327–9633); **Avis** (tel. 800/331–1212, 800/879–2847 in Canada); **Budget** (tel. 800/527–0700); **Dollar** (tel. 800/800–4000); **Hertz** (tel. 800/654–3131, 800/263–0600 in Canada); and **National Interrent** (tel. 800/227–7368). You will also find **Thrifty** (tel. 800/367–2277). Prices are not the same throughout the state: At present, for example, rates for a compact with unlimited mileage are lower in Flagstaff (about $145) than in Phoenix (anywhere from $160 to $205); this does not include tax.

Extra Charges Picking up the car in one city and leaving it in another may entail substantial drop-off charges or one-way service fees. The cost of a collision or loss-damage waiver (*see below*) can also be high. Some rental agencies will charge you extra if you return the car *before* the time specified on your contract. Ask before making unscheduled drop-offs. Fill the tank before you turn in the vehicle to avoid being charged for refueling at what you'll swear is the most expensive pump in town. By prior arrangement, you can also rent four-wheel-drive vehicles, trucks, and or campers.

Cutting Costs Major international companies have programs that discount their standard rates by 15%–30% if you make the reservation before departure (anywhere from 24 hours to 14 days), rent for a minimum number of days (typically three or four), and prepay the rental. More economical rentals may come as part of fly/drive or other packages, even bare-bones deals that only combine the rental and an airline ticket (*see* Tours and Packages, *above*).

Insurance and Collision-Damage Waiver Before you rent a car, find out exactly what coverage, if any, is provided by your personal auto insurer and by the rental company. Don't assume that you are covered. If you do want insurance from the rental company, secondary coverage may be the only type offered. You may already have secondary coverage if you charge the rental to a credit card. Only Diners Club (tel. 800/234–6377) provides primary coverage in the United States and worldwide.

In general, if you have an accident you are responsible for the automobile. Car rental companies may offer a CDW, which ranges in cost from $4 to $14 a day. You should decline the CDW only if you are certain you are covered through your personal insurer or credit-card company. In many states, laws mandate that renters be told what the CDW costs, that it's optional, and that their own auto insurance may provide the same protection.

By Train

The *Southwest Chief* operates daily between Los Angeles and Chicago, stopping in Kingman, Flagstaff, and Winslow. The *Sunset Limited* travels three times each week between Los Angeles and Miami, with stops at Yuma, Phoenix, Tempe, Coolidge, Tucson, and Benson. For details, contact **Amtrak** (tel. 800/872–7245).

By Bus

Greyhound (tel. 800/231–2222) provides service to many Arizona destinations from most parts of the United States.

Staying in Arizona

Shopping

Many tourists come to Arizona for no other reason than to purchase fine **Native American jewelry and crafts.** Collectibles include Navajo rugs and sand paintings, Hopi kachina dolls (intricately carved and colorful representations of Hopi spiritual beings) and pottery, Tohonó O'odham (Papago) basketry, and Apache beadwork, as well as the highly prized silver and turquoise jewelry produced by several different tribes. Many of these items are sold in big-city shops and malls, but going directly to the reservation often gives shoppers additional rewards.

Museums and trading posts on the Navajo and Hopi reservations in the state's northeastern region offer introductions to crafts and their history and have gift shops where you can make purchases. Demonstrations of silversmithing, rug-weaving, and pottery-making techniques are often held on the premises. Roadside stands also offer wares for sale.

You can find exquisite baskets and other crafts of the Tohonó O'odham at the plaza outside the San Xavier Mission on the outskirts of Tucson, as well as at shops in Sells, the tribe's headquarters, about 60 miles southwest of Tucson. Apache beadwork, baskets, wood carvings, and jewelry are sold at reservation trading posts in the eastern part of the state.

Bear in mind that the high quality of Native American arts and crafts is reflected in the prices they fetch. Bargaining is the exception, not the rule. In general, the best buys are to be had in the fall, after most of the tourists have gone home.

Mineral rich Arizona is also a haven for **rock and mineral** collectors. An astounding variety of specimens include agate, jasper, tourmaline, petrified wood, quartz, turquoise, amethyst, precious opal, and fire agate. Buy them at specialty shops or at one of the state's year-round rock and gem shows. The largest shows, generally held from late January to mid-February, are at Quartzsite, about 19 miles from the California border, and Tucson.

Sports and the Outdoors

Ballooning Both Phoenix and Tucson have a large number of hot-air-balloon operators, whose pilots will take you hovering above metropolitan areas as well as the Sonoran Desert. Some companies offer flights year-round, though most will fly only during the cooler months. Tours last about one hour and are customarily followed by a champagne celebration.

Baseball Baseball fans visiting Arizona in March have a chance to watch major-league teams during spring training. Exhibition games begin in early March, but the eight Cactus League teams start practice at training camps as much as three weeks earlier. The free drills—held in the morning before an exhibition game—are fun to watch, and there's a good chance you might be able to chat with the players before or after these sessions.

The Phoenix area, where seven of the eight teams practice, is the best place to see Cactus League baseball: The **Chicago Cubs** play at Hohokam Park in Mesa (tel. 602/964–4467), the **Oakland Athletics** at Phoenix Municipal Stadium (tel. 602/392–0217), the **San Francisco Giants** at Scottsdale Stadium (tel. 602/990–7972), the **California Angels** at Diablo Stadium in Tempe (tel. 602/438–9300), and the **Milwaukee Brewers** at the Compadre Stadium in Chandler (tel. 602/895–1200). Both the **San Diego Padres** and the **Seattle Mariners** train at Peoria Stadium (tel. 602/412–4213), in another Phoenix suburb. In 1993 the **Colorado Rockies** practiced for their first major-league games in Tucson's Hi Corbett field (tel. 602/327–9467).

In some cases, reserved seats sell out the fall before the season, but you can almost always get general-admission seats on the day of the games. For current information on all aspects of Cactus League baseball, contact the **Mesa Convention and Visitor's Bureau** (120 North Center St., Mesa 85201, tel. 602/969–1307 or 800/283–6372).

Bicycling Cyclists can ride on city streets, desert trails, mountain passes, or the open road. Start off with a bike in good repair, a maintenance kit, a sturdy bicycle helmet, and plenty of water. If you're not used to long-distance cycling, don't push yourself. Begin with short jaunts and work up to longer journeys. A lightweight touring bike and extra-low gears for mountain grades will help you along. Most bicycle shops can provide you with tour guides, tips, and, if you decide to go pro, a current racing schedule. Call the county **Parks and Recreation Department** in the area you're visiting for information on nearby bike paths. **The Arizona Bicycle Club, Inc.** (Box 7191, Phoenix 85011) publishes a schedule of the many bicycle races that take place throughout the state.

Boating and Lake Activities Visitors may be surprised to find so many lakes in this state noted for its desert life. Choices range from secluded, get-away-from-it-all oases to big and boisterous canyon-bound water resorts. The two national recreational areas, Glen Canyon (Lake Powell), in the north-central region, and Lake Mead (including Lake Mohave), in the northwest, offer many facilities, including marinas, launching ramps, and boat and ski rentals. At both lakes you can sign up for a paddle-wheeler tour or take the wheel yourself in a fully equipped houseboat. Lake Havasu, fed by the Colorado River in the western part of the state, is another favored site for boating, waterskiing, windsurfing, and jet-skiing; in the background is the rather surreal vision of London Bridge, which was moved block by block from England and reassembled at this lakeside resort. In all locations, check ahead on the availability of rental equipment.

Saguaro and Canyon lakes, just east of Scottsdale, offer good boating and waterskiing for those based in the Phoenix area who are looking for a convenient day trip.

Other Water Sports **Swimmers** can take a cool plunge in a mountain lake, dive into an Olympic-size pool, or splash in the acres and acres of water at one of the recreational mega-resorts. Virtually every hotel and motel has a swimming pool of some size, and nearly all Arizona cities have at least one public pool; most are heated, and in the northern region many are indoors. You can cavort in the man-made waves at a number of water parks in the Phoenix area, including Water World and Golfland/Sunsplash (in Mesa), and even **surf** the 3- to 5-foot-high waves at Big Surf in Tempe. Bring your own board, or rent one on site. **Tubing** is a popular sport along the Salt River, east of Mesa. Tubes can be rented, and a shuttle bus will pick up or drop off at any of five points, enabling you to choose the length of your float.

Camping *See* Lodging, *below.*

Canoeing Swift currents without rapids make the day-long Topock Gorge trip on the Colorado River a favorite outing. Beginning at Topock, canoeists travel through a wildlife refuge to Castle Rock at the top end of Lake Havasu. Another route, made dramatic by the Black Canyon cliffs, is along the Colorado River below Hoover Dam to Willow Beach. Canoe rentals are available at both locations.

Fishing Fish practically jump out of Arizona's cool mountain streams, major rivers, and man-made lakes and are especially plentiful at the Colorado River resorts. Rainbow, brown, brook, and cutthroat trout, as well as catfish, crappie, bass, pike, and bluegill, are the main species. San Carlos Lake is tops for bass, and the trout are plentiful at Lees Ferry. Fishing licenses are required and can be obtained from the **Arizona Game and Fish Department** (2221 W. Greenway Rd., Phoenix 85023, tel. 602/942–3000).

Golf Your clubs won't gather dust in Arizona. Aside from the big-draw Phoenix and Tucson opens (*see* Festivals and Seasonal Events, *above*), golfers flock to this state to tee off at the myriad top-rank private and municipal courses. The year-round desert courses offer cheaper greens fees during the summer, and those in the northern part of the state usually shut down for winter. Just about every resort has its own course or is affiliated with a private club. For a listing of Arizona's golfing facilities, contact the **Arizona Golf Association** (7226 N. 16th St., Suite 200, Phoenix 85020, tel. 602/944–3035).

Hiking Hikers can choose from trails that wind through the desert, head over the mountains, delve deep into the forests, or circumnavigate the cities. Whatever your choice of direction, you'll find thousands of miles of marked paths. Protect against sunburn and, if you're hiking in the desert areas, beware of heatstroke; if you're going through dense scrub, it's a good idea to keep a lookout for snakes. In general, only backcountry hikers need worry about meeting up with Gila monsters.

Grand Canyon hikers should be well prepared before starting out. Summer months mean extreme heat, while the winter season can turn alternately snowy, rainy, or sunny. One of the biggest dangers of winter hikes is hypothermia, caused by exposure to cold, wet weather. In summer, hikers to the inner Canyon must head out carrying a gallon of water for each day they plan to hike. There is no shade, so a hat and sunglasses are crucial. It is not advisable to hike remote areas alone. **The Backcountry Reservations Office** (tel. 602/638–7888) provides hikers with trail details, weather conditions, and packing suggestions.

For hikers who prefer to travel with a group, the **Sierra Club** (tel. 602/253–8633) leads a variety of wilderness treks; there are chapters in Phoenix, Tucson, Kingman, Prescott, Sedona, Flagstaff, and Yuma.

Horseback Riding Traveling by horseback through the somewhat wild West or the scenic high country is perhaps the most appropriate way to explore Arizona. Stables offer a selection of mountain- or desert-trail rides lasting a half day, two days, or as long as two weeks. In the northern regions the season is from May through October. If riding is the focus of your Arizona holiday, however, you might consider staying at a dude ranch where you can saddle up every day.

River Rafting Rafting and kayaking trips down the Colorado River and through the Grand Canyon are experiences that keep visitors returning year after year. Trips run from one day to two weeks and operate during the summer season. Other rafting expeditions are offered on the Salt and Verde rivers, through the Sonoran Desert, near Scottsdale. Contact the **Arizona Office of Tourism** (*see* Tourist Information, *above*) for an extensive list of operators.

Rockhounding Arizona is rock-hound heaven, its deserts and mountains laden with a dazzling variety of rocks and minerals. **The Department of Mines and Mineral Resources** (1502 W. Washington St., Phoenix 85007, tel. 602/255–3795) is an excellent source of information about the specimens that can be found in each part of the state; the department offers a fine Mining and Mineral Museum as well as a rockhounding reference library. Inquire about restrictions before you fill your pockets; taking rocks is illegal on the Navajo and Hopi reservations, for example.

Skiing　Cross-country skiing is featured at **Mormon Lake Ski Touring**
Cross-Country　**Center** (tel. 602/354–2240), southeast of Flagstaff; at the **North Rim Nordic Center** (tel. 602/526–0924 or 800/525–0924 outside AZ); and along the miles of crisscrossing trails around **Alpine** (tel. 602/339–4384). Equipment and instruction are readily available, though it's best to make reservations for the high season.

Downhill　**Sunrise Park Resort** in McNary (tel. 800/772–7669), owned and operated by the White Mountain Apache Indians, encompasses three mountain peaks and is the state's largest ski area. Other popular resorts are **Arizona Snowbowl,** near Flagstaff (tel. 602/779–1951), and **Mt. Lemmon Ski Valley,** near Tucson (tel. 602/576–1321). Ski resorts cater to all levels, from beginner to expert, and provide instruction and equipment rental.

Tennis　Arizona offers a multitude of tennis opportunities, from hard courts at city parks and university campuses to full-scale programs at ultraposh tennis-oriented resorts such as **John Gardiner's Tennis Ranch** (5700 E. McDonald Dr., Scottsdale 85253, tel. 602/948–2100 or 800/245–2051), one of the country's best. Most hotels either have their own courts or are affiliated with a private or municipal facility.

National and State Parks and Monuments

National　Arizona's two national parks are the granddaddy Grand Canyon
Parks　National Park (1,218,375 acres) and Petrified Forest National Park (93,533 acres). The **Grand Canyon,** northwest of Flagstaff, has achieved status as one of the Seven Natural Wonders of the World. Travelers come from all parts of the globe to hike, camp, raft, helicopter, or simply ooh and aah at the spectacular views and ever-changing colors, shadows, and light. **Petrified Forest National Park,** east of Flagstaff, features rainbow-colored petrified logs, tree fragments, and chunks of rock—preserved-in-stone remnants of a forest dating from the dinosaur age.

National　**Saguaro National Monument,** which flanks Tucson's east and
Monuments　west sides, boasts the most specimens in the United States of the towering saguaro cactus, which can live over 200 years. **Organ Pipe National Monument,** in the southwest part of the state, abounds in examples of the saguaro's many-armed cousin. For Native American ruins in scenic settings, visit **Walnut Canyon National Monument** and **Wupatki National Monument** in the Flagstaff area, **Tuzigoot National Monument** south of Sedona, and **Navajo National Monument** near Monument Valley. Little-visited spots of unusual beauty include **Sunset Crater Volcano National Monument,** west of Flagstaff, its black lava flows contrasted against a lush green forest; and **Chiricahua National Monument** in the southeast, where odd rock formations preside over woods that celebrate spring and autumn at the same time.

State Parks Arizona's state parks range from relatively tiny **Slide Rock** (54 acres), near Sedona, to 13,000-acre **Lake Havasu**; both feature water-based activities. Boating and water-sports enthusiasts also like to congregate at **Alamo Lake State Park,** north of Wenden, **Roper Lake State Park,** at the foot of Mt. Graham in the southeast, and **Lyman Lake State Park,** in the White Mountains area. **Catalina** and **Picacho Peak state parks,** near Tucson, and **Lost Dutchman State Park,** east of Phoenix, are the best bets for desert activities. **Painted Rocks State Park,** west of Gila Bend, is distinctive for its Indian rock carvings. Those interested in the lively frontier history of this state should enjoy **Riordon Historical State Park** in Flagstaff, **Jerome State Historic Park** and **Fort Verde State Historic Park** in north-central Arizona, and **Tombstone Courthouse State Historic Park** and **Yuma Territorial Prison State Historic Park,** both in the south. For a complete listing of all state parks and their facilities, contact the **Arizona State Parks Department** (1300 W. Washington St., Phoenix 85007, tel. 602/542–4174).

Fragile Life Don't be tempted to pull any of Arizona's century-old saguaro cacti out by the roots. The state flower is protected by law, as are most slow-growing desert plants and flowers. Theft or vandalism carries stiff penalties. Similarly, the dry and easily desecrated desert floor takes centuries to overcome human damage. Consequently, it is illegal for four-wheel-drive and all-terrain vehicles and motorcycles to travel off established roadways.

Indian Reservations

Individual tribes own their respective lands. If you venture off main highways that traverse the reservations to do extensive backcountry exploring, you must request permission from the village leader; any local should be able to direct you. Never take photographs without first securing consent and paying a fee, if required. Visitors are occasionally allowed to watch certain tribal ceremonies, but all cameras, tape recorders, and even sketch pads are forbidden. Remember that you are a guest on private property. **The Native American Tourism Center** (4130 N. Goldwater Blvd., Scottsdale 85251, tel. 602/945–0771) sells a map of the Arizona reservations, which includes a listing of their annual festivals, and also offers tourism brochures and a calendar of events on and off the reservations. In addition, the center can help you contact any of the 14 tribal councils in the state.

Dining

Outside the main cities, Arizona cuisine leans mainly toward Western-style steaks, barbecued ribs and beans, biscuits with gravy, and chuck wagon–type fare. The Navajo taco (beans, tomatoes, lettuce, and cheese on Indian fry bread) and a few Hopi recipes served on the reservation blend Native American and Mexican food traditions. Mexican food is plentiful everywhere in the state. Phoenix and Tucson offer fine Continental dining, an eclectic mix of ethnic eateries, and, most important, the acclaimed Southwestern international-style cuisine, featuring indigenous ingredients prepared in an innovative fashion. Make advance reservations at the better restaurants, and don't be misled by the casual lifestyle—ask about dress codes first to avoid being turned away at the door. A few of the tonier establishments, including some at the swank resorts, require men to wear a jacket and tie.

Lodging

Arizona's hotels and motels run the gamut from world-class resorts to budget chains, with historic inns, bed-and-breakfasts, mountain lodges, dude ranches, campgrounds, and RV parks providing even more options. Most nationwide and international companies are represented within the state. Big resorts offer extensive recreational and dining facilities, while modest motels may provide nothing more than a small swimming pool and complimentary coffee. Make reservations well in advance for the high season—winter in the desert south and summer in the high country. Tremendous bargains can be found in the off-season, when even the ultraswank spots cut their rates by half.

Bed-and-Breakfasts Many areas of the state offer B&B lodging, in anything from a ranch in the country to a Victorian adobe in the city. Moderate prices and personalized, homey hospitality are the hallmarks of this type of accommodation. Arizona B&B organizations include **Mi Casa Su Casa** (Box 950, Tempe 85280, tel. 602/990–0682 or 800/456–0682, fax 602/990–3390), **Bed & Breakfast Inn Arizona** (Gallery 3 Plaza, 3819 N. 3rd St., Phoenix, AZ 85012, tel. 602/ 265–9511, reservations only 800/266–7829, fax 602/263–7762), and the **Arizona Association of Bed and Breakfast Inns** (3101 North Central Ave., Suite 560, Phoenix 85712, tel. 602/277– 0775). The Arizona Office of Tourism (*see* Tourist Information, *above*) has a statewide list of bed and breakfasts.

Dude Ranches Down-home Western lifestyle, cooking, and activities are the focus of guest ranches, situated primarily in Tucson and Wickenburg. Some are resortlike properties where guests are pampered, while the smaller family-run ranches expect *everyone* to join in the chores. Horseback riding and other outdoor recreational activities are emphasized. Most dude ranches are closed during summer months. Contact the Arizona Office of Tourism (*see* Tourist Information, *above*) for the names and addresses of dude ranches throughout the state.

Home Exchange You can find a house, apartment, or other vacation property to exchange for your own by becoming a member of a home-exchange organization, which then sends you its annual directories listing available exchanges and includes your own listing in at least one of them. Arrangements for the actual exchange are made by the two parties to it, not by the organization. For more information contact the **International Home Exchange Association** (IHEA, 41 Sutter St., Suite 1090, San Francisco, CA 94104, tel. 415/673–0347 or 800/788–2489). **Intervac International** (Box 590504, San Francisco, CA 94159, tel. 415/435–3497) has three annual directories; membership is $62, or $72 if you want to receive the directories but remain unlisted. **Loan-a-Home** (2 Park La., Apt. 6E, Mount Vernon, NY 10552, tel. 914/664–7640) specializes in long-term exchanges; there is no charge to list your home, but the directories cost $35 or $45 depending on the number you receive.

Apartment and Villa Rentals If you want a home base that's roomy enough for a family and comes with cooking facilities, a furnished rental may be the solution. It's generally cost-efficient too, although not always—some rentals are luxury properties (economical only when your party is large). Home-exchange directories do list rentals—often second homes owned by prospective house swappers—and some services search for a house or apartment for you (even a castle if that's your fancy) and also handle the paperwork. Some send an illustrated catalogue and others send photographs of specific properties, sometimes at a charge; up-front registration fees may apply. Among the companies is **Rent-a-Home International** (7200 34th Ave. NW, Seattle, WA 98117, tel. 206/789–9377 or 800/488–7368). **Hideaways International** (767 Islington St., Box 4433, Portsmouth, NH 03802, tel. 603/430–4433 or 800/843–4433) functions as a travel club. Membership ($99 yearly per person or family at the same address) includes two annual guides plus quarterly newsletters; rentals are arranged directly between members, not by the club staff.

Camping and Campgrounds Campers can choose from a feast of federal, state, Native American, or private campgrounds in virtually all parts of the state. Facilities range from deluxe parks with swimming pools and recreation rooms to primitive backcountry wilderness sites. Most campgrounds provide toilets, drinking water, showers, and hookups. Camping is also permitted in Arizona's seven national forests, but be forewarned that there are no facilities whatsoever.

Campers should pack according to season, region, and length of trip. Basic gear should include a sleeping bag, a tent (optional, and forbidden in some RV parks), a camp stove, cooking utensils, food and water supplies, a first-aid kit, insect repellent, sunscreen, a lantern, trash bags, a rope, and a tarp. In case you forget something, almost every camping item is available for sale or rent at one of Arizona's many sporting-goods shops.

Individual campgrounds should be contacted before travel for suggestions as to specific equipment to bring, as well as necessary reservations, advance deposits, and permits. Most state parks have a 15-day maximum-stay limit. For further details, contact the **National Park Service** (202 E. Earll Dr., Suite 115, Phoenix 85012, tel. 602/640–5250), **Bureau of Land Management** (Box 16563, Phoenix 85011, tel. 602/650–0528), **Arizona State Parks Department** (*see* State Parks, *above*), **Apache Sitgreaves National Forest** (Box 640, Springerville 85938, tel. 602/333–4301), **Coconino National Forest** (2323 E. Greenlaw La., Flagstaff 86004, tel. 602/527–3600), **Coronado National Forest** (Federal Bldg., 300 W. Congress St., Tucson 85701, tel. 602/670–4552), **Kaibab National Forest** (800 S. 6th St., Williams 86046, tel. 602/635–2681), **Prescott National Forest** (344 S. Cortez, Prescott 86303, tel. 602/445–1762), or **Tonto National Forest** (2324 E. McDowell Rd., Phoenix 85010, tel. 602/225–5200). The **National Forest Service hot line** (tel. 602/225–5296) gives recorded information and campground updates.

Credit Cards

The following credit-card abbreviations are used throughout this guide: AE, American Express; D, Discover; DC, Diners Club; MC, MasterCard; V, Visa.

2 Portraits of Arizona

The What and the Why of Desert Country

By Joseph
Wood Krutch

On the brightest and warmest days my desert is most it-self because sunshine and warmth are the very essence of its character. The air is lambent with light; the ca-ressing warmth envelops everything in its ardent embrace. Even when outlanders complain that the sun is too dazzling and too hot, we desert lovers are prone to reply, "At worst that is only too much of a good thing."

Unfortunately, this is the time when the tourist is least likely to see it. Even the winter visitor who comes for a month or six weeks is mostly likely to choose January or February because he is thinking about what he is escaping at home rather than of what he is coming to here. True, the still warm sun and the usu-ally bright skies make a dramatic contrast with what he has left behind. In the gardens of his hotel or guest ranch, flowers still bloom and some of the more obstreperous birds make cheerful sounds, even though they do not exactly sing at this season. The more enthusiastic visitors talk about "perpetual summer" and sometimes ask if we do not find the lack of seasons monotonous. But this is nonsense. Winter is winter even in the desert.

At Tucson's 2,300 feet it often gets quite cold at night even though shade temperatures during the day may rise to 75° Fahrenheit or even higher. Most vegetation is pausing, though few animals hibernate. This is a sort of neutral time when the desert environment is least characteristically itself. It is almost like late September or early October, just after the first frost, in southern New England. For those who are thinking of nothing except getting away from something, rather than learning to know a new world, this is all very well. But you can't become ac-quainted with the desert itself at that time of year.

By April the desert is just beginning to come into its own. The air and the skies are summery without being hot; the roadsides and many of the desert flats are thickly carpeted with a profu-sion of wildflowers such as only California can rival. The desert is smiling before it begins to laugh, and October or November are much the same. But June is the month for those who want to know what the desert is really like. That is the time to decide once and for all if it is, as for many it turns out to be, "your coun-try."

It so happens that I am writing this not long after the 21st of June, and I took especial note of that astronomically significant date. This year, summer began at precisely 10 hours and no min-utes, mountain standard time. That means that the sun rose higher and stayed longer in the sky than on any other day of the year. In the North there is often a considerable lag in the sea-sons as the earth warms up, but here, where it is never very cold, the longest day and the hottest are likely to coincide pretty closely. So it was this year. On June 21 the sun rose almost to the zenith so that at noon he cast almost no shadow. And he was showing what he is capable of.

Even in this dry air, 109° Fahrenheit in the shade is pretty warm. Under the open sky the sun's rays strike with an almost physical force, pouring down from a blue dome unmarked by the faintest suspicion of even a fleck of cloud. The year has been unusually dry even for the desert. During the four months just past, no rain—not even a light shower—has fallen. The surface of the ground is as dry as powder. And yet, when I look out of the window, the dominant color of the landscape is incredibly green.

On the low foothills surrounding the steep rocky slopes of the mountains, which are actually 10 to 12 miles away but seem in the clear air much closer at hand, this greenness ends in a curving line following the contour of the mountains' base and inevitably suggesting the waves of a green sea lapping the irregular shoreline of some island rising abruptly from the ocean. Between me and that shoreline the desert is sprinkled with hundreds, probably thousands, of evenly placed shrubs, varied now and then by a small tree—usually a mesquite or what is called locally a cat's-claw acacia.

More than a month ago all the little annual flowers and weeds which spring up after the winter rains and rush from seed to seed again in six weeks gave up the ghost at the end of their short lives. Their hope of posterity lies now invisible, either upon the surface of the bare ground or just below it. Yet when the summer thunderstorms come in late July or August, they will not make the mistake of germinating. They are triggered to explode into life only when they are both moist and cool—which they will not be until next February or March when their season begins. Neither the shrubs nor the trees seem to know that no rain has fallen during the long months. The leathery, somewhat resinous, leaves of the dominant shrub—the attractive plant unattractively dubbed "creosote bush"—are not at all parched or wilted. Neither are the deciduous leaves of the mesquite.

Not many months ago the creosote was covered with bright yellow pealike flowers; the mesquite with pale yellow catkins. Now the former is heavy with gray seed and on the mesquite are forming long pods which Indians once ate and which cattle now find an unusually rich food.

It looks almost as though the shrubs and trees could live without water. But of course they cannot. Every desert plant has its secret, though it is not always the same one. In the case of the mesquite and the creosote it is that their roots go deep and that, so the ecologists say, there is in the desert no wet or dry season below 6 feet. What little moisture is there is pretty constant through the seasons of the year and through the dry years as well as the wet. Like the temperature in some caves, it never varies. The mesquite and creosote are not compelled to care whether it has rained for four months or not. And unlike many other plants they flourish whether there has been less rain or more than usual.

Those plants which have substantial root systems but nevertheless do not reach so deep are more exuberant some years than others. Thus the Encelia, or brittlebush, which, in normal years, literally covers many slopes with thousands of yellow, daisylike flowers, demands a normal year. Though I have never seen it fail, I am told that in very dry years it comes into leaf but does not flower, while in really catastrophic droughts it does not come up at all, as the roots lie dormant and hope for better times. Even the creosote bush, which never fails, can, nevertheless, profit from surface water, and when it gets the benefit of a few thunderstorms in late July or August, it will flower and fruit a second time so that the expanse which is now all green will be again sprinkled with yellow. . . .

Obviously the animals and plants that share this country with me take it for granted. To them it is just "the way things are." By now I am beginning to take it for granted myself. But being a man I must ask what they cannot: What *is* a desert, and why is it what it is? At latitude 32 one expects the climate to be warm. But the desert is much more than merely warm. It is a consistent world with a special landscape, a special geography, and, to go with them, a special flora and fauna adapted to that geography and that climate.

Nearly every striking feature of this special world, whether it be the shape of the mountains or the habits of its plant and animal inhabitants, goes back ultimately to the grand fact of dryness—the dryness of the ground, of the air, of the whole sum total. And the most inclusive cause of the dryness is simply that out here it doesn't rain very much.

Some comparisons with regions where it rains more may help us understand what that means. Take, for example, southern New England. By world standards it gets a lot—namely some 40 inches of rain per year. Certain parts of the southern states get even more: about 50 inches for east Tennessee, nearly 60 for New Orleans. Some areas on the West Coast get fantastic amounts, like the 75 inches at Crescent City, California, and the unbelievable 153 inches, or nearly four times what New York City gets, recorded one year in Del Norde County, California.

Nevertheless, New England's 40 is a lot of water, either comparatively or absolutely. The region around Paris, for instance, gets little more than half that amount. Forty inches is, in absolute terms, more than most people imagine. One inch of rain falling on an acre of ground means more than 27,000 gallons of water. No wonder that irrigation in dry regions is quite a formidable task even for modern technology.

In terms of what vegetation can use, 40 inches is ample for the kind of agriculture and natural growth which we tend to think of as "normal." It means luxuriant grass, rapid development of second-growth woodland, a veritable jungle of weeds and bushes in midsummer. In inland America, the rainfall tends to be less than in the coastal regions. As one moves westward from the Mississippi it declines sharply and begins to drop below 20 inches a year at about the one-hundredth meridian or, very roughly, at a line drawn from Columbus, Ohio, through Oklahoma City. This means too little water for most broad-leaved trees and explains why the southern Great Plains were as treeless when the white man first saw them as they are today.

Our true deserts—the Great Basin Desert in Utah and Nevada, the Chihuahuan in New Mexico, the Sonoran in Arizona, and the Mohave in California—all lie still farther to the west. The four differ among themselves but they are all dry and hot, and they all fulfill what is probably the most satisfactory definition of "desert"—namely, a region where the ground cover is not continuous; where, that is, the earth remains bare of vegetation between such plants as manage to grow. Over these American deserts the rainfall varies considerably, and with it the character and extent of the vegetation. In southern Arizona, for instance, it is about 4 inches at Yuma, nearly 11 near Tucson. Four inches means sand dunes which look like those pictures of the Sahara, which the word "desert" calls to most people's minds. Eleven means that where the soil is suitable, well-separated individuals of such desert plants as the cacti and the paloverde trees will flourish.

But if scanty rainfall makes for deserts, what makes for scanty rainfall? To that there are two important answers. One is simply that most regions other than the mountainous ones tend to be dry if they lie in that belt of permanently high atmospheric pressure which extends some 30 or 35 degrees on each side of the equator where calms are frequent and winds erratic. Old sailors used to call this region "the horse latitudes," though nobody knows why and you can take your choice of three equally unconvincing explanations. One is that it was because horses tended to die when the ships lay long in the hot calms. Another, because the boisterous changeableness of the winds when they do come suggests unruly horses. A third is that they were originally called after the English explorer, Ross, which was mistaken by the Germans for their old word for "horse." In any event, the latitude of Tucson puts it just within the "horse latitudes." Most of the important deserts of the world, including the Sahara and the Gobi, lie within this same belt.

The other important answer to the question "What makes for scanty rainfall?" is, "Mountains lying across the path of such moist winds as do blow." In our case, the Coast Ranges of California lie between us and the Pacific. From my front porch, which looks directly across the desert to some nearer mountains of the southernmost Rockies, I can see, on a small scale, what happens. Many, many times a moisture-laden mass of air reaches as far as these closest mountains. Dark clouds form, sometimes the whole range is blotted out. Torrential rains are falling. But on me not a drop. Either the sky is blue overhead or the high clouds which have blown my way dissolve visibly as the warm air rising from my sun-drenched flats reaches them. I am in what the geographers call a "rain shadow" cast by the mountains. Up at their summit the rainfall is nearly twice as much as it is down here, and they are clothed with pines beginning at 6,000 or 7,000 feet and going on up to the 19,000-foot peak. When I do get rain in midwinter and in midsummer, it is usually because winds have brought moisture up from the Gulf of Mexico by an unobstructed southern route, or because in summer a purely local thundershower has been formed out of the hot air rising from the sun-beaten desert floor. Most of the time the sun is hot, even in winter, and the air is usually fantastically dry, the relative humidity being often less than 10.

Naturally the plants and animals living in such a region must be specially adapted to survive under such conditions, but the casual visitor usually notices the strangeness of the landscape before he is aware of the flora or the fauna. And the peculiar features of the landscape are also the result of dryness, even in ways that are not immediately obvious.

The nude mountains reveal their contours, or veil them as lightly as the late Greek sculptors veiled their nudes, because only near the summits of the mountains can anything tall enough to obscure the outlines grow. A little less obvious is the fact that the beautiful "monuments" of northern Arizona and southern Utah owe their unusual forms to the sculpturing of windblown sand, or that sheer cliffs often rise from a sloping cone of rocks and boulders because the talus slopes can accumulate in just that way only where there is not enough draining water to distribute them over the whole surrounding plain, as they would be distributed in regions of heavier rainfall. But the most striking example of all is the greatest single scenic wonder of the region, the Grand Canyon itself. This narrow gash, cut a mile deep through successive strata until the river flows at last over some of the oldest rock exposed anywhere on earth, could have been formed only in a very dry climate.

As recently as 200 years ago the best-informed observer would have taken it for granted that the river was running between those sheer walls at the bottom of the gorge simply because it had found them out. Today few visitors are not aware that the truth lies the other way around, that the river cut its own course through the rock. But most laymen do not ask the next questions: Why is the Grand Canyon unique, or why are such canyons, even on a smaller scale, rare? And the answer to those questions is that a set of very special conditions was necessary.

First there must be a thick series of rock strata slowly rising as a considerable river flows over it. Second, that considerable river must carry an unusual amount of hard sand or stone fragments in suspension so that it will be able to cut downward at least as rapidly as the rock over which it flows is rising. Third, that considerable river must be flowing through very arid country. Otherwise rain, washing over the edges of the cut, will widen it at the top as the cut goes deeper. That is why broad valleys are characteristic of regions with normal rainfall; canyons, large and small, of arid country.

And Grand Canyon is the grandest of all canyons because at that particular place all the necessary conditions were fulfilled more exuberantly than at any other place in the whole world. The Colorado River carries water from a relatively wet country through a dry one, it bears with it a fantastic amount of abrasive material, the rock over which it flows has been slowly rising during several millions of years, and too little rain falls to widen very rapidly the gash which it cuts. Thus in desert country everything from the color of a mouse or the shape of a leaf to the largest features of the mountains themselves is more likely than not to have the same explanation: dryness.

So far as living things go, all this adds up to what even an ecologist may so far forget himself as to call an "unfavorable environment." But like all such pronouncements this one doesn't mean much unless we ask "unfavorable for what and for whom?" For many plants, for many animals, and for some men it is very favorable indeed. Many of the first two would languish and die, transferred to some region where conditions were "more favorable." It is here, and here only, that they flourish. Many men feel healthier and happier in the bright dry air than they do anywhere else. And since I happen to be one of them, I not unnaturally have a special interest in the plants and animals that share my liking for just these conditions. For five years now I have been amusing myself by inquiring of them directly what habits and what adjustments they have found most satisfactory. Many of them are delightfully ingenious and eminently sensible. . . .

Men of most races have long been accustomed to speak with scorn of the few peoples who happen to live where nature makes things too easy. In the inclemency of their weather, the stoniness of their soil, or the rigors of their winter they find secret virtues so that even the London fog has occasionally found Englishmen to praise it. No doubt part of all this is mere prejudice at worst, making a virtue out of necessity at best. But undoubtedly there is also something in it. We grow strong against the pressure of a difficulty, and ingenious by solving problems. Individuality and character are developed by challenge. We tend to admire trees, as well as men, who bear the stamp of their successful struggles with a certain amount of adversity. People who have not had too easy a time of it develop flavor. And there is no doubt about the fact that desert life has character. Plants and animals are so obviously and visibly what they are because of the problems they have solved. They are part of some whole. They belong. Animals and plants, as well as men, become especially interesting when they do fit their environment, when to some extent they reveal what their response to it has been. And nowhere more than in the desert do they reveal it.

Arizona Crafts

By Suzanne Carmichael

Suzanne Carmichael is the author of The Traveler's Guide to American Crafts: East of the Mississippi *and* West of the Mississippi *and travel and craft articles for such publications as* The New York Times, USA Weekend, *and* Northwest Magazine.

Whether you have $10 or $1,000 to spend, shopping for crafts can make your trip to Arizona memorable, and not only for what you'll take home with you. The pursuit of local wares may take you down desert roads to remote crafts studios, introduce you to snazzy urban galleries and historic trading posts, or involve you in lively festivals. Regional crafts also provide an intimate introduction to an area's history, culture, and peoples, as well as its contemporary interests and trends.

In the Southwest, several cultures have developed strong crafts traditions, some predating European contact by more than 1,000 years. Native American, cowboy, and contemporary crafts—many made from native materials or by capturing local colors, themes, and spirit—are all well developed in this region.

Native American Crafts

Arizona visitors will see Native American crafts everywhere—in specialty shops, airports, motel gift shops, drugstores, and even gas stations. The problem is finding top-notch, authentic work. Some so-called Native American crafts are made in Taiwan or Mexico. Others labeled "genuine Indian made" are mass-produced with shoddy material and inferior workmanship.

If you haven't read any books on the subject, study Native American collections at the Heard Museum (Phoenix) or the Museum of Northern Arizona (Flagstaff). These museums also have their own gift shops, which sell good-quality items at reasonable prices. Long-established trading posts, galleries, and Native American dealers are another option. Most first-rate shops will have a range of prices and knowledgeable salespeople who can answer your questions. If everything in a shop is inexpensive, it's probably attributable to the poor quality of the goods rather than to a low overhead. It's a good idea to shop elsewhere.

One way to ensure authenticity and at the same time add an adventurous detour to your trip is to buy directly from craftspeople on the reservations. Look for signs that say "pottery," "rugs," or "baskets" hanging outside homes. Although visiting craftspeople is not a guarantee of quality, it does provide an opportunity to ask questions and learn about the work you are purchasing. And it's fun to watch artisans at work, to see their raw materials being turned into finished pieces.

Reservation gift shops are another option for authentic wares, although quality and prices vary tremendously. And crafts are generally sold at Native American festivals, fairs, and powwows (ceremonial gatherings), which exhibit the work of many artisans and also showcase tribal dancing, storytelling, and food.

One recommended event is Flagstaff's annual six-week Festival of Native American Arts held each summer at the Coconino Center for the Arts (2300 N. Valley Rd., U.S. 180, Flagstaff, tel. 602/779–6921). This juried festival offers high-quality traditional and contemporary tribal arts, including work rarely found elsewhere, such as colorful Pueblo moccasins and miniature pottery. Visitors can also watch jewelry-making, cloth- or basket-weaving demonstrations or participate in various workshops, including one that teaches children how to make Native American masks.

Arizona's Native American crafts legacy includes distinctive tribal arts made by many of the state's 14 tribes. Although the work of the Hopi, Navajo, and Tohonó O'odham (Papago) are best known, equally fine items are produced by the Chemehuevi, Maricopa, Mojave, Paiute, and Pima tribes.

Hopi pottery, baskets, and weaving reflect ancient traditions and techniques, while the tribe's silver work is of more recent vintage. Artisans of the Hopi tribe live on one of the reservation's three mesas, each of which has a craft specialty. First Mesa is home to potters who fashion hand-coiled vessels with pale cream or deep red glazes decorated with stylized birds and figures. Second Mesa's specialty is baskets of thickly coiled yucca joined with colorfully dyed lengths of yucca leaves; wicker baskets decorated with brightly colored designs can be found on Third Mesa. When buying pottery and baskets, look for symmetrical shapes, smooth rims, and neatly painted or evenly woven designs.

Tribal artisans also create kachina dolls, colorfully costumed, masked figures embellished with feathers, textiles, and leather. Modeled after the Hopi religion's kachina ceremonial dancers, the dolls are used to teach children their religious heritage. Hopi weaving, which is done exclusively by men, creates colorful sashes and narrow decorative bands that are used on clothing. Both of these items are woven on belt looms. The vertical threads (warp) on these unusual looms stretch around one rod tied to a tree to another rod held taut by a belt wrapped around the weaver's waist. While making a sash, the weaver leans forward to loosen the warp, backward to tighten it. Although Hopi woven fabric is created primarily for personal use, some pieces are occasionally available through the reservation's crafts cooperative.

Hopi silver work, a craft that was begun in the late 1890s, reflects a creative collaboration between contemporary silver-working techniques and ancient motifs. Hopi silversmiths use two layers of silver to create some of the Southwest's finest jewelry. Designs, which range from simple sun shapes to those depicting elaborate tribal legends, are carefully cut through the top layer, which is then soldered to the bottom layer. Tiny parallel lines are chiseled inside the design, and the piece is then oxidized to make the motif stand out from the polished silver surrounding it. The best pieces have smoothly cut patterns with neatly stamped, parallel interior lines.

Navajo jewelry traces its origin to the mid-19th century. Tribal craftsmen learned smithery from Mexican artisans, later adding their own styles and designs. Early pieces were made from hammered silver coins and decorated with stamp work. Although turquoise beads date from prehistoric times, Navajos did not combine the stone with silver until the late 1800s. Today, in addition to turquoise, artisans sometimes incorporate coral, lapis, and other semiprecious stones into their designs.

Contemporary Navajo jewelry ranges from simple rings and cast silver bracelets to massive necklaces and concha belts (named for the stamped silver disks strung together on narrow leather strips). Because there are so many variables in the quality of stones and workmanship, you should purchase Navajo jewelry only from reputable dealers. Many Indian traders and jewelry shops throughout the Southwest have one case displaying items of Native American–made jewelry that have been pawned and not retrieved by their owners. Although you can occasionally find older pieces of exquisite quality in these cases, be leery of assertions as to an item's age or caliber.

Navajos are also known for the variety and quality of their woven wool rugs. Sheepherders for centuries, Navajos learned their weaving skills from Pueblo Indians during the 18th century. At first they produced blankets and clothing in natural brown-and-white stripes. During the late 19th century, colors, particularly red, and a wide range of complex designs were added. At this time, most weavers also switched from producing items for personal use to creating rugs for traders. Today Navajo rug patterns range from traditional eye dazzlers with bold zigzag patterns and pictorials featuring animals and other figures to *yei* rugs that duplicate sandpainting designs and two-faced rugs with different patterns on each surface.

If you purchase a Navajo rug, make sure that it is made entirely of wool (no linen or cotton threads), that the wool is of even thickness throughout the piece, that the design is neatly woven, and that the colors are uniform throughout. A good source of Navajo rugs and other Native American crafts is the Hubbell Trading Post, a National Historic Site in Ganado, on the Navajo reservation 22 miles west of Window Rock. Established in 1878, the post looks exactly as it did in the 19th century when Navajos brought John Lorenzo Hubbell their rugs and jewelry to trade for groceries and other goods. These artisans still bring their crafts for sale or trade, but now they arrive in pickups instead of on horseback.

While Hopi and Navajo crafts are the best-known Arizona Native American arts, other tribes also produce good-quality items that provide an introduction to their cultural history. Among these are traditional Tohonó O'odham baskets. Tohonó O'odham artisans create coiled, waterproof baskets with intricate designs using techniques and materials that have remained virtually unchanged for more than 11 centuries. Most baskets are broad, slightly sloping vessels with geometric patterns and are made from two Southwestern desert plants. Black designs, the most highly prized, are fashioned from black devil's claw, an increasingly rare plant that yields very strong strips of jet-black fiber. Red motifs are woven with the root of banana yucca, a more common plant found in Arizona's higher elevations. One traditional Tohonó O'odham design is the legendary Man in the Maze, a stylized male figure standing at the top of the basket, about to enter a complex white-and-black labyrinth.

Baskets are also made by the Pima and Paiute. The Pima use coils of cattail stems bound with willow and favor complex zig-zag designs. Traditional Paiute baskets have plain, functional shapes, reflecting the fact that they were once used to carry water, harvest or store seeds, and cradle babies. Mojave, Maricopa, and Chemehuevi tribal arts are more difficult to find, but they are worth the effort. Mojave beadwork can be exquisite, especially large, collar-shapenecklaces created in traditional network designs resembling intricate lace. Maricopa artisans specialize in cream-colored pottery, decorated with black designs that incorporate both geometric shapes and curvilinear symbols. Finely woven Chemehuevi baskets, another rare but exquisite craft, are made from coiled fiber, sometimes decorated with colorful feathers.

Cowboy Crafts

Even if you don't own horses or cattle, consider buying cowboy crafts: They can add pizzazz to your decor or an unusual flair to your wardrobe and provide an intriguing diversion as you watch them being created by talented artisans.

Arizona ranchers may use computers to keep track of their businesses, but no one has devised the technology to replace cowboys. Although his (and sometimes her) job may include time in a pickup, the daily routine is still dominated by horses, cattle, and traditional equipment rarely influenced by 20th-century innovations. The items cowboys use every day—from saddles and spurs to bridles and hats—form a crafts tradition that spans centuries. Some items originated with Native Americans, while others were adopted from Mexican or California-Spanish traditions.

Arizona cowboy crafts can be found in many shops, and even in department stores, but it's more fun to buy them directly from craftspeople or in tack shops that sell everything a horse and its rider need, from saddles to cowboy hats. Look in telephone books under tack shops, horse furnishings, or specific crafts such as saddlery or hats. For a thorough immersion, attend Flagstaff's annual 5½-week Trappings of the American West Festival, sponsored by the Coconino Center for the Arts; it runs from early May until the second week of June. The festival includes cowboy crafts demonstrations and workshops where you can learn rawhide braiding and boot making.

Although cowboy crafts are often decorative, they are first of all functional tools of the trade. Hats protect the wearer from weather, branches, and rocks and double as containers for carrying water and feed. Boots, designed to be pulled off easily and fit comfortably in stirrups, protect feet from mud and brush. Chaps shield the legs from prickly cactus and other hazards. The brush in Arizona is particularly heavy, so cowboys here prefer Arizona bell-bottom chaps made from very heavy leather that is flared at the bottom so they bend with the leg. The best of each? Hats made from beaver-fur felt, custom-made boots, and used chaps with that trail-worn look.

Saddles, which are custom-made to fit horse and rider, are often covered with carved or stamped designs of elaborate floral and leaf motifs. Some cowboys claim that deep carving keeps them from slipping in the saddle. For urban cowpokes, many saddlers create stamped or carved leather purses, belts, wallets, and even wastebaskets.

The oldest cowboy craft is leather and horsehair braiding. Conceived by Native Americans, braiding was later adopted by Mexican and American cowboys. Complex patterns decorate braided horse gear, from bridles and reins to other items whose exotic names belie their practicality: bosals and hobbles, romals and quirts. Look also for braided hatbands, belts, and bracelets.

Other cowboy accoutrements include bits and spurs with ornate inlaid designs that are seen only by the cowboy and his horse. Texas cowboys generally favor massive inlaid silver stars and geometric patterns, while California and Arizona cowboys prefer gear embellished with flowers and flourishes. Many smiths also fashion decorative silver work for saddles, as well as buckles, money clips, and jewelry. Knives, another cowboy necessity, can be found in great variety. Look for those with handles that are made from exotic materials, engraved, or inlaid with precious metal and stones.

Contemporary Crafts

Arizona's contemporary artisans work in every medium, but particularly in ceramics, textiles, and wood. Although the focus of their work varies from abstract to functional, many of the crafts reflect Arizona colors: the splashy hues of a desert sunset, the subtle pastels of cactus flowers, the myriad reds of Sedona's cliffs. There's also a healthy dose of humor in many items: prickly ceramic cactus vases, howling wood dogs, flirty roadrunner sculptures, chairs with coyote armrests. The use of native materials is also common—for example, you may come across cactus-spine baskets or mesquite armoires.

Phoenix, Scottsdale, and Tucson offer a bonanza of contemporary crafts galleries. On a smaller scale, Tubac, an artists' community 35 miles south of Tucson, has numerous crafts studios open to the public. Tubac artisans create everything from avant-garde jewelry and textiles to copper fountains shaped like cacti. To find galleries throughout Arizona, consult *Art Life*, two comprehensive guides (one covers northern Arizona, the other southern Arizona) that describe galleries, provide detailed maps, and include indexes arranged by style, subject, and medium. Available free in many Arizona galleries, the guides can also be ordered by calling Yoakum Publishing (tel. 602/797–1271).

3 The Grand Canyon and Northwest Arizona

By William
E. Hafford
and Edie
Jarolim

Although millions of words have been devoted to describing the Grand Canyon, writers have generally conceded that the Earth's greatest gorge is beyond the scope of language. Southwestern author Frank Waters has come closer than most to capturing its power. "It is the sum total," he writes, "of all the aspects of nature combined in one integrated whole. It is at once the smile and frown upon the face of nature. In its heart is the savage, uncontrollable fury of all the inanimate Universe, and at the same time the immeasurable serenity that succeeds it. It is Creation."

To appreciate the Grand Canyon, you must see it. Not even the finest photographs pack a fraction of the impact of a personal glimpse of this vast, beautiful scar on the surface of our planet—277 miles long, 18 miles across at its widest spot, and more than a mile below the rim at its deepest point. The Grand Canyon is the quintessence of the high drama of the American western landscape.

More than 65 million years ago, a great wrenching of the earth pushed the land in the region of the canyon up into a domed tableland, today called the Colorado Plateau. Then the Colorado River, racing south through present-day Utah, began chewing at the uplifted region. The river is responsible for much of the erosion, but many side gullies and canyons were formed by melting snow and fierce rainstorms that sent water rushing into the gorge through smaller tributaries. Softer rock formations were washed away by the Colorado and carried to the distant sea; the harder formations remained as great cliffs and buttes. Above the twisting line of river are otherworldly stone monuments with colors that range from muted pastels to deep purples, vibrant yellows, fiery reds, and soft blues. This palette shifts with the hours: What you see at midmorning is repainted by the setting sun.

This is also a land of ancient peoples. In some of the deepest, most inaccessible reaches of the Grand Canyon, evidence of early human habitation exists. Stone ruins high in the cliffs reveal the archaeological secrets of a culture more than 4,000 years old. In the higher country above the rims, both north and south, are the ruins of a prehistoric Pueblo civilization, which existed in the area until about AD 1200. It is believed that the people left the region during a period of harsh and sustained drought. Today's Hopi Indians, who live on high rock mesas about 150 miles east of the canyon, may be descendants of that group.

In the year 1540, a small group of Spanish soldiers under the command of Captain García López de Cárdenas became the first white men to look into the canyon. The members of the expedition, dispatched by Francisco Coronado to find an Indian village, were disinclined to stay very long—or to return. Spanish Franciscan missionary and explorer Francisco Tomás Garcés visited a Havasupai Indian village in the canyon in 1776, and Lieutenant Joseph Ives went on an official mission for the U.S. government to explore the area in 1857. But no one thought it worth much attention until 1869, when John Wesley Powell, a

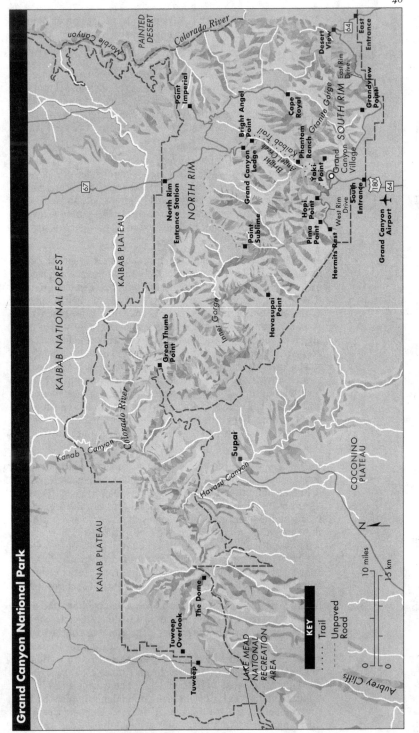

Grand Canyon National Park

one-armed adventurer and scholar, put rough-hewn boats into the Colorado and let the swirling white water of the mighty river take him along its length.

During the last years of the 19th century, almost all development at or near the canyon was related to mining. In fact, the earliest trails down into the canyon were built by miners searching for precious minerals. Shortly after the beginning of the 20th century, the Santa Fe Railroad completed a line to the South Rim of the canyon, ushering in the era of tourism. In 1903 Theodore Roosevelt visited and drew public interest to the site; it was declared a national park in 1919. Today close to 5 million visitors come each year from around the world to peer into this gorge in amazement.

The Fred Harvey Company opened the world-famous El Tovar Hotel on the rim of the canyon in 1905, heralding the beginning of Grand Canyon Village. Now there are more than 900 motel and hotel rooms in the Village, but the ever-increasing visitor population makes even that number of accommodations insufficient in summer. If you can arrange it, try to visit the Grand Canyon in the fall or spring. You might encounter cold weather during those periods, but chances are good that most of the days will be clear and will range from pleasantly cool to warm. In autumn and spring, when the crowds have thinned, reservations are much easier to arrange, and, in some cases, prices drop. Or consider a winter visit. The snow on the ground only enhances the site's sublime beauty.

The North Rim, in the isolated Arizona Strip, draws only about 10% of the Grand Canyon's visitors but is every bit as gorgeous as the South Rim. From southern Arizona, there's only one highway into this area, 210 miles of lonely road to the north and west of Flagstaff. Set in deep forest near the 9,000-foot crest of the Kaibab Plateau, the North Rim is, for many visitors, worth the extra miles. But truth to tell, there's virtually no place along either rim or in the depths of the Grand Canyon that will fail to startle and impress you.

Essential Information

Important Addresses and Numbers

Tourist Information **Grand Canyon Lodge** (TW Recreation Services, Inc., Box 400, Cedar City, UT 84720, tel. 801/586–7686, fax 801/586–3157) has lodging and general information about the North Rim year-round. For information on local services during the season in which the North Rim is open (generally mid-May through late October, depending on the weather), you can phone the lodge directly (tel. 602/638–2611).

Grand Canyon National Park Lodges (Box 699, Grand Canyon 86023, tel. 602/638–2401, fax 602/638–9247) can provide information on lodging, tours, and all other recreation inside the park at the South Rim.

Grand Canyon National Park (Box 129, Grand Canyon 86023, tel. 602/638–7888) is the contact for general information. Write ahead for a complimentary *Trip Planner*, updated regularly by the National Park Service.

Kaibab Visitor Center (204 W. Railroad Ave., at Grand Canyon Blvd., Williams, 86046, tel. 602/635–4061) is run jointly by the National Forest Service and the city of Williams and has information on Williams, Kaibab Forest, and the entire Grand Canyon area.

North and South Rim camping (MISTIX, Box 85705, San Diego, CA 92138, tel. 800/365–2267 or 619/452–0150 outside the U.S.). When you call this computer-operated system, have the exact dates you'd like to camp on hand.

Every arriving visitor at the South or North Rim is given a detailed map of the area. Both rims also publish a free newspaper, *The Guide*, which contains a detailed area map; it is available at the visitor center and many of the lodging facilities and stores.

The park also distributes "Accessibility Guide," a free newsletter that details the facilities available for those with special needs.

Emergencies **Police, fire,** or **ambulance** (tel. 911).

Medical **Grand Canyon Health Center** (Grand Canyon Village, tel. 602/
South Rim 638–2551 or 602/638–2469) offers physician services and receives patients weekdays 8–5:30, Saturday 9–noon. After-hours care and 24-hour emergency services are also available. Dental care (tel. 602/638–2395) is offered by appointment only.

North Rim The **North Rim Clinic** (Grand Canyon Lodge, Cabin 1, tel. 602/
638–2611, ext. 222) is staffed by a nurse practitioner. The clinic is open for walk-ins and appointments on Monday and Friday–Sunday 9–noon and 3–6, and on Tuesday 9–noon; it's closed on Wednesday. For emergency service dial 911.

Pharmacies At the South Rim there is a well-stocked drugstore at Grand Canyon Village (tel. 602/638–2460), open weekdays 8:30–5:30 year-round, and also Saturday morning in the summer; it's generally closed for an hour at lunchtime during the week. There is no pharmacy at the North Rim.

Road Service At Grand Canyon Village, the **Fred Harvey Public Garage** (tel.
South Rim 602/638–2225) is a fully equipped AAA garage that provides auto and RV repair as well as 24-hour emergency service. About ¾ mile down the road, across from the visitor center, **Fred Harvey Chevron** (tel. 602/638–2631) does oil and tire changes and minor repairs, and carries propane and diesel fuel.

North Rim The **Chevron** service station (tel. 602/638–2611), offering auto repairs, is located inside the park on the access road leading to the North Rim Campground. No diesel fuel is available at the North Rim.

Food and Camping Supplies
South Rim
Babbitt's General Store (tel. 602/638–2262) has three locations in the South Rim area: at Grand Canyon Village, in the nearby village of Tusayan, and at Desert View near the east park entrance. The main store, in Grand Canyon Village, is a department store that has a deli and sells a full line of camping, hiking, and backpacking supplies in addition to groceries.

North Rim
The **North Rim General Store** (tel. 602/638–2611), which is in the park across from the North Rim Campground, carries groceries, some clothing, and travelers' supplies.

Banks
An office of **Bank One** (tel. 602/638–2437) is located at the South Rim across from the visitor center in Grand Canyon Village. Services include a 24-hour teller machine operating with Bank One, Plus (Visa), Star, Arizona Interchange Network, and Cirrus (MasterCard) access cards. The bank cashes traveler's checks and exchanges foreign currency, but it does not cash personal checks. Banking hours are weekdays 10–3. No banking facilities are located within Grand Canyon National Park at the North Rim.

Arriving and Departing by Plane

Because most of Arizona's scenic highlights are many miles apart, an automobile is the most practical mode of transportation for touring the state. You won't really need a car, however, if you're planning to visit only the Grand Canyon's most popular area, the South Rim. Many people choose to fly to the Grand Canyon and then hike, catch a shuttle or taxi, or sign on for bus tours or mule rides in Grand Canyon Village.

Airports
McCarran International Airport in Las Vegas (tel. 702/261–5743) is the primary air hub for flights to **Grand Canyon National Park Airport** (tel. 602/638–2446). You can also make connections into the Grand Canyon from **Sky Harbor International Airport** in Phoenix (tel. 602/273–3300). Ground transportation and air-shuttle service (*see* By Air Shuttle and By Taxi, *below*) are available from the Grand Canyon Airport either to Grand Canyon Village or to the small tourist community of Tusayan, 6 miles from the South Rim.

Airlines
The many carriers that fly to the Grand Canyon from Las Vegas include **Air Nevada** (tel. 800/634–6377), **Grand Airways** (tel. 800/634–6616), **Las Vegas Fliers** (tel. 800/343–2632), and **Scenic Airlines** (tel. 800/634–6801).

From Phoenix, **Scenic Airlines** (tel. 800/535–4448) offers two daily flights to Grand Canyon Airport; flights via **Arizona Pacific Airways** (tel. 800/221–7904) depart from Phoenix on Monday, Wednesday, Friday, and Saturday. Phoenix Sky Harbor Airport is served by virtually all the major U.S. commercial airlines (*see* Chapter 6, Phoenix and Central Arizona).

TWA Express (tel. 800/221–2000) has daily service from Los Angeles' LAX to Grand Canyon Village.

Between the Airport and Grand Canyon Village/ Tusayan
By Air Shuttle

The **Tusayan/Grand Canyon Shuttle** (tel. 602/638–2475) operates between Grand Canyon Airport and the nearby towns of Tusayan and Grand Canyon Village; it makes hourly runs daily between 8:15 AM and 5:15 PM, with additional trips in the summer months. A day pass for unlimited trips costs $8 for adults and $5 for children under age 12; if you're only going one-way, the cost is $5 for adults, $3 for children under 12. Children under age 6 travel free. Those with large families might consider the $20 family pass, which allows unlimited travel back and forth throughout the day; often the company will extend the pass to 48 or even 72 hours for the same rate.

By Taxi

Fred Harvey Transportation Company (tel. 602/638–2822 or 602/638–2631) offers 24-hour taxi service at Grand Canyon Airport, Grand Canyon Village, and the nearby village of Tusayan; taxis also make trips to other destinations in and around Grand Canyon National Park.

Transportation Services

In summer, transportation services desks are maintained at **Bright Angel Lodge, Maswik Lodge,** and **Yavapai Lodge** in Grand Canyon Village; in winter, only the desk at Bright Angel Lodge is open. The desks provide information and handle bookings, sightseeing tours, taxi and bus services, mule and horseback rides, and accommodations at Phantom Ranch (at the bottom of the Grand Canyon). The service desks are geared primarily to in-person visits, but you can call (tel. 602/638–2631) for additional information.

Arriving and Departing by Train or Bus

By Train

Amtrak (tel. 800/872–7245) provides daily service to Arizona from both the east and west, with its most convenient stop (for Grand Canyon access) at Flagstaff. From Flagstaff, bus connections can be made for the final leg of the trip to the South Rim through **Nava-Hopi Tours** (tel. 602/774–5003 or 800/892–8687).

An alternative way to complete your journey is a scenic rail trip: Travel from Flagstaff to Williams by bus—the cost is included in the price of the Amtrak ticket—then continue to the Grand Canyon in an old but beautifully restored steam train on the Grand Canyon Railway (*see* Guided Tours, *below*).

By Bus

Greyhound Lines (tel. 800/231–2222) provides bus service from all points in the United States to Flagstaff or Williams, both considered gateway communities to the Grand Canyon.

From either Flagstaff or Williams, bus service to the South Rim of the Grand Canyon is offered by **Nava-Hopi Tours** (tel. 602/774–5003 or 800/892–8687).

Getting Around

By Car

If you are traveling to Arizona by car from the east, or coming up from the southern part of the state, your best access to the Grand Canyon is from Flagstaff. You can take U.S. 180 northwest (81 miles) to Grand Canyon Village on the South Rim. Or, for a scenic route with stopping points along the canyon rim, drive north on U.S. 89 from Flagstaff, then turn left at the junction of AZ 64 (52 miles north of Flagstaff) and proceed west for an additional 57 miles.

To visit the North Rim of the canyon, proceed north from Flagstaff on U.S. 89 to Bitter Springs, then take U.S. 89A to the junction of AZ 67, which leads to the North Rim, a distance of approximately 210 miles from Flagstaff.

If you are crossing Arizona on I–40 from the west, your most direct route to the South Rim is on AZ 64 (U.S. 180), which runs north from Williams for 58 miles to Grand Canyon Village.

Keep in mind that summer car traffic leading to the South Rim is heavy, and downright congested in the vicinity of Grand Canyon Village and the various parking areas along the rim. If you visit from October through April, you should experience only light to moderate traffic in the vicinity of the canyon. The more remote North Rim, which reaches elevations of more than 7,000 feet, has no services available from late October through mid-May; the road is open for day use only until the first heavy snowfall of the year (generally in November or December), at which point the roads close until spring. The South Rim stays open to auto traffic all year, though access to the West Rim is restricted in summer because of overcrowded roads.

Rental Cars It's imperative to make reservations in advance for the busy summer months; for the rest of the year, you'll avoid disappointment if you book a car well ahead of time. Be sure to ask about weekly rates and unlimited mileage opportunities.

Major companies serving Phoenix and Flagstaff include **Avis** (tel. 800/331–1212), **Budget** (tel. 800/527–0700), **Dollar** (tel. 800/800–4000), **Hertz** (tel. 800/654–3131), and **National Interrent** (tel. 800/227–7368). Budget and Dollar are located at Grand Canyon Airport.

By Shuttle Bus In summer, free shuttle service offered by the **National Park Service** (tel. 602/638–7888) runs from Grand Canyon Village to Hermits Rest and Yaki Point, popular viewing areas on the South Rim. Generally, this service, which offers shuttles approximately every 15 minutes from 6:30 AM to 6:45 PM, is available late May through September. Also under the aegis of the National Park Service, CTS runs a year-round shuttle that takes hikers from the Backcountry Reservations Office (across from the visitor center), Maswik Lodge, and Bright Angel Lodge to South Kaibab Trailhead at Yaki Point; the price is $3, and there are two departures every morning. Check for times upon arrival. From May 15 through the end of October, **Trans Canyon Van Service** (tel. 602/638–2820), a South Rim to North Rim shuttle, leaves from Bright Angel Lodge at 1:30 PM and arrives at the North Rim at about 6 PM; the return from Grand Canyon Lodge is at 7 AM, with arrival at the South Rim at about 11:30 AM. The fare is $60 each way ($100 round-trip), and a 50% deposit is required two weeks in advance.

Guided Tours

By Train The Grand Canyon Railway began running from Williams to the
South Rim in 1989, offering a modern version of a route that was
first established in 1901. The railroad had been out of operation
since 1968, but an $85 million restoration put the old steam en-
gines and Pullman cars back in business. The ride from the renovated station in Williams, about 2½ hours each way, features
refreshments, commentary, and corny but fun on-board entertainment. Upgraded Club Class and Chief Class service is available for an additional $10 and $30, respectively. Even if you
don't take the train, the impressive 1908 depot, with its free railroad museum and gift shop, are worth visiting. *518 E. Bill Williams Ave., Williams 86046, tel. 800/THE–TRAIN. Round-trip
fare: $47 adults, $23.50 ages 13–19, $14.50 12 and under. Depar-
ture from Williams Mar. 23–Oct. 30, daily 9:30 AM, return ar-
rives in Williams at 5:30 PM; call for details on the more limited
schedule the rest of the year.*

By Plane Flights over the Grand Canyon by airplane or helicopter are offered by a number of companies operating either from Grand
Canyon Airport or from heliports in Tusayan. **Air Grand Canyon**
(tel. 602/638–2618 or 800/247–4726), **Grand Canyon Airlines** (tel.
602/638–2407 or 800/528–2413), and **Windrock Aviation** (tel. 602/
638–9591 or 800/247–6259) fly small planes, while **AirStar Helicopters** (tel. 602/638–2622 or 800/962–3869), **Papillon Helicopters** (tel. 602/638–2419 or 800/528–2418), and **Kenai Helicopters**
(tel. 602/638–2412 or 800/541–4537) operate whirlybirds. Prices
and length of flights vary greatly with tours, but they start at
about $60 per person for short airplane flights and $95 per person for short helicopter runs. Inquiries and reservations can
also be made at any Grand Canyon lodge transportation desk
(*see* Transportation Services, *above*).

By Bus From late May to late September, a free **shuttle bus service** is
offered by the National Park Service (*see* By Shuttle Bus in Getting Around, *above*) in the South Rim area. This does not provide a guided tour, but you can get a good feel for the region by
taking advantage of trips through Grand Canyon Village, to
Yavapai Museum, and to Hermits Rest on the West Rim. In addition, the **Fred Harvey Transportation Company** (tel. 602/638–
2822 or 602/638–2631) in Grand Canyon Village provides a veritable menu of daily motor-coach sightseeing trips along the
South Rim and to destinations as far away as Monument Valley
on the Navajo reservation. Prices range from $11 for short trips
to $75 for all-day tours. Children's half-price fares apply to those
under 16 for in-park tours, under 12 on the longer out-of-park
tours. For schedules, call the South Rim reservations number
(tel. 602/638–2401) or inquire at any transportation desk (*see*
Transportation Services, *above*). **TW Recreational Services, Inc.**
(tel. 801/586–7686) offers an interpretive van tour of the North
Rim ($20 adults, $10 children ages 4–12); schedules and other
details are available in the lobby of the Grand Canyon Lodge.

By Mule Mule trips down the precipitous trails to the Inner Gorge of the Grand Canyon are nearly as well known as the canyon itself. But, especially for the summer season, it's very hard to get reservations unless you make them months in advance; write Reservations Department (Box 699, Grand Canyon 86023, tel. 602/638–2401). These trips have been conducted since the early 1900s, and no one has ever been killed by a mule falling off a cliff. Nevertheless, the treks are not for the faint of heart or people in questionable health. Riders must be at least 4 feet 7 inches tall, weigh less than 200 pounds, understand English, and they cannot be visibly pregnant. Children under 15 must be accompanied by an adult. The all-day ride to Plateau Point costs $87 (lunch included). An overnight with a stay at Phantom Ranch at the bottom of the canyon (*see* Lodging, *below*) is $259 ($464 for two) for one night, $359 ($608 for two) for two nights; meals are included in these prices. *See* What to See and Do with Children, *below*, for information on the shorter mule rides from the North Rim.

Weather

Weather information and road conditions for both the North and South rims, updated at 7 AM daily, can be obtained by calling 602/638–7888.

In general, the South Rim, with an elevation of 7,000 feet, has summer temperatures that range from lows in the 50s to highs in the upper 80s. There are frequent afternoon thunderstorms. Winter temperatures have average lows of around 20°F and average highs near 50°F, with the mercury occasionally dropping below zero. In spring and fall, temperatures generally stay above 32°F and often climb into the 70s. The North Rim, accessed through country that ranges in altitude from 8,000 to 9,000 feet, gets heavy winter snows and thus is open to the public only from mid-May through October. Temperatures during this open season go from lows in the 30s to highs in the 70s. It frequently rains in the afternoon; in May and October, it occasionally snows as well. As you proceed down either rim into the canyon toward the Inner Gorge, temperatures rise. In summer along the Colorado River—at an elevation of about 2,400 feet—temperatures range from lows in the 70s to highs above 100°F. Winter sees lows in the 30s, highs around 50. It rarely snows at the bottom of the Grand Canyon, even in winter; the snow on the rims usually turns to rain as it falls into the Inner Gorge.

Telephones

It's often hard to get through to the Grand Canyon: The trunk lines into the area are limited and often overloaded with people calling this most popular of Arizona's attractions. You'll get a fast busy signal if this is the case. In addition, when you do get through to the National Park Service or South Rim Reservations numbers—which handle many of the services listed in this chapter—you'll have to punch a lot of numbers on a computer-voice system before you reach the service you want. Be patient; it's possible to get through to a human being eventually. Writing ahead for the information-packed *Trip Planner* (*see* Tourist Information, *above*) is likely to save you a phone call. Remember, too, that the park does not accept reservations for backcountry permits by phone; they must be made in writing.

Safety Tips

Be careful when you or your children are near the edge of the canyon or walking any of the trails that descend into it. Guardrails exist only on portions of the rims. Tragically, a few visitors are killed each year in falls from viewing points. Before engaging in any strenuous exercise, be aware that the canyon rims are more than 7,000 feet in altitude. Being at this height can cause some people to become dizzy or faint. Before hiking down into the canyon, assess the distance of the proposed hike against your physical condition. Descending into the canyon is not especially difficult, but going back up can be very strenuous. Be sure to take sufficient water and food on hikes into the canyon (*see* Hiking in Sports and the Outdoors, *below*). During summer months, temperatures in the Inner Gorge can climb above 105°F.

Entrance Fees

The fees levied by the National Park Service vary depending on your method of entering Grand Canyon National Park. If you arrive by automobile, the fee is $10, regardless of the number of passengers. Individuals arriving by public conveyance (bus, taxi, or train) pay $4. The entrance gates are open 24 hours a day but are generally supervised from about 7 AM until 6 PM. If you arrive when there's no one at the gate, you may enter legally without paying.

Exploring the Grand Canyon

Both the South Rim and the North Rim areas of the Grand Canyon were established as recreational and sightseeing enclaves under the direction of the National Park Service. Unfortunately, most of Grand Canyon Village at the South Rim was laid out before the Park Service existed, so the area is not well equipped to accommodate the large crowds that converge on the area every summer (and, increasingly, throughout the spring and fall as well).

In truth, the South Rim is a bit of a circus in summer. It's hard to commune with one of nature's great spectacles when you've just spent two hours looking for a parking spot and are now being asked to step out of the range of someone else's video camera. Not even a descent into the canyon itself guarantees a getaway at this time of year. For your sake as well as that of the canyon, it's best to avoid the South Rim in its busiest season.

There are two ways to discover the canyon: walking or driving along its rim (Tours 1–6) and hiking down into its depths (*see* Hiking in Sports and the Outdoors, *below*). The first view of the canyon will stay with you a lifetime. After a half-dozen lookouts, however, your sense of wonder will begin to diminish. The problem is that it's impossible to establish a personal relationship with so much grandeur. Traveling along the rim, you will easily tire of putting your nose up against this beauty and safely, almost antiseptically, peering in. By all means stop along the rim, but we can't encourage you strongly enough to take a walk, however brief, into the canyon itself. Bright Angel Trail is easiest, the South Kaibab Trail steeper but more spectacular. A 20-minute walk into the maw of this abyss will open up a totally new perspective and permit you to develop a personal relationship with the canyon that is unattainable at the rim.

Highlights for First-Time Visitors

South Rim Country
Bright Angel or Kaibab Trails (*see* Tours 2 and 3)
Desert View and The Watchtower (*see* Tour 2)
El Tovar Hotel (*see* Tour 3)
Hermits Rest Overlook (*see* Tour 4)
Lookout Studio (*see* Tour 3)
Powell Memorial (*see* Tour 4)
Visitor Center (*see* Tour 1)

North Rim Country
Cape Royal (*see* Tour 6)
Grand Canyon Lodge and Bright Angel Point (*see* Tour 6)
Lees Ferry (*see* Tour 5)
Vermilion Cliffs (*see* Tour 5)

Tour 1: Approaching the South Rim

Numbers in the margin correspond to points of interest on the South Rim: Tours 1 and 2 map.

Because the approach to the South Rim of the Grand Canyon is across the relatively level surface of the 7,000-foot Coconino Plateau, you won't see the great gorge until you're practically at its edge. **Mather Point** gives you your first glimpse of the canyon from one of the most impressive and accessible vista points on the rim; it's easily reached from Grand Canyon National Park's east entrance (on AZ 64) or from the south entrance (on AZ 180). If you're arriving from the east, you might be tempted to stop at Desert View, just inside the park, but we suggest that you save this and other vista points on the eastern approach for a later East Rim tour (*see* Tour 2, *below*).

❶ Located on the outskirts of Grand Canyon Village, **Mather Point** is approximately 24 miles from the east entrance and 4 miles from the south entrance. Whether you enter the park from the east or south, you'll arrive at the junction of AZ 64 and AZ 180. Proceed in the direction of Grand Canyon Village for less than a mile, and you'll see a large parking area with a sign for Mather Point.

This overlook of the canyon, named for the National Park Service's first director, Stephen Mather, affords an extraordinary view of the Inner Gorge of the canyon and of numerous buttes that rise out of the eroded chasm: Wotan's Throne, Brahma Temple, Zoroaster Temple, and many others. The Grand Canyon Lodge, on the North Rim, is almost directly north from Mather Point and only 10 miles away—yet you have to drive nearly 210 miles to get from one spot to the other.

2 After your first view of the canyon, proceed to **Grand Canyon Village,** and stop in at the **National Park Service's Visitor Center,** which has something for even the most independent traveler. Not only does the center orient you to many facets of the site (history, geology, and sightseeing), but it's also an excellent place for gathering information whether you're interested in escapist hikes or group tours. At the visitor center, you'll get an intriguing profile of the area's natural and human history. The region's first inhabitants were probably Paleo-Indians, who lived here more than 11,000 years ago. Artifacts from the Archaic culture that followed are on display here: perfectly preserved figurines of animals, made more than 4,000 years ago from willow twigs and found in caves deep in the canyon. Sometime after AD 1, the Anasazi culture flourished, but it disappeared about AD 1200. The museum also traces the arrival of the early Spanish explorers, including Captain García López de Cárdenas, leader of the first expedition of white men to see the Grand Canyon (1540), and of John Wesley Powell, an American who was the first person to travel through the canyon by boat. The various crafts that have navigated the white-water rapids of the Colorado River are on display.

The visitor center also presents short movies and slide shows on the canyon, and its bookstore carries a wide variety of printed matter, videotapes, and slides. Park rangers are on hand to answer questions and aid in planning Grand Canyon excursions. The center also has a schedule for ranger-guided walks along the South Rim. *East side of Grand Canyon Village, about 1 mi east of El Tovar Hotel, tel. 602/638–7888. Admission free. Open Memorial Day–Labor Day, daily 8 AM–6 PM; the rest of the year, daily 8–5.*

Tour 2: East Rim

This breathtaking drive on the East Rim proceeds east for about 25 miles along the South Rim from Grand Canyon Village to Desert View. Before beginning the drive, consider stopping to see the exhibits and attend the free minilectures offered by park naturalists at Yavapai Observation Station, ¾ mile east of the visitor center. There are four posted picnic areas along the route and rest rooms at Tusayan Museum and Desert View.

3 To get to **Yaki Point,** the first stop on the tour, from the village, head east to the junction of AZ 180 and AZ 64. Turn onto AZ 64 and continue east. From this vantage point, look to the northeast for an exceptional view of Wotan's Throne, a majestic flat-

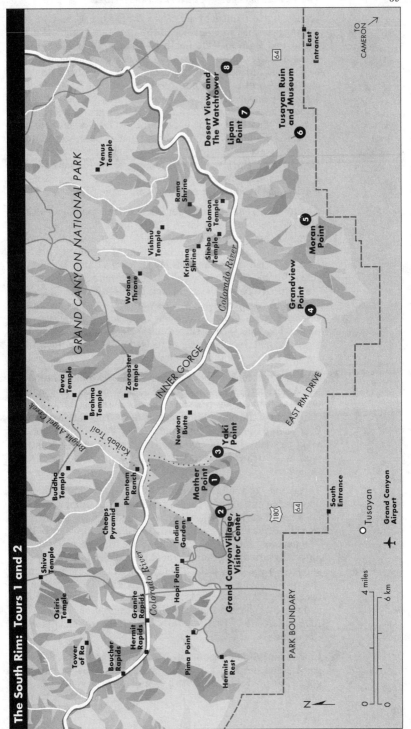

The South Rim: Tours 1 and 2

topped butte named by François Matthes, a U.S. Geological Survey scientist who developed the first topographical map of the Grand Canyon. Due north is Buddha Temple, capped by limestone; Newton Butte, with its flat top of red sandstone, lies to the east. At Yaki Point the popular Kaibab Trail starts the canyon descent to the Inner Gorge, crosses the Colorado over a steel suspension bridge, and wends its way to rustic Phantom Ranch, the only lodging facility at the bottom of the Grand Canyon. You might take this opportunity to hike a short distance down the Kaibab Trail, just to get a feel for a descent into the canyon. If you plan to go more than a mile, carry water with you (*see* Hiking in Sports and the Outdoors, *below*). If you encounter a mule train, be aware that the animals have the right-of-way. Move to the inside of the trail and wait as they pass.

❹ About 7 miles east of Yaki Point, **Grandview Point,** at an altitude of 7,496 feet, supports large stands of ponderosa pine, piñon pine, oak, and juniper. The view from here is one of the finest in the canyon. To the northeast is a group of dominant buttes, including Krishna Shrine, Vishnu Temple, Rama Shrine, and Shiva Temple. A short stretch of the Colorado River is also visible. Directly below the point and accessed by the Grandview Trail is Horseshoe Mesa, where you can see ruins of the Last Chance Copper Mine. Grandview Point was also the site of the Grandview Hotel, constructed in the 1890s but closed in 1908; logs salvaged from the hotel were used for the Kiva Room of the Desert View Watchtower (*see below*).

❺ The next overlook is about 5 miles east at **Moran Point,** named for American landscape artist Thomas Moran, who painted Grand Canyon scenes from many points on the rim but was especially fond of the play of light and shadows from this location. He first visited the canyon with John Wesley Powell in 1873, and his vivid canvases helped convince Congress to create a national park at the Grand Canyon. This is also a favorite spot for photographers.

❻ Three miles east of Moran Point, on the south side of the highway, is the entrance to **Tusayan Ruin and Museum,** which offer evidence of early habitation in the Grand Canyon and information about the lifestyles of the Anasazi people (circa AD 1–1200). The partially intact rock dwellings here were occupied for perhaps 20 years by a group of about 30 Indian hunters, farmers, and gatherers. They left suddenly, driven to a new location, archaeologists believe, by a severe drought. The museum and bookstore feature artifacts, models of the Anasazi dwellings, and exhibits on more modern tribes of the region. *Tel. 602/638–2305. Admission free. Open daily 8–5; closed Thanksgiving and Christmas.*

❼ **Lipan Point,** 1 mile east of Tusayan Ruin, is the canyon's widest point. From here you can get an astonishing visual profile of the gorge's geologic history, with a view of every eroded layer of the canyon.

8 **Desert View and The Watchtower** offer a climactic final stop. At 7,500 feet, Desert View is the highest point along the tour, and the vista is spectacular. If you climb to the top of the 70-foot stone-and-mortar Watchtower, built in 1932 by the Fred Harvey Company in the style of Southwest Indian structures, you can see the muted pastel hues of the distant Painted Desert to the east and the 3,000-foot-high Vermilion Cliffs rising from a high plateau near the Utah border. You also get an extraordinary glimpse of the upper reaches of the canyon as it angles away to the north toward Marble Canyon, and at this point an impressive stretch of the Colorado River reveals itself. The Watchtower houses a glass-enclosed observatory with powerful telescopes, as well as galleries decorated with reproductions of ancient Indian pictographs, and a curio shop where paintings, jewelry, and other handicrafts by contemporary Native American artists are sold. *Watchtower tel. 602/638-2736, trading post tel. 602/638-2360. Admission free, but there is a 25¢ charge to climb Watchtower. Trading post open Memorial Day–Labor Day daily 8–8; rest of year daily 8–6. Watchtower closes ½ hour before trading post.*

Tour 3: The Village Rim

Numbers in the margin correspond to points of interest on the South Rim: Tours 3 and 4 map.

This is a fairly short walking tour (about 1 mile round-trip) over level ground via a paved pathway that runs along the rim. The **9** **Hopi House** is a good place to begin (if you're driving, leave your car at the nearby El Tovar parking lot). This multistoried structure of rock and mortar was modeled after buildings found in the Hopi village of Oraibi, Arizona, the oldest continually inhabited community in the United States (*see* Chapter 4, The Northeast). Part of an attempt by the Fred Harvey Company to encourage Southwest Indian crafts at the turn of the century, Hopi House was established as one of the first curio stores in the Grand Canyon. It has the air of a museum, with some artifacts too priceless to sell today, but it remains one of the best-stocked gift shops in the vicinity (*see* Shopping, *below*).

A few yards to the west of Hopi House is the most renowned hotel in the nation's National Park System, the historic **El Tovar Hotel.** Built in 1905 to resemble the great hunting lodges of Europe, this massive log structure underwent a major renovation in 1991, but it retains the ambience of its early days. If the weather is cool, stop in front of the massive stone fireplace to warm your hands. The rustic lobby, with its numerous stuffed and mounted animal heads, is a great place for people-watching.

From El Tovar, return to the rim and pick up the trail heading **11** west toward **Lookout Studio.** Built in 1914 as a lookout point, the Pueblo-style building was later used as a photography studio. Today it's a combination lookout point, museum, and gift shop, and it has an extensive collection of geologic samples from around the world as well as many fossil specimens. An upstairs

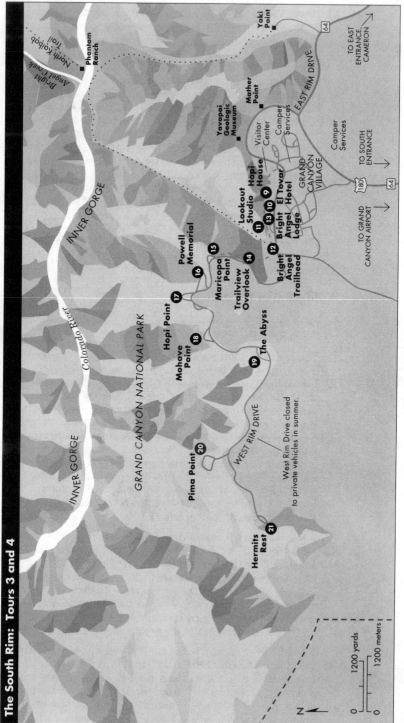

The South Rim: Tours 3 and 4

loft provides another excellent overlook into the mighty gorge below.

⑫ Not many yards to the west of Lookout Studio is **Bright Angel Trailhead,** the starting point for perhaps the best-known of all the trails that descend to the bottom of the canyon. It was originally a bighorn sheep path and was later used by the Havasupai Indians; in 1890–91 it was widened for prospectors trying to reach mining claims in the canyon. Today Bright Angel Trail is a well-maintained avenue for mule and foot traffic. If you intend to go very far—the trail descends 4,460 feet to the Colorado River—you should be prepared with proper shoes, clothing, equipment, and water (*see* Hiking in Sports and the Outdoors, *below*); discuss your intentions with the Park Service representatives at the visitor center before you go.

Bright Angel Trailhead is the turnaround point on this short walking tour. If you'd like to go farther west, *see* Tour 4: West Rim Drive, *below*. From Bright Angel Trailhead, walk directly east rather than returning to the rim trail. You'll pass the barn that houses some of the tour mules; it's worth a brief stop, especially if children are along. Continue east to **Bright Angel Lodge,** which was built in 1935 of logs and native stone; there are rustic cabins set away from the main building. It's another good place to people-watch, especially in the area of the "geologic" fireplace, made of regional rocks arranged in the order in which they are layered in the Grand Canyon. A history room displays memorabilia from early years at the South Rim.

Time Out For light snacks—cold sandwiches, ice cream, and soft drinks—try the **Soda Fountain** in the Bright Angel Lodge. *Tel. 602/638-2631. Open May–Sept., daily 11–9.*

From Bright Angel Lodge, take the village road back to your parking spot near El Tovar.

Tour 4: West Rim Drive

This tour cannot be made by car in the summer months; at that time the West Rim Road is closed to auto traffic because of congestion. From Memorial Day weekend to October 1, a free shuttle bus makes most of the stops on the described itinerary (*see* By Shuttle Bus in Getting Around, *above*).

Originally called the Hermit Rim Road, the **West Rim Drive** was constructed by the Santa Fe Company in 1912 as a scenic tour route. Cars were banned on the road because they frightened horses pulling the open-topped touring stages. West Rim Drive today offers 10 scenic overlooks spread out over 8 miles (one-way). Consider covering half on the first leg of the trip and the others on the way back; there's easy access to the lookout points from both sides of the road.

Start out at **Bright Angel Lodge** and head west for about a mile ⑭ until you come to **Trailview Overlook.** If you turn and look away from the canyon toward the south you'll have a wonderful, unobstructed view of the distant San Francisco Peaks, Arizona's highest mountains (the tallest is 12,633 feet), as well as of Bill Williams Mountain (on the horizon) and Red Butte (about 15 miles south of the canyon rim). As its name suggests, this overlook also affords a dramatic view of the Bright Angel and Plateau Point trails as they zigzag down the canyon. In the deep gorge to the north flows Bright Angel Creek, one of the few permanent tributary streams of the Colorado River in the region.

⑮ **Maricopa Point,** about ⁷/₁₀ of a mile from Trailview, merits a stop not only for the arresting scenery, which features a clear view of the Colorado River below, but also for its towering headframe of an early Grand Canyon mining operation. On the rim to your left, as you face the canyon, are the Orphan Mine and, in the canyon below, a mine shaft and cable lines leading up to the rim. The copper ore in the mine, which started operations in 1893, was of excellent quality, but the cost of removing it from the canyon finally brought the venture to a halt.

⑯ About ½ mile beyond Maricopa Point, the large granite **Powell Memorial** stands as a tribute to the first man to ride the wild rapids of the Colorado River through the canyon in 1869. John Wesley Powell, a one-armed Civil War hero and explorer, measured, charted, and named many of the canyons and creeks of the river. It was here that the dedication ceremony for Grand Canyon National Park took place on April 3, 1920.

⑰ From **Hopi Point** (elevation 7,071 feet), ½ mile down the road, you can see a large section of the Colorado River; although it appears as a thin line from here, the river is nearly 350 feet wide below this overlook. Across the canyon to the north is Shiva Temple, which, until 1937, remained an isolated section of the Kaibab Plateau. In that year, Harold Anthony of the American Museum of Natural History led an expedition to the rock formation in the belief that it supported life that had been cut off from the rest of the canyon. Imagine the expedition members' surprise when they found an empty Kodak film box on top of the temple.

⑱ Four-fifths of a mile to the west, **Mohave Point** also affords spectacular views of the Colorado River. In addition, Granite and Salt Creek rapids can be seen from this point.

⑲ **The Abyss,** 1 mile farther, is one of the most awesome stops on this tour, revealing a sheer canyon drop of 3,000 feet to the Tonto Platform in the gorge below. From this spot, you'll also see several impressive isolated sandstone columns, the largest of which is called The Monument.

⑳ **Pima Point,** 3 miles away, provides a bird's-eye view of the Tonto Platform and the Tonto Trail, which wends its way through the canyon for more than 70 miles. If you look down on the plateau toward the west, you may be able to see the foundations of an old tourist camp built in the first decade of the century and used until 1930. Also to the west, two dark, cone-shaped mountains—Mt. Trumbull and Mt. Logan—are visible on clear days. They rise in stark contrast to the surrounding flat-topped mesas and buttes.

㉑ **Hermits Rest,** the westernmost viewpoint, and the Boucher Trail that descends from it (*see* Hiking in Sports and the Outdoors, *below*) were named for the "hermit" Louis Boucher, a 19th-century prospector who had a number of mining claims and a roughly built home down in the canyon. Canyon views from here include Hermit Rapids and the towering cliffs of the Supai and Redwall formations. The stone building at Hermits Rest sells curios and refreshments and provides the only rest rooms on the West Rim tour.

Tour 5: The Drive to North Rim

Numbers in the margin correspond to points of interest on the North Rim: Tours 5 and 6 map.

This tour is not an option during the winter, when heavy snows close highway access to, and facilities in, the North Rim.

㉒ This long excursion—about 210 miles, whether you start out from Grand Canyon Village on the South Rim of the canyon or from Flagstaff—is the best way to get to the North Rim and offers plenty to see along the way. It begins at the **Cameron Trading Post,** on U.S. 89, 1 mile north of the junction with AZ 64 (which you will be on if you're coming from Grand Canyon Village) and 53 miles north of Flagstaff. Founded in 1916, this historic trading post, one of the few remaining in the Southwest, has an extensive stock of Native American jewelry, rugs, baskets, and pottery. Most of the items sold here are made by nearby Navajo and Hopi artisans, but some are created by New Mexico's Zuni and Pueblo Indians. In addition to the main building, which sells wares in all price categories, there's also a separate gallery that offers more expensive, museum-quality goods.

Time Out The **Cameron Trading Post** restaurant (tel. 602/679–2231) serves American food that ranges from light snacks to complete dinners; try the huge Navajo tacos on fry bread, heaped with cheese, chopped meat, guacamole, and salad. The high-ceiling room, decorated with Native American art and furniture, is an appealing eatery, but service can be a bit slow; if you're in a rush, try the new cafeteria next door, where you can get hot and cold sandwiches and other buffet-style fare.

㉓ The route north on U.S. 89 affords a wide and unobstructed view of the **Painted Desert** off to the right. The desert, which covers thousands of square miles and extends far to the south and east, is a vision of harsh beauty, with windswept plains and mesas, isolated buttes, and barren valleys in delicate patterns of soft pastels. In the few places in which there is vegetation, it is mostly desert scrub, which provides sustenance for only the hardiest wildlife. Most of the undulating hills belong to the Chinle formation, deposited more than 200 million years ago and containing countless fossil records of ancient plants and animals.

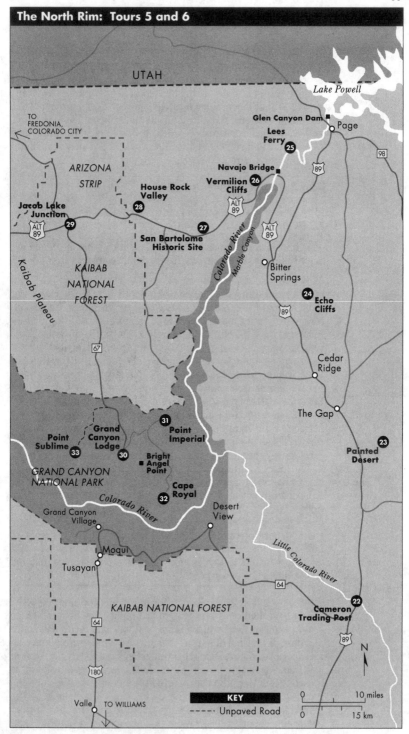

The North Rim: Tours 5 and 6

UTAH

Lake Powell

TO FREDONIA, COLORADO CITY

ARIZONA STRIP

Glen Canyon Dam

Page

Lees Ferry **25**

Navajo Bridge **26**

Vermilion Cliffs

ALT 89

98

89

House Rock Valley **28**

Jacob Lake Junction **29**

ALT 89

San Bartolome Historic Site **27**

Colorado River

Marble Canyon

ALT 89

Bitter Springs

KAIBAB NATIONAL FOREST

Kaibab Plateau

Echo Cliffs **24**

89

67

Cedar Ridge

The Gap

Painted Desert **23**

Point Sublime **33**

Grand Canyon Lodge **30**

Point Imperial **31**

Bright Angel Point

GRAND CANYON NATIONAL PARK

Cape Royal **32**

Colorado River

Grand Canyon Village

Desert View

Little Colorado River

Moqui

Tusayan

64

KAIBAB NATIONAL FOREST

Cameron Trading Post **22**

89

64

180

Valle

TO WILLIAMS

N

KEY
--- Unpaved Road

0 — 10 miles
0 — 15 km

About 30 miles north of the Cameron Trading Post, the Painted Desert country gives way to soaring sandstone cliffs that run for many miles off to the right. Brilliantly hued, and ranging in color from light pink to deep orange, the **Echo Cliffs** rise to well over 1,000 feet in many places. They are also essentially devoid of vegetation, but in a few isolated places high up, you'll spot thick patches of tall cottonwood and poplar trees, nurtured by springs and water seepage from the rock escarpments.

At Bitter Springs, 60 miles north of Cameron, leave U.S. 89 and take U.S. 89A north. Fourteen miles out of Bitter Springs, **Marble Canyon,** actually the beginning of the Grand Canyon, comes into view. Like the rest of the Grand Canyon, Marble Canyon has been carved by the force of the Colorado River. Traversing a gorge nearly 500 feet deep is **Navajo Bridge,** a narrow steel span built in 1929; until the bridge at Glen Canyon Dam was constructed in 1959, this was the only bridge crossing of the Colorado for the 600 miles from Moab, Utah, to the Hoover Dam. It's still used for car traffic, but will soon function only as a pedestrian overpass; a new, wider bridge, being built 120 feet downriver, should be completed by 1996.

When you come to Marble Canyon Lodge, about a mile past Navajo Bridge, you'll see a turnoff for historic **Lees Ferry,** 3 miles away. Situated on a sharp bend in the Colorado River at a break in the surrounding Echo Cliffs, Lees Ferry is considered mile zero of the river, the point from which all distances on the river system are measured. It's also at the eastern edge of Arizona Strip country (*see* Off the Beaten Track, *below*), and it was one of the last areas in the mainland United States to be completely charted. This spot was first visited by non-Indians in 1776, when Spanish priests Fray Francisco Atanasio Domínguez and Fray Silvestre Velez de Escalante tried but failed to cross the Colorado. Explorer John Wesley Powell also visited in 1870 on an expedition with Mormon leaders. After the ferry was established, it became part of the Honeymoon Trail, a gateway to Utah for young couples who wanted their civil marriages in Arizona sanctified at the Latter-day Saints temple in St. George. It also became a crossing and a supply point for miners and other pioneers who shaped much of the American West.

Lees Ferry retains a number of vestiges of the mining era, but it's now primarily known as the spot where most of the Grand Canyon river rafts put into the water. In addition, huge trout lurk in the river near here, so there are several places to pick up angling gear and/or a guide. If you go out on your own, be sure you have an Arizona fishing license before casting a line (*see* Fishing in Participant Sports, *below*).

Heading west from Navajo Bridge, you'll be treated to views of some of the world's most spectacular geologic formations. Rising to the right of the highway are the sheer **Vermilion Cliffs,** in many places more than 3,000 feet high.

As you continue the journey to the North Rim, the immense blue-green bulk of the Kaibab Plateau stretches out before you.

㉗ About 18 miles past Navajo Bridge, a sign directs you to the **San Bartolome Historic Site,** which tells the story of the Domínguez–Escalante expedition of 1776.

㉘ Proceeding about 2 miles west, you'll enter **House Rock Valley,** where a large sign on the road announces the House Rock Buffalo Ranch, operated by the Arizona Division of Wildlife. A 23-mile dirt road leads to the home of one of the largest herds of American bison in the Southwest. You may drive out to the ranch, but be aware that you may not see any buffalo: The expanse of their range is so great that they frequently cannot be spotted from a car.

About 25 miles west of Marble Canyon on U.S. 89A, you'll start climbing to the top of the Kaibab Plateau, heavily forested, rife with animals and birds, and more than 9,000 feet at its highest point. The rapid change from barren desert to lush forest is dramatic. At an elevation of 7,900 feet, the **Jacob Lake junction** is a
㉙ good place to stop for groceries and gas. Turn left (south) from the junction to access AZ 67. From here to the North Rim, a distance of 44 miles, you drive through one of the thickest stands of ponderosa pine in the United States. Watch for wildlife along the way. Visitors frequently see mule deer and, once in a while, catch a glimpse of rare Kaibab squirrels; you can recognize them by their all-white tails and ears with long tufts of white hair.

Tour 6: Bright Angel Point, Point Imperial, Cape Royal, Point Sublime

㉚ When you arrive at the historic **Grand Canyon Lodge** you are, literally, at the end of the road; there are no meandering streets as there are at South Rim. A massive stone structure built in 1928 by the Union Pacific Railroad, the lodge is listed in the National Register of Historic Places. Inside, the huge lounge area with hardwood floors and high, beamed ceilings affords a marvelous view of the canyon through massive plate-glass windows. On warm days, visitors sit in the sun and drink in the surrounding beauty at an equally spacious outdoor viewing deck.

The trail to Bright Angel Point, one of the most awe-inspiring overlooks on either rim, starts on the grounds of the Grand Canyon Lodge and proceeds along the crest of a point of rocks that juts into the canyon for several hundred yards. The walk is only 1 mile round-trip, but the trek is exciting because there are sheer drops just a few feet away on each side of the trail. In a few spots, where the route is extremely narrow, metal railings along the path ensure visitors' safety. The trail is quite safe, but visitors have been known to clamber out to precarious perches to have their pictures taken. Be very careful: There have been tragic falls at the Grand Canyon.

If you'd like to take another walk, this time through the deep forest, head for the beginning of the Transept Trail near the corner of the lodge's east patio. This 3-mile (round-trip) trail stays near the rim for part of the distance, then it plunges into the forest, ending at the North Rim Campground and General Store, 1½ miles from the lodge.

Time Out Lunch, dinner, or a snack in the huge, high-ceiling, rock-and-log dining room of the **Grand Canyon Lodge** (tel. 602/638–2611) is an integral part of the North Rim experience. The moderately priced menu, which changes every season, is surprisingly sophisticated for the rustic locale: You might find marinated pork kebabs, grilled swordfish, or linguine with cilantro and pesto among the entrées. Or, just buy a drink at the lodge's Pizza Place, sit out on the viewing deck, and watch the sun set over the canyon.

To get to the North Rim's most popular lookouts—Point Imperial and Cape Royal—drive north from Grand Canyon Lodge and **③** veer right at the signed fork in the road. **Point Imperial,** 11 miles from the lodge, is the highest vista point (elevation 8,803 feet) on either rim, offering magnificent views of both the canyon and the distant country for many miles around: the Vermilion Cliffs to the north, the 10,000-foot Navajo Mountain to the northeast in Utah, the Painted Desert to the east, and the Little Colorado River canyon to the southeast.

Return west to the signed junction and turn left (south) to reach **③** **Cape Royal,** about 23 miles from your starting point at the lodge. From the parking lot at the road's end, it's a short, scenic walk on a paved road to this southernmost viewpoint on the North Rim. In addition to another large slice of the Grand Canyon, Angel's Window, a giant, erosion-formed hole can be seen through the projecting ridge of Cape Royal. If you would like to experience a very pleasant walk in this area of the rim, drive north about ⅓ mile to Angel's Window Overlook. At this point, Cliff Springs Trail starts its 1-mile route (round-trip) through a forested ravine. The trail, narrow and precarious in spots, passes an Anasazi ruin, winds beneath a limestone overhang, and terminates at Cliff Springs, where the forest opens on another impressive view of the canyon walls.

An excellent option for those who want to get off the beaten **③** path, the trip to **Point Sublime** is intended only for visitors driving vehicles with high-road clearance (pickups and four-wheel-drive vehicles). It is also necessary to be properly equipped for wilderness road travel: Check with a park ranger or at the information desk at Grand Canyon Lodge before taking this journey. The road winds for 17 miles through gorgeous high country to Point Sublime, an overlook that lives up to its name. You may camp here, but only after obtaining a permit from the Backcountry Reservations Office at the park ranger station (*see* Hiking in Sports and the Outdoors, *below*).

What to See and Do with Children

The Grand Canyon is family vacation country, and most activities can be enjoyed by all ages. However, many of the daily activities at both the North and South rims, detailed in the free

Grand Canyon newspaper, *The Guide*, will appeal especially to children. In addition, the Junior Ranger program, geared toward those ages 4 through 12, introduces kids to the concept of caring for the national parks via an activities checklist found in *Young Adventurer*, a publication available at the South Rim Visitor Center and the Tusayan and Yavapai museums.

Animal Rides You can rent extremely gentle horses at the **Apache Stables** at Moqui Lodge (tel. 602/638–2891) in the village of Tusayan, South Rim. The cost is $20 an hour, $34 for two hours. A four-hour East Rim ride goes for $55, a campfire horse and haywagon ride for $25 ($7.50 if you ride in the wagon rather than on your own horse). Children 6 and up are permitted on the hour-long ride, 10 and up on the two-hour ride, 14 and up on the half-day trip. The rides are offered, weather permitting, when Moqui Lodge is open (mid-Feb.–Nov. 30), and sometimes year-round.

Canyon Trail Rides (tel. 801/679–8665 preseason, tel. 602/638–2292 after May 15 at Grand Canyon Lodge) operates short mule rides suitable for children on the easier trails along the North Rim. A one-hour ride, available to those 6 and older, runs about $10. Half-day trips on the rim or into the canyon (minimum age 8) cost $30; full-day trips (minimum age 12), which include lunch, go for $70. These excursions are very popular, so try to make reservations in advance. Rides are available daily from May 15 to the end of October.

Films of the An enjoyable 34-minute documentary, *Grand Canyon—The*
Canyon *Hidden Secrets*, is shown on the 70-foot-high screen at the IMAX Theater. The script is informative, and some of the shots—especially those of boats running the rapids—are positively dizzying. *Tusayan, tel. 602/638–2203. Admission: $7 adults, $4 children ages 3–11. Open Mar. 1–Oct. 31, daily 8:30–8:30; Nov. 1–Feb. 28, daily 10:30–6:30; shows every hour starting on the half-hour.*

The computer-controlled *Over the Edge* multimedia show tells the Grand Canyon story in words and song—with the help of 12 projectors and strobe effects. The photography is often stunning. *Community Building, Grand Canyon Village, tel. 602/638–2229. Admission: $4 adults, $3.50 senior citizens 55 and older, $2 children 8–15, children 7 and under free. Open Mar.–Oct., daily 9–9; Nov.–Feb., daily 10–6; shows every 30 min. on the hour and half-hour.*

Off the Beaten Track

Arizona Strip The **Arizona Strip** is the 12,000-square-mile northwestern portion of the state, cut off from the rest of Arizona by the giant scar created by the Colorado River as it comes out of Utah and winds its way through the Grand Canyon to the western border of the state. Sometimes called the American Tibet because it's so isolated, the area boasts only two small towns: the farming and lumbering community of Fredonia and, near the Utah border, the polygamous Mormon town of Colorado City. Their combined population is less than 7,000, and fewer than 700 permanent residents—including 150 members of the Kaibab–Paiute tribe—live in the rest of the strip. An information center for this area, a good one- or two-day side trip from the Grand Canyon's North Rim, is open at Jacob Lake (tel. 602/643-7298) from May 1 through the end of October.

The first of the two main destinations in the area is **Pipe Spring National Monument,** 90 miles from the North Rim. Head north from the rim on AZ 67, and at Jacob Lake take AZ 89A to Fredonia; continue 14 miles beyond Fredonia on the same highway (now called AZ 389). Located at Pipe Spring, one of the few reliable sources of water in the Arizona Strip, the park features a restored rock fort and ranch, with exhibits of Southwestern frontier life; in summer there are living-history demonstrations that focus on such things as ranching operations or weaving. The fort was completed in 1871 to fend off Indian attacks (which never came because a peace treaty was signed before it was finished), and it was originally built as a ranch for the managers sent to oversee the Mormon church's tithed herds. It ended up functioning mainly as headquarters for a dairy operation, and in 1871 became the first telegraph station in the Arizona territory. Also on the site are a well-stocked bookstore and gift shop, a coffee shop, and a visitor center with exhibits. About ½ mile north of the monument is a campground and picnic area run by the Kaibab–Paiute tribe. *HC 65, Box 5, Fredonia 86022, tel. 602/643-7105. Admission: $2 adults, children 16 and under and senior citizens over 62 free. Historic structures open daily 8-4; visitor center/museum open daily 8-4:30; closed Thanksgiving, Christmas, and New Year's Day.*

After touring the old fort, backtrack on AZ 389 for 6 miles, then take a right turn on the dirt road to **Toroweap Overlook,** a distance of approximately 60 miles. You'll be riding through starkly beautiful, uninhabited country. Toroweap, a lonely and awesome overlook, is the narrowest stretch of the canyon (less than 1 mile across) and also the point with the deepest sheer cliff (more than 3,000 feet straight down). From this vantage point, you can see upstream to sedimentary ledges, cliffs, and talus slopes. Looking downstream, you can see miles of the lava flow that forms steep deltas, some of which look like black waterfalls frozen on the cliff.

Be sure you have plenty of gas, drinking water, good tires, and a reliable car; a high-clearance vehicle (one that sits high up off the ground, like a pickup truck) is best for this trip. Don't try to go in wet weather, when the dirt road is likely to be washed out. There's a ranger station near the rim as well as a primitive campground. If you plan to return the same day, you should make motel reservations in advance at one of the Arizona Strip motels (*see* Lodging, *below*).

Havasu Canyon, South Rim For those who want to get away from the crowds, Havasu Canyon, south of the middle part of the national park, exhibits a Shangri-la–like beauty. It is the home of some 500 Havasupai, a tribe that has populated this beautiful, isolated country for centuries. Spectacular waterfalls (one drops 200 feet) cascade over the red cliffs, spilling blue-green water into immense travertine pools that are surrounded by thick foliage and sheltering trees.

From Grand Canyon Village, head south on U.S. 180 (AZ 64) for 57 miles to Williams, then take I–40 west 44 miles to Seligman. From there, go 34 miles west on AZ 66 until you come to Indian Route 18. A drive 60 miles north will take you to the head of the 8-mile-long Hualapai Trail. You can hike into the canyon or ride a horse or mule down for about $70; the trail twists along the edges of rock walls that go straight down for hundreds of feet. The hurried—or faint of heart—can take a helicopter; **Papillon Helicopters** (tel. 800/528–2418) offers round-trips for $372 per person for a day excursion, $412 for an overnight. You'll definitely want to stay overnight if you're hiking or riding (*see* Lodging, *below*). All visitors are charged a $12 fee to enter the Havasupai tribal lands. For additional information, contact Havasupai Tourist Enterprise (Supai 86435, tel. 602/448–2121 [tourist office] or 602/448–2111 [lodging]).

Shopping

At the South Rim, nearly every lodging facility and retail store offers Native American artifacts and Grand Canyon souvenirs. In truth, you'll find that after visiting a few of the curio and jewelry shops, all the merchandise begins to look alike. However, the items at most of the lodges and at major gift shops are authentic. The most interesting places for browsing or buying in the immediate area are **Desert View Trading Post** (East Rim Dr. near The Watchtower at Desert View, tel. 602/638–2360), which sells a mix of traditional Southwestern souvenirs and authentic Native American pottery; the **El Tovar Hotel Gift Shop** (near the rim in Grand Canyon Village, tel. 602/638–2631), which carries Native American jewelry, rather expensive casual wear, and souvenir gifts; and **Hopi House** (east of El Tovar Hotel, tel. 602/638–2631), which opened in 1905 and still offers one of the widest selections of Native American artifacts—some of museum quality and not for sale—in the vicinity of the Grand Canyon. The far less commercial North Rim has only one gift shop, at the Grand Canyon Lodge, where you'll find some better-quality items mixed in with a largely schlocky selection of souvenirs.

The huge **Cameron Trading Post** (*see* Tour 5 in Exploring, *above*) stocks crafts of the Navajo, Hopi, Zuni, and New Mexico Pueblo peoples. The vast array of goods and prices will satisfy everyone's taste and purse, but it helps to come armed with knowledge of Native American artisanship if you're looking at high-ticket items. *On U.S. 89 1 mi north of junction with AZ 64, tel. 602/679–2231 or 800/338–7385. Open Apr.–Oct., daily 6 AM–10 PM; Nov.–May, daily 7 AM–9 PM.*

Sports and the Outdoors

Participant Sports

Bicycling Bicycles are not permitted on any of the Grand Canyon trails, but there are miles of scenic paved thoroughfares in the national park. Be aware, however, that the park roads have narrow shoulders and are heavily trafficked; use extreme caution. From June 15 through October 14, **North Rim Mountain Bike Tours** (tel. 602/638–2389 or 602/526–0924 in Flagstaff) conducts daily interpretive excursions from Kaibab Lodge (*see* Lodging, *below*). Rates range from $35 for a morning tour to $50 for a lunch or sunset tour and include bike rental, helmet, and water bottle (prices are lower if you're staying at the Kaibab Lodge or have your own bike). There are no rentals or tours available at the South Rim.

Camping Camping inside Grand Canyon National Park is permitted only in designated areas. (For information about campgrounds in and around the park, *see* Lodging, *below*.)

Fishing In the vicinity of Lees Ferry, just across Marble Canyon Bridge on U.S. 89 (the route to the North Rim), the Colorado River is known for its huge trout. Fishing for trout, along with crappie, catfish, and small-mouth bass, is also popular at a number of lakes surrounding Williams, near the South Rim. You can get an Arizona fishing license at many sporting goods stores around the state, at Babbitt's General Store at the South Rim, and at Marble Canyon Lodge, near Lees Ferry, but you won't be able to obtain one at the North Rim; if you'd like a license in advance of your visit, contact the **Arizona Game and Fish Department** (2221 W. Greenway Rd., Phoenix, AZ 85023, tel. 602/942–3000). For details on fishing regulations, check with the Backcountry Reservations Office (*see* Hiking, *below*). **Lees Ferry Anglers** (HC-67 Box 2, Marble Canyon, AZ 86036, tel. 602/355–2261 or 800/962–9755 outside AZ) offers guided fishing trips, including lunch, starting from $225 per day; they're the only guide service in the area that practices year-round catch and release.

Hiking Hiking trails are numerous and the scenery always spectacular in Grand Canyon country. Opportunities range from leisurely walks on well-defined paths through level or easy-rolling country to arduous treks to the bottom of the canyon—even all the way across it to the other rim. Easy hikes can be found in the Exploring section (*see* Tour 3 and Tour 6, *above*). In addition to some of the most popular trails outlined below, national park rangers or visitor center personnel will gladly provide you with hiking information and local maps of trails that vary in degree of difficulty.

Note: Overnight hikes require a permit that can be obtained by written request only to the **Backcountry Reservations Office** (Box 129, Grand Canyon, AZ 86023). Permits are limited, so it's wise to make reservations in advance. If you arrive without one, go to the Backcountry Reservations Office at either rim: South

Rim near the entrance to Mather Campground, North Rim at the ranger station.

Bright Angel Trail, South Rim One of the most popular and scenic hiking paths from the South Rim to the bottom of the canyon (9 miles), the well-maintained Bright Angel Trail was used in the late 1800s as a route to mining claims. There are rest houses for hikers at the 1½- and 3-mile points and at Indian Garden. Plateau Point, about 175 feet below Indian Garden, is a good turnaround point for a day hike. Because the climb out from the bottom of the canyon is an ascent of 4,460 feet, the trip should be attempted only by those in good physical condition and is not recommended during the summer.

Hermit Trail, South Rim This 9-mile trail, which starts at Hermits Rest (8 miles west of Grand Canyon Village), is unmaintained, steep, and suitable only for experienced long-distance hikers; a particularly tricky area is a ⅓-mile section of rock slides. No water is available along the way. The route, which leads to the Colorado River, offers some inspiring views of Hermit Gorge and the Redwall and Supai formations. It's 6 miles from the trailhead to now-abandoned Hermit Camp, operated as a tourist resort by the Santa Fe Railroad after 1912.

South and North Kaibab Trails, South and North Rims South Kaibab Trail, which begins near Yaki Point on East Rim Drive near Grand Canyon Village, connects at the bottom of the canyon (after the Kaibab Bridge across the Colorado) with the North Kaibab Trail, the only maintained trail into the canyon on the North Rim. Plan on three days if you want to hike the gorge from rim to rim. South Kaibab Trail is steep, descending 4,800 feet in just 7 miles, with no campgrounds or water and very little shade; if you're going back up to the South Rim, ascend via the Bright Angel Trail. Accommodations for hikers along the way include the campgrounds at Indian Garden and Bright Angel or Phantom Ranch (*see* Lodging, *below*).

Safety Tips Water must be carried for hikes into the Inner Gorge—at least 1–1½ gallons per day. To avoid dehydration, it is important to drink frequently, about every 10 minutes, especially during summer months. To avoid fatigue, take food—preferably energy snacks such as trail mix, bananas, and fig bars. Wear hiking boots or running shoes that have been broken in and proven on previous hikes. In case of a medical emergency, stay with the distressed person and ask the next hiker to go for help. Do not attempt to make the round-trip to the Colorado River in one day. The trek down is deceptively easy, the route back up very fatiguing.

Mule Trips Almost everyone who knows anything about the Grand Canyon has heard of the mule rides to the bottom of the canyon. For South Rim rides, *see* the Guided Tours section, *above*; for the North Rim, *see* What to See and Do with Children, *above*.

Rafting Many people who have made the white-water trip down the Colorado River through the Grand Canyon say it is the adventure highlight of a lifetime. White-water trips embark from Lees Ferry, below Glen Canyon Dam near Page, Arizona. Trips that run the length of the canyon (a distance of more than 200 miles) can last from three days to three weeks. Shorter trips, which also start at Lees Ferry, let passengers off at Phantom Ranch at the bottom of Grand Canyon (a distance of about 100 miles); these pass through a great amount of white water, including Lava Falls rapids (on the longer trips), considered the wildest navigable rapids in North America. For those who would like a more tranquil turn on the Colorado, there are also one-day, quiet-water raft cruises just below Glen Canyon Dam near Page. Although more than 25 companies currently offer these excursions, reservations for raft trips (excluding the smooth-water, one-day cruises) often must be made more than six months in advance. For a complete list of river-raft companies, call 602/638–7888 from a Touch-Tone telephone and press 1-3-71, or write Grand Canyon National Park, Box 129, Grand Canyon, AZ 86023 to request a *Trip Planner*. White-water companies include **Canyoneers, Inc.** (tel. 602/526–0924 or 800/525–0924 outside AZ), **Diamond River Adventures** (tel. 602/645–8866 or 800/343–3121), **Expeditions Inc.** (tel. 602/779–3769), and **Wilderness River Adventures** (tel. 602/645–3296, 800/992–8022, or 800/528–6154 for reservations more than a week in advance). Smooth-water, one-day-trip companies include **Fred Harvey Transportation Company** (tel. 602/638–2822) and **Wilderness River Adventures** (tel. 602/645–3279; see above for toll-free numbers). Prices for river-raft trips vary greatly, depending on type and length. Day trips on smooth water run as low as $39 per person; trips that negotiate the entire length of the canyon and take as long as 12 days can cost close to $2,000.

Skiing Though you can't schuss down into the Grand Canyon, you can hit the slopes at the nearby **Williams Ski Area** (Box 953, Williams 86046, tel. 602/635–9330), open when there's snow in the region (usually mid-December through March); take South 4th Street for 2 miles, then turn right at the sign and go another 1½ miles. There are four groomed runs (including one for beginners) and a variety of trails for downhill skiers as well as areas suitable for cross-country enthusiasts. Lift tickets range from $8 to $19 depending on your age and level of expertise; lessons are available on a group ($15 per person) and individual ($25) basis. In ski season, when the road to the national park is closed, the **North Rim Nordic Center** (c/o Canyoneers, Inc., Box 2997, Flagstaff 86003, tel. 602/526–0924 or 800/525–0924 outside AZ) transports visitors via SnowVan from Jacob Lake to the Kaibab Lodge, where they can traverse 25 miles of regularly groomed trails in a spectacular wooded setting. Call or write for information on packages, some of which include a helicopter flight from the South Rim.

Dining and Lodging

Dining Throughout Grand Canyon country and the vast areas of northwestern Arizona, restaurants cater to tourists who generally move from one place to another at a good clip. Therefore, most establishments offer standard American fare, prepared quickly and offered at reasonable prices. However, there are a few dining opportunities, noted below, that merit mention. In addition, for a quick meal at reasonable prices, there are cafeterias on the South Rim in Grand Canyon Village at **Yavapai Lodge** and **Maswik Lodge** (tel. 602/638–2401 for both) or at **Desert View Trading Post** (AZ 64, 23 mi east of Grand Canyon Village, tel. 602/638–2360). On the North Rim, the cafeteria is in **Grand Canyon Lodge** (tel. 602/638–2611). Restaurants are open daily unless otherwise noted.

Highly recommended restaurants are indicated by a star ★.

Category	Cost*
$$$$	over $25
$$$	$17–$25
$$	$10–$17
$	under $10

per person, excluding drinks, service, and 5% sales tax

Lodging When it comes to lodging in Grand Canyon country, there is one thing to be aware of above all else. The popular South Rim is very crowded during the summer. The North Rim is less crowded, but that area has limited lodging facilities. You would be well advised to make reservations as soon as your itinerary has been decided, even as early as six months in advance. If you can't find accommodations in the immediate area of the South Rim, you'll probably find something in the nearby communities of Williams or Flagstaff (*see* Chapter 5, North-Central Arizona). For those going to the North Rim, we list the three lodgings in the sparsely populated Arizona Strip country on the approach to the North Rim on U.S. 89A. Prices at many of the hotels and motels in Grand Canyon country are lower in spring, fall, and winter.

Highly recommended lodgings are indicated by a star ★.

Category	Cost*
$$$$	over $100
$$$	$75–$100
$$	$50–$75
$	under $50

All prices are for a standard double room, excluding 5.5%–6.7% tax.

South Rim **El Tovar Hotel.** Built in 1905 of native stone and heavy pine logs, *Dining and* El Tovar is reminiscent of a grand European hunting lodge. *Lodging* Maintaining its tradition of excellent service and luxury, the ho- ★ tel is, as when first built, operated by the Fred Harvey Company. Some rooms have a canyon view. For decades the hotel's world-class restaurant has enjoyed a reputation for fine food served in a classic 19th-century room of hand-hewn logs and beamed ceilings. The Continental menu changes seasonally but includes a daily vegetarian special along with innovatively prepared fish, poultry, and meat dishes: Free-range chicken breast with lemon wasabi sauce or Creole-style crab cakes might be among your dinner options. *Box 699, Grand Canyon 86023, tel. 602/638–2401 (reservations) or 602/638–2631 (switchboard), fax 602/638–9247. 78 rooms and 10 suites, all with bath. Facilities: cocktail lounge, gift shop, dining room, air-conditioning, phones, TV, room service. AE, D, DC, MC, V. $$$$*

★ **Bright Angel Lodge.** Designed by Mary Jane Colter for the Fred Harvey Company in 1935, this log-and-native-stone structure sits within a few yards of the canyon rim and offers rooms in the main lodge or in the quaint cabins (some with fireplaces) that are scattered among the pines. Don't come for luxury but for a historic structure that blends superbly with the spectacular natural environment in which the lodge is set. The Bright Angel Restaurant is a memorable but informal spot for breakfast, lunch, or dinner; the Arizona Steak House is open for dinner only. *Box 699, Grand Canyon 86023, tel. 602/638–2401 (reservations) or 602/638–2631 (switchboard), fax 602/638–9247. 11 rooms with bath, 13 rooms with half-bath (sink and toilet only), 6 rooms without bath, 42 cabins with bath. Facilities: coffee shop, restaurant, cocktail lounge, soda fountain, gift shop, TV, phones. AE, D, DC, MC, V. $$–$$$$*

Dining **The Steak House.** This is a warmly appointed, typical Southwestern steak house—right down to the black-and-white-cowhide-pattern tablecloths, massive brick fireplace, displays of Native American and Western art, and traditional country music on the jukebox. The John Wayne bar is lined with memorabilia of the actor. The food is well prepared, and there's plenty of it, with the menu consisting almost entirely of mesquite-grilled steaks and barbecued chicken entrées; a Mexican plate is always offered, as are specials for senior citizens and a children's menu. *Junction of U.S. 180 and AZ 64, 2 mi south of Grand Canyon entrance, directly north of the IMAX Theater, tel. 602/638–2780. Reservations accepted for 8 or more. Dress: casual. No credit cards. Open early Mar.–mid-Dec., daily 6:30 AM–2 PM and 5–10 PM. $–$$*

Lodging **Best Western Grand Canyon Squire Inn.** Located 1 mile from the national park entrance, this motel lacks some of the historic charm of the older lodges at the canyon rim, but it offers a much longer list of amenities. The spacious, cheerful rooms are nicely appointed with Southwestern-style furnishings. Ask for one with a view of the woods; others face the highway. *Box 130, Grand Canyon 86023, tel. 602/638–2681 or 800/6–CANYON, fax 602/638–2782. 250 rooms with bath. Facilities: dining room, lounge, coffee shop, outdoor heated pool (in season), tennis courts (in season), indoor whirlpool, exercise room, sauna, bowling, billiards, playroom, gift shop, tour desk, beauty salon. AE, D, DC, MC, V. $$$$*

Quality Inn. The design and interior of this facility in Tusayan, 6 miles south of the South Rim on U.S. 180, are typical of Quality Inns elsewhere—unpretentious, but offering a satisfactory comfort level in a land where motel vacancies can be difficult to find in the busy summer season. Rooms are done in soothing shades of light blue, peach, or tan. In contrast to many other chain hotels, individual service is emphasized here. *Box 520, AZ 64 and U.S. 180, Grand Canyon, 86023, tel. 602/638–2673 or 800/221–2222, fax 602/638–9537. 176 rooms with bath. Facilities: outdoor pool (in season), Jacuzzi, air-conditioning, TV, phones, gift shop. AE, D, DC, MC, V. $$$$*

Fred Harvey Motels. The Fred Harvey Company has seven lodges on the South Rim. Of them, El Tovar and Bright Angel (*see above*) are outstanding, but Maswik Lodge, Yavapai Lodge, Moqui Lodge, Kachina Lodge, and Thunderbird Lodge are all comfortable and nicely appointed. In addition to lodge rooms, Maswik offers rustic cabins. Moqui is on U.S. 180, just outside the national park. The others are in Grand Canyon Village. With the exception of Maswik Lodge, which has rooms in the $$ range, accommodations in all the motels fall into the $$$ or $$$$ price categories. Note: Moqui Lodge is only open from March through November. *Box 699, Grand Canyon 86023, tel. 602/638–2401 (reservations) or 602/638–2631 (switchboard), fax 602/638–9247. (The postal box, tel., and fax nos. are the same for all Fred Harvey accommodations on South Rim.) 855 rooms with bath. Facilities: phones, TV, restaurant on site or close by. AE, D, DC, MC, V. $$–$$$$*

Camping Camping inside Grand Canyon National Park is permitted only in designated areas. Campgrounds at the South Rim are listed below.

Desert View Campground, 23 miles east of Grand Canyon Village off AZ 64, offers RV and tent sites, flush toilets, and water but no hookups. The cost is $10 per site, with no reservations. *Box 129, Grand Canyon 86023, tel. 602/638–7888. Open May–Oct.*

Mather Campground in Grand Canyon Village has 97 RV and 190 tent sites (no hookups), flush toilets, water, showers, and a laundromat; the cost is $10 per site. *Reservations through MISTIX (Box 85705, San Diego, CA 92138, tel. 800/365–2267 or 619/452–0150 outside the U.S. Open all year; no reservations taken from Dec. 1–Mar. 1.*

Trailer Village, in Grand Canyon Village, has 78 RV sites with full hookups for $17 per site. *Box 699, Grand Canyon 86023, tel. 602/638–2401 (reservations) or 602/638–2631 (switchboard), fax 602/638–9247. Open all year.*

Commercial and Forest Service campgrounds outside the park include:

Flintstone Bedrock City, 30 miles south of the park, offers 28 tent and 32 partial RV hookups. Basic rates are $12 per site for two people; add $3 for electricity hookup, $2.50 for water hookup, and $1.50 for each additional person. *Grand Canyon Hwy., HCR 34, Box A, Williams 86046, tel. 602/635–2600. Open Apr.–Oct.*

Grand Canyon Camper Village in Tusayan, 6 miles south of the rim, has 250 RV hookups, some partial, some full ($22 for two people, plus $2 for each additional person over the age of 12) and

100 tent sites ($15 for two people). *Box 490, Grand Canyon 86023, tel. 602/638-2887.*

Ten X Campground is run by the Forest Service about 9 miles south of the park. It offers 70 family sites plus a group site (available for groups of up to 100 people), water, and pit toilets for $10 per day but no hookups. No reservations are accepted (except for the group site). *Kaibab National Forest, Tusayan Ranger District, Box 3088, Grand Canyon 86023, tel. 602/638-2443. Open May 1–Sept. 30.*

Bottom of the Canyon
Dining and Lodging

Phantom Ranch. Built on the site of an earlier hunting camp in 1932, this group of wood-and-stone buildings is set among a grove of cottonwood trees at the bottom of the canyon. For hikers (who need a backcountry permit to come down here), dormitory accommodations—20 beds for men and 20 for women—are available, as are two cabins (one sleeping four people, the other 10). There are also seven cabins reserved exclusively for mule riders; lodging, meals, and mule rides are offered as a package (*see* Guided Tours in Essential Information, *above*). The restaurant at Phantom Ranch, probably the most remote eating establishment in the United States, has a limited menu. All meals are served family style, with breakfast, dinner (including a selection for vegetarians), and box lunches available. Arrangements—and payment—for both food and lodging should be made 9 to 11 months in advance. *Box 699, Grand Canyon 86023, tel. 602/638-2401 (reservations) or 602/638-2631, ext. 6015 (switchboard). 4 dormitories for hikers with shared bath, 11 cabins for mule riders with shower outside. Facilities: dining room. AE, D, DC, MC, V. $*

Camping

There are two free campgrounds en route to Phantom Ranch: **Indian Garden,** about halfway down the canyon, and **Bright Angel,** closer to the bottom. Both offer toilet facilities and running water (no showers). A backcountry permit, which serves as a reservation, is required. For information, contact Backcountry Reservations Office (Box 129, Grand Canyon 86023, tel. 602/638-7888).

Havasu Canyon
Dining and Lodging

Havasupai Lodge. The lodge and restaurant at the bottom of Havasu Canyon, operated by the Havasupai tribe, offers clean, comfortable rooms at about $80 for a double (this rate is in addition to the $12 per person fee to enter the Havasupai tribal lands). The restaurant serves three meals a day, generally sandwiches and fast-food-type fare, and a special daily meal; dinner prices are around $8–$10. For information about camping in the canyon, call the Havasupai Tourist Enterprise (tel. 602/448-2121). *Supai 86435, tel. 602/448-2111 (lodge), or 602/448-2981 (restaurant). 24 rooms. No credit cards accepted at any facilities; personal checks accepted for deposit, traveler's checks or cash required upon arrival. $$$*

En Route to the North Rim/Arizona Strip

Dining and Lodging

★ **Cameron Trading Post.** In 1993 the 1930s-era inn abutting the historic trading post was razed and replaced by a two-building motel complex. Rooms still have a Southwestern-style decor, attractive hand-carved oak furniture, tile baths, and balconies overlooking the Colorado, but now have such contemporary amenities as remote-control TVs. The original native-stone landscaping—including fossilized dinosaur tracks—was retained, as was the small, well-kept garden with lilacs, roses, and crab apple trees. A new cafeteria, designed to serve the tour-bus trade, is unusually elegant, with an antique back bar and light fixtures; the older dining room, with its original tinwork ceilings, kiva fireplace, and beautiful oak sideboards, offers hearty meals at good prices. The trading post is on the Navajo reservation, so no alcohol is served here. *Box 339, Cameron 86020, tel. 602/679–2231 or 800/338–7385, ext. 407; fax 602/679–2350. 66 rooms with bath, 3 suites. Facilities: market, restaurant, cafeteria, gift shop, art gallery. AE, DC, MC, V. $$$*

Cliff Dwellers Lodge. Originated in 1949 in the Marble Canyon area of the Arizona Strip, this dining and lodging complex sits right at the foot of the Vermilion Cliffs. Rooms in the modern motel building are attractive and clean. In summer, the lodge offers four-wheel-drive and hiking tours of the area, and a river expedition company is headquartered right next door. *AZ 89A, 9 mi west of Navajo Bridge, HC 67–30, Marble Canyon 86036, tel. 602/355–2228 or 800/433–2543, fax 602/355–2229. 21 rooms with bath. Facilities: restaurant and bar, patio, convenience store, gas station. D, MC, V. $$*

Jacob Lake Inn. This modest but clean lodging complex, on 5 acres in Kaibab National Forest (at the junction of U.S. 89A and AZ 67, 45 miles north of the North Rim), is a good option for lodging in the area. Both basic cabins and standard motel-type units are available. All rooms have modern, motel-style appointments, with some rustic touches; most overlook the highways. The bustling lodge center, a popular stop for those heading to the North Rim, has a grocery, a coffee shop, a restaurant, and a large gift shop. *Jacob Lake 86022, tel. 602/643–7232. 11 motel units, 3 family units, 22 cabins, all with bath. Facilities: restaurant, gas station, gift shop, grocery, café. AE, D, DC, MC, V. $$*

★ **Marble Canyon Lodge.** This Arizona Strip lodge opened in 1929, on the same day the Navajo Bridge was dedicated. It is currently owned by Jane Foster, who first came here in 1950 with her father. Three types of accommodations are available: rooms with lace curtains, brass beds, and hardwood floors in the original building; standard motel rooms in the newer building across the street; and apartments (which can sleep up to eight) in a 1991 complex. Guests can sit on the porch swing of the native-rock lodge building and look out on the Vermilion Cliffs and the desert, or they can play the piano that was brought over on Lees Ferry in the 1920s. Zane Grey and Gary Cooper are among the well-known guests who have stayed here. *1/2 mi west of Navajo Bridge on AZ 89A, Marble Canyon 86036, tel. 602/355–2225 or 800/726–1789, fax 602/355–2227. 63 units with bath. Facilities: restaurant, gift shop, gas station, landing strip, laundry, coin-op showers. MC, V. $$*

Lees Ferry Lodge. Geared toward the Lees Ferry trout-fishing trade, this lodge will outfit you, guide you, and freeze or cold-store your catch. At the end of the day you can sit out on one of the garden patios of this rustic building, constructed of native stone and rough-hewn beams in 1929. Rooms are charming, if a bit quirky in their plumbing. The hotel's Vermilion Cliffs Bar and Grill is a popular gathering spot for the men and women who pilot and guide the river rafts through the Grand Canyon, and it serves good American fare—especially the steaks and seafood—in an authentic Western setting. *3 mi west of Navajo Bridge on AZ 89A, HC67, Box 1, Marble Canyon 86036, tel. 602/ 355-2231. 8 rooms with shower, 5-person trailer with bath. Facilities: restaurant, fly/curio shop, boat for rent. MC, V. $*

Camping   **Jacob Lake Campground,** at the junction of U.S. 89A and AZ 67, 45 miles north of the North Rim, has family and group RV and tent sites (no hookups) for $10 per vehicle per day. In summer, rangers present interpretive programs in the evening. No reservations accepted (except for large groups). *Southwest Natural and Cultural Heritage Association, Box 620, Fredonia 86022, tel. 602/643-7395. Open May-Oct.*

Jacob Lake RV Park, on AZ 67 ¼ mile south of Jacob Lake junction, has 50 tent sites ($10 for two people, $1 for each additional person) and 80 RV and trailer sites ($16 for two people, $1 for each additional person; full hookups). Reservations are accepted. *Jacob Lake 86022, tel. 602/643-7804. Open May 1-Oct. 15.*

North Rim
Dining and
Lodging
★

Grand Canyon Lodge. This historic property offers a range of accommodations in a setting of extraordinary beauty; it's the premier lodging facility in the remote, sparsely populated North Rim area. The main building was constructed in the 1920s and has massive limestone walls and timbered ceilings. Room choices include small, very rustic cabins; newer, larger cabins (some with a canyon view and some with two bedrooms); and traditional motel rooms. The hotel's huge, high-ceiling dining room offers spectacular views and very good food. *TW Recreational Services, Box 400, Cedar City, UT 84721, tel. 801/586-7686 (reservations) or 602/638-2611 (switchboard), fax 801/586-3157. 40 rooms with bath, 54 Western cabins (for up to 5 people), 82 Frontier cabins (up to 3 people), 21 Pioneer cabins (4 or 5 people), 4 cabins accessible to travelers with disabilities. Facilities: dining room, cafeteria, cocktail lounge, gift shop, visitor center, talks and programs. D, MC, V. $$*

Kaibab Lodge. In a lovely wooded setting just 5 miles from the entrance to Grand Canyon National Park's North Rim, this 1920s property offers rustic cabins with plain, motel-style furnishings. When they're not out looking into the abyss, guests can sit around the lodge's huge stone fireplace or participate in one of its sports programs: mountain biking in summer, or Nordic skiing in winter (*see* Sports and the Outdoors, *above*). Open mid-May-Nov. 1 for summer season, early Dec.-early Apr. for skiing season. *AZ 67, HC 64, Box 30, Fredonia 86022, tel. 602/ 638-2389. 24 cabins with shower. D, MC, V. $$*

Camping On the North Rim there is only one designated campground inside Grand Canyon National Park. **North Rim Campground,** located 3 miles north of the rim, has 83 RV and tent sites (no hookups) for $10 per day. *Reservations through MISTIX (Box 85705, San Diego, CA 92138, tel. 800/365–2267 or 619/452–0150 outside the U.S). Open May 15–Oct. 26.*

Forest Service campgrounds outside the park include **Demotte Campground,** 16 miles north of the rim, with 22 single-unit RV and tent sites, but no hookups, for $10 per day. There are interpretive campfire programs in summer. No reservations accepted. *Southwest Natural and Cultural Heritage Association, Box 620, Fredonia 86022, tel. 602/643–7395. Open mid-May/ early June–Oct.*

The Arts and Nightlife

Unless you head for nearby Williams or Flagstaff after dark, nightlife in this part of the Southwest consists of watching a full moon above the soaring buttes of the Grand Canyon, roasting marshmallows over a crackling fire, crawling into your bedroll beside some lonely canyon trail, or attending a free evening program on the history of the Grand Canyon. Dinner at **El Tovar Restaurant** (it has an excellent wine list) would be a memorable evening. In addition, the following Grand Canyon properties have cocktail lounges: **El Tovar Hotel** (piano bar), **Bright Angel Lodge** (live entertainment), **Maswik Lodge** (sports bar), **Yavapai Lodge** (dancing), and **Moqui Lodge** (live entertainment). Call 602/638–2401 for reservations and further information.

Similarly, there's little in the way of cultural events in the area, but every fall the **Grand Canyon Chamber Music Festival** is held in the Shrine of the Ages auditorium at the South Rim visitor center. For schedule information and advance tickets, call or write Box 1332, Grand Canyon 86023, tel. 602/638–9215. A **lecture series** on scientific topics, cosponsored by the National Park Service and the Grand Canyon History Association, is scheduled to coincide with the chamber music festival; ask for details at any of the area lodges or at the visitor center.

Northwest Arizona, Lake Mead, and Laughlin

If the Grand Canyon is the most dramatic natural attraction in northwest Arizona, it is by no means all there is to see. Towns like Williams and Kingman hearken back to the glory days of old Route 66, while the ghost towns of Chloride and Oatman bear testament to the mining madness that once reigned in the region. Water-sports fans, or those who just want to laze on a houseboat, will enjoy Lake Mead, just across the Nevada border, or Lake Havasu, over which London Bridge somewhat surrealistically presides. Another bridge across the Colorado leads to Nevada and the casinos of Laughlin, more low-key and casual than those of Las Vegas. Perhaps the most fitting adjunct to a visit to the Grand Canyon is a visit to Hoover Dam, that most impressive example of human dominion over the force of the Colorado.

Exploring

Numbers in the margin correspond to points of interest on the Northwest Arizona and Lake Mead map.

❶ Often considered just a jumping-off point for the Grand Canyon, **Williams** retains its own funky frontier charm, despite a proliferation of motels and fast-food restaurants on its main street (named, like the town itself, after mountain man Bill Williams). Due to its elevation of 6,700 feet, the area is wooded and pleasantly temperate in summer, and in winter a small ski area (*see* Sports and the Outdoors, *above*) operates.

Although the town is no longer on an east–west rail link, the route north to the Grand Canyon was restored in 1989 (*see* Guided Tours in Essential Information, *above*). Even if you don't take the train, stop by the **Williams Depot** (518 E. Bill Williams Ave., tel. 602/635–4000), built in 1908. Attractions here include a passenger car and the locomotive of a turn-of-the-century steam train, a small but interesting railroad museum (admission free), and a gift shop where you can find such kitschy souvenirs as a tie that plays "I've Been Working on the Railroad." Reasonably priced antiques shops and retailers selling Native American crafts and jewelry can also be found lining the main drag, where a number of historic buildings have been restored and period lampposts installed.

In addition to the many familiar budget chain motels represented in town, **The Mountain Side Inn & Resort** (642 E. Bill Williams Ave., Williams 86046, tel. 602/635–4431 or 800/462–9381) has comfortable rooms, a good restaurant, and live country-and-western bands in summer. At the no-frills **Norris Motel** (1001 W. Bill Williams Ave., Williams 86046, tel. 602/635–2202 or 800/341–8000), you'll find clean accommodations at good rates (look for the British flag out front). For more information about hotels, restaurants, and exploring, including a self-guided walking tour brochure, contact the **Williams Chamber of Commerce** (820 W. Bill Williams Ave., Box 235, Williams 86046, tel. 602/635–4061). In addition, the **Kaibab Visitor Center** (204 W. Railroad Ave., at Grand Canyon Blvd., Williams 86046, tel. 602/635–4061) has information on the entire Grand Canyon area, as well as on the Kaibab Forest and the city of Williams.

❷ From Williams, take I–40 west to **Kingman,** surrounded by mountains on three sides and host to the longest remaining stretch of old Route 66. In town, the neon-lined roadway is named for native son Andy Devine, the gravelly voiced actor who played the leading man's sidekick in innumerable Westerns. Because I–40, U.S. 93, AZ 68, and Route 66 all converge in Kingman, which is also served by Amtrak, Greyhound, and America West airlines (offering three flights a day from Phoe-

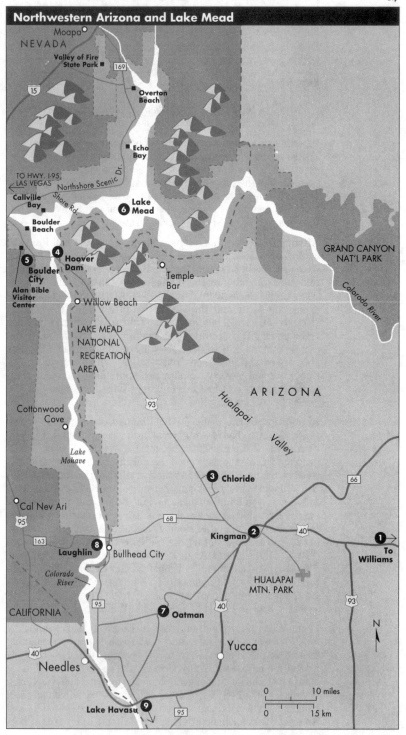

Northwestern Arizona and Lake Mead

NEVADA

Moapa

Valley of Fire State Park ■ 169

15

Overton Beach ■

Echo Bay ■

TO HWY. I-95,
LAS VEGAS
← Northshore Scenic Dr.

Callville Bay

Shore Rd.

6 Lake Mead

Boulder Beach ■

4 Hoover Dam

5 Boulder City

Alan Bible Visitor Center

GRAND CANYON NAT'L PARK

Temple Bar

Colorado River

Willow Beach

LAKE MEAD NATIONAL RECREATION AREA

ARIZONA

93

Hualapai Valley

Cottonwood Cove

Lake Mohave

3 Chloride

66

Cal Nev Ari

95

68

Kingman **2** 40

1 →
To
Williams

163

8 Laughlin Bullhead City

HUALAPAI MTN. PARK

Colorado River

CALIFORNIA

95

7 Oatman

40

93

N

40

Needles

Yucca

Lake Havasu 95
↓

0   10 miles
0   15 km

nix), it is a hub for such area attractions as Hoover Dam, Laughlin, and Lake Havasu.

Once in town, the **Kingman Area Chamber of Commerce** (333 W. Andy Devine Ave., Box 1150, Kingman 86402, tel. 602/753–6106), which carries T-shirts, postcards, and the usual brochures, can acquaint you with local attractions. The **Mohave Museum of History and Arts** (400 W. Beale St., tel. 602/753–3195), includes an Andy Devine Room; an exhibit of carved Kingman turquoise; and a diorama depicting the expedition of Lt. Edward Beale, who led his ill-fated camel-cavalry unit to the area in search of a wagon road along the 35th parallel. The **Bonelli House** (430 E. Spring St., no phone), an excellent example of the Anglo Territorial architecture popular in 1915, is one of 62 buildings in the business district listed on the National Register of Historic Places. A 15-mile drive from town up Hualapai Mountain Road will take you to **Hualapai Mountain Park,** where more than 2,200 wooded acres at elevations ranging from 6,000 to 8,400 feet host 6 miles of hiking trails as well as picnic areas, rustic cabins, and RV and tenting areas; contact the Mohave County Parks Department (tel. 602/753–0739) for details.

There are some 35 motels in this modest (pop. about 13,000) town, most of them along Andy Devine Avenue; the **Quality Inn** (1400 W. Andy Devine Ave., 86401, tel. 602/753–4747 or 800/221–2222) has comfortable rooms and a coffee shop stocked with Route 66 memorabilia. Right next door, **JR's** (1410 Andy Devine Ave., tel. 602/753–1066) serves up large portions of American and Mexican food at reasonable prices.

If you're heading on to Hoover Dam and Lake Mead, take U.S. 93 north; you'll come to a marked turnoff for the ghost town of ❸ **Chloride**, which takes its name from a type of silver ore mined in the area. Many buildings were lost to fires that ravaged the town in its heyday, but some historic treasures still stand, including the old bank vault, now a museum; the 1890 Jim Fritz house; and the Tennessee Saloon, now a general store and dance hall. Don't miss the huge murals painted on the rocks at the outskirts of town by Western artist Roy Purcell, who worked the mines here in his youth.

❹ Continue along U.S. 93 to reach **Hoover Dam.** The visual impact of its incredible mass and height often compels visitors to make this the first stop on a visit to the Lake Mead area. Created for flood control and to generate electricity, the dam is 727 feet high (the equivalent of a 70-story building) and 660 feet thick (more than the length of two football fields). Its construction required 4.4 million cubic yards of concrete, enough to build a two-lane highway from San Francisco to New York. Every year more than 700,000 people take the Bureau of Reclamation's guided tour, which takes visitors deep inside the structure for a look at its inner workings; the tours leave every few minutes from the exhibit building at the top of the dam. A huge new visitor center, scheduled to open on the Nevada side in spring 1995, will feature three revolving theaters, an exhibition gallery, an observation tower, and a much-needed five-story parking garage. *Tel. 702/ 293–8367. Admission free. Guided tours: $3 adults, $1.50 senior citizens over 62 with Golden Age Pass, children under 12 free. Open Memorial Day–Labor Day, daily 8–7:15; Labor Day–Memorial Day, daily 9–4:15; closed Christmas.*

❺ About 8 miles west of Hoover Dam on U.S. 93 **Boulder City,** Nevada is a small, pleasant town with a movie theater, numerous gift shops and eateries, and a small hotel. Developed in the early 1930s to house the 4,000 Hoover Dam workers and to deter them from spending their hard-earned dollars on wine, women, and Las Vegas, Boulder City is the only community in Nevada where gambling is to this day illegal. When the dam was completed, the city served as a center for the management and maintenance of the site. The **Boulder City Chamber of Commerce** (1497 Nevada Hwy., Boulder City, NV 89005, tel. 702/293–2034) has information about the town and nearby attractions.

Just northeast of Boulder City, at the intersection of U.S. 93 (also called Nevada Highway here) and Lakeshore Scenic Drive (NV 166), you'll come to the **Alan Bible Visitor Center** (601 Nevada Hwy., Boulder City, NV 89005, tel. 702/293–8906), the best place to become acquainted with the Lake Mead area.

Turn left out of the visitor center and go down the hill to pick up Lakeshore Scenic Drive (NV 166). This route wends its way
❻ along the shore of **Lake Mead,** the largest man-made body of water in the United States, with a surface covering 229 square miles and an irregular shoreline extending for 550 miles. It was formed when Hoover Dam was built in 1935 to hold back the Colorado River. The recreation areas here include Boulder Beach, Callville Bay, Echo Bay, and Overton Beach, all of which host marinas.

If you didn't bring your own boat, your rental options include houseboats, patio boats, fishing boats, and ski boats—pick up a list of marinas at the Alan Bible Visitor Center (*see above*). Houseboat rentals are available at **Callville Bay Resort and Marina** (tel. 702/565–7340) or at **Echo Bay Resort** (tel. 702/394–4066). Smaller boats are available at these locations and at **Lake Mead Resort** (Boulder Beach, tel. 702/293–3484), in addition to other marinas.

For those who want to leave the navigating to someone else, a 1½-hour cruise of the Hoover Dam area on a 250-passenger stern-wheeler is available through **Lake Mead Cruises** (Lake Mead Marina, near Boulder Beach, tel. 702/293–6180) and a 15-mile motorized raft trip on the Colorado from the base of Hoover Dam down Black Canyon to Willow Beach is offered by **Gray Line Tours** (tel. 702/384–1234 or 800/634–6579).

If you're heading to Laughlin from Kingman, but you're not
❼ overanxious to hit the slots, the ghost town of **Oatman** is a worthwhile detour via old Route 66; it's a straight shot across the Mohave Desert valley for a while, but then the road narrows and winds precipitously for about 15 miles through the Black Mountains. The main street of this former gold-mining town is

right out of the Old West; in fact, a number of films, including *How the West Was Won*, were shot here. You can wander into one of the three saloons or visit the Oatman Hotel, where Clark Gable and Carole Lombard honeymooned in 1939 after they were secretly married in Kingman, but the burros that often come in from the nearby hills and meander down the street are the real draw; a couple of stores sell hay to visitors who want to feed these "wild" beasts.

North Oatman Road will take you to Bullhead City, where you ❽ can cross the Colorado River to reach **Laughlin,** Nevada. Don Laughlin opened the first casino here in 1966, but the town didn't really take off until the early 1980s. Though often considered just a smaller version of Las Vegas, Laughlin has a character of its own. It generally attracts older, retired travelers who spend at least part of the winter in Arizona, and other folks who prefer the low-pressure, low-minimum tables, the cheap food, the low-cost rooms, and the slots galore. The dealers are generally friendlier, the bettors more relaxed, and, especially compared to the shuttered rooms in Las Vegas, Laughlin casinos have a bright, airy, open feeling, lent by large picture windows that overlook the Colorado. When you've finished at the tables, Laughlin's outdoor activities include water sports, golf, tennis, and strolls along the tree-lined River Walk. The **Laughlin Chamber of Commerce** (1725 Casino Dr., Box 2280, Laughlin 89029, tel. 702/298–2214 or 800/227–5245) can provide further information on the area, which is served six times daily by America West flights from Phoenix to Bullhead City.

The gambling halls lining Casino Drive include **Riverside Resort** (1650 S. Casino Dr., tel. 702/298–2535 or 800/227–3849), **Flamingo Hilton** (1900 S. Casino Dr., tel. 702/298–5111 or 800/352–6464), **Regency Casino** (1950 S. Casino Dr., tel. 702/298–2439), **Edgewater** (2020 S. Casino Dr., tel. 702/298–2453 or 800/257–0300), **Colorado Belle** (2100 S. Casino Dr., tel. 702/298–4000 or 800/458–9500), **Pioneer Hotel** (2200 S. Casino Dr., tel. 702/298–2442 or 800/634–3469), **Ramada Express** (2121 S. Casino Dr., tel. 702/298–4200 or 800/272–6232), **Golden Nugget** (2300 S. Casino Dr., tel. 702/298–7111 or 800/237–1739), **Gold River** (2700 S. Casino Dr., tel. 702/298–2242 or 800/835–7903), and **Harrah's** (2900 S. Casino Dr., tel. 702/298–4600 or 800/447–8700).

❾ From Bullhead City, drive 19 miles south on AZ 95 to reach **Lake Havasu,** renowned for hosting London Bridge. A brilliant stroke of entrepreneurship turned what might have been just another desert town on the Colorado into a crowd-drawing curiosity: When the City of London put the sinking bridge up for sale in 1967, developer Robert McCulloch decided it would make the perfect centerpiece for the community he had planned on the shores of the lake. He bought the historic bridge for nearly $2.5 million, had it dismantled stone by stone, shipped, and precisely reassembled (all 10,000 tons of it) to span a narrow arm of Lake Havasu.

An Olde English theme is played to the hilt here: A Tudor-style village replete with pub, red London telephone booths, and other Britobilia abuts the base of the bridge. But Havasu City is on a lake, and in Arizona after all, so the sunshine, water sports, and fishing can amuse visitors after they've seen the surprising span. The weather is wonderful in spring, fall, and winter, but summers often see temperatures that exceed 100°F. Among the recreational opportunities on and around 45-mile-long Lake Havasu are houseboat, ski-boat, Jet Ski, and sailboat rentals; marinas, RV parks, and campgrounds; golf, tennis, and guided fishing expeditions. Those who are interested in exploring the desert—including old mines and a wildlife refuge—might consider booking a four-wheel-drive tour with Outback Off-Road Adventures (2169 Swanson Ave. #4, tel. 602/680–6151).

The area has more than 20 lodging establishments—from inexpensive roadside motels to posh resorts—and more than 40 restaurants, from fast-food emporiums to fine-dining establishments. For more information on Lake Havasu City, contact the **Lake Havasu Chamber of Commerce** (1930 Mesquite Ave., Lake Havasu City 86403, tel. 602/453–3444 or 800/242–8278).

4 The Northeast

*Petrified Forest,
Hopi and Navajo Country,
Lake Powell*

*By William
E. Hafford*

*Updated by
Edie Jarolim*

If you like wide-open spaces, you'll want to visit northeastern Arizona, a vast and lonely land of shifting red dunes and soaring buttes, where horizons capped by pure blue skies are almost always 100 miles or more away. Covering more than 30,000 square miles, most of the northeast belongs to the Navajo and Hopi peoples, who have held on to their ancient cultural traditions—based on strong spiritual values and an affinity for nature—to the present day. Excellent Native American arts and crafts can be found in shops, galleries, and trading posts throughout the region. Visiting here is like crossing into a foreign country—one that is, sadly, less prosperous than much of the rest of the United States. In some respects, life on the Hopi Mesas does not seem very different from what it must have been in the last century, and it's not uncommon to hear the Navajo language spoken in towns such as Tuba City and Window Rock.

The sprawling Navajo reservation (known to its people as the Navajo Nation) incorporates about 25,000 square miles of the entire northeastern corner of Arizona; in its approximate center lie the 4,000 square miles of Hopi reservation, a series of stone and adobe villages built on high mesas that overlook agricultural land. Within the stunning landscape of Navajo National Monument and Canyon de Chelly rest the mysterious ruins of the ancient Anasazi Indian tribes, who first wandered here thousands of years ago.

Outside the borders of the Navajo Nation, you'll find two of the most popular attractions in the area. Just below the southeastern boundary of the reservation, straddling I–40, is Petrified Forest National Park, an intriguing geologic open book of the Earth's distant past. The park includes a large portion of the famed Painted Desert, with its stratified bands of multicolored hills in which ancient life-forms and huge fallen tree trunks have petrified over hundreds of millions of years. Abutting the far northwestern corner of the Navajo reservation on U.S. 89 lies Glen Canyon Dam—and behind it, more than 120 miles of Lake Powell's emerald waters held in precipitous canyons of erosion-carved stone. Many find Lake Powell one of the most serene and beautiful spots in the world.

Most of the northeast is arid land, with soil and rock formations ranging in color from delicate salmon pink to rusty orange—and sometimes nearly red. Driving for long distances, you'll generally see immense vistas of mesas, rock spires, canyons, and cliffs, but you'll also pass some impressive mountain ranges. The Chuska Mountains to the north and east of Canyon de Chelly are covered with striking stands of ponderosa pine, and Navajo Mountain to the north and west in Utah soars above 10,000 feet.

Essential Information

Important Addresses and Numbers

Tourist
Information
For more information regarding Indian country, contact the **Navajoland Tourism Department** (Box 663, Window Rock 86515, tel. 602/871–6659, 871–7371, or 871–6436) and the **Hopi Tribe Office of Public Relations** (Box 123, Kykotsmovi 86039, tel. 602/734–2441); both publish tourist-oriented newspapers. The **Native American Tourism Center** (4130 N. Goldwater Blvd., Scottsdale 85251, tel. 602/945–0771) sells a map of the Arizona reservations, which includes a list of their annual festivals, and also offers tourism brochures and a calendar of Indian events on and off the reservations. In addition, the center can help you contact any of the 14 tribal councils in the state. The **Page/Lake Powell Chamber of Commerce** (110 S. Lake Powell Blvd., Box 727, Page 86040, tel. 602/645–2741) and the **National Park Service/Glen Canyon Recreation Area** (Box 1507, Page 86040, tel. 602/645–8200) are both excellent sources for Lake Powell vacation information and prices.

Emergencies
Police
Navajo tribal police: Chinle (tel. 602/674–5291), **Tuba City** (tel. 602/283–5242, **Window Rock** (tel. 602/871–6113 or 871–6116); **Hopi tribal police: Hopi Mesas** (tel. 602/738–2233).

Hospitals/
Medical
Clinics
Medical care in Indian country is not as easily accessible as in heavily populated urban areas. People with chronic medical conditions or those in frail health may wish to avoid a trip into Arizona's sparsely populated northeast. Hospital emergency care is generally not more than 60 minutes' driving time from any location on a paved highway.

Sage Memorial Hospital (tel. 602/755–3411), a public hospital located in Ganado, on the Navajo reservation, offers medical and dental services. **Monument Valley Hospital** (tel. 801/727–3241) in Utah (near Goulding's Trading Post off U.S. 163 at the Arizona–Utah border) has medical and dental services. Emergency care through the U.S. Public Health Service Indian Hospitals is available in the reservation communities of Fort Defiance (tel. 602/729–5741), Chinle (tel. 602/674–5281), Tuba City (tel. 602/283–6211), and Keams Canyon (tel. 602/738–2211). Another option in a medical emergency is to contact the Navajo or Hopi tribal police (*see* Police, *above*).

Page Hospital (N. Navajo and Vista Aves., tel. 602/645–2424) has emergency-room service.

Pharmacies
There are no pharmacies on the Navajo or Hopi reservation; for emergency medical supplies, go to the private or public hospitals noted in the Hospital/Medical Clinics section, above.

In Page, **Safeway** (Page Plaza, tel. 602/645–5714 or 602/645–5068) is open Monday through Friday 9–9, Saturday 10–6, and Sunday 10–4.

Road Service **Fed Mart Automotive** (AZ 264 near Window Rock, tel. 602/871–4764), **Tuba City Motors** (corner of Birch and Oak Sts., Tuba City, tel. 602/283–5330 during the day, 602/283–5300 at night), **Kayenta Discount Auto Parts** (Kayenta on Hwy. 160, tel. 602/697–3200), **Onsae Auto Repair** (Second Mesa, across from the Hopi Cultural Center, Hopi Mesas, tel. 602/734–2211).

Arriving and Departing by Plane

No major airlines fly directly to Indian country. To get closer to the northeastern part of the state, travelers will need to make flight connections in Phoenix to travel either on to Flagstaff, on I–40 near the southwestern corner of the Navajo reservation, or the community of Page, on U.S. 89 near Lake Powell and the northern border of Arizona. At the end of your flight, you'll need to rent a car for the rest of the journey (*see* Rental Cars, *below*).

Airports and **Sky Harbor International Airport** (tel. 602/273–3300) in Phoenix
Airlines is the primary hub for air travel coming into Arizona from points out of state. **Flagstaff Pullium Airport** (tel. 602/556–1234) and **Page Municipal Airport** (tel. 602/645–2494) are both small but modern. **Skywest** (tel. 800/453–9417) has daily flights from Phoenix to Page. (*See* Chapter 6, Phoenix and Central Arizona, and Chapter 5, North-Central Arizona, for information on airlines that service Phoenix and Flagstaff.)

Arriving and Departing by Train or Bus

By Train **Amtrak** (tel. 800/872–7245) provides daily service into Arizona from both the east and the west. It makes scheduled stops in Flagstaff, which is a good jumping-off point for a car trip into Indian country. No passenger train enters the interior of the Navajo or Hopi reservation.

By Bus **Greyhound Lines** (tel. 800/231–2222) has numerous Arizona destinations, but there is no service into Indian country. If you're coming from out of state and wish to tour northeastern Arizona, you can take a bus to Phoenix or Flagstaff and then rent a car.

Getting Around

By Car If you are arriving from southern California or southern Arizona, Flagstaff is the most likely entry point into northeastern Arizona (*see* Chapter 5, North-Central Arizona, for directions to Flagstaff). If you are traveling from the north or northwest, you might choose to come in from Utah via U.S. 89, starting your tour at Page, Arizona. For those driving south from Colorado, a logical entry point is west from Farmington, New Mexico, via U.S. 64. Gallup, New Mexico, or Flagstaff, Arizona—both on I–40—are convenient starting points for those arriving from most eastern locations.

Road Maps Because a tour of Indian country involves driving long distances among widely scattered communities, a detailed, recently published road map is absolutely essential. A wrong turn in this lonely country could send you many miles out of your way. Gas stations carry adequate state maps, but two other maps are especially recommended: the Automobile Association of America's guide to Indian country or the excellent map of the northeastern region prepared by the **Navajoland Tourism Department** (*see* Important Addresses and Numbers, *above*).

Road Service It isn't easy to find a place to service your car here; we recom-
and Weather mend that you make sure your car is inspected and serviced before your trip. Also, seek weather information if you see ominous rain clouds in summer or signs of snow in winter. Never drive into dips or low-lying road areas during a heavy rainstorm; they could be flooded. (For road service locations and emergency and weather information, *see* Important Addresses and Numbers, *above*, and Weather, *below*.) If you heed these simple precautions, car travel through Indian country will be as safe as travel anywhere else. Paved highways in the interior are well maintained and patrolled by police officers.

Rental Cars Rental cars in heavily touristed Arizona are plentiful and usually available, but it's still smart to reserve a car in advance of your arrival. Major companies serving Phoenix and Flagstaff include **Avis** (tel. 800/331–1212), **Budget** (tel. 800/527–0700), **Hertz** (tel. 800/654–3131), and **National** (tel. 800/227–7368). Avis and Budget also offer rentals in Page. Weekly rates for a compact with unlimited mileage are most reasonable in Flagstaff (about $140 without any discounts), slightly higher in Phoenix (about $150), and much higher in Page (around $225).

By Bus The **Navajo Transit System** (Drawer 1330, Window Rock 86515, tel. 602/729–5449, 602/729–5457 or, at Navajo Nation Inn, tel. 602/871–4108) offers regular service on fixed routes throughout the Navajo reservation as well as charter service; write ahead for schedules. The buses are modern, in good condition, and generally on time. However, this method of travel, across vast areas of Indian country where towns and bus stops are many miles apart, may be too slow for some visitors.

Guided Tours

Except during winter months, the **Navajo Transit System** (*see above*) offers tours of Indian country departing from Window Rock, the tribal capital. Destinations include Canyon de Chelly, the Painted Desert, and the Petrified Forest. **Nava-Hopi Tours, Inc.** (tel. 602/774–5003 or 800/892–8687), an affiliate of Gray Line, schedules tours into Indian country from Flagstaff. **Crawley's Monument Valley Tours** (tel. 602/697–3463) leaves from the small town of Kayenta, and **Goulding's Monument Valley Tours** (tel. 801/727–3231) departs from Goulding's Lodge (*see* Lodging, *below*). Half- and full-day truck and Jeep tours into Canyon de Chelly on the Navajo reservation depart from nearby **Thunderbird Lodge** (tel. 602/674–5841); the half-day tours leave twice daily (when there is a minimum of six passengers) throughout the year, while full-day tours are available only from April to October. The newspaper published by the

Navajoland Tourism Department (*see* Important Addresses and Numbers, *above*) has a listing of operators offering Jeep and horseback tours on the Navajo reservation.

Unless you have a four-wheel-drive vehicle or don't mind hiking 8 miles (round-trip) through sand, you'll want to take a guided tour to Corkscrew Canyon, one of the most arresting sights in the Page/Lake Powell area (*see* Off the Beaten Path, *below*). **Duck Tours** (tel. 602/645–8881, code 81; tickets also available at the Page Chamber of Commerce and the John Wesley Powell Museum) uses a 30-foot-long, bright-yellow, World War II–vintage amphibious vehicle for its forays into the canyon; if company owner Lee Woods is your guide, you're in for a fascinating introduction to the area.

Weather

With elevations generally between 4,000 and 7,000 feet, the region's summer temperatures average about 87°F but can climb beyond 100°F. Winter daytime temperatures range from the 30s to the 60s but can drop to zero or below. While the area gets less than 10 inches of rainfall in an average year, fierce summer thunderstorms can quickly fill the arroyos and turn them into raging torrents. Sometimes during the winter months, heavy snows virtually stop all traffic on the dirt back roads.

KTNN radio (AM 660), provides periodic weather information. This station serves the Hopi and Navajo reservations from studios in Window Rock. Some of the programming is in Navajo, but there are news and weather reports in English. You might also telephone the Canyon de Chelly (tel. 602/674–5500) or the Navajo or Hopi tribal police (*see* Emergencies, *above*) for weather updates.

Time

Unlike the rest of Arizona (including the Hopi reservation), the Navajo reservation observes daylight saving time. Thus for half the year—April to October—it's an hour later on the Navajo reservation than everywhere else in the state.

Banks

Citibank has branch offices in Window Rock and Tuba City on the Navajo reservation, but there are no automated teller machines (ATMs) at these locations. The Arizona communities of Flagstaff, Page, Winslow, and Holbrook, all adjacent to the reservation, have banks and ATMs.

The Hopi and the Navajo

No one knows where the ancestors of today's Hopi Indians came from, and archaeologists cannot pinpoint exactly when they arrived. However, the Hopi consider themselves to be the first people to arrive in the Americas, and their oral history has it that these ancestors came by sea, crossing on boats or rafts from one "stepping-stone" to the next. They may have island-hopped across the Pacific rather than crossed the frozen land of the Bering Straits. Many anthropologists think the Hopi are descended from the Anasazi people. Hopi stories suggest that they probably migrated widely for a very long time before being spiritually guided to the mesas that are their present home. It is believed that Oraibi, the earliest village, was established in about AD 1150. Over the years the Hopi have been an extremely peaceful people, taking a warlike posture only when Spanish priests came to the area around 1630, hoping to convert them to Christianity. In 1680, they joined the Indians of the New Mexico pueblos in a revolt that destroyed the Spanish missions and drove the intruders away.

The Navajo, a more warlike tribe believed to be related to the Athabascans of northeastern Canada, arrived in the Southwest sometime after the Hopi, probably around AD 1300. Thanks to the Pueblo Indians already established in the area, they learned the skills of pottery and weaving, and they also raised livestock and became expert horsemen after the arrival of the Spanish in the 17th century; the Navajo have continued farming and creating arts and crafts to this day. In the years 1863 and 1864, the U.S. Army descended on the Navajo and forced them to make the infamous Long Walk to a virtual concentration camp in eastern New Mexico, releasing them four years later. In 1868 the U.S. government established the Navajo Indian reservation, today the largest in the country, occupying not only the entire northeastern portion of Arizona but also spilling over into Utah and New Mexico. The much smaller Hopi territory, smack in the middle of the Navajo holdings, was ceded to the tribe by the federal government in 1882. Border disputes between the two tribes continue, negotiated in court and before Congress. Differences are evident in their way of life, too: The Hopi tend to live together in villages, whereas the Navajo dwellings are usually dispersed.

Although the Navajo and Hopi peoples fall under certain federal laws, they are essentially self-governing. In earlier days, the Navajo were ruled largely by a complex clan system, but in 1923, they established a tribal government that consists of an elected tribal president, vice president, and more than 80 council members representing the various chapters throughout the Navajo Nation. In 1868, when the reservation was established, there were fewer than 8,000 Navajo, but now this democratically governed Native American community has more than 185,000 people.

The Hopi live in 15 villages, nine of which are on three primary mesas, with a population of about 10,000. Their government, like that of the Navajo, is solidly based on democratic principles. Although both the Navajo and Hopi peoples rely on their own tribal governments and adhere tenaciously to ancestral traditions, they are patriotic Americans as well; large numbers of

Hopi and Navajo have served in the U.S. military with distinction.

Courtesy in Indian Country

Both the Hopi and Navajo peoples are friendly to tourists. However, their privacy, customs, and laws should be respected.

Do not wander across residential areas or disturb property.

Always ask permission before taking photographs of the locals; you may have to pay to take the picture.

Do not litter.

No open fires are allowed; fires are permitted only in grills and fireplaces. Bring your own wood or charcoal.

Observe quiet hours from 11 PM until 6 AM at all camping areas.

Do not disturb or remove animals, plants, rocks, or artifacts. They are protected by Tribal Antiquity and federal laws, which are strictly enforced.

The possession and consumption of alcoholic beverages or drugs is illegal.

No off-trail hiking or rock climbing is allowed.

A permit is required for fishing in lakes or streams or hunting for game; the use of firearms is otherwise prohibited.

Off-road travel by four-wheel-drive vehicles, dune buggies, Jeeps, and motorcycles is not allowed.

Do not wear bikinis or similar scanty clothing in public.

Pets should be kept on a leash or in a confined area.

On the Hopi reservation, taking photographs or making videos, tape recordings, and sketches of villages and ceremonies is strictly prohibited. At all sacred events, neat attire and a respectful demeanor are requested. Camping is permitted for a maximum of two nights, but only in designated areas. All Hopi villages have separate rules about visitors; check with the individual village Community Development Offices (*see* Tour 2: The Hopi Mesas, *below*), or call the **Hopi Tribe Office of Public Relations** (tel. 602/ 734–2441) in advance for information.

Hopi Ceremonies

The Hopi are well known for their colorful ceremonial dances, many of which are supplications for rain, fertile crops, and harmony with nature. Most of these ceremonies take place in village plazas and kivas (underground ceremonial chambers) and last two days or longer; outsiders are permitted to watch only certain segments and are never allowed into the kivas. The dances may involve masks, beaded costumes, drums, and chanting. The best-known is the snake dance, in which participants carry live snakes, including poisonous rattlers, but this ceremony has not been open to the public in recent years. The seasonal kachina dances have also been restricted: Now only those in Moenkopi, Old Oraibi, Hotevilla, and Kykotsmovi may be observed by those who are not Native American.

The dances that visitors are allowed to watch usually take place on weekends, extending through the day until dusk. Each of the tribal clans has its own sacred rituals, and starting times and dates are determined by tribal elders. Visitors should be respectful and adhere to the proper etiquette while observing the dances. For more information, contact the **Hopi Tribe Office of Public Relations** (*see above*).

Exploring the Northeast

Excursions into northeastern Arizona can range from a brief, one-day tour to an extended sojourn of seven days or more. The tours that follow all begin at Flagstaff, the city from which most travelers set out. If you choose one of the other entry points (*see* Getting Around, *above*), you'll need to adjust the recommended tours accordingly.

Tour 1 of the Petrified Forest National Park and the Painted Desert may be included as part of Tour 3 of the southern Indian country if time permits. Tour 2 of the Hopi Mesas may be incorporated into both Tour 3 and Tour 4 of the northern Indian country.

Highlights for First-Time Visitors

Canyon de Chelly (*see* Tour 3)
The Hopi Mesas (*see* Tour 2)
Lake Powell and Rainbow Bridge (*see* Tour 5)
Monument Valley (*see* Tour 4)
Navajo National Monument (*see* Tour 4)
Petrified Forest National Park and the Painted Desert (*see* Tour 1)

Tour 1: Petrified Forest National Park and the Painted Desert

Numbers in the margin correspond to points of interest on the Northeastern Arizona map.

❶ From **Flagstaff,** drive east on I–40 for 115 miles to the north en-
❷ trance (25 miles east of Holbrook) of **Petrified Forest National Park,** a geologic trip back in time. In 1984 the fossil remains of one of the oldest dinosaurs ever unearthed—more than 225 million years old, dating from the Triassic period of the Mesozoic era—were discovered here; other plant and animal fossils in the park date from the same period. Remnants of ancient human beings and their artifacts, dating from some 8,000 years ago, have been recovered at more than 500 sites in this national park. The park derives its name from the fact that the grounds are also covered with tree trunks whose wood cells were replaced over centuries by brightly hued mineral deposits—including silica,

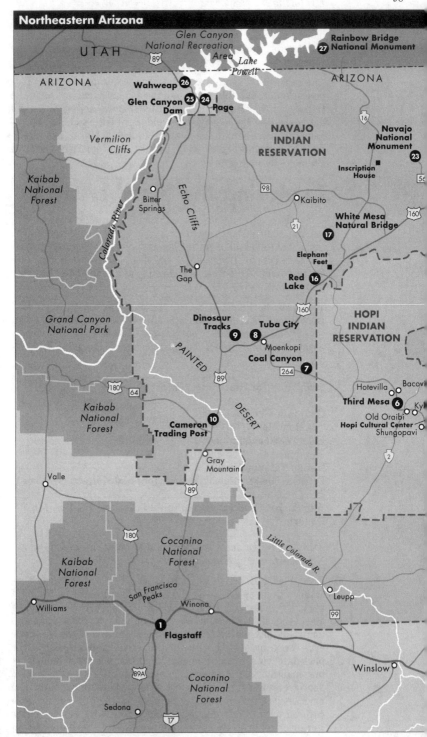

Northeastern Arizona

UTAH

ARIZONA

Glen Canyon
National Recreation
Area

**Rainbow Bridge
National Monument** ㉗

Lake
Powell

㊵

ARIZONA

Wahweap ㉖

**Glen Canyon
Dam** ㉕ ㉔ **Page**

**NAVAJO
INDIAN
RESERVATION**

㊶

**Navajo
National
Monument**
㉓

Vermilion
Cliffs

*Kaibab
National
Forest*

Echo Cliffs

Bitter
Springs

**Inscription
House** ■

㊷

98

Kaibito

White Mesa
Natural Bridge**
㉗

㊶

The
Gap

㉑

**Elephant
Feet** ■

**Red
Lake** ㉖

*Grand Canyon
National Park*

160

**HOPI
INDIAN
RESERVATION**

**Dinosaur
Tracks** ㉙ ⑧ **Tuba City**

Moenkopi

Coal Canyon ⑦
264

*Kaibab
National
Forest*

PAINTED

89

US
180 64

Hotevilla

Bacovi

Third Mesa ⑥

Ky

Old Oraibi
Hopi Cultural Center
Shungopavi

**Cameron
Trading Post** ⑩

DESERT

2

Valle

Gray
Mountain

89

*Kaibab
National
Forest*

Little Colorado R.

180

*Coconino
National
Forest*

*San Francisco
Peaks*

Williams

Winona

Leupp

99

⑴ **Flagstaff**

89A

*Coconino
National
Forest*

Winslow

Sedona

17

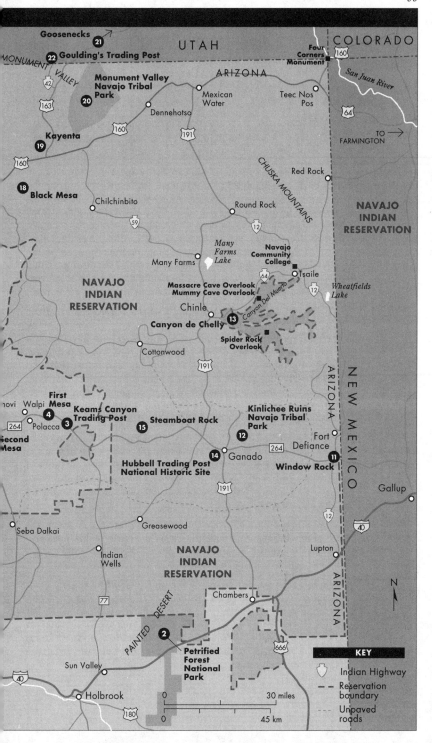

iron oxide, manganese, aluminum, copper, lithium, and carbon—and fossilized; in many places, the petrified logs scattered about the landscape resemble giant jackstraws. Most of the park's 94,000 acres include portions of the vast, lunarlike landscape known as the Painted Desert. In the northern area of the park, this colorful but essentially barren and waterless series of windswept plains, hills, and mesas is considered by geologists to be part of the Chinle formation, deposited at an early stage of the Triassic period. The colors are the most dramatic at dawn and sunset, when the oblique light causes shadows to deepen and makes the smaller chasms glow bright red.

If your schedule permits, you can easily spend most of a day in the park, which has 28 miles of paved roads with walking trails, parking areas, and spur roads. Along the way you can see some spectacular desert scenery and visit several petrified-wood sites. During the early years of this century, looters hauled away pieces of wood in large quantities. In 1906, President Theodore Roosevelt created a national monument in the area, and to this day, it is illegal to remove even a small sliver of petrified wood from the park (there are plenty of pieces on sale at the visitor center gift shop if you want a souvenir).

The **Rainbow Forest Museum and Visitor Center,** located at the south entrance (off U.S. 180), features three skeletons from the Triassic period, including that of the ferocious phytosaur, a crocodilelike carnivore. The museum has numerous exhibits relating to the world of cycads (tropical plants), ferns, fish, and other early life, as well as artifacts and tools of ancient humans. The self-guided **Giant Logs Trail** starts at the museum and visitor center and loops through ½ mile of huge fallen trees. The base of one specimen stands taller than 6 feet.

A movie entitled *The Stone Forest,* which traces the natural history of the area, is shown at regular intervals each day in the **Painted Desert Visitor Center,** located at the north entrance of the park (off I–40). Within the park's boundaries, visitors also have access to gift shops, a restaurant, a soda fountain, and a service station.

Picnicking is allowed inside the park, but there are no overnight accommodations. You may hike into the nearby wilderness areas, but you must obtain a park permit for an overnight stay. Free permits are issued at both visitor centers (*see above*).

North entrance: off I–40, 25 mi east of Holbrook. South entrance: off U.S. 180, 19 mi southeast of Holbrook. Box 2217, Petrified Forest, AZ 86028, tel. 602/524–6228. Admission: $5 per vehicle, free with Golden Eagle, Golden Age, or Golden Access pass. Open daily 8–5 (budget permitting, 1995 summer hours may be extended; call ahead to inquire). Park closed Christmas and New Year's Day.

Tour 2: The Hopi Mesas

From Flagstaff, drive east on I–40. AZ 99, 87, and 77 all go north into the Hopi reservation, but the best of these highways is AZ 87, the turnoff for which is 62 miles east of Flagstaff (4 miles past Winslow). From here, head north 58 miles to the Hopi's Second Mesa, where you will intersect AZ 264.

❸ Drive 21 miles east on AZ 264 to start your tour at the **Keams Canyon Trading Post,** established by Thomas Keam in 1875. Originally, it served only the Indians of the area, but today the trading post also includes a modest motel, a primitive campground, a restaurant (*see* Dining, *below*), and a shopping center (*see* Shopping, *below*). An administrative center for the Bureau of Indian Affairs, Keams Canyon also hosts a number of government buildings. The first 3 miles of the canyon running toward the northeast can be seen by car. At Inscription Rock, about 2 miles down the road, early frontiersman Kit Carson engraved his name in stone. Though there are several picnic spots in the wooded canyon, the main attraction here is the trading post, which offers authentic Native American arts and crafts. Don't expect anything on the scale of the historic Cameron or Hubbell trading posts (*see below*) on the Navajo reservation, though.

From Keams Canyon, head west on AZ 264 for a tour of the Hopi villages, most of which are situated on the top of or at the base of a trio of mesas: First Mesa, Second Mesa, and Third Mesa. You'll need permission beforehand to visit the Hopi villages. For information, call the **Hopi Tribe Office of Public Relations** (tel. 602/734–2441), which also provides phone numbers for village leaders or village community development offices.

❹ On **First Mesa,** 15 miles west of Keams Canyon, you will initially approach **Polacca;** the older and more impressive villages of **Hano, Sichomovi,** and **Walpi** are situated at the top of the mesa. From Polacca, a paved road (off AZ 264) angles up to a parking lot near the village of Sichomovi. For permission to visit Hano, Sichomovi, and Walpi, or for information on the guided walking tours of these villages, call the **First Mesa Visitor's Center at Ponsli Hall** (tel. 602/737–2262). Guided tours can be arranged between 9 AM and 4 PM daily, except when ceremonies are being held; the tours are free, but a contribution is suggested.

All the older Hopi villages have structures built of rock and adobe mortar in a simple architectural style. **Hano** actually belongs to the Tewa, a Pueblo tribe that fled from the Spanish in 1696 and secured permission from the Hopi to build a new home on First Mesa. **Sichomovi** is built so close to Hano that only the residents know the actual boundary line. Constructed in the mid-1600s, this village is believed to have been built to ease overcrowding at Walpi, the highest point on the mesa.

For most outsiders, **Walpi** is usually the most impressive stop on the Hopi reservation, but it can be visited only if you are accompanied by a Hopi guide. Built on solid rock and surrounded by steep cliffs, Walpi stands against an immense expanse of distant earth and sky. At its narrowest point, the mesa measures only 15 feet across. Inhabited for more than 500 years, Walpi's cliff-edge houses seem to be an extension of the nearby terrain. Today, only about 30 residents occupy this settlement, which has neither electricity nor running water. Important ceremonial dances frequently take place here. You can purchase kachina dolls made by the local men and authentic Hopi pottery created by the local women.

❺ Second Mesa, accessed by AZ 264, is 10 miles west of Polacca. The small villages of **Sipaulovi** and **Mishongnovi** are situated off a paved road that goes north from 264, about ⅕ mile east of the Hopi Cultural Center. Both communities lie on a projection of the Second Mesa; Mishongnovi, the easternmost settlement, was built in the late 1600s. If you'd like to visit Sipaulovi, the most recently established village, call the Sipaulovi Village Community Center (tel. 602/737–2570).

Shungopavi, the largest and oldest village on Second Mesa, may be reached by a paved road angling south off AZ 264, between the junction of AZ 87 and the Hopi Cultural Center. The famous Hopi snake dances (now closed to the public) are held here in August during even-numbered years. For permission to visit Shungopavi, call the village's **Community Development Office** (tel. 602/734–2262).

One of the livelier spots on Second Mesa is the **Hopi Cultural Center,** on the north side of AZ 264, west of the junction at AZ 87. A cluster of shops carry the work of the Hopi artisans who live in the area; the selection is very good and the prices are reasonable. In addition, the center features a pueblo-style museum, a good restaurant that serves American and Native American dishes and a decent motel (*see* Dining and Lodging, *below*). The cultural center is not only a good spot for an overnight stop, but it is also one of the best places on the reservation from which to obtain information. *Tel. 602/734–2401 (restaurant and motel), tel. 602/734–6650 (museum). Museum admission: $3 adults, $1 children under 13. Open mid-May–Oct., weekdays 8–5, weekends 9–4; Nov.–mid-May, weekdays 8–5, closed weekends.*

If you drive 8 miles to the west of the Hopi Cultural Center on **❻** AZ 264, you'll approach **Kykotsmovi** at the eastern base of **Third Mesa.** Hopi from Old Oraibi (*see below*) descended from the mesa and built this village in a canyon with a perennial spring; the community is known for its greenery and its peach orchards. The town also serves as the home of the **Hopi Tribal Headquarters** and the **Office of Public Relations** (tel. 602/734–2441), another good source of information regarding ceremonies and dances.

Old Oraibi, a few miles west and on top of Third Mesa, is widely believed to be the oldest continually inhabited community in the United States, dating from around AD 1150. It was also the site of a rare, bloodless conflict between two groups of the Hopi people; in 1906, a dispute, settled uniquely by a "pushing contest," sent the losers off to establish Hotevilla (*see below*). Oraibi is a dusty spot, and as an act of courtesy, tourists are asked to park their cars outside and approach the village on foot.

As you continue to drive west on AZ 264, you'll pass more crafts shops and art galleries. The Third Mesa villages are known for their baskets, kachina dolls, weaving, and jewelry.

Hotevilla and **Bacavi** are about 4 miles west of Oraibi, and their inhabitants are descended from the former residents of that village. The men of Hotevilla continue to plant crops along the mesa slopes, and in warmer months these gardens on the cliffs are lovely to behold.

Beyond Hotevilla, AZ 264 descends from Third Mesa, and you will soon exit the Hopi reservation and cross Navajo land. About ❼ 30 miles west of Hotevilla, you'll pass **Coal Canyon,** where Indians have long mined coal from the dark seam just below the rim. This canyon of colorful mudstone, dark lines of coal, and bleached white rock has an eerie, ghostlike appearance, especially by the light of the moon.

Another 20 miles to the west is **Moenkopi,** the last Hopi outpost, just before Tuba City at the junction of AZ 264 and U.S. 160. Established as a farming community, it was also settled by the ❽ descendants of former Oraibi residents. Across U.S. 160, **Tuba City** is the administrative center for the western portion of the Navajo Nation, with about 5,000 permanent residents. In addition to a motel, a hostel, and a few restaurants, this small town has a hospital, a bank, and a historic trading post. Founded in the early 1880s and recently restored, the octagonal **Tuba City Trading Post** (Main St., tel. 602/283–5441) carries authentic Indian rugs, pottery, baskets, and jewelry; it also sells groceries.

From Tuba City, take U.S. 160 west. About 5½ miles from the city, between mileposts 316 and 317, you'll see a small sign for ❾ **Dinosaur Tracks.** More than 200 million years ago, dilophosaurus, carnivorous bipedal reptiles more than 10 feet tall, left their imprints in soft mud that subsequently turned to sandstone. There's no charge for a look.

Four miles west of the Dinosaur Tracks on U.S. 160, you'll come to the junction with U.S. 89. This is one of the most colorful regions of the Painted Desert, with amphitheaters of maroon, orange, and red rocks facing west; it's especially glorious at sunset. If you turn left on U.S. 89 and drive 16 miles south, you ❿ will arrive at the **Cameron Trading Post** (tel. 602/679–2231). Established in 1916, this is one of the few remaining authentic trading posts in the Southwest. *See* Chapter 3, The Grand Canyon and Northwest Arizona, for details.

From the Cameron Trading Post, it's another 52 miles back to Flagstaff. To see the Hopi Mesas at a reasonable pace, it's a good idea to take at least one overnight on this tour, either at the Hopi Cultural Center on Second Mesa or, if you're planning to head north into Navajo country, at a hotel in Tuba City (*see* Dining and Lodging, *below*).

Tour 3: Indian Country—Southern Tour

To take the complete tour, allow at least three days and two nights. Begin your drive at **Petrified Forest National Park** and the **Painted Desert** (*see* Tour 1, *above*), if you haven't stopped here before.

From the Petrified Forest, continue east on I–40 to Lupton; turn north on Indian Highway 12, which will take you to **Window Rock;** the total distance is 82 miles. Named for an immense hole in a massive sandstone ridge nearby, Window Rock is the capital of the Navajo Nation. With a population of less than 5,000, this small community serves as the shopping, business, and social center for countless Navajo families from the surrounding areas. It is also the home of the **Navajo Nation Council Chambers** (turn east off Indian Highway 12, about ½ mile from AZ 264), a handsome structure that resembles a large hogan—the traditional six-sided Navajo house with a domed roof. Visitors can observe sessions of the council, where 88 delegates representing 100 reservation communities meet on the third Monday of January, April, July, and October. The sessions are conducted mostly in the Navajo language. When the council is not being held, you can walk around the chamber, where colorful murals decorate the circular walls. Near the Council Chambers lies Window Rock Navajo Tribal Park, a pleasant picnic area with juniper trees that allows you to get a close view of the huge rock with a circular opening that gives the town its name.

A short drive south of Tribal Park is the **Navajo Tribal Museum,** a small space devoted to the art and culture of the region and the history of the Navajo people; there's an excellent selection of books on the Navajo Nation here. *On AZ 264, next to Navajo Nation Inn, tel. 602/871–6673. Admission free. Open Mon.– Fri. 8–4:45.*

In the same building, the **Navajo Arts and Crafts Enterprise** has local creative works on view, including pottery, jewelry, and blankets. *Tel. 602/871–4095. Admission free. Open Apr.–Oct., Mon.–Sat. 8–6; Nov.–Mar., weekdays 8–5 (often later during busy season from Thanksgiving to New Year's Day).*

If you're curious about wildlife in northeastern Arizona, stop at the **Navajo Nation Zoological Park,** just east of the Navajo Tribal Museum. At this small zoo—set amid sandstone monoliths— you'll find golden eagles, hawks, elk, wolves, cougars, coyotes, and many other birds, reptiles, and mammals from the area. *East of Navajo Nation Inn and north of AZ 264, tel. 602/871– 6573. Admission free. Open daily 8–5.*

Window Rock is a good place to stop for lunch, supplies, and gas. The restaurants here serve standard American fare, Navajo dishes, and fast food. Near the center of downtown is the **Navajo Tribal Fairgrounds,** the site of many all-Indian rodeos (in the Navajo Nation, many Indians are cowboys). The community hosts the annual July 4 Powwow, with a major rodeo, ceremonial dances, and a parade; and the Navajo Nation Tribal Fair, much like a traditional state fair, with a Navajo accent, in early September. For more information about both events, call the Navajo Nation Fair Office (tel. 602/871–6478).

⓬ **Kinlichee Ruins Navajo Tribal Park** lies 22 miles west of Window Rock on AZ 264; a marked turnoff leads to this 640-acre park. A complex of ruins here dates from the early Anasazi, a culture of prehistoric Native Americans who mysteriously abandoned their Southwestern dwellings prior to AD 1300. The park, which is always open, has a self-guided trail that takes you past the ruins and trailside exhibits (you are not permitted to descend into the pit, where the kiva is); it also offers picnic areas and a primitive campground. A camping fee of $1 per person may be collected.

Next, drive 6 miles west on AZ 264, passing through the community of **Ganado,** and continue for another 5 miles until you reach the intersection of U.S. 191 north; turn right and drive 30 miles to **Chinle,** the closest town to Canyon de Chelly. There are three good lodgings with restaurants here (*see* Dining and Lodging, *below*), as well as a few fast-food places, a large supermarket, and a campground. You should call ahead for hotel reservations, especially in summer.

⓭ The nearly 84,000-acre **Canyon de Chelly** (pronounced deh-SHAY) near Chinle is one of the most spectacular national monuments in the Southwest. Its main gorges—the 26-mile-long **Canyon de Chelly** and the adjoining 35-mile-long **Canyon del Muerto**—have sheer, heavily eroded sandstone walls that reach up to 1,000 feet; ancient pictographs decorate some of the cliffs. Gigantic stone formations rise hundreds of feet above small streams, hogans, tilled fields, peach orchards, and grazing lands.

The first inhabitants in the canyons, the Anasazi people, arrived more than 2,000 years ago and built stone cliff dwellings. After the Anasazi disappeared around 1300, Hopi farmers settled here, followed by the Navajo, beginning around 1700. Centuries-old traditions have been passed down to the Navajo families who now live, farm and raise sheep here. Although the monument is administered by the National Park Service, the land itself belongs to the Navajo.

Canyon de Chelly and Canyon del Muerto each have a paved rim drive that offers marvelous views of the massive canyons; prehistoric ruins sometimes lie near the base of cliffs and other times perch on high sheltering ledges. Occasionally you will also see the modern dwellings and cultivated fields of the present-day Navajo in the flatlands between the cliffs. Each canyon drive takes about two hours.

The **South Rim Drive** (36 miles round-trip) of Canyon de Chelly starts at the visitor center and ends at **Spider Rock Overlook,** where the cliffs drop 1,000 feet. Here you'll have a view of two pinnacles, Speaking Rock and Spider Rock; the latter rises about 800 feet from the canyon floor. Other highlights on the South Rim Drive are **Junction Overlook,** where Canyon del

Muerto joins Canyon de Chelly; **White House Overlook,** which allows access to the canyon floor (*see below*); and **Sliding House Overlook,** where you can see ruins on a narrow, sloped ledge across the canyon.

The **North Rim Drive** (34 miles round-trip) of Canyon del Muerto also begins at the visitor center and continues northeast on Indian Highway 64 toward Tsaile, the site of Navajo Community College. Major stops on this drive include **Antelope House Overlook,** the site of a large ruin named for the animals painted on an adjacent cliff; the **Mummy Cave Overlook,** where two mummies were found inside a remarkably unspoiled pueblo dwelling, the monument's largest; and **Massacre Cave Overlook,** the last stop on the drive, which marks the spot where 115 Navajo were killed by the Spanish in 1805.

Within the monument, only one hike—the **White House Ruin Trail,** on the South Rim Drive—can be done without an authorized guide. The easy-to-negotiate trail starts near White House Overlook and runs along sheer walls that drop about 550 feet. The trail leads to the White House Ruin, with dwelling remains of nearly 60 rooms and several kivas. Bring your own water for this 2½-mile hike (round-trip).

Visitors can explore the area of Canyon de Chelly National Monument by taking truck and Jeep tours (*see* Guided Tours in Essential Information, *above*), or by hiking with rangers and paid guides. (*see* Hiking in Sports and the Outdoors, *below*). The **visitor center** features exhibits on the history of the Anasazi cliff dwellers and provides information on scheduled hikes, tours, and other programs within the national monument; it also has a good selection of books on the area and on Navajo culture. *Box 588, Chinle 86503, tel. 602/674–5500 or 602/674–6601. Admission free. Open Memorial Day–Labor Day, daily 8–6; Labor Day–Memorial Day, daily 8–5.*

Retrace your steps after you depart Canyon de Chelly: Head back south for about 30 miles on U.S. 191, then turn east onto **⑭** AZ 264 and continue on for several miles to **Hubbell Trading Post National Historic Site.** This trading post was established in 1878 by John Lorenzo Hubbell, a native of the Southwest who was born in Pajarito, New Mexico. To the Navajo, Hubbell was not only a merchant but also a good friend and teacher who translated letters, settled family quarrels, explained government policy, and helped the sick. During the 1886 smallpox epidemic in the area, he turned his home into a hospital and personally ministered to the sick and dying. Hubbell died in 1930 and is buried not far from the trading post.

Today the Hubbell Trading Post operates much as it did more than a century ago. At the visitor center, National Park Service exhibits illustrate the post's history, and Navajo men and women frequently demonstrate the crafts of making jewelry and rugs. You may also take a guided tour of Hubbell's house, which contains one of the finest personal collections of Native American artistry anywhere, including rugs and paintings; tours are given six times daily in summer, four in winter. The affiliated shop, run by the Southwest Parks and Monuments Association, specializes in Navajo rugs (*see* Shopping, *below*). *On AZ 264, 1 mi west of Ganado, tel. 602/755–3475. Admission free. Open June–Sept., daily 8–6; Oct.–May, daily 8–5. Closed major holidays.*

About 20 miles west of the trading post on the north side of AZ 264 is **Steamboat Rock,** an immense, jutting peninsula of stone that resembles an early steamboat, complete with a geologically formed waterline.

At Steamboat Rock, you are only 5 miles from the eastern boundary line of the Hopi reservation, where you can visit the **Hopi Mesas** (*see* Tour 2, *above*). After driving through the mesas on AZ 264, you can join Tour 4 (*see below*) at Tuba City, 50 miles west of the Hopi village of Hotevilla.

Tour 4: Indian Country—Northern Tour

Twenty-two miles northeast of Tuba City on U.S. 160 is the tiny community of **Red Lake.** Off to the left of the highway is a geologic phenomenon known as **Elephant Feet.** These massive eroded sandstone buttes make a good photo stop.

If time permits, you might enjoy a short side trip to real Navajo backcountry and a look at **White Mesa Natural Bridge,** about 17 miles north of Red Lake on Indian Highway 21, a graded dirt road. The payoff is a view of a massive arch of white sandstone that extends from the edge of White Mesa. Return by the same route to Red Lake.

About 30 miles north of Red Lake on U.S. 160, you'll come to the turnoff for Navajo National Monument (*see below*).

Continue northeast from this turnoff and take note of the plateau to the right, the long **Black Mesa,** which will remain in view for about the next 15 miles. Above the prominent escarpments of this land formation, mining operations—a major source of revenue for the Navajo Nation—are busy delving into the more than 20 billion tons of coal deposited there.

Turn more directly north from U.S. 160 onto U.S. 163; you'll soon approach **Kayenta,** a small town with a few grocery stores, two motels, and a hospital. Kayenta is near the magnificent **Monument Valley,** which stretches to the northeast into Utah. At an altitude of approximately 5,500 feet, this sprawling expanse was originally populated by the ancient Anasazi and has also been home to generations of Navajo who have farmed and herded livestock in this arid country. With its soaring red buttes, eroded mesas, deep canyons, and naturally sculpted rock formations, Monument Valley is best enjoyed by simply driving through and pausing from time to time at roadside stops. Many Westerns, including *Stagecoach, She Wore a Yellow Ribbon,* and *How the West Was Won,* have been filmed here.

20 Within this vast area lies the 30,000-acre **Monument Valley Navajo Tribal Park.** The visitor center is 3½ miles off U.S. 163 and about 24 miles north of Kayenta. The park offers a scenic 17-mile self-guided tour, but the road is unpaved and rutted; if you don't want to wear out the shocks on your car, consider taking one of the many guided tours offered by operators in and around the visitor center; most take visitors around in enclosed vans and charge about $15 for 2½ hours. Also at the visitor center are an Indian crafts shop and exhibits devoted to both ancient and modern Indian history within the area. The park has a 100-site campground, which closes from early October through April. *Visitor center, tel. 801/727-3287. Park entrance fee: $2.50 adults, $1 senior citizens 60 and older, children under 5 free. Visitor center open May–Sept., daily 7–7; Oct.–Apr., daily 8–5. Closed major holidays.*

Monument Valley's scenic route, U.S. 163, continues from Arizona into Utah, where the land is crossed, east to west, by a
21 stretch of the San Juan River known as the **Goosenecks**—so named for the type of twists and curves it takes at the bottom of a wildly carved canyon. Set in a lonely, untrafficked domain, this barren, erosion-blasted gorge has a stark beauty that is nearly as awesome as that of the Grand Canyon. The scenic overlook for the Goosenecks is reached by turning west from U.S. 163 onto UT 261, 4 miles north of the small community of **Mexican Hat** (named for the sombrerolike rock formation you'll see on the hills to your right as you drive north), then proceeding on UT 261 for 1 mile to a directional sign at the road's junction with UT 316. Turn left onto UT 316 and proceed 4 miles to the vista-point parking lot. If you visit during the week, you're likely to find yourself alone there, or perhaps joined by one or two Navajo women selling crafts.

After a stop at the Goosenecks vista point, backtrack along U.S. 163 and then take Indian Highway 42 one-half mile west to
22 **Goulding's Trading Post.** Established in 1924 by Harry Goulding and his wife, this remote outlet was used as a headquarters by director John Ford when he filmed the Western classic *Stagecoach.* Because of the numerous Westerns that have been shot in the area, the trading post, motel, and restaurant have gained a measure of international fame. In the old trading-post building, a museum showcases prehistoric and modern Indian artifacts as well as memorabilia of the Goulding family. The lodge here is an ideal place for an overnight stay, but call in advance for reservations. Alternatively, you can overnight in or near Kayenta, where there are three motels (*see* Dining and Lodging, *below*).

Take Indian Highway 42 back to the junction with U.S. 163, and proceed south until you reach U.S. 160; continue south, making
23 a right turn on AZ 564 and traveling 9 miles to **Navajo National Monument.** Here two unoccupied 13th-century cliff pueblos, **Keet Seel** and **Betatakin,** stand under the overhang of soaring orange and ocher cliffs. The largest Indian ruins in Arizona, these pueblos were built by the Anasazi people, whose reasons for abandoning the pueblos prior to AD 1300 are still disputed by

scholars. The two large stone-and-mortar complexes were obviously built for permanent occupancy, yet the Anasazi had lived in them for only about three decades when they disappeared. Betatakin (Navajo for "ledge house") consists of a well-preserved, 135-room ruin situated in a large alcove. Keet Seel (Navajo for "broken pottery") is also in good condition, with 160 rooms and five kivas in a serene setting.

For an impressive view of Betatakin, walk to the rim overlook about ½ mile from the visitor center. You can also hike to Betatakin (5 miles round-trip from the visitor center), but only on tours with ranger guides, offered between early May and mid-October. The trips, which leave once a day in early May, most of September, and early October, and twice a day from Memorial Day to Labor Day (weather permitting), are limited to groups of 25. No reservations are accepted; tours are on a first-come, first-served basis.

Explorations of Keet Seel, which lies at an elevation of 7,000 feet and is 17 miles (round-trip) from the visitor center, are even more restricted: Only 20 people are allowed to visit per day, and only between Memorial Day and Labor Day, when a ranger is present at the site. A permit—which also allows campers to stay overnight near the ruins—is required. Those interested in horseback trips can make arrangements at the visitor center to rent horses and guides from a Navajo family. Trips to Keet Seel are very popular, and reservations are taken up to (but not beyond) two months in advance; call 602/672–2367 to reserve a visitor's permit (and, if you like, a horse) as soon you know the date you're coming.

The visitor center houses a small museum, exhibits of prehistoric pottery, and a crafts shop. Free campground and picnic areas are nearby, and rangers sometimes present campfire programs in summer. No food, gasoline, or lodging is available at the monument. *Navajo National Monument, HC71 Box 3, Tonalea 86044, tel. 602/672–2366. Admission free. Open Memorial Day–Labor Day, daily 8–6; Dec.–Feb., daily 8–4:30; rest of the year, daily 8–5. Closed major holidays.*

This tour may be followed by a visit to Page, Lake Powell, Glen Canyon Dam, and Rainbow Bridge (*see* Tour 5, *below*). To reach Page from the Navajo National Monument, return to U.S. 160 and travel south for 12 miles, then take AZ 98 for 66 miles. If, on the other hand, you'd like to follow this tour with a visit to Canyon de Chelly (*see* Tour 3, *above*), stop at Navajo National Monument before you go on to Monument Valley. Then, from Kayenta, take U.S. 160 east for 41 miles and, just before Mexican Water, pick up U.S. 191; it's another 62 miles south to Chinle.

Tour 5: Glen Canyon Dam and Lake Powell

From Flagstaff, take U.S. 89 on a route almost directly north and drive 136 miles to Page and nearby Glen Canyon Dam and Lake Powell. For many miles of this trip, you'll pass an impressive stretch of the Painted Desert off to the right of the highway, with a multihued geography almost identical to that of the Painted Desert contained within the boundaries of Petrified Forest National Park (*see* Tour 1, *above*). Farther north, this landscape gives way to the immense Echo Cliffs, orange sandstone formations that rise well over 1,000 feet above the highway in some places. At Bitter Springs, the highway ascends the cliffs and provides a spectacular view of the 9,000-square-mile expanse of the Arizona Strip to the west and the sheer, 3,000-foot Vermilion Cliffs to the northwest.

㉔ Prior to 1957, the broad mesa on which the community of **Page** is situated was essentially barren land, but when construction of Glen Canyon Dam commenced that year, Page was born. Initially a construction camp, after the completion of the dam and the formation of Lake Powell, Page became a tourist stop and gradually grew to its present population of about 7,000—the largest community in far northern Arizona.

Most of the motels, restaurants, and strip shopping centers in Page can be found along Lake Powell Boulevard, the name given to U.S. 89 as it loops through the town's business district in a roughly northwest direction. At the corner of Navajo Drive is the **John Wesley Powell Memorial Museum,** a small building honoring the work of explorer John Wesley Powell, who, between 1869 and 1872, led the first expeditions down the Green River and the rapids-choked Colorado through the Grand Canyon. The one-armed Civil War hero mapped, explored, and kept detailed records of his trips, naming the Grand Canyon and many other geographic points of interest in northern Arizona. The displays—drawings and photographs of the expedition, area fossils, minerals, and Native American crafts—are rather unimpressive, but the museum serves as an information center for the area and a place to book river and lake trips and scenic flights. It also has a good selection of regional books and maps. *6 N. Lake Powell Blvd., tel. 602/645–9496. Requested donation: $1 adults, 50¢ children. Open May–Oct., Mon.–Sat. 8–6:30, Sun. 10–6:30; Nov. and Mar., weekdays 9–5; Apr., weekdays 8–6. Closed Dec.–Feb.*

㉕ Once you leave the Page business district, the **Glen Canyon Dam** and Lake Powell behind it immediately become visible. Completed in September 1963, the construction of this concrete-arch dam and its power plant was an engineering feat that rivaled the building of Hoover Dam. Nearly 5 million cubic feet of concrete were required. The dam's crest is 1,560 feet across and rises 710 feet from bedrock and 583 feet above the waters of the Colorado River. Lake Powell is 560 feet deep at the dam at full pool elevation.

Just off the highway at the north end of the bridge is the **Carl Hayden Visitor Center,** a museumlike facility dedicated to telling the story of the creation of Glen Canyon Dam and Lake Powell. Among the several exhibits is a giant, three-dimensional topographic map of Lake Powell country. The center's huge reception and observation room, with floor-to-ceiling glass, provides panoramic views of the dam, the wildly sculpted cliffs that border Lake Powell, and the immense sandstone buttes that protrude, islandlike, from the lake's emerald waters. Between May and October, free guided tours of the dam are offered daily between 8:30 and 3:30 every hour on the half-hour. The rest of the year, visitors can take a 40-minute self-guided tour through the dam complex. *Glen Canyon Dam, tel. 602/645-2511 or 602/ 645-8404. Admission free. Open Memorial Day–Labor Day, daily 7–7; Labor Day–Memorial Day, daily 8–5. Closed Christmas and New Year's Day.*

Lake Powell, with more than 1,900 miles of shoreline, is the heart of the huge (1,255,400-acre) Glen Canyon National Recreation Area. Created by the barrier of Glen Canyon Dam and fed by the mighty Colorado River (as well as five others), the jade-green lake extends through eroded canyon country that is nearly devoid of vegetation and so rugged that it was the last major area of the United States to be mapped. The waters of Lake Powell are confined by immense red cliffs that twist off from the main body of the lake into 96 major canyons and countless inlets and coves—so many, in fact, that no single person claims to have explored all of them. In a number of places, huge sandstone buttes jut from the water. Seeing the stark, stunning geography of Lake Powell often makes tourists feel as if they are visiting another planet.

The most popular destination on the lake, which stretches 180 miles through northern Arizona and southern Utah, is **Wahweap,** a vacation village 5 miles north of the Glen Canyon Dam on U.S. 89. Most of the recreational activity in the region takes place around here, where everything needed for a water-oriented holiday is available. Visitors can easily rent boats and a wide variety of water-sports equipment (*see* Sports and the Outdoors, *below*). Stop at **Wahweap Lodge** (*see* Dining and Lodging, *below*) for an excellent view of the lake area. In addition to Wahweap, three other full-service marinas operate year-round on the perimeter of Lake Powell. **Bullfrog** (tel. 801/684-2233) and, across from it, **Halls Crossing** (tel. 801/684-2261) are around mid-lake, while **Hite Marina** (tel. 801/684-2278), the smallest, is the farthest north, just off UT 95. A fifth marina 40 miles north of Wahweap, Dangling Rope, has limited services and can be reached only by boat.

Summer is a busy time in the Lake Powell area, and reservations for accommodations are essential. Travelers seeking a quieter vacation should plan a visit during late October through early May, when there are fewer people and lower prices. Skies in the Lake Powell area are blue nearly all year, and only about 8 inches of rain falls annually. Summer temperatures range from the 60s to the 90s (sometimes they rise to more than 100°F). Many fall and spring days are balmy, with daytime temperatures often in the 70s and 80s, but it is possible for chilly weather to set in. In winter, the risk of a cold spell increases, but all-weather houseboats and tour boats make year-round cruising possible.

The best way to appreciate the beauty of Lake Powell is by boat. If you don't have access to one, the five-hour excursion cruise to **Rainbow Bridge National Monument** is the way to go. Along the 52-mile route (one-way from Wahweap Marina), you're treated to ever-changing, beautiful and bizarre scenery, including huge monoliths that look like people turned into stone and a butte that resembles a dinosaur. You might also see eagles perched on ragged outcrops of rock. Finally, after gliding through a deep and twisting canyon waterway, the boat docks near Rainbow Bridge, the massive 290-foot red sandstone arch that straddles a cove of the lake. The world's largest natural stone bridge, it can be reached only by water or by an arduous hike from a remote point on the Navajo reservation (*see* Sports and the Outdoors, *below*).

The excursion boats, which leave Wahweap daily, are two-tiered craft with sun decks upstairs and interior seating with windows downstairs. Experienced pilots provide commentary throughout the trip. Pack a lunch or take snacks; no food is sold on the boats, though coffee and water are provided. And be sure to bring your camera.

Other cruises are offered at the Wahweap Marina, including an all-day trip that stops at Rainbow Bridge and then proceeds farther into the Utah portion of the lake. (*See* Boating and Cruises in Sports and the Outdoors, *below*, for information on prices and reservations.)

Off the Beaten Track

Most of the 25,000 square miles of the Navajo reservation and other areas of northeastern Arizona are actually off the beaten track. Many visitors to the northeast generally stay on the paved roads, but this vast, sparsely populated region is crisscrossed with dirt roads. If you don't have the equipment for wilderness travel—including a four-wheel-drive vehicle, water, food, tools, and bedrolls—and do not have backcountry experience, we recommend that you stay off the dirt roads unless they are signed and graded, and the skies are clear.

Antelope Canyon. You'll probably recognize it from one of many photographs: Red sandstone rising majestically in a corkscrew formation, dramatically illuminated by a chink of light streaming in from above. And, in fact, you're likely to see assorted shutterbugs standing patiently next to tripods, waiting hours for just the right shot. A highlight of any trip to the Lake Powell area, Antelope Canyon is on the Navajo reservation, about 3 miles from Page. If you don't have a four-wheel-drive vehicle (or the time to wait for the rather erratic—and limited—hours that the gate to the site is open), book a tour from Page (*see* Guided Tours in Essential Information, *above*).

Chuska Mountains. These impressive mountains in Navajo high country are covered with huge stands of ponderosa pine. To explore this part of the reservation, take Indian Highway 64 from the Canyon de Chelly visitor center to the community of Tsaile

(23 miles). Here Navajo medicine men worked in conjunction with architects to design Tsaile's **Navajo Community College** (tel. 602/724–3311). Because all important Navajo activities traditionally take place in a circle (a hogan is essentially circular), the campus was laid out in the round with all of the buildings within its perimeter. The college's **Hatathli Museum** is devoted to Native American culture. *Tel. 602/724–3311. Donations accepted. Open weekdays 8:30–noon and 1–4; groups by appointment.*

Two miles northeast of Tsaile, turn left on Indian Highway 12 and continue 26 miles to Round Rock, where Indian Highway 12 meets U.S. 191. During your drive, the high country will rise off to the right. Dirt roads traverse the mountains, but they are often unsuitable for passenger cars. At U.S. 191, turn left and head back south to Chinle if you are following Tour 3, *above*.

Four Corners Monument. A simple concrete slab inlaid into the ground marks the only point in the United States where four states meet: Arizona, New Mexico, Colorado, and Utah. Most visitors—in summer, nearly 2,000 a day—stay only a few minutes to record the spot on film; you'll see many people posed awkwardly, with an arm or a leg in each state. *Off U.S. 160, 7 mi northwest of the U.S. 160–NM 502 junction (near Teec Nos Pos). The monument is a 75-mi drive from Kayenta, near Monument Valley.*

What to See and Do with Children

Although northeastern Arizona is an extremely popular area for families on vacation, the region has no attractions designed specifically for children. However, many youngsters will be fascinated by the area's scenic beauty and Indian culture. They will particularly enjoy the Navajo Nation Zoological Park in Window Rock (*see* Tour 3, *above*). At the Petrified Forest (*see* Tour 1, *above*), Canyon de Chelly (*see* Tour 3, *above*), and Navajo National Monument (*see* Tour 4, *above*), they'll have plenty of space for running around and exploring. Children may be bored on some of the longer lake excursions, but many motels in the Lake Powell area (*see* Tour 5, *above*) have swimming pools, and there are numerous water-related recreational activities for children.

Younger children may get restless during some of the long and lonely stretches on the Indian reservations, so it's a good idea to bring along lots of toys and books for the car.

Shopping

Groceries, over-the-counter medicines, gasoline, and other supplies can be purchased in all of the major communities and trading posts on the Navajo and Hopi reservations, including Page, Window Rock, Fort Defiance, Ganado, Chinle, Hopi Second Mesa, Keams Canyon, Tuba City, Kayenta, Goulding's Trading Post, and Cameron Trading Post. Some of the smaller communities offer limited supplies; in general, don't count on a wide selection. Plan your gas stops for the locations cited.

Beyond the necessities for travel, most visitors to Indian country are looking for pottery, turquoise and sterling-silver jewelry, handwoven baskets, beautiful and often expensive Navajo wool rugs, and other examples of Native American crafts. In addition to the work of Hopi and Navajo artisans, many of the trading posts also carry the work of New Mexico's tribes, including exquisite Zuni jewelry and the world-acclaimed pottery of the Pueblo Indians. Many vendors have roadside stands that resemble Navajo shade arbors. Most products offered on the Hopi and Navajo reservations are authentic, but the possibility of imitations still exists. The trading posts are usually reliable.

Telephone lines—and thus connections with credit-card verification sources—are often iffy at the Hopi Mesas. It's a good idea to carry cash or traveler's checks to make purchases here or anywhere else outside of the trading posts.

Outlets of **Navajo Arts and Crafts Enterprises,** in Window Rock (off AZ 264, next to Navajo Nation Inn, tel. 602/871–4090 or 602/871–4095) and Cameron (on U.S. 89 at the junction with AZ 64, tel. 602/679–2244) stock fine authentic Navajo products. The nearby **Cameron Trading Post** has a large selection of goods from a variety of tribes; *see* Chapter 3, Grand Canyon Country and Lake Mead, for details. The **Hopi Cultural Center** (off AZ 264, Hopi Second Mesa, tel. 602/734–2463) has a collection of shops that feature the work of local artists and artisans. Just to the west, the **Hopi Arts and Crafts/Silvercrafts Cooperative Guild** (no phone) hosts many craftspeople selling their wares; you might even see some silversmiths at work here. **Keams Canyon Arts and Crafts** (Keams Canyon, tel. 602/738–2295) also sells Hopi wares. The gift shop at **Navajo National Monument** (tel. 602/672–2366) has an excellent selection of jewelry. **Hubbell Trading Post** (off AZ 264, 1 mi west of Ganado, tel. 602/755–3254) is famous for its "Ganado red" Navajo rugs; the quality is outstanding but prices are accordingly high. Be forewarned, though: It's hard to resist these beautiful designs and colors. The **swap meet** held every Friday from 8 AM on in Tuba City (on Main St., behind the community center and next to the baseball field) has good prices on jewelry, rugs, pottery, and other arts and crafts; there are also food concessions and booths selling herbs.

Although you may feel more comfortable shopping at an established store, you may find exactly what you want, at a good price, at a reservation roadside vendor. If you would like some tips on quality, the **Navajoland Tourism Office** (*see* Important Addresses and Numbers in Essential Information, *above*) has printed material on the subject.

In the Lake Powell area, **Page Factory Stores** (644 N. Navajo Dr. at Lake Powell Blvd., tel. 602/645–5975) has discount outlets for London Fog, Benetton, and Polo Ralph Lauren. On South Lake Powell Blvd., just east of Hwy. 89, **Corral West Ranchwear**

(Gateway Park mall, tel. 602/645–9391) carries a good selection of cowboy and cowgirl duds.

Sports and the Outdoors

Bicycling For biking enthusiasts, the news is good and bad. If you carry a bike on your car, as many cyclists do these days, you will find endless miles of paved roads, and most of the time, traffic is very light. The bad news is that the mostly two-lane highways do not have paved shoulders, and local motorists and tourists alike are unaccustomed to encountering cyclists. As a result, you should practice extreme caution when riding. For safe bike rides, the roads at Canyon de Chelly National Monument, Navajo National Monument, Monument Valley Navajo Tribal Park, and Kinlichee Navajo Tribal Park are your best bets. There are no bicycle-rental companies in Indian country.

Boating **Lake Powell.** The boating opportunities on Lake Powell are almost limitless. If you have your own boat, docks and launching ramps are available at State Line Marina, 1½ miles north of Wahweap Lodge. In addition, there are four full-service marinas at the lake at which to rent small or excursion boats, including houseboats, and water-sports equipment, including ski packages, water sleds, and motorized wave cutters: **Wahweap** (tel. 602/278–8888), **Bullfrog** (tel. 801/684–2233), **Halls Crossing** (tel. 801/684–2261), and **Hite Marina** (tel. 801/684–2278). Wahweap, 5 miles north of Page on U.S. 89, is the largest, with 850 slips and the most facilities. Houseboats range widely in size and price; one that sleeps six (in three double beds) may cost $675 for three nights. New houseboats are being added to the fleet, and many are being upgraded—some boats now have air-conditioning, TVs, VCRs, microwaves, and other amenities. Houseboats should be reserved well in advance. Small boats, too, vary in size and price. An 18-foot powerboat for eight passengers runs about $185 per day. Most of these prices drop after the summer months. A variety of boat-tour and lodging packages are also available. For detailed information on all the Lake Powell options and prices, contact ARA Leisure Services (Box 56909, Phoenix 85079, tel. 800/528–6154, fax 602/331–5258).

Camping and Although Indian country stretches thousands of square miles
RV Parks across an open and sparsely populated region, visitors are allowed to camp only in posted authorized areas. Most campgrounds are primitive, in many cases nothing more than open, level areas where sleeping bags can be laid out or RVs can be parked; outside the Lake Powell area, only Monument Valley has developed camping facilities. If you plan to stay in national monument and park areas, camping permission can be obtained on-site; for other camping situations, contact the **Navajo Parks and Recreation Department** (Box 308, Window Rock 86515, tel. 602/871–6647) to find out whether you need a permit. (*See* Dining and Lodging, *below,* for some of the recommended campsites in the area.)

Cruises
Lake Powell
A variety of excursions on double-decker scenic cruisers piloted by experienced guides leave from the dock of Lake Powell's Wahweap Lodge (off U.S. 89, 5 mi north of Page, tel. 602/645–2433 or 800/528–6154). The most popular is the one to Rainbow Bridge National Monument, a 290-foot arch that spans an isolated cove 50 miles from Wahweap. Half-day cruises cost $51.30 adults, $27.30 children; full-days are $64.65 adults, $34.50 children. A 2½-hour sunset dinner cruise also departs from Wahweap. A buffet-style dinner is served on the fully glassed lower deck of the 95-foot Canyon King Paddlewheeler, an 1800s riverboat. The meal includes prime rib with fresh garden vegetables and a baked potato, a salad, and dessert; cocktails are available at an extra charge. The cost of the dinner cruise is $41.20 for both children and adults; adults who wish to take the cruise without eating pay $19.65, children $13.10.

Guided, piloted, 4½-hour **rafting excursions** cover a portion of the Colorado River that is relatively calm, with no white-water rapids. The scenery through Glen Canyon Dam is spectacular as the rafts glide beneath multicolored sandstone cliffs that are frequently adorned with Indian petroglyphs. The point of departure is the Wilderness River Adventures office in Page (50 S. Lake Powell Blvd, tel. 602/645–3279 or 800/528–6154); transportation is furnished to the launch site and back from Lees Ferry, where the raft trip ends. The cost is $38.70 adults, $31 children under 12.

Fishing
Indian country has scattered lakes, most of them remote and small, that contain game fish. Two of the more popular and accessible lakes are in the eastern portion of the Navajo reservation in the vicinity of Canyon de Chelly: **Wheatfields Lake,** on Indian Highway 12 about 11 miles south of the community of Tsaile, and **Many Farms Lake,** near the community of Many Farms, on U.S. 191. Permits are always required for fishing on the reservation. Contact the **Navajo Fish and Wildlife Office** (Box 1480, Window Rock 86515, tel. 602/871–6451 or 602/871–6452).

Lake Powell and the area below Glen Canyon Dam are excellent fishing sites. Lake Powell hosts 16 varieties of fish, including largemouth bass, black crappie, striped bass, bluegill, green sunfish, carp, smallmouth bass, threadfin, shad, walleye, rainbow trout, channel catfish, brown trout, and northern pike, while the Colorado River below Glen Canyon Dam is known for its large trout. Keep in mind that Lake Powell stretches through both Arizona and Utah, and the appropriate permit is required depending on where you fish; *see* Chapter 1, Essential Information, for more information on fishing permits). Fishing licenses are available at the Wahweap Marina (off U.S. 89, 5 mi north of Page) and at Stix Market in Page (5 S. Lake Powell Blvd., tel. 602/645–2891). If you want a fishing guide for the lake or the Colorado River at Lees Ferry, about 15 miles below the Glen Canyon Dam en route to the North Rim of the Grand Canyon, contact Ed Strasburg (Box 2699, Page 86040, tel. 602/645–9489).

Hiking There are many excellent places to hike at the national monuments, tribal parks, and other points of interest in Indian country, but the following merit special mention.

In **Canyon de Chelly,** some of the best hiking is up the streambed between the soaring orange sandstone cliffs, with the ruins of the old Anasazi communities frequently in view. Guides, required for all but the White Horse Ruin Trail, currently charge about $10 per hour for groups of up to four people for day hikes. For overnights, there's a $20 surcharge for the guide and usually a $30 charge for permission to stay on private land in the area to which the guide will take you; groups of up to 15 people can be accommodated. From Memorial Day through Labor Day, free three-hour ranger-led hikes leave from the visitor center at 9 AM (*see* Tour 3, *above*). Also during the summer, four-hour hikes costing $10 per person leave from the visitor center in the morning and afternoon; rates for two-hour evening hikes are $5 per person. Some of the hikes are a bit strenuous and precipitous, without clearly defined or gently graded trails. Visitors with health problems or a fear of heights should question the guide about the difficulty of the hike they're considering.

In addition to casual hikes along the rim areas where the ruins of Betatakin can be viewed, in spring and summer **Navajo National Monument** offers a guided 5-mile (round-trip) hike to Betatakin once a day between early May and mid-October, twice a day from Memorial Day through Labor Day; visitors may also obtain permits to hike 17 miles (round-trip) on their own to the Keet Seel ruins from Memorial Day to Labor Day. *See* Tour 4, *above*, for details.

Seasoned hikers in good physical condition might want to try either of the two trails leading to **Rainbow Bridge,** the 290-foot sandstone arch in a remote cove on Lake Powell; each runs about 26–28 miles round-trip. Take Indian Highway 16 north toward the Utah state border. When you come to a fork in the road, go down either "prong" for about 5 miles and you'll come to a trailhead leading to Rainbow Bridge. Excursion boats pull in at the dock at the arch, but no supplies are sold there. For a backcountry hiking permit, contact the **Navajo Parks and Recreation Department** (Box 308, Window Rock 86515, tel. 602/871–6647). Note, too, that the trails are often poorly marked and ill maintained in this wilderness area. The **Glen Canyon Natural History Association** (Box 581, Page 86040, tel. 602/645–3532) sells good topographical maps of the region as well as useful publications on hiking here.

Horseback Riding **Justin's Horse Rental** (Box 881, Chinle 86503, tel. 602/674–5678), near the South Rim Drive entrance of Canyon de Chelly, offers trips into the canyon for $8 per hour for each horse plus $8 per hour for a guide.

Native American guides conduct horseback tours to Keet Seel at Navajo National Monument daily from Memorial Day weekend through Labor Day weekend; rates are approximately $50 per day. Reservations should be made two months in advance;

there's often a waiting list. Contact **Virginia Austin** (c/o Navajo National Monument, HC-71 Box 3, Tonalea, AZ 86044, tel. 602/672–2366 or 602/672–2367) for details.

If you've always wanted to ride off into the sunset at Monument Valley, get in touch with **Ed Black's Horseback Riding Tours** (Box 155, Mexican Hat, UT 84531, tel. 800/551–4039). Prices for trail rides, which can be as short as 1½ hours or as long as five days, range from $20 to $65 (per overnight); rides leave from the corral, ½ mile north of the Monument Valley Visitor Center.

Rainbow Trails & Tours (Box 7218, Shonto, AZ 86054, tel. 602/672–2397) runs pack trips in Lake Powell country from May through September. Tailored to individual interests and skills, Navajo-guided rides include a day trip to Rainbow Bridge and an overnight with tepee accommodations at Desha Canyon near Navajo Mountain. Rates are $75 per person per day, including meals. Shorter trail rides in the Lake Powell area are available in Page from **Rope & Saddle Promotions** (Vermilion Downs on Haul Road, tel. 602/645–2752 or 602/645–2077); the fee is $20 for the first hour for adults and $10 for each additional hour, $10 for the first hour for children and $5 for each additional hour.

Dining and Lodging

Dining Northeastern Arizona offers few restaurants for fine dining. For the most part, dress is casual, seating is on a first-come, first-served basis, and prices are reasonable. Only in the Page/Lake Powell area at the height of the summer season is it advisable to make reservations.

Because northeastern Arizona is a vast area and few communities offer eating establishments, visitors should keep in mind that the following major locations have restaurants and fast-food service: Page, Window Rock, Fort Defiance, Ganado, Chinle, Hopi Second Mesa, Keams Canyon, Tuba City, Kayenta, Goulding's Trading Post/Monument Valley, and Cameron. Most serve standard American fare, and some also feature Mexican and Native American dishes. In some of the smaller reservation communities, only fast food may be available.

Restaurants are open daily unless otherwise noted. Highly recommended restaurants are indicated by a star ★.

Category	Cost*
$$$$	over $25
$$$	$15–$25
$$	$10–$15
$	under $10

per person, excluding drinks, service, and sales tax (9.5% in Page), except on the Hopi and Navajo reservations, where no tax is charged

Lodging Northeastern Arizona is a big land with few people and long distances between communities. When you travel here, a top priority is making sure that you have a place to lay your head at the end of the day. Half the battle is knowing which of the scattered communities have motels. During summer months, it is especially wise to make reservations. Fortunately, most of the motels in Indian country are clean and comfortable, and the majority of the dozen motels and hotels in Page and at Lake Powell are also well maintained.

Because of a demand for accommodations in the area, bed-and-breakfasts have begun to proliferate in Page in the last few years. Zoning restrictions currently prevent them from being anything other than informal homestays, but that is likely to change soon. Among the recommended B&Bs are **Dottie's Country Cottage** (Box 188, Page 86040, tel. 602/645–9740), **A Place Above the Cliff** (Box 2456, Page 86040, tel. 602/645–3162), and the **American Bed & Breakfast** (Box 213, Page 86040, tel. 602/ 645–9752). A brochure listing all the other members of the new Page/Lake Powell Bed & Breakfast Association is available from the Page/Lake Powell Chamber of Commerce (110 S. Lake Powell Blvd., Box 727, Page 86040, tel. 602/645–2741).

Unless otherwise indicated, all the establishments listed have air-conditioning, private baths, telephones, and TVs in their rooms. Highly recommended establishments are indicated by a star ★.

Category	Cost*
$$$	over $80
$$	$50–$80
$	under $50

All prices are for a standard double room at summer rates (rates may be lower at other times), excluding hotel tax: 10.5% in the Page area, 8% on the Navajo reservation. No hotel tax is charged on the Hopi reservation.

Cameron

Dining and Lodging **Cameron Trading Post and Motel.** This is a good place to stop if you're driving from the Hopi Mesas to the Grand Canyon. (*See* Dining and Lodging in Chapter 3, The Grand Canyon and Northwest Arizona, for details.)

Camping **Cameron RV Park** (on U.S. 89, 26 mi southwest of Tuba City, tel. 602/679–2231 or 800/338–7385) is adjacent to the Cameron Trading Post, with its restaurant, grocery store, and post office. The fee with hookup is $14 per day. The park is open all year.

Canyon de Chelly/Chinle/Tsaile

Dining and Lodging **Holiday Inn Canyon de Chelly.** The newest (1992) lodging near Canyon de Chelly is less generic than you might expect: This territorial-style, Navajo-staffed complex stands on the site of a former trading post and incorporates part of the historic structure. Rooms, on the other hand, are predictably pastel and contemporary. The lobby restaurant, low-key by most standards, is the most upscale eatery in town, serving well-prepared Native American dishes, fish and vegetarian entrées, and steaks and burgers. *BIA Rte. 7, Box 1889, Chinle 86503, tel. 602/674–5000 or 800/234–6835, fax 602/674–8264. 108 rooms. Facilities: restaurant, pool, gift shop, Native American music and dance evenings in season. AE, D, DC, MC, V. $$$*

Thunderbird Lodge. Set in an ideal spot at the mouth of Canyon de Chelly, this pleasant establishment has stone and adobe units that match the architecture of the site's original 1896 trading post. Inviting rooms feature roughly hewn beamed ceilings, rustic wooden furniture, and Navajo decor. The staff is friendly and knowledgeable about the locale. The manicured lawns and large, sheltering cottonwood trees help create a resortlike atmosphere. A traditional cafeteria offers an inexpensive American menu that ranges from soup, salads, and sandwiches to complete meals, including charbroiled steaks, prepared by an all-Navajo staff. *Box 548 (½ mi south of Canyon de Chelly visitor center), Chinle 86503, tel. 602/674–5841. 72 rooms. Facilities: cafeteria, gift shop, Jeep tours. AE, D, DC, MC, V. $$$*

Coyote Pass Hospitality. You're not likely to encounter a more unusual lodging than this roving B&B run by the Coyote Pass clan of the Navajo Nation. It's not for everyone: You sleep on a mattress on the dirt floor of a hogan (its location depends on the season, but most are near Canyon de Chelly), use an outhouse, and eat a traditional Navajo breakfast prepared on a wood-burning stove. But if you don't mind roughing it a bit, this is a rare opportunity to immerse yourself in Native American culture in beautiful surroundings. Guided hikes, nature programs, and other meals are optional extras. *Contact Will Tsosie, Jr., Box 91, Tsaile 86556, tel. 602/724–3383 or 602/674–9655. Rates per night: $75 1 person, $10 each additional person; call for tour and additional meal rates. $$*

Lodging **Canyon de Chelly Motel.** This two-story, Western-style motel, about a mile from Canyon de Chelly, has modern, cheerful rooms with light oak furnishings and Native American–print bedspreads and drapes. All rooms have cable TV and coffeemakers. *Box 295 (on Rte. 7, ¼ mi east of U.S. 191), Chinle 86503, tel. 602/674–5875, 602/674–5288, or 800/327–0354. 102 rooms. Facilities: restaurant, indoor pool, gift shop. AE, D, DC, MC, V. $$$*

Camping **Cottonwood Campground** (Canyon de Chelly National Monument, near visitor center, Chinle, tel. 602/674–5500) offers free, first-come, first-served camping at 52 RV sites (maximum length 35 feet; no hookups) and 95 tent sites on grounds with cottonwood trees and a picnic area. The campground is open all year, with water and flush toilets available April–September.

Hopi Reservation–Second Mesa

Dining **Tunosvongya Restaurant.** Also known as the Hopi Cultural Center Restaurant, this clean, comfortable establishment operated by Native Americans provides the opportunity to sample traditional dishes, including Indian tacos, Hopi blue-corn pancakes, fry bread (not unlike a soft pizza crust), and *nok qui vi*, Hopi lamb stew. *On AZ 264 on Second Mesa, tel. 602/734–2401. DC, MC, V. $*

Lodging **Hopi Cultural Center Motel.** The only accommodation in the area, this pleasant pueblo-style lodging set high atop a Hopi mesa offers basic but clean rooms. One drawback: There's not always a night manager on the premises; guests are given a phone number to reach someone in case there are any problems. *Box 67 (on AZ 264, at Hopi Cultural Center), Second Mesa 86043, tel. 602/734–2401, fax 602/734–2435 Attn: Hopi Cultural Center. 33 units. Facilities: restaurant, museum, gift shop. AE, DC, MC, V. $$*

Camping **Hopi Cultural Center Campground.** There's no charge to stay at the modest camping and picnic area on the west side of the Hopi Cultural Center. There are no water hookups, but campers can use the rest rooms in the cultural center, and showers there are available during the morning hours for a small fee. Inquire at the Hopi Cultural Center Motel (*see above*).

Kayenta

Dining and **Anasazi Inn at Tsegi.** This unpretentious roadside motel, conve-
Lodging nient to both Navajo National Monument and Monument Valley, offers clean, comfortable accommodations and striking views of Tsegi Canyon from its rear-facing rooms. Its restaurant, which features tasty Navajo fry-bread sandwiches and tacos, is one of the best in the area. *Box 1543 (on U.S. 160, 10 mi west of Kayenta), Kayenta 86033, tel. and fax 602/697–3793. 56 units. Facilities: restaurant. AE, D, DC, MC, V. $$*

Lodging **Holiday Inn.** Except for the contemporary Southwestern-style decor, this accommodation about ½ mile from Monument Valley provides what you would expect from the Holiday Inn chain. It has one of the few swimming pools in the western section of Indian country. Children under 19 stay in their parents' room free. *Box 307 (south of junction of U.S. 160 and U.S. 163), Kayenta 86033, tel. 602/697–3221 or 800/465–4329, fax 602/697–3349. 160 rooms. Facilities: restaurant, gift shop, swimming pool, Monument Valley tours. AE, D, DC, MC, V. $$$*
Wetherill Inn Motel. Named for John Wetherill, a frontier rancher, trader, and explorer who discovered many of the major prehistoric Native American ruins in Arizona, this clean, cheerful, two-story motel without frills has orange-and-brown room decor and a well-stocked gift shop. *Box 175 (on U.S. 163), Kayenta 86033, tel. 602/697–3231. 54 rooms. Facilities: gift shop, nearby café. AE, D, DC, MC, V. $$*

Keams Canyon

Dining **Keams Canyon Restaurant.** At this typical rural roadside dining spot, functionally furnished with Formica tabletops, you can choose from American dishes and a few Native American items, including Navajo tacos, made with Indian fry bread heaped with ground beef, chili, beans, lettuce, and grated cheese. (Note: The inexpensive motel in the same complex cannot be recommended.) *Keams Canyon Shopping Center (near AZ 264), tel. 602/738–2296. MC, V. Open weekdays 7 AM–8 PM, weekends until 6 PM.* $

Monument Valley

Dining and **Goulding's Lodge.** Built near the base of an immense red sand-
Lodging stone butte with spectacular views of Monument Valley from all
★ the rooms, this comfortable motel often serves as headquarters for the location crews of filmmakers. The lodge has handsome pueblo-style buildings stuccoed in a deep reddish brown that makes them appear to be a part of the surrounding red-rock formations. The cozy rooms are furnished in contemporary style, with Southwestern colors and Navajo-design bedspreads. The on-premises Stagecoach restaurant, serving good standard American fare, is decked with memorabilia from movies shot in the area; service is excellent, and large windows provide a splendid view across the valley. *Box 1 (2 mi west of U.S. 163, just north of Utah border), Monument Valley, UT 84536, tel. 801/ 727–3231 or 800/874–0902. 62 rooms. Facilities: museum, heated pool (both closed Nov. 15–Mar. 15), restaurant, Monument Valley tours. AE, D, DC, MC, V.* $$$

Camping **Goulding's Good Sam Campground** (off U.S. 163, near Goulding's Trading Post, 27 mi north of Kayenta, tel. 801/727–3231, ext. 425) has tents and RV sites. The fee is $14 with no hookups, $22 with hookups (plus tax). *Open Mar. 15–Oct. 15.*

Mitten View Campground (Monument Valley Navajo Tribal Park, near visitor center, off U.S. 163, 25 mi north of Kayenta, tel. 801/727–3287) has sites with a table, a grill, and a deck. Water is available, but no hookups; the fee is $5 per site, with hot showers extra. More sites are open in summer, but 10 or 15 are open year-round.

Navajo National Monument

Camping **Navajo National Monument** (reached by turnoff on U.S. 160, 21 mi south of Kayenta, tel. 602/672–2366) has a campground with RV and tent sites, water, and rest rooms, but no hookups. Camping here is free and is available May–October.

Page/Lake Powell

Dining **Rainbow Room in Wahweap Lodge.** You can't beat the beautiful setting of this attractive semicircular restaurant with panoramic views of Lake Powell and a colony of houseboats bobbing off-

shore. An extensive menu features Southwestern, standard American, and some Continental fare, accompanied by a good wine selection. Specialties include Southwest chicken breast marinated in a honey-and-jalapeño-pepper sauce, and coho salmon with a Dijon-mustard cream sauce. *Wahweap Lodge (on U.S. 89, 5 mi north of Page), tel. 602/645–2433 or 800/528–6154. Reservations accepted in summer. AE, D, DC, MC, V. $$–$$$*
Salsa Brava. This cheerful Mexican restaurant, with green upholstered booths, lots of windows, and beamed ceilings, emphasizes charbroiled rather than fried preparations and uses vegetable oil instead of lard. Good versions of the standard burritos, tamales, and enchiladas are available along with more unusual fare such as *carnitas* (slow-cooked pork), chicken with mole sauce, and fish tacos. There's an outdoor patio and a dark and clubby bar. *635 Elm St., Page, tel. 602/645–9058. MC, V. $$*

Lodging **Wahweap Lodge.** On a promontory above Lake Powell, Wahweap
★ Lodge serves as the center for recreational activities in the area. This attractively landscaped property offers accommodations with oak furnishings and balconies or patios; many of the rooms have a lake view (rates are a bit higher for these). The brightly colored, Southwestern-style suites in the newest building are particularly attractive. Guests can enjoy two pools, a cocktail lounge, a marina, and the Rainbow Room (*see above*) for dining. Off-season rates are very reasonable. *Box 1597 (on U.S. 89, 5 mi north of Page), Page 86040, tel. 602/645–2433 or 800/528–6154. 350 rooms. Facilities: rental boats, cruises, fishing and water-skiing equipment, river-rafting excursions, houseboats, 2 gift shops. AE, D, DC, MC, V. $$$*
Inn at Lake Powell. It's neither an inn nor on Lake Powell, but never mind: This modern, well-run motel on a high bluff at the northern end of Page has large rooms with queen-size beds and Southwestern-print bedspreads. And, at a slightly higher room rate, you can get views of Lake Powell and Glen Canyon Dam. *Box C (716 Rim View Dr.), Page 86040, tel. 602/645–2466 or 800/ 826–2718. 103 rooms. Facilities: restaurant, cocktail lounge, conference rooms, pool, hot tub. AE, D, DC, MC, V. $$–$$$*
Weston's Empire House. Built in 1962, this classic 1950s-style motel on Page's main street recently renovated its comfortable rooms, which have individual air-conditioning and heating units. The smoky Western bar has a huge jukebox and a big-screen TV. *Box 1747 (107 S. Lake Powell Blvd.), Page 86040, tel. 602/645–2406 or 800/551–9005, fax 602/645–2647. 69 rooms. Facilities: restaurant, bar/lounge, outdoor pool, cable TV. MC, V. $$*

Camping **Page–Lake Powell Campground** (849 Hwy. 98, tel. 602/645–3374) has more than 70 full-hookup RV sites ($18 per night, $2 extra for cable-TV hookup), and eight tent sites ($15). A coin-op laundry, an indoor swimming pool, and two sets of men's and women's bathrooms and showers are available for no extra charge to both tenters and RVers. The campground is open year-round, and accepts reservations.

Wahweap RV Park (5 mi north of Page on U.S. 89 near shore of Lake Powell, tel. 602/645–1004 or 800/528–6154 [reservations]) offers 120 full-service sites with full hookups, showers, and a laundromat; the fee is $21.50. It's open year-round and reservations are accepted. The adjacent **Wahweap Campground** (tel. 602/645–1059) has 180 sites, some near the marina. The fee for campsites with drinking water is $8.50; campers can use the coin-op laundry and showers ($2 extra) at the RV park. Open Apr. 1–Oct. 31, the campground operates on a first-come, first-served basis.

Tuba City

Dining   **Pancho's Family Restaurant.** The main fare here is Mexican, but the menu also features American and Navajo dishes. Mexican entrées are abundant and traditionally prepared, with chicken enchiladas and beef tamales as good as any you'll find south of the border. The large dining room looks like a Western coffee shop but has beamed wooden ceilings and incorporates such Native American touches as handmade pottery chandeliers and Navajo rugs on the walls. *Main St., adjacent to Tuba City Motel and Trading Post, tel. 602/283–5260. AE, D, DC, MC, V. $*

Lodging   **Tuba City Motel.** In the largest community in the western part of Indian country, this property is conveniently situated near Pancho's Family Restaurant (*see* Dining, *above*), a trading post, and shops for essentials, gifts, and souvenirs. The spacious, well-maintained rooms are fine for an overnight stopover before or after a visit to the Hopi Mesas. *Box 247 (at AZ 264-U.S. 160 junction), Tuba City 86045, tel. 602/283–4545 or 800/644–8383, fax 602/283–4144. 80 rooms. Facilities: gift shop, nearby restaurants, post office, trading post. AE, D, DC, MC, V. $$*

Grey Hills Inn. Students at Grey Hills High School run this unusual lodging, a former dorm that offers large, clean accommodations. The queen-size beds are comfortable, and pastel Native American–print bedspreads and kitschy paintings add character to the otherwise plain rooms. Bathrooms and showers are down the hall, and it's hard to find your way to the inn's entrance in the large high-school complex at night, but the rates are reasonable, especially for Youth Hostel members. *Box 160 (off U.S. 160, ½ mi north of junction with AZ 264), Tuba City 86045, tel. 602/283–6271, ext. 141 or 602/283–6273 (on weekends or after school hours). 32 rooms. No credit cards. $–$$*

Window Rock

Dining and   **Navajo Nation Inn.** Indian officials in town on government busi-
Lodging   ness frequently stay in this motel in the Navajo Nation's tribal capital. The exterior is typical of contemporary roadside motels, but the rooms have been pleasantly decorated with Spanish Colonial furniture and Navajo art. The inexpensive restaurant serves standard American as well as Navajo entrées; the mutton stew is hearty, and the tasty fry-bread taco could easily feed two. *48 W. Hwy 264, Box 2340, Window Rock 86515, tel. 602/*

*871–4108 or 800/662–6189 (reservations only), fax 602/871–
5466. 56 units. Facilities: restaurant, conference rooms, nearby
shopping and services. AE, DC, MC, V. $$*

Camping   **Summit Campground** (off AZ 264, 9 mi west of Window Rock,
tel. 602/871–6645) has picnic tables but no water. The camp-
ground is open year-round and may charge a fee of $1 per per-
son.

Tse Bonito Tribal Park (near AZ 264, Window Rock, tel. 602/
871–6645), set among sandstone monoliths, is a historically sig-
nificant site: The Navajo camped here before being forced on the
Long Walk to Fort Summer. The campground has shaded picnic
tables and nearby rest rooms but no water. A fee of $2 per per-
son may be charged. *Open year-round except Christmas and
New Year's Day.*

Nightlife

Aside from sitting by a campfire, nightlife in northeastern Ar-
izona is minimal. The Page/Lake Powell area offers the most op-
tions. The cocktail lounge at **Wahweap Lodge** (on U.S. 89, 5 mi
north of Page, tel. 602/645–2433) on the shore of Lake Powell
and the **sunset dinner cruise** that departs from the dock at
Wahweap Lodge (*see* Dining and Lodging, *above*) are two possi-
bilities. Page also has a movie house, **Mesa Theater** (42 S. Lake
Powell Blvd., tel. 602/645–9565); a combination bowling alley/
off-track betting parlor/comedy club/bistro called **Canyon Bowl**
(24 N. Lake Powell Blvd. tel. 602/645–2682); and **Ken's Old West**
(718 Vista Rd., tel. 602/645–5160), a country-and-western music
and dancing spot where you can also get a pretty good steak or
barbecued chicken dinner. In addition, there's an inexpensive
first-run movie theater in Tuba City.

Keep in mind that no alcoholic beverages are sold on the Navajo
and Hopi reservations, and possession or consumption of alcohol
is against the law in these areas.

5 North-Central Arizona

Sedona and the Verde Valley, Flagstaff

*By Edie
Jarolim and
Trudy
Thompson
Rice*

Rich in natural attractions, north-central Arizona draws visitors to the striking red-rock formations of Sedona; to the limestone hills and desert scrub of the Verde Valley; and, just north of Flagstaff, to the San Francisco volcanic field, which hosts the highest peaks in the state as well as ancient lava flows and cinder cones. Sedona sits at the southern end of Oak Creek Canyon, where the Colorado Plateau meets the Sonora Desert to the south; Highway 89A, which traverses this wooded canyon en route to Flagstaff, is one of the most scenic drives in the state.

The area is also rich in artifacts from its earliest inhabitants: Several national and state parks hold well-preserved evidence of the architectural accomplishments of the Native American settlers who made their homes in the Verde Valley and in the region near the San Francisco peaks—particularly the Sinagua people, who disappeared as mysteriously as the Anasazi did. Nor will those interested in exploring the West's wild and woolly days be disappointed: The preserved fort at Camp Verde gives an excellent feel for rugged frontier life, and funky old Jerome is living testament to Arizona's days of mining madness.

The towns of Verde Valley—Cornville, Clarkdale, Cottonwood—are as sleepy as their names suggest; a visit to the historic sites in the region will take you through a part of America that seems to have changed little since the 1950s. Sedona couldn't provide a greater contrast, with its chic shops, sophisticated restaurants, upscale accommodations, and New Age entrepreneurs. Flagstaff, the largest city in north-central Arizona and long considered a jumping-off point for tours of the region, is becoming recognized as an appealing destination in its own right, offering some of the best skiing in the state at reasonable prices, and lots of opportunities to explore Arizona history, astronomy, and Native American culture.

Essential Information

Important Addresses and Numbers

**Tourist
Information**
One of the busiest tourist information offices in the country, the **Flagstaff Visitors Center** (1 Rte. 66, tel. 602/774–9541 or 800/842–7293) is open every day of the year, including Christmas: Monday–Saturday 8 AM–9 PM, Sunday 8 AM–5 PM. In 1994, the center moved downtown, into the refurbished historic train depot, which it shares with Amtrak.

For hiking maps and camping tips, contact the **U.S. Forest Service** (2323 Greenlaw La., tel. 602/527–3600).

The **Sedona–Oak Creek Canyon Chamber of Commerce,** at the corner of North Highway 89A and Forest Road (Box 478, Sedona 86339, tel. 602/282–7722 or 800/288–7336), is staffed with knowledgeable residents who can guide you to points of special interest; it's open Monday to Saturday 9–5, Sunday 9–3.

You can get some information about the Verde Valley from the Chamber of Commerce offices in **Jerome** (Main St., tel. 602/634–2900), **Clarkdale** (Main St., tel. 602/634–8700), **Cottonwood** (1010 S. Main St., tel. 602/634–7593), and **Camp Verde** (Main St., tel. 602/567–9294); the addresses give a clue to the size of these towns.

Emergencies Call 911 to reach the **fire department, police,** and **emergency medical services.**

Hospitals and At an altitude of nearly 7,000 feet, Flagstaff has "thin" air; heart
Doctors and respiratory patients may experience difficulty here, particularly upon exertion.

Flagstaff Medical Center, a full-service hospital, has a 24-hour emergency room downtown (1200 N. Beaver St., tel. 602/779–3366), about nine blocks north of Route 66. The facility also provides referrals to local doctors and dentists.

The **Sedona Medical Center** has a doctor on call 24 hours. *75 Kallof Pl., tel. 602/282–1285. Walk-in hours Mon.–Fri. 8–5, Sat. 9–2.*

Late-Night The pharmacy at the **Flagstaff Medical Center** (*see above*) is open
Pharmacies 24 hours. **Walgreen's** (1500 E. Cedar Ave., tel. 602/773–1011), a few blocks north of downtown, is open Monday–Saturday 9 AM–10 PM, Sunday 9 AM–8 PM; the pharmacy at **Smith's Food and Drug** (201 Switzer Canyon Rd., corner Route 66, tel. 602/774–2719) is open Monday–Saturday 9 AM–9 PM, Sunday 10 AM–4 PM.

In Sedona **Walgreen's** (180 Coffee Pot Dr., tel. 602/282–2528) stays open until 9 Monday–Saturday, until 8 on Sunday; **Payless** (2350 W. Hwy. 89A, tel. 602/282–9577) closes at 9 every day except Sunday, when it closes at 7.

Arriving and Departing by Plane

Flagstaff Air travelers arrive at the newly refurbished **Flagstaff Pullium Airport** (tel. 602/556–1234), 4 miles south of town off I–17 at exit 337.

Both **America West Express/Mesa** (tel. 800/247–5692) and **Skywest** (tel. 800/453–9417), a division of Delta Airlines, have frequent daily flights into Flagstaff from Phoenix. If you plan to rent a car, the most cost-effective plan might be to fly into Phoenix, which has more flight options, and rent a car there. The drive from Phoenix to Flagstaff is a pretty one, climbing almost 5,000 feet in 134 miles.

Sedona The tiny **Sedona Airport** (tel. 602/282–4487) has a very scenic location up on Airport Mesa; from West Sedona, take Highway 89A to the top of Airport Road.

Scenic Airlines (1225 Airport Rd., Suite 3, Sedona, tel. 602/282–7935 or 800/535–4448) has four daily round-trips between Phoenix and Sedona year-round; the cost is $95 to $110 round-trip.

Airport to A taxi ride from the airport to the downtown area should cost
Downtown about $10. Cabs are not regulated; some, but not all, have me-
Flagstaff ters. It's wise to agree on a rate before you contract with a driv-
By Taxi er to take you to your destination. **Alpine Taxi Cab** (tel. 602/526–
7162) and **Northland Taxi** (tel. 602/556–0041) are two reliable op-
tions.

By Bus There is no public bus from the airport to downtown. Some hotels offer a shuttle service; inquire when making reservations.

By Rental Car Rental-car agencies represented at the airport include **Avis** (tel.
800/331–1212), **Budget** (tel. 800/527–0700), and **Hertz** (tel. 800/
654–3131). Ask about a rate that allows you unlimited mileage,
as you're likely to drive several hundred miles while you're in
this part of the state.

To reach downtown from the airport, follow the signs out of the
airport to I–17 (the airport is just off the highway). Turn right
(north) on I–17, then exit at the downtown turnoff, less than 5
miles away.

Airport to While there are no cabs waiting at the airport, if you call **Bob's**
Downtown **Sedona Taxi** (tel. 602/282–1234), they will dispatch a car, which
Sedona should show up in about five minutes. A ride to town will run you
By Taxi about $7 or $8.

By Rental Car **Budget Rent-A-Car** (tel. 602/282–4602 or 800/527–0700) has an
office at the Sedona Airport.

Arriving and Departing by Car, Train, and Bus

By Car **Flagstaff** lies at the crossroads of I–40 (running east–west) and
I–17 (running south from Flagstaff). It's 134 miles from Phoenix via I–17 (also known in Phoenix as Black Canyon Freeway)
north. The road is a four-lane divided highway the entire way;
there are several steep climbs and descents (you'll see a number
of runaway-truck ramps—emergency stopping places for
truckers who have lost their brakes on the steep declines). In
winter, snowstorms can occasionally restrict travel to vehicles
with snow chains.

To get to **Sedona** from Phoenix, take I–17 north for 113 miles,
then drive another 15 miles on AZ 179; the trip should take
about 2½ hours. The 27-mile drive from Flagstaff to Sedona on
Highway 89A through Oak Creek Canyon is breathtaking because of both the stunning scenery and the precipitous, winding
road.

By Train Flagstaff is a railroad town: The tracks that gave rise to the
city's growth still run through the town today. **Amtrak** (tel. 602/
774–8679 or 800/872–7245) comes into the downtown station at 1
Route 66 twice daily.

There is no rail service into Sedona.

By Bus In **Flagstaff,** the **Greyhound Lines** station is downtown at 399
South Malpais Lane (tel. 602/774–4573 or 800/231–2222). There
are daily connections to Phoenix, but none to Sedona. Buses also

serve San Francisco, Los Angeles, Las Vegas, and other cities. **Nava-Hopi** buses also depart daily to the Grand Canyon and offer sightseeing trips to Sedona (*see* Special-Interest Tours, *below*).

The **Sedona/Phoenix Shuttle Service** (Box 3342, West Sedona 86340, tel. 602/282–2066 or 800/448–7988 in Arizona) makes four trips daily between those cities; the fare is $30 one-way, $55 round-trip. You can catch the bus at three terminals of Sky Harbor International Airport in Phoenix.

Getting Around

Flagstaff is a compact town, much of it situated along the railroad tracks. Just north of, and roughly parallel to, the tracks is the busy street that was called Santa Fe Avenue for many years; in 1992 it officially resumed its famous original name, Route 66. Not all the signs in town have been changed yet, however, and many maps—and most locals—still refer to Santa Fe Avenue, so the change will probably cause confusion for some time. I–40 lies to the south of the tracks and also runs east–west; the main north–south thoroughfare is I–17, which turns into Milton Road, Humphreys Street, and then U.S. 180 as you drive north through town. Fast-food restaurants and motels line all these major roads.

Because Flagstaff is the gateway to the Grand Canyon, most people on the road here are from out of town; keep that in mind when you ask for directions!

Sedona is even more compact than Flagstaff, with Highway 89A, which runs roughly east–west through town, as the main thoroughfare. Highway 89A is bisected by AZ 179. The more commercial section of Highway 89A east of AZ 179 is known as Uptown; locals tend to frequent the shops on the other side, called West Sedona. To the south of Highway 89A, AZ 179 is lined with upscale retailers for a couple of miles. There is no public transportation in Sedona; if you don't have your own wheels, you'll need to rent a car or Jeep (*see* By Car and By Jeep, *below*) or take a taxi (*see* Airport to Downtown Sedona, *above*).

By Bus In Flagstaff, **Pine Country Transit** (tel. 602/779–6624) offers clean and reliable service throughout the city for 75¢. Senior citizens age 60 and older, riders with disabilities, and children 7–17 pay only 60¢ a ride; children age 6 and under ride free. Three bus lines run weekdays 6:15 AM–7:10 PM; only one bus line, on a more limited schedule, operates Saturday and holidays, and there is no service on Sunday. Passengers with disabilities should check with the office to find out which buses are outfitted to accommodate wheelchairs.

By Car It makes sense to rent a car at the airport if you fly into Flagstaff or Sedona (*see* Airport to Downtown sections, *above*). In downtown Sedona **Super Star Rent A Car** (2730 W. Hwy. 89A, tel. 602/282–2897) offers reliable service.

By Jeep If you want to explore the back roads of Sedona's red rocks on your own, you can rent a four-wheel-drive vehicle from **Sedona**

Jeep Rentals (Sedona Airport, tel. 602/282–2227) or **Sedona Vacation Rentals** (Oak Creek Terrace Resort, Hwy. 89A, tel. 602/282–6061).

Opening and Closing Times

Flagstaff is a town of travelers and students, so restaurants tend to stay open late, some of them 24 hours. Sedona, on the other hand, is a resort that caters to retirees, so restaurants tend to close earlier, many of them by 10 PM. In both places banking can be done at odd hours by way of automated teller machines (ATMs) located all over town. Some banks stay open until 6 PM on Friday. In summer, shops and attractions are open longer: 9–9 Monday through Saturday and noon–5 on Sunday.

Guided Tours

Orientation
Flagstaff
For self-guided tour maps of Flagstaff itself, stop at the **Flagstaff Visitors Center** (*see* Tourist Information, *above*); if you're going to spend any time in town, it's well worth taking the route outlined in the "Historic Downtown Walking Tour" pamphlet. If you're interested in a look at the **Northern Arizona University** campus (tel. 602/523–2491), from September through May (except during spring break and holiday weekends) tours are conducted Monday–Saturday; from June through August, they're offered during the week only. Call ahead to check the schedule and to reserve a place.

Sedona
Sedona Trolley (tel. 602/282–6826) offers two types of daily orientation tours, both departing from the main bus stop in Uptown and lasting less than an hour. One goes along AZ 179 to the Chapel of the Holy Cross, with stops at Tlaquepaque and some of the resorts; the other passes through West Sedona to Boynton Canyon. Rates are $6 each, or $9 for both.

Special-Interest Tours
Flagstaff
The Gray Line of Flagstaff, operated by **Nava-Hopi Tours** (114 W. Route 66 [Box 339], Flagstaff 86002, tel. 602/774–5003 or 800/892–8687), runs bus trips from its downtown bus station to the **Grand Canyon** ($38 round-trip, including park entry fee). A tour of **Sedona** costs $36 per person; there are no drop-offs—that is, all passengers must return to Flagstaff on the same bus that evening. The company also offers a variety of package tours, such as the one to the **Hopi Indian Reservation** ($62 round-trip, including lunch). All require reservations, which are taken until two hours before departure. Free hotel and motel pickups are included in the price.

The Ventures program, run by the education department of the **Museum of Northern Arizona** (3001 N. Fort Valley Rd. [Box 720], Flagstaff 86001, tel. 602/774–5213), offers tours of the area led by local scientists, artists, and historians. Trips might include rafting excursions down the San Juan and lower Verde rivers, hikes into the Grand Canyon or Arizona Strip Country, or bus tours into Albuquerque or Santa Fe. Prices start at $300 and go up to $1,300, with most tours in the $300 to $600 range.

Alpine Air Service (Box 252, Flagstaff 86002, tel. 602/779–5178) plane tours of the area's attractions leave from Flagstaff Pullium Airport. The cost for the pilot and plane, which carries three passengers, is $90 an hour plus tax. FAA regulations prevent tour companies, including this one, from flying over the Grand Canyon.

Sedona One of the most popular things to do in the Sedona area is to take a **Jeep tour;** several operators headquartered along Sedona's main Uptown drag offer a variety of excursions, some focusing on geology, some on vegetation, some on vortices, and some on all three. In addition to the ubiquitous **Pink Jeep Tours** (Box 1447, Sedona 86339, tel. 602/282–5000 or 800/8–SEDONA), **Sedona Adventures** (Box 1478, Sedona 86339, tel. 602/282–3500 or 800/888–9494), **Sedona Red Rock Jeep Tours** (Box 10305, Sedona 86339, tel. 602/282–6826 or 800/848–7728), and **Time Expeditions** (Box 2936, Sedona 86339, tel. 602/282–2137 or 800/999–2137) are all reliable operators. Prices start at about $18 per person for one hour, $40 per person for two hours. Car seats are available for youngsters; check with your operator before you book. Although all the excursions are safe, those who dislike heights should choose one that's easy on the nerves.

Rahelio (10 Traumeri La., Sedona 86339, tel. 602/282–6735) offers vortex tours, vision quests, a variety of mystical hikes, and adventures. Those interested in Native American culture and spirituality should contact **Anasazi Healing Tours** (Box 3448, West Sedona 86340, tel. 602/204–1053); Steven Alish-TaSen is an excellent guide to the Hopi Mesas and other Native American sites.

A **hot-air-balloon tour** of Sedona provides a unique perspective of the red-rock landscape. Prices generally start at $135 per person for a one- to two-hour tour. Plan to spend about three or four hours on this venture, including driving time to the launch site and a champagne picnic. The only two companies with permits to fly over Sedona are **Northern Light Balloon Expeditions** (Box 1695, Sedona 86339, tel. 602/282–2274) and **Red Rock Balloon Adventures** (Box 2759, Sedona 86339, tel. 602/284–0040 or 800/258–3754).

It's the rare visitor who won't snap a roll or two of film in beautiful Sedona; **Sedona Photo Tours** (Box 1650, Sedona 86336, tel. 602/282–4320) will take you to all the prime spots and help you take your best shot. Rates are $35 per person for a basic two-hour tour; it's an additional $15 per hour for more technical expert advice.

Those interested in the photographs of others—and in art in general—might consider a tour of some of the galleries in town; contact **Sedona Art Tours** (Box 10578, Sedona 86339, tel. 602/282–7686) for information.

Exploring North-Central Arizona

Highlights for First-Time Visitors

Jerome (*see* The Verde Valley)
Montezuma Castle (*see* The Verde Valley)
Museum of Northern Arizona (*see* Flagstaff and Environs)
Oak Creek Canyon (*see* Sedona and Environs)
The red rocks of Sedona (*see* Sedona and Environs)
Riordan Mansion (*see* Flagstaff and Environs)
Sunset Crater Volcano and Wupatki National Monuments (*see* Flagstaff and Environs)
The Verde River Canyon Excursion Train (*see* The Verde Valley)

The Verde Valley

About 100 miles north of Phoenix, as you round a curve approaching exit 285 of I–17, the valley of the Verde River suddenly unfolds in a stunning panorama of grayish-white cliffs, tinted red in the distance and dotted with desert scrub, cottonwood, and pine. With the exception of bustling Sedona at its northern edge, the valley is rather sleepy, but for hundreds of years it was home to many active Native American communities, especially those of the Southern Sinagua people. In the second half of the 19th century the discovery of silver and gold in the Black Hills, which border the valley on the southwest, gave rise to such boomtowns as Jerome—and to military installations such as Fort Verde, set up to protect the white settlers and wealth-seekers from the Native American tribes they displaced.

Numbers in the margin correspond to points of interest on the North-Central Arizona map.

If you get off at any of the three Camp Verde exits of I–17, signs
❶ will direct you to **Fort Verde State Historic Park,** set on 10 acres overlooking the Verde Valley. Established in 1871–73 as the third of three military posts designed to protect miners and their suppliers from Tonto Apache and Yavapai raids, this fort oversaw the movement of nearly 1,500 Indians to the San Carlos and Fort Apache reservations. A museum details the history of the area's military installations, and three furnished officers' quarters show the day-to-day living conditions of the top brass; even on the frontier, the married men lived far more comfortably than their bachelor counterparts. *Box 397, Camp Verde, 86322, tel. 602/567–3275. Admission: $2 adults, $1 children 13–17. Open daily 8–5. Closed Christmas Day.*

Returning to Camp Verde's Main Street, you'll see a sign for the Montezuma Castle Road; it's about 3 miles from here to
❷ **Montezuma Castle National Monument** (if you're on 1–17, take exit 289 and follow the signs for 3 miles). Mistakenly named by early explorers who believed it had been built by the Aztecs, this

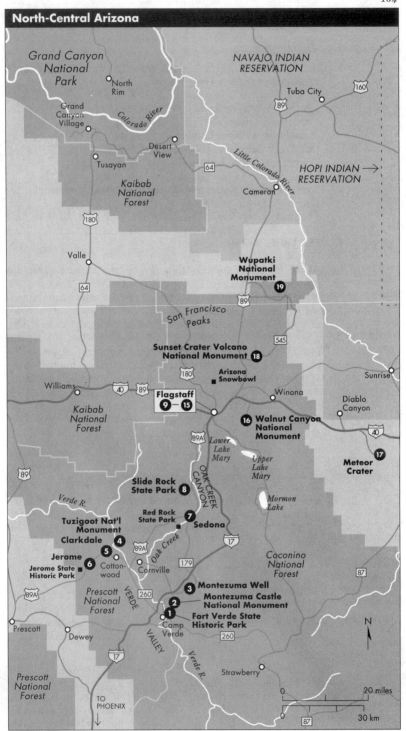

North-Central Arizona

Grand Canyon National Park

NAVAJO INDIAN RESERVATION

North Rim

Tuba City

89

160

Grand Canyon Village

Colorado River

Desert View

64

Little Colorado River

HOPI INDIAN RESERVATION →

Tusayan

Kaibab National Forest

Cameron

180

Valle

Wupatki National Monument 19

64

89

San Francisco Peaks

Sunset Crater Volcano National Monument 18

545

Williams

40 89

180

Arizona Snowbowl

Sunrise

Flagstaff 9 — 15

Winona

Diablo Canyon

Kaibab National Forest

16 Walnut Canyon National Monument

40

89

Lower Lake Mary

Meteor Crater 17

Upper Lake Mary

Slide Rock State Park 8

OAK CREEK CANYON

Mormon Lake

Verde R.

Red Rock State Park 7

89A

Tuzigoot Nat'l Monument Clarkdale 4

Sedona

Coconino National Forest

Jerome 6

5

Oak Creek

17

Jerome State Historic Park

Cotton-wood

89

Cornville

179

87

89A

260

VERDE

3 Montezuma Well

Prescott National Forest

2

Montezuma Castle National Monument

1

Fort Verde State Historic Park

Prescott

Dewey

Camp Verde

260

17

Verde R.

Strawberry

N

Prescott National Forest

TO PHOENIX ↓

0   20 miles

0   30 km

87

five-story, 20-room cliff dwelling of the southern Sinagua Indians is one of the best-preserved prehistoric ruins in North America—and one of the most accessible. An easy, paved trail (⅓ mile round-trip) leads to the structure and to the adjacent Castle A, a badly deteriorated six-story apartment with about 45 rooms. Visitors are not permitted to enter the ruins, but the viewing area is very close by. *Box 219, Camp Verde, 86322, tel. 602/567-3322. Admission: $2 adults 17 and over. Open 8-5 in winter, 8-6 in spring, 8-7 in summer.*

❸ Somewhat less accessible but equally striking is the **Montezuma Well** unit of the national monument, 4 miles off Exit 293 of I-17. Although there are some Sinagua and Hohokam ruins here, the limestone sinkhole containing a limpid blue-green pool in the middle of the desert is the site's main attraction. This sink—55 feet deep and 365 feet across—is all that's left of an ancient subterranean cavern; the water remains at a constant 76°F year-round. It's a short hike up here, but the serene setting and the views of the Verde Valley amply reward the effort. *Tel. 602/567-4521. No entrance fee. Open same hours as Montezuma Castle.*

❹ Not as well preserved as Montezuma's Castle but more impressive in scope is **Tuzigoot National Monument,** another complex of ruins of the Sinagua Indians, who lived on this land overlooking the Verde Valley from about AD 1125 through 1400. Items used for food preparation, as well as jewelry, weapons, and farming tools excavated from the site, are displayed in the visitor center, where there is also a reconstructed room from the pueblo. The site, near the town of Clarkdale, is off Highway 89A; you can take AZ 260 east from Camp Verde, or drive west from Sedona. *Box 68, Clarkdale 86324, tel. 602/634-5564. Admission: $2 adults, children under 17 and senior citizens free. Open Memorial Day–Labor Day, daily 8-7; Labor Day–Feb., daily 8-5; Mar.–May, daily 8-6 (call ahead in Apr. and May to check; schedule is affected by Easter holidays).*

Time Out   Two restaurants in Cornville, roughly between Camp Verde and Clarkdale, are worth a detour. The **Manzanita Restaurant & Lounge** (11425 E. Cornville Rd., tel. 602/634-8851) serves reasonably priced Continental fare in a lace-curtained dining room; you can lunch on bratwurst with sauerkraut and spaetzle for $5.50, including soup or salad, or enjoy a dinner of roast half-duckling with orange sauce for $11.95. **Page Springs Bar & Restaurant** (Page Springs Rd., tel. 602/634-9954) serves more of what you might expect to find out west: great chili, burgers, and steaks served up in two rustic, wood-paneled rooms, both overlooking Oak Creek.

❺ There's little to see in **Clarkdale** itself, but the now sleepy town was once home to the smeltery for the copper mines in nearby Jerome; the original settlement is said to have arisen from an encampment of prostitutes and hard-core gamblers who were tossed out of the rowdy mining camp in one of its periodic purges of sinners. These days, Clarkdale draws a somewhat more sedate group of train buffs who come to catch the **Verde River Can-**

yon Excursion Train. Knowledgeable announcers regale riders on this scenic 22-mile route with the colorful history of the area, pointing out natural attractions along the way—say, a bald eagle's nest in the side of a cliff. A cowboy balladeer entertains passengers on the way back. This trip, which takes about four hours, is especially popular during the fall-foliage season and in the spring when the desert wildflowers bloom; make reservations well in advance. The train sells snacks, drinks, and sandwiches; for an additional fee you can ride the comfy, living-room-like first-class cars; hot hors d'oeuvres, coffee, and champagne are included in the price. *Arizona Central Railroad, 300 N. Broadway, Clarkdale 86324, tel. 602/639–0010. Round-trip rides: $32.95 adults, $29.95 senior citizens over 65, $17.95 children under 12. First class: $49.95. Trains run June–Mar., Wed.–Sun.; Apr.–May, Wed.–Mon. Call for times.*

❻ From Clarkdale, it's 4 miles up the mountain to **Jerome,** once known as the Billion Dollar Copper Camp; the road is windy on this side of the mountain but the grades are not very steep. After the last mines closed in 1953, a booming population of 15,000 dwindled to a low of 50 determined souls, earning Jerome the "ghost town" designation it still holds. The town saw a slight revival during the mid-1960s, when hippies moved in and turned it into a funky art colony of sorts. Today some 400 people reside here full-time, but tourists keep the place alive. Worth a visit for its historic interest as well as for its scenery, Jerome is literally built into the side of Cleopatra Hill, and from here you can see Sedona's red rocks, Flagstaff's San Francisco Peaks, and even eastern Arizona's Mogollon Rim country (*see* Chapter 6, Phoenix and Central Arizona).

Jerome sits about a mile above sea level, but structures within town sit at elevations that vary by as much as 1,500 feet, depending on whether they're perched on Cleopatra Hill or at its foot. Blasting at the mines regularly shook buildings off their foundations, and the town's jail slid across a road and down a hillside, where it can still be seen today. That's not all that was unsteady about Jerome. In 1903, a reporter from a New York newspaper called Jerome "the wickedest town in America" because of its abundance of drinking and gaming establishments; 1880 town records list 24 saloons. Whether due to divine retribution or drunken accidents, the town was burned down several times—some historians say five, others two or three. The mine's financial backers were a bit more respectable: Eugene Jerome, for whom the town was named, was first cousin to Jenny Jerome, Winston Churchill's mother.

Of the three mining museums in town, the most comprehensive is at **Jerome State Historic Park;** just outside town, signs on Highway 89A will direct you to the turnoff for the park, reached by a short but precipitous road with speed limits of 15 miles per hour. The museum occupies the mansion of Jerome's mining king, Dr. James "Rawhide Jimmy" Douglas, Jr., who purchased Little Daisy Mine in 1912; the house was built in 1917 at the height of Little Daisy's success. (Rawhide Jimmy's first mining fortune was made in southern Arizona; *see* the town of Douglas in Chapter 7, Tucson and Southern Arizona.) On the grounds you'll see some of the tools and heavy equipment used to grind ore. A video details the history of Jerome; the bawdy parts have been left out, but you can read between the lines for some sense of the town's wild mining days. Views from the mansion and its surrounding grounds are spectacular. *State Park Rd., tel. 602/ 634–5381. Admission: $2 adults, $1 children 12–17. Open daily 8–5.*

The other worthwhile mining museum, **The Mine Museum,** is downtown. Staffed by the Jerome Historical Society, the museum's collection of mining stock certificates alone is worth the (small) price of admission—the amount of money that changed hands in this town 100 years ago boggles the mind. *Main St., tel. 602/634–5477. Admission: 50¢. Open daily 9–4:30.*

Jerome, like Sedona on a smaller, less expensive scale, is a scenic shopper's haven. Chic, artsy boutiques and galleries carrying local and imported goods line the streets in the tiny downtown area (*see* Shopping, *below*).

Time Out **Teri's Jerome Market** (515 Main St., tel. 602/639–2218), serving freshly made sandwiches, salads, and soups, is a good place to refuel after sightseeing and shopping. You can order your food from the deli counter and take it to one of the tables next door; in summer, there's outdoor seating.

For those who plan to continue from Jerome to Prescott (*see* Chapter 6, Phoenix and Central Arizona), the 34-mile drive southwest down a mountainous section of Highway 89A is gorgeous (if somewhat harrowing in bad weather), filled with twists and turns through the Prescott National Forest.

Sedona and Environs

❼ **Sedona,** at the north rim of the Verde Valley, is perhaps the most attractive stopover en route north to the Grand Canyon. With its numerous galleries, shops, resorts, and restaurants, as well as a splendid setting in the midst of red-rock country, Sedona also makes a fine weekend destination in its own right.

The former artists' colony is now home to some 15,000 residents, many retired, and many (alas) more interested in making money than in creating beauty. Expansion during the past 10 years has been rapid, and the lack of planning has taken its toll in increased traffic and congestion, especially on weekends and during the busy summer months, when Phoenix residents, overcome by heat, flee north to higher elevations.

That said, it's easy to see what draws so many visitors to Sedona. The deep-red rocks poke holes in what is almost always a clear blue sky—which seems even bluer above the dark green of the forests. The wilderness—canyons, creeks, Indian ruins, and always a dreamscape of twisted red rock—is readily accessible on foot or on any number of Jeep tours. The rugged landscape once attracted filmmakers, who shot more than 80 Westerns in the area in the 1940s and '50s. These days, Sedona—which seems likely to become the next Santa Fe—draws enterprising restaurateurs and gallery owners from the East and West coasts. The town has also become a center of interest to New Age followers, who believe that the area contains some of the more important vortices (energy centers) of the Earth. The town has become something of a haven for artists, the tofu set, and others in between. Several entrepreneurs have set up crystal shops or New Age bookshops here, catering to the curious as well as to true devotees.

Exploring Sedona Visitors have a choice of Jeep tours (*see* Special-Interest Tours in Essential Information, *above*) and a number of attractive hikes among the red rocks; the entire region is crisscrossed with trails. For free detailed maps and advice, speak to the rangers at the **Sedona Ranger District** office (250 Brewer Rd., tel. 602/282–4119), which is open Monday–Friday 7:30–4:30. Ask here or at your hotel for directions to trailheads for Devil's Kitchen, Long Canyon, or the Indian ruins in Boynton Canyon. Nearby Red Rock State Park and Slide Rock State Park (*see below*), both within 10 miles of Sedona, also offer many trekking opportunities.

Those who don't have the time or the inclination to get out of their cars for long won't lack for photo opportunities either. The drive out to the Enchantment Resort, in Boynton Canyon, is stunning; even if you're not staying there, consider stopping in for a scenic lunch or a late-afternoon drink. The views from the Chapel of the Holy Cross (*see below*) are also outstanding. Weather permitting, the Schnebly Hill Scenic Drive is another ooh-and-ah–inspiring option, and the vistas of the town from Airport Mesa at sunset can't be beat. Many of the most picturesque spots in Sedona are considered energy centers; vortex maps of the area are available at most of Sedona's New Age stores.

Although it's set in an area that was inhabited by Native Americans for centuries, the town of Sedona itself is very new—it wasn't incorporated until 1988—so there are few historical sights for visitors to peruse. The main activity here is shopping, mostly for Southwestern-style paintings, rugs, jewelry, and Native American artifacts. During the warmer months it makes sense to visit the air-conditioned shops at midday and save the hiking and Jeep tours for very early morning or late afternoon, when the light is softer and the heat less oppressive. The so-called **Uptown shopping area** is cut in half by Highway 89A; the stores in this area tend to cater primarily to the tour-bus trade. **Native & Nature** (248 N. Hwy. 89A, tel. 602/282–7870 is outstanding for its regional books and Southwest artifacts; at the end of the strip, **North Wind** (450 N. Hwy. 89A, tel. 602/282–6505) is a comfortable gallery that hosts some unusual Native American pieces.

Time Out The tiny **Sedona Coffee House & Bakery** (293 N. Hwy. 89A, tel. 602/282–2241) offers good home-baked breads, healthy sandwiches, and soups Uptown; most of the seating is outside. Nearby, you'll find the expected chili and nachos at the **Cowboy Club** (241 N. Hwy. 89A, tel. 602/282–4200)—along with more unusual western fare such as snake bites (breaded and fried pieces of rattlesnake meat) and stuffed corn cakes.

For more upscale shopping, drive less than a minute south to the attractive **Tlaquepaque** development (AZ 179, tel. 602/282–4838), where more than 100 artists, most of them painters and sculptors, sell their works. Prices tend to be high here; when asked how to pronounce the name of this shopping complex, locals joke that it's "to-lock-your-pocket." **Isadora** (tel. 602/282–6232) has beautiful handwoven jackets and shawls, and **Carusetta** (tel. 602/282–7793) showcases gold, silver, lapis, and turquoise jewelry; **Estaban's** (tel. 602/282–4686) focuses on ceramics. Some good bets for Southwestern art are **El Prado Galleries** (tel. 602/282–7390) and **Aguajito del Sol** (in the bell tower, tel. 602/282–5258).

A half-mile south of Tlaquepaque (take a right out of the parking lot), at the junction of AZ 179 and Schnebly Hill Road, a small strip of shops includes **Garland's Navajo Rugs** (tel. 602/282–4070), with its huge collection of new and antique carpets, as well as Native American kachina dolls, pottery, and baskets. Next door to Garland's, **Sedona Pottery** (tel. 602/282–1192) features unusual pieces, including life-size ceramic statues by shop owner Mary Margaret Sather.

The next cluster of shops you'll come to on the same side of the road is the **Hozho Center** (431 AZ 179, tel. 602/282–1038), a small, upscale complex set in a beige Santa Fe–style building. The center's **Lanning Gallery** (Bldg. A, tel. 602/282–6865) sells attractive Southwestern art and jewelry. Drive another minute or two south on AZ 179 and you'll come to the **Hillside Courtyard & Marketplace** (671 AZ 179, tel. 602/282–4500). Among the 23 shops and galleries, **Chula** (tel. 602/282–3899) carries a good selection of folk art from all over the world, and **Soderberg/Stevenson** (tel. 602/282–3818) specializes in Western sculpture. Across the street from Hillside, **Ratliff-Williams Gallery** (556 AZ 179, tel. 602/282–1404) has two floors of Southwestern art, much of it by not-yet-established artists; well-heeled buyers can find lots of fun, functional pieces.

You don't have to be religious to be inspired by the setting and the architecture of the **Chapel of the Holy Cross** (tel. 602/282–4069; look for the Chapel Road turnoff on AZ 179 about 2 mi south of the Hillside mall, then drive another mile to the top of the road). Built by Marguerite Brunwige Staude, a disciple of Frank Lloyd Wright, this striking modern structure, with a huge cross on the facade, rises between two red-rock peaks; the vistas of the town and the surrounding area are spectacular. There are no regular services, but visitors are welcome to come in daily 9–5 (9–6 in summer) for quiet meditation. A small gift shop sells religious articles and books.

Inveterate bargain hunters will want to continue south on AZ 179 for another 2 miles to the village of Oak Creek; at the **Oak Creek Factory Stores** (6657 S. AZ 179, tel. 602/284–2150), Corning/Revere, Mikasa, Anne Klein, Van Heusen, and many other manufacturers have factory outlets.

Two miles west of Sedona on Highway 89A, you'll come to the turnoff for the 286-acre **Red Rock State Park;** drive another 3 miles to enter one of the newest state parks in Arizona (opened in 1991), and one of the most beautiful. An ideal place to enjoy both the red-rock formations of the Sedona area and lovely Oak Creek, it's also a less crowded alternative to the popular Slide Rock State Park (*see below*). The five park trails (all fairly easy and short—the longest is 1.9 miles) are well marked and provide beautiful vistas. One trail leads to the House of Apache Fire, an unfinished residence started in 1946 by the former owners of the land, Jack and Helen Fry. (He was president of TWA.) You can enter the house only on ranger-led tours, offered daily; birdwatching tours and nature walks are also given every day, weather permitting. *Box 3864, West Sedona 86340, tel. 602/282–6907. Admission: $5 per car. Open daily 8–5 winter, 8–6 spring, 8–7 summer.*

Other Area Attractions Whether you want to swim, hike, picnic, or enjoy beautiful scenery framed through a car window, head north on U.S. 89A through the wooded **Oak Creek Canyon.** This is the most attractive route to Flagstaff and the Grand Canyon. Although the forest is primarily evergreen, there are enough changing colors in the fall to make the view especially glorious then. The road winds through a steep-walled canyon, and visitors crane their necks for views of the dramatic rock formations above. Oak Creek, which runs along the bottom of the canyon, is lined with tent campgrounds, fishing camps, cabins, motels, and restaurants.

❽ Look for **Slide Rock State Park** on your left, 7 miles north of Sedona. It's a good place for a picnic and a hike back into the forest. On a hot day, you can plunge down a natural rock slide into a swimming hole—a delightful experience. (Bring an extra pair of jeans to wear on the slide.) About 3 miles farther north is the popular West Fork Trail, which follows a creek where you can cool off in summer. The only downside to this trip is the traffic, particularly on summer weekends. *Box 10358, Sedona 86339, tel. 602/282–3034. Admission: $3 per car Oct.–Mar., $5 per car Apr.–Sept. Open daily 8–5 winter, 8–6 spring, 8–7 summer.*

Flagstaff and Environs

Few visitors slow down long enough to explore Flagstaff, a town of 42,000, known locally as "Flag"; most stop only to spend the night at one of the town's many motels before making the last leg of the trip to the Grand Canyon, 80 miles north. But the city, set against a lovely backdrop of pine forests and the snowcapped

San Francisco Peaks, retains a frontier flavor downtown and is home to several attractions, including the excellent Museum of Northern Arizona, the Riordan mansion, and the Lowell Observatory. Festivals celebrating summer often fill Flagstaff's streets with parades and its sidewalks with Native American art exhibits and crafts sales.

Flagstaff has more fast-food outlets per permanent resident than most cities do, no doubt because of the incredible demand for it: Two major interstate highways crisscross the town; thousands of tourists drive through on the way to the Grand Canyon; thousands of students attending Northern Arizona University reside here; and many Native Americans come in from nearby reservations. The city is also packed with motels, although there are no major hotels or resorts. Traffic to the Grand Canyon is heavy all year, but in the summertime it skyrockets, increasing the number of overnight visitors. During that time of year, the streets are also filled with Phoenix residents seeking relief from the desert heat.

Phoenicians also come to Flagstaff in winter to ski at the Arizona Snowbowl, a small ski resort about 15 miles northeast of town among the San Francisco Peaks. Accommodation rates are low at this time of year, making winter visits an excellent option for downhill and cross-country enthusiasts. At any time of the year, temperatures in Flagstaff are approximately 20°F cooler than in Phoenix. It's wise to reserve a room ahead of time in Flagstaff, and during the summer months, it's essential.

Central Flagstaff *Numbers in the margin correspond to points of interest on the Flagstaff map.*

The **downtown historic district** offers a glimpse of Flagstaff in its prime, with some excellent examples of late Victorian and early Art Deco architecture. Allowed to become somewhat seedy over the years, downtown is currently undergoing a major restoration under the auspices of the national Main Street organization. A walking-tour map of the area, prepared by the Arizona Historical Society, is available at the **Visitors Center** (*see* Important Addresses and Numbers, *above*), now in the Tudor Revival–style Santa Fe Depot and an excellent place to begin the tour. Highlights include the Monte Vista Hotel (*see* Lodging, *below*) and the gabled-roof Orpheum Theatre. You may notice a lot of structures that bear the name Babbitt, after one of Flagstaff's wealthiest founding families. Former Arizona governor and current Secretary of the Interior Bruce Babbitt is just the latest member of the family to wield power and influence. This is also the part of town in which the most interesting shops are concentrated (*see* Shopping, *below*); it's fun to stroll around the area and poke around in stores selling everything from sporting goods to Native American crafts.

Time Out Chili-pepper strings, a neon cactus, and a pastel mural all add to the upbeat atmosphere at **Café Olé** (119 S. San Francisco St., tel. 602/774–8272), a tiny, family-run restaurant. Vegetarian green-chile-and-cheese tamales are among the Mexican special-

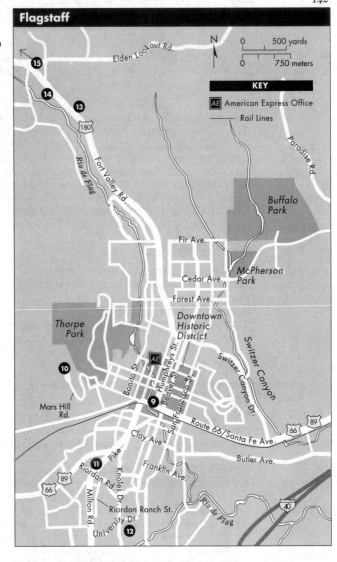

Flagstaff

KEY

AE American Express Office

Rail Lines

ties here. Part art gallery, part bakery, and totally hip, **Café
Express** (16 N. San Francisco St., tel. 602/774–0541) serves up
heaping portions of tasty food that's good for you: Mediterranean salads, tempeh burgers, pita pizzas, and (maybe-not-so-
healthy) chocolate-chip cookies.

10 To reach **Lowell Observatory**, less than 2 miles from downtown,
drive west on Route 66 (which resumes its former name, Santa
Fe Avenue, before it merges into Mars Hill Road). This scientific
institution was founded in 1894 by Boston businessman, author,
and scientist Percival Lowell, who studied the planet Mars from
here. His predictions of the existence of a ninth planet led to the

discovery of Pluto at Lowell in 1930 by Clyde Tombaugh. V. M. Slipher's observations here between 1912 and 1920 led to the theory of the expanding universe.

A new 6,500-square-foot visitor center, opened in 1994, hosts exhibits, a lecture hall, and a gift shop; a "Tools of the Astronomer" display explains what professional stargazers do. During the day, the staff welcomes guests and offers slide lectures and tours, including a look at the 24-inch Clark telescope. Hours change every month, so call when you're in town, or when you know on what date you plan to visit. There are several interactive exhibits (simple, but interesting) for children, who will especially enjoy the Pluto Walk, a scaled-down version of our solar system that is designed for exploring.

On different evenings every month except January, weather permitting, the public is invited to peer through the telescope. The greatest number of viewings (four a week) are offered from June through August; again, call ahead for a schedule. The observatory dome is open and unheated—any change in temperature would affect the telescope lens—so dress for an outdoor rather than an indoor activity. *1400 W. Mars Hill Rd., tel. 602/ 774–2096. Admission: $2.50 adults, $1 children 6–18. Hours vary, so call ahead.*

⓫ A unique artifact of Flagstaff's logging heyday, **Riordan State Historic Park,** near Northern Arizona University, is a must-see. Its centerpiece is a mansion built in 1904 for Michael and Timothy Riordan, lumber-baron brothers who married two sisters. The 13,300-square-foot, 40-room log-and-stone structure—designed by Charles Whittlesley, who was also responsible for the El Tovar Hotel at the Grand Canyon—contains a good deal of furniture by Gustav Stickley, father of the American Arts and Crafts design movement. Fascinating details abound; one room holds "Paul Bunyan's shoes," a two-foot-long pair of boots made by Timothy in his workshop. Everything on display—from books to family photos and clothes—is original to the house, half of which was occupied by members of the family until 1986. The mansion may be explored on a guided tour only. Special evening tours given during Halloween week are very popular; they're limited to groups of 20, so book at least a month in advance if you want to be spooked. *1300 Riordan Ranch St., tel. 602/779–4395. Admission: $3 adults, $2 children 12–17. Park open mid-May– mid-Sept. daily 8–5, with tours at 9, 10, 11, 1, 2, 3, and 4; mid-Sept.–mid-May, daily 12:30–5, with tours at 1, 2, 3, and 4. Closed Dec. 24 and 25.*

⓬ Riordan State Park lies near **Northern Arizona University.** Go two blocks south on Milton Road, then make a left onto University Drive. After about ½ mile, turn right on San Francisco Street and continue to the university's **observatory.** The observatory and 24-inch telescope were built in 1952 by Dr. Arthur Adel, who had been a scientist at Lowell Observatory until he joined the college faculty as a professor of mathematics. His work on infrared astronomy pioneered research into molecules that absorb light passing through the Earth's atmosphere. Today's studies of our planet's shrinking ozone layer rely on some of Dr. Adel's early work. Visitors to the observatory—which houses one of the largest telescopes that the public is allowed to move and manipulate—are usually hosted by friendly students and faculty members of the university's Department of Physics and Astronomy.

Public viewings take place every clear Friday night from 7:30 PM to 10 PM. Tours for individuals and small groups can be arranged any day except Friday by calling at least 24 hours in advance. *Northern Arizona Campus Observatory, c/o Dept. of Physics and Astronomy, S. San Francisco St., tel. 602/523–7170. Admission free.*

Flagstaff Museums and the Arizona Snowbowl In a wooded residential section at the northwest end of town, the Pioneer Historical Museum, Coconino Center for the Arts, and the Museum of Northern Arizona give visitors an introduction to the natural and cultural history of the area. They're all on the way to the Arizona Snowbowl, which is worth visiting even in the summertime, when a ski lift to the top of the San Francisco Peaks affords marvelous views of the area.

From downtown, drive north on Humphreys Street, which turns into U.S. 180 after veering a block to the left. Once you're on U.S. 180, you'll soon see a large brown sign on the right-hand side of the road for the Pioneer Historical Museum and the Coconino Center for the Arts.

The first building as you enter the Fort Valley Park complex is **⑬** the **Pioneer Historical Museum,** operated by the Arizona Historical Society in a volcanic rock building constructed in 1908—Coconino County's first hospital for the poor. You can still see one of the depressingly small patients' rooms, an old iron lung, and a reconstructed doctor's office, but most of the displays touch on more cheerful aspects of Flagstaff history—for example, road signs and children's toys. The museum hosts a folk-crafts festival on the Fourth of July, where you can watch traditional tradespeople, such as blacksmiths, weavers, spinners, quilters, and candle makers, at work. Their crafts, and those of other local artisans, are sold in the museum's gift shop, a tiny space filled with teddy bears, dolls, hand-dipped candles, and hand-stitched quilts. *2340 N. Fort Valley Rd., tel. 602/774–6272. Suggested donation: $1 per individual, $3 per family. Open Mon.–Sat. 9–5.*

Walk a few hundred feet up a gentle hill to reach the **Coconino Center for the Arts,** a nonprofit community center that puts on two major annual arts-and-crafts festivals (*see* the Arts and Nightlife, *below*) and hosts exhibits, performing arts events, and educational programs throughout the year. A gallery features the work of local artists, from photographers to sculptors and lithographers, on a rotating basis; write or phone for a calendar of events. Warning: The gift shop, filled with handcrafted jewelry, pottery, and posters by featured artists, can be detrimental to your pocketbook. All proceeds go to the center, though, so you're shopping for a worthy cause—and there's no tax on your purchases. *2300 N. Fort Valley Rd., Box 296, Flagstaff 86002, tel. 602/779–6921. Admission free. Open Apr.–Sept., Tues.–Sun. 10–5; Oct.–Mar., Tues.–Sat. 10–5. Closed Easter, Thanksgiving, and Dec. 24–Jan. 6.*

When you leave the complex, turn right out of the parking lot and drive 1 mile northwest on U.S. 180; on your left you'll see the ⓮ **Museum of Northern Arizona,** a large stone building shaded with trees. Founded in 1928, the museum is now respected worldwide for its research and for its collections centering on the natural and cultural history of the Colorado Plateau; only 1% of its vast holdings on the archaeology, ethnology, geology, biology, and fine arts of the region is on display at any given time. Among the permanent exhibitions are an extensive collection of Navajo rugs as well as an authentic Hopi kiva (men's ceremonial chamber). Every summer, the museum hosts exhibits and sales by Native American artists, whose wares are also sold in the museum gift shop (*see* The Arts in Arts and Nightlife, *below*).

Two interesting outdoor features are a life-zone exhibit, which shows the changing vegetation in the area from the bottom of the Grand Canyon to the highest peak in Flagstaff (the equivalent of a trip from Mexico to Canada), and a nature trail that heads down across a small stream into a canyon and up into an aspen grove (open only in summer).

Two galleries—one devoted to the biology and the other to the geology of the area—opened in 1992. The latter includes a cast of the dilophosaurus; this medium-size carnivorous dinosaur, unique to northern Arizona, roamed the area back when much of it was swampland.

The museum is not particularly child-oriented, but both of the above galleries include some hands-on displays. Docent-led tours are available for individuals or groups, but appointments must be made at least two weeks in advance. In addition, the museum's education department sponsors excellent tours of the area and some as far away as New Mexico and California (*see* Guided Tours in Essential Information, *above*). *3001 N. Fort Valley Rd., tel. 602/774–5213. Admission: $4 adults, $3 senior citizens over 55, $2 children and students under 21. Open daily 9–5. Closed major holidays.*

Five miles farther along the same road is the turnoff for the ⓯ **Arizona Snowbowl.** The Fort Valley Lodge to the right is a good place to stop for groceries and clean rest rooms, as well as for information about skiing and other recreational opportunities at the Snowbowl; it's open in the daytime only. If there's a crowd visiting the ski area or a recent heavy snow that makes travel difficult, park here and ride the shuttle to the top; it runs continuously and costs $5 per person round-trip.

After you leave U.S. 180, it's another 7 paved miles on Snowbowl Road to the **Arizona Snowbowl Skyride,** which takes you through the Coconino National Forest to a height of 11,500 feet in 25 minutes. From this vantage point, you can see up to 70 miles; views include the North Rim of the Grand Canyon.

There's a lodge nearby with a restaurant and bar. *Tel. 602/779–1951. Tickets: $8 adults, $6 senior citizens over 64, $4.50 children 6–12. Group discounts are available. The ride operates daily mid-June–Labor Day, weekends only (weather permitting) Labor Day–mid-Oct. Operating hours and prices may change, so call before you go.*

There is plenty of **hiking** here in Arizona's alpine tundra, where more than 80 species of plants grow on the upper elevations of the San Francisco Peaks. The habitat is fragile, so hikers are asked to stay on established trails (and there are lots of them). The Humphreys Peak Trail is 9 miles round-trip, with a vertical climb of 3,133 feet to the summit of Arizona's highest mountain (12,633 feet). Those who don't want a long hike will be well rewarded if they do just the first mile of the 8-mile-long Kachina Trail; completely flat, this route is surrounded by huge stands of aspen and offers fantastic vistas. It's particularly worthwhile in fall, when the changing leaves paint the landscape shades of yellow, russet, and amber. All trails are well marked and maintained by the **Coconino National Forest** (tel. 602/527–3600). The altitude here will make even the hardiest hikers breathe a little harder, so individuals with cardiac or respiratory problems should be cautious of overexertion.

In winter the Arizona Snowbowl offers an average of 250 inches of snow and 32 trails of varying difficulty (30% beginner, 40% intermediate, and 30% advanced) for **skiing.** Enthusiasts who favor the challenging slopes of Colorado's Rockies might find the Snowbowl a bit disappointing, but it's just fine for skiers of beginning or moderate ability. Senior citizens age 65 and older pay only $8, and children 7 and younger ski for free; all-day lift tickets for adults run $29. Half-day discounts are available, and group-lesson packages (including two hours of instruction, an all-day lift ticket, and equipment rental) are a good buy at $45. Many Flagstaff motels offer ski packages, including transportation to the Snowbowl. Write or call the Arizona Snowbowl Ski Area (Box 40, Flagstaff 86002, tel. 602/779–1950 or 800/828–7285) for more information. For the current snow report, call 602/779–4577.

East of Flagstaff *Numbers in the margin correspond to points of interest on the North-Central Arizona map.*

The area east of Flagstaff is often overlooked by visitors to the region because there's little, regardless of beauty or historical significance, that can compete with the Grand Canyon. But traveling east has its unique rewards. If you don't have enough time to do everything, opt for taking the quick drive to Walnut Canyon—only about 15 minutes out of town—and staying in this lovely spot for as long as you can.

16 **Walnut Canyon National Monument** is 7½ miles east of Flagstaff (exit 204 off I–40), then 3 miles south. Towering Douglas firs, piñon pines, and alligator juniper trees keep the area green— hundreds of shades of green—year-round; the canyon is especially beautiful on a snowy winter day.

The Sinagua Indians (possibly ancestors of today's Pueblo Indians) lived and farmed the area starting in approximately AD 800. They vanished around 1250; archaeologists have speculated that they left because of a drought—the name Sinagua means "without water"—or because invaders chased them out. The more than 300 cliff dwellings abandoned by the Sinagua were discovered in 1883 by Mormon settlers from Utah, who regarded the ruins as curiosities but nothing more.

You can see many of the cliff dwellings at close range—a number of them in near-perfect condition—by descending 185 feet by way of the mile-long stepped Island Trail, which starts at the visitor center. The dwellings are in such good condition because they were carefully constructed under the protection of overhanging cliffs, because the weather here is dry and temperate, and because visitors are forbidden to enter them. The Island Trail, which closes one hour before the park closes, takes about an hour to complete. Those with health problems should opt for the easier Rim Trail (a ½-mile route that most people can complete in about a half-hour), which takes visitors past several overlooks from which the dwellings can be viewed, as well as an excavated and reconstructed pit house. Attractive picnic areas dot the grounds and line the roads leading to the park. Park service guides conduct tours daily in summer and on weekends in winter. *Walnut Canyon Rd., tel. 602/526–3367. Admission: $2 per person entering by bus or bicycle, $4 per car. Open Labor Day–Memorial Day, daily 7–6; off-season, daily 8–5.*

⓱ To reach **Meteor Crater** from Walnut Canyon, drive about 33 miles farther east on I–40, get off at Exit 233, then go 6 miles south on Meteor Crater Road. This natural phenomenon, set in a privately owned and run park, is impressive if for no other reason than its sheer size. A hole in the ground 600 feet deep, nearly a mile across, and more than 3 miles in circumference, Meteor Crater is large enough to accommodate the Washington Monument or 20 football fields. It was created when a meteorite came hurtling through space at a speed of 43,000 miles per hour and crashed here some 49,000 years ago. The area looks so much like the surface of the moon that NASA made it one of the official training sites for the *Apollo* astronauts.

Visitors can't descend into the crater because of the efforts of its owners to maintain its excellent condition—scientists consider this to be the best-preserved crater on Earth—but a 3-mile rim trail gives visitors a bird's-eye view of the hole. Two short, rather corny films, which play every half-hour, detail the history of the crater and of astronaut training here. A small snack bar sells soft drinks, coffee, and sandwiches. Rock hounds will enjoy the Lapidary Shop, filled with raw specimens from the area as well as with jewelry made from native stones. *Meteor Crater Rd., tel. 602/289–2362. For information, write or call administrative offices, 603 N. Beaver St., Suite C, Flagstaff 86001, tel. 602/774–8350. Admission: $7 adults, $6 senior citizens 65 and over, $4 students, $2 children 13–17, $1 children 6–12. Open May 16–Sept. 14, daily 6–6; Sept. 15–May 15, daily 8–5.*

San North of Flagstaff, the San Francisco Volcanic Field encom-
Francisco passes 2,000 square miles of fascinating geological phenome-
Volcanic na—the San Francisco Peaks themselves, some of which soar to
Field almost 13,000 feet; ancient volcanoes; cinder cones; and valleys
carved by water and ice—as well as some of the most extensive
Native American ruins in the Southwest. If you have any time at
all, don't miss Sunset Crater and Wupatki; these national monuments are not only extremely interesting but can be explored in
relative solitude during a large part of the year. The area is
short on services, so fill up on gas and consider taking along a
picnic; there are plenty of lovely spots for lunch along the way. A
good source for hiking and camping information in this area is
the Peaks Ranger Station (5010 N. U.S. 89, tel. 602/526–0866).

⑱ To get to **Sunset Crater Volcano National Monument,** take Santa
Fe Avenue east of Flagstaff to U.S. 89, and drive north for about
20 miles. Turn right onto the road marked Sunset Crater—it's
another 2 miles from here to the visitor center.

Sunset Crater, a cinder cone that rises some 1,000 feet into the
air, was an active volcano 900 years ago. The final eruption contained iron and sulfur, which gives the rim of the crater its glow
and thus its name, Sunset. You can walk around the base, but
you can't descend into the huge but fragile cone. If you take the
Lava Flow Trail, a half-hour, mile-long self-guided walk, you'll
have a good view of the evidence of the volcano's fiery power:
lava formations and holes in the rock where volcanic gases
vented to the surface. Three smaller cones to the southeast were
formed at the same time, and along the same fissure, as Sunset
Crater.

If you're interested in hiking a volcano, head to **Lenox Crater,**
about a mile east of the visitor center. It's 280 feet to the top of
the cinder cone. Wear closed, sturdy shoes if you plan to do this;
the cinder is soft and crumbly, without vegetation. From
O'Leary Peak, 5 miles from the visitor center on Forest Route
545A (an unpaved but decent road), there are great views of the
San Francisco Peaks, the Painted Desert, and beyond. *HC 33,
Box 4441, Flagstaff 86004, tel. 602/556–7042. Admission: $4 per
car, $2 to enter on foot or by nonmotorized vehicle; fees include
admission into Wupatki National Monument (see below). Open
daily 8–6 Memorial Day–Labor Day, 8–5 the rest of the year.*

Drive 20 miles north of the Sunset Crater visitor center along
⑲ AZ 545 to get to the entrance of **Wupatki National Monument.**
En route, parts of the Painted Desert are visible in the distance;
the immediately surrounding landscape is starkly beautiful,
without much vegetation. In summer, rangers give interpretive
lectures on the history of the region.

Some 2,700 identified sites contain archaeological evidence of
Native American settlement in this area. Families from the
Sinagua, Anasazi, and perhaps other cultures are believed to
have lived together in harmony here, farming and trading with
one another and with others who passed through their "city."
The eruption of Sunset Crater, 20 miles away, may have caused

migration to this area—and may have disrupted the settlement more than once around 1064. The earliest inhabitants are believed to have settled here around AD 600, and some anthropologists think the last of them had abandoned the land by about AD 1300 because of a drought; others conjecture that poor soil conservation or social unrest may have led to the desertion of the pueblo.

The site for which the national monument was named, the **Wupatki**, originally three stories high, was built above a system of unexplored natural caves. The structure had almost 100 rooms and a large, open ball court, which was probably the site of religious ceremonies. Next to the ball court is a blowhole, a geologic phenomenon in which air is forced upward by underground pressure; scientists speculate that early inhabitants may have attached some spiritual significance to the many blowholes in the region.

Although there are extensive, easily viewed remnants of Native American settlements at Wupatki National Monument, most of them are closed to casual visitors. Many are being studied by professional archaeologists (the park service can provide information on these research projects). Permits are available from the park service for limited access beyond the open areas, but rules regarding entering closed sites are strictly enforced.
If you are interested in an in-depth tour of the area, consider taking a ranger-led overnight hike to the **Crack-in-the-Rock Ruin.** The 14-mile trek (round-trip) covers areas marked by ancient petroglyphs and dotted with well-preserved ruins. The cost is $25; anyone who is interested should contact the rangers for details. There are a limited number of trips, conducted in April and October; it's best to call in February and August if you'd like to take part in the lottery for one of the 100 available places on these hikes. *HC 33, Box 444A, Flagstaff 86004, tel. 602/556–7040. Admission (collected at Sunset Crater): $4 per car, $2 to enter by foot or nonmotorized vehicle. Open Oct. 1– May 31, daily 8–5, June 1–Sept. 30, daily 8–6.*

The archaeological site in the park closest to U.S. 89 (the most direct route back to Flagstaff) is the **Citadel Ruin,** a pueblo that sits on a knoll above a limestone sink. It's 9 miles northwest of the visitor center on the main loop road. Between the Wupatki and Citadel ruins, the **Doney cinder hole** affords 360° views of the Painted Desert and the San Francisco Volcanic Fields. It's a perfect spot for a sunset picnic.

What to See and Do with Children

Small children should enjoy the **Grand Canyon Deer Farm,** 25 miles west of Flagstaff on I–40, at Exit 171 (8 miles east of Williams). Visitors can pet and feed the deer, including the tiny fawns born every June and July. There are also pygmy goats, llamas, and other animals to pet. *105 Deer Farm Rd., Williams 86046, tel. 602/635–4073. Admission: $4.75 adults, $3.50 senior citizens over 62, $2.50 children 3–13. Open Mar.–May, daily 9–*

dusk; June–Aug., daily 8–dusk; Sept.–Oct., daily 9–dusk; Nov.–Feb., daily 10–5 if the weather is good. Closed Thanksgiving and Christmas.

Anglers young and old will enjoy the sure catch at the **Rainbow Trout Farm**. For $1 you'll get a cane pole with a hook and bait. There's a charge for every fish you catch: $3 for anything under 10 inches, $3.50 for 10–13-inchers, and another 50¢ an inch for everything bigger. The real bargain is that the staff will clean your fish for 50¢ each and pack them in ice for you. *3 mi north of Sedona on Hwy. 89A, tel. 602/282–3379. Open weekdays 9–5, weekends 8–6; summer, daily 8–7, weather permitting.*

Youngsters will love the plunge down the **natural rock slide** into the water at Slide Rock State Park in Oak Creek Canyon (*see* Sedona and Environs, *above*).

School-age children will be impressed by **Meteor Crater** (*see* Flagstaff and Environs, *above*). All ages enjoy **Jeep tours** in Sedona (*see* Special-Interest Tours in Essential Information, *above*). The **train from Clarkdale** (*see* Sedona and Environs, *above*) also keeps children entertained.

Shopping

Flagstaff

Downtown is Flagstaff's prime shopping area; even if you're not looking for anything in particular, it's fun to stroll along San Francisco Street and along Route 66, where most of the interesting shops—many in historic buildings—are concentrated. **The Carriage House** (413 N. San Francisco St., tel. 602/774–1337) is a collection of 19 antiques shops that offer old clothes, furniture, fine china, and jewelry. The **Old Highway Trading Post** (698 E. Rte. 66, tel. 602/774–0035) also brings together a number of purveyors of advertising art, jewelry, clothing, and other collectibles. For fine arts and crafts—everything from ceramics and stained glass to weaving and painting—visit **The Artists Gallery** (17 N. San Francisco St., tel. 602/773–0985), a cooperative that carries the work of more than 30 local artists. **Old Town Gallery** (2 W. Rte. 66, tel. 602/774–7770), owned by anthropologist Bruce Hudgens, features fine art and Native American jewelry. **Crystal Magic** (5 N. San Francisco St., tel. 602/779–2528) sells New Age books, records, tapes, and crystals. **McGaugh's Newsstand** (24 N. San Francisco St., tel. 602/774–2131) is the place to come for international newspapers and books on any topic you can think of; even nonsmokers will enjoy the aroma of the pipe tobacco sold in the back. Don't worry if you've come to town without all your hiking supplies; at **The Edge** (12 E. Aspen Ave., tel. 602/774–4775) you can pick up any sporting-goods items you might be missing.

The **Coconino Arts Center** gift shop (*see* Flagstaff Museums and the Arizona Snowbowl, *above*) carries high-quality art posters and crafts.

The **Flagstaff Mall** (4650 N. U.S. 89, tel. 602/526–4827) is just east of town off Exit 201 of I–40. Small by most standards, this mall has the greatest number of department and specialty stores in the area, including Dillards, Sears, and JC Penney; a huge Target store has just opened here. It's a good place for travelers who need camping gear, car-repair items, or warm clothing to cope with the area's cool nights.

Jerome

Shoppers in Jerome will find a variety of boutiques in houses perched precariously on the side of Cleopatra Hill. The town has its share of art galleries, but they're likely to be a bit more on the funky side than the ones you'll find in Sedona. An exception is the **Anderson-Mandette Art Studios** (Old Mingus High School, Bldg. C, tel. 602/634–3438). Robin Anderson and Margo Mandette made the building their workplace in 1978; at almost 20,000 square feet, it is considered by many to be the largest private art studio and gallery in the United States. The gallery is open Thurs.–Tues. 11–6; guided tours are available on request. Shopping is easy in Jerome; all you need to do is stroll up and down Main Street. Your eyes may begin to glaze over after browsing one boutique after another, each offering tasteful Southwestern goods. At the bottom of Main, **Aurum** (tel. 602/634–3330) carries lovely imported and locally made jewelry, much of it silver. Next door, you'll be drawn in by the bright patterns and attractively styled women's clothing of **Designs on You** (tel. 602/634–7879). Farther up the hill, **Sky Fire** (tel. 602/634–8081) has two floors of items to adorn your person and your house, ranging from wrapping paper and confetti to a $1,000 fabric bench in the shape of an iguana. **Nellie Bly** (tel. 602/634–0255) offers a wide range of kaleidoscopes in addition to a good selection of silver jewelry.

Sedona

See Exploring Sedona, *above.*

Sports and the Outdoors

Biking A map of the Urban Trails System, available at the Flagstaff Visitors Center (*see* Important Address and Telephone Numbers, *above*), details biking and hiking options in the area.

Camping There are more than 50 campgrounds in the Flagstaff, Sedona, and Jerome areas. The best way to learn about them is to consult the *Arizona Camping and Campgrounds Guide*, available from the **Arizona Office of Tourism** (*see* Chapter 1, Essential Information).

In **Coconino National Forest,** near Flagstaff (ranger's tel. 602/527–3600), the campgrounds near Mormon Lake and Lake Mary—including Pinegrove, Lakeview, Forked Pine, Double

Springs, and Dairy Springs—are popular to the point of over-crowding in summer.

Campgrounds close to **Sedona** often fill up in the summertime, especially those along Oak Creek in Oak Creek Canyon; two good places to try are Manzanita and Banjo Bill (ranger's tel. 602/282–4119).

Jerome's campgrounds are generally less crowded. Try Jerome State Historic Park (tel. 602/634–5381) or Mingus Mountain and Potato Patch (tel. 602/634–8851).

If you're camping in winter, remember that this area gets quite cold, with frequent snowstorms. In summer, night tempera-tures can dip to the 40s, while daytime temperatures can reach 90°F.

Golf In addition to the many private clubs in the Flagstaff–Sedona area, golfers will find semiprivate courses, which accept a lim-ited number of nonmembers, as well as public courses. Among the recommended ones in the **Flagstaff** vicinity are the Fairfield Flagstaff resort's **Elden Hills Country Club** (2380 N. Oakmont Dr., Flagstaff, 602/526–5125), a public course, and **Pinewood Country Club** (395 E. Pinewood Blvd., Munds Park, tel. 602/ 286–1110), which is semiprivate. In the **Sedona** area, the **Oak Creek Country Club** (690 Bell Rock Blvd., Sedona, tel. 602/284–1660) is a good semiprivate option. The public is also welcome at the **Sedona Golf Resort** (7260 Hwy. 179, Oak Creek, tel. 602/ 284–9355), where the 18-hole course was designed by Gary Panks.

Hiking Hikers will find an abundance of trails all across the region. In **Sedona,** contact the **Sedona Ranger District** office (250 Brewer Rd., tel. 602/282–4119) for detailed hiking maps. Just **north of Flagstaff,** but still in town, the **Peaks Ranger Station** (5075 N. U.S. 89, tel. 602/527–3630) also has excellent hiking and recrea-tional guides. Around Mormon Lake, **south of Flagstaff,** the **Happy Jack Ranger Station** (Forest Hwy. 3, Happy Jack, tel. 602/527–7371) provides information about treks in the area. The **Verde Ranger District** office of the **Prescott National Forest** (Gen-eral Crook Trail, Camp Verde, tel. 602/567–4121) is a good re-source for places to hike—as well as to fish and boat—along the Verde River. The **Coconino National Forest** north and east of Camp Verde is mapped by the **Beaver Creek Ranger District** (Forest Service Rd. 618, Rimrock, tel. 602/567–4501). (*See* Red Rock State Park and the Arizona Snowbowl in Exploring, *above*, for other hiking options.)

Horseback Spring, summer, and fall are the best times of the year to ride in **Riding** this area. In **Flagstaff,** the wranglers at **Hitchin' Post Stables** (Box 448, Lake Mary Rd., tel. 602/774–1719 or 602/774–7131) lead rides into Walnut Canyon as well as horseback or horse drawn–wagon rides with sunset barbecues. In **Sedona, Kachina Riding Stable** (5 J La., Lower Red Rock Loop Rd., West Sedona, tel. 602/282–7252) offers a package that includes an Oak Creek swim and a picnic lunch. Weight limit for riders is 225 pounds.

Skiing The ski season usually starts in mid-November and ends in mid-April. A good option for downhill skiers is the **Arizona Snowbowl** (*see* Flagstaff and Environs in Exploring, *above*). Cross-country skiers can find well-groomed trails in several places around Flagstaff, among them **Mormon Lake Ski Center** (21 mi southeast of Flagstaff by way of Lake Mary Rd., Mormon Lake, tel. 602/354–2240) and **Montezuma Nordic Ski Center** (just north of Mormon Lake, tel. 602/354–2220).

Dining and Lodging

When it comes to lodging, Flagstaff and Sedona are like Jack Sprat and his wife: Flagstaff has very little in the way of fat, while Sedona offers practically nothing lean. You'll find many comfortable motels in Flagstaff (all the familiar U.S. chains are represented here) but no real luxury; there are stunning settings and outstanding amenities in Sedona but few bargains.

Prices in Flagstaff are highest in summer; those in Sedona tend to stay pretty much the same year-round. There aren't many hotel rooms in tiny Jerome; if you think you might want to spend the night there, be sure to book in advance. Dining choices in Flagstaff and Sedona are much more evenly balanced than lodging options. Though many places in Flagstaff are of the fast-food or down-home variety, you won't have trouble finding a nice, elegant meal in town. And although many Sedona eateries tend toward the upscale, a number of good, low-key places can be found. By city ordinance, all the restaurants in Flagstaff are nosmoking. Note: A number of Sedona restaurants close for stretches in January and February; be sure to call ahead during those months.

Dining Highly recommended restaurants are indicated by a star ★.

Category	Cost*
$$$$	over $35
$$$	$25–$35
$$	$15–$25
$	under $15

per person, excluding drinks, service, and sales tax (6% in Flagstaff, 7% in Sedona)

Lodging Highly recommended lodgings are indicated by a star ★.

Category	Cost*
$$$$	over $140
$$$	$100–$140

$$	$60–$100
$	under $60

All prices are for a standard double room in high (summer) season, excluding room tax (8% in Flagstaff, 10½% in Sedona).

Flagstaff

Dining **Chez Marc Bistro.** This classic French restaurant, run by the Cannes-born former head chef of L'Auberge de Sedona resort, is set in a restored mansion, built in 1911 by the influential Babbitt family. In three pretty Country French–style dining rooms you can enjoy such entrées as blackened *ahi* tuna atop pink and green lentils or roast quail with elephant garlic and lobster mushrooms. The setting is romantic and the food generally fine, but don't expect the sophisticated service or attention to culinary detail you'd find in a major city. *503 Humphreys St., tel. 602/774–1343. Reservations advised. Dress: casual but neat. AE, D, DC, MC, V. Closed Sun. $$–$$$*

★ **Brix Grill & Wine Bar.** Tucked away in a nondescript strip mall near the university, Brix is probably the most interesting new restaurant in town. Innovative Southwestern cuisine and a nice selection of wines by the glass are served in an appropriately pared-down (but comfortable) room. Entrées, which change daily, might include grilled polenta with hazelnut pesto and mozzarella, or New Zealand rack of lamb with rosemary and red-wine sauce; everything, including the excellent breads and desserts, is prepared on the premises. Service can be a bit erratic, but it's always friendly. *801 S. Milton Rd., tel. 602/779–5117. Dress: casual but neat. AE, DC, MC, V. $$*

Cottage Place. Another unexpectedly elegant spot in a town known for hearty food and drive-through service, this cozy restaurant in a 50-year old cottage has intimate dining rooms decorated in Country French style. The menu focuses on classic Continental cuisine, with many innovative touches. Dishes range from Turkish-style braised lamb casserole with rice pilaf to grilled polenta layered with fresh vegetables and baked with Cheddar cheese. The mushrooms stuffed with herbed sausage and nuts make a wonderful starter, but dinners include both soup and salad, and you'll want to save room for the excellent desserts. *126 W. Cottage Ave., tel. 602/774–8431. Reservations advised. Dress: casual but neat. AE, MC, V. Dinner only, closed Mon. $$*

Horsemen Lodge & Restaurant. Three miles north of Flagstaff Mall, in a ranch-style stone building decorated with hunting trophies (the furry kind that stare at you during dinner), this restaurant is very "Flagstaff," reflecting the blend of Native American and frontier cultures that shaped the area. The knotty-pine beams and huge stone fireplace make this a perfect place to spend a snowy evening. The menu emphasizes traditional American fare, prepared without pretense for the hearty appetite. *8500 N. U.S. 89, tel. 602/526–2655. Reservations advised. Dress: casual but neat. MC, V. Dinner only, closed Sun. $$*

★ **Sakura Restaurant.** The oddness of finding a good sushi bar in Flagstaff is compounded by the fact that the only other entrées available at Sakura are prepared *teppan* (Japanese grill) style. If your dining companion doesn't like raw fish, you'll be eating yours at a large table to the accompaniment of a grill chef's pyrotechnics. That said, the fish, flown in every other day from the West Coast, is excellent; the spicy sushi-style tuna salad will knock your socks off. And even if you haven't set foot in a Benihana's in years, you'll probably enjoy the well-seasoned, large portions of steak or seafood with vegetables being flipped around in front of you. *1175 W. Hwy. 66, tel. 602/773–9118. Reservations accepted. Dress: casual. AE, D, DC, MC, V. Closed Sun. lunch. $$*

Buster's Restaurant. At lunchtime, families and students from nearby Arizona State University (ASU) frequent the comfortable booths and tables of this popular restaurant. The menu is varied—fresh seafood, homemade soups, salads, giant burgers, and mesquite-grilled steaks. Try the *lahvosh* appetizer—a giant cracker heaped with a choice of toppings ranging from smoked salmon to mushrooms—or the Caesar salad with grilled Cajun chicken. Upscale single professionals and skiers crowd the bar at night. *1800 S. Milton Rd., tel. 602/774–5155. Reservations advised. Dress: casual. AE, D, DC, MC, V. $–$$*

Pasto. This downtown Italian restaurant proved so popular with a young crowd that, a little more than a year after it opened, it took over another historic building next door. The expanded digs are still intimate, though no longer cramped, and the food is as good and plentiful as before. Such standards as spaghetti with meatballs and marinara sauce appear on the menu along with more innovative fare like artichoke orzo, and there's a nice selection of beers, soft drinks, and coffees along with the wines. A backyard patio, tucked away among higher buildings, has a romantic urban feel. *16 N. San Francisco St., tel. 602/774–0541. Dress: casual. Reservations suggested. MC, V. $–$$*

Kachina Cafe. Tables in this family-style Mexican restaurant are Formica and chairs are vinyl, but the food is well prepared, spicy, and served in copious portions. The combination plates are a real bargain; you can get an enchilada, taco, and tostada with beans and rice, a *sopapilla* (fried dough coated with powdered sugar), plus coffee for $6. There are terrific breakfast specials too, and the selection of Mexican and American beers is unusually large. *2220 E. Route 66, tel. 602/556–0363; and Kachina Downtown, 522 E. Route 66, tel. 602/779–1944. Reservations accepted. Dress: casual. MC, V. Closed Tues. and Wed.; downtown location open daily. $*

Macy's. Students, skiers, nouveau and aging hippies, and just about everyone who likes good coffee jams into Macy's for the best cup in town. The beans are roasted on the premises in the huge red machine that dominates one wall of this bustling spot. Though coffee—including a variety of espressos and cappuccinos—is the focus, good fresh pastas, soups, and salads are also offered for lunch and early dinner: Macy's opens at 6 AM every day, but the kitchen closes at 7 PM Sun.–Wed., and 8 PM

Thurs.–Sat. *14 S. Beaver St., tel. 602/774–2243. No reservations. Dress: casual. No credit cards. $*

Salsa Brava. This cheerful Mexican restaurant, with light-wood booths and bold, colorful designs, eschews heavy Sonoran-style fare in favor of the grilled dishes found in Guadalajara (determined artery-cloggers will still find enough cheese-smothered items on the menu). The fish tacos are particularly popular, and this place has the only salsa bar in town. One annoyance: After the first bowl, additional tortilla chips cost extra. *1800 S. Milton Rd., tel. 602/774–1083. Dress: casual. Reservations advised. AE, MC, V. $*

Lodging

Hotels and Motels

Best Western Woodlands Plaza Hotel. This upscale link in the Best Western chain is the glitziest accommodation in town—which isn't saying much in Flagstaff. The brass-and-marble lobby, although tasteful, is somewhat oddly eclectic in style. But the hotel is conveniently located near downtown and the main outbound roads; the rooms are large, comfortable, and nicely furnished in Southwestern pastels; and there are two good restaurants on the premises, including Sakura (*see* Dining, *above*). *1175 W. Hwy. 66, 86001, tel. 602/773–8888 or 800/528–1234, fax 602/773–0597. 183 rooms with bath. Facilities: cocktail lounge, fitness center, outdoor pool, indoor and outdoor spa, gift shop. AE, D, DC, MC, V. $$$*

Residence Inn. Good for families and for skiers, who can buy lift tickets at the front desk, this motel offers attractive modern accommodations with kitchen facilities (dishes, full-size refrigerator, microwave); many of the two-bedroom suites have fireplaces. Continental breakfast, a newspaper, and cocktails are included in the room rate. The inn is convenient to I–40 and a nearby golf course. *3440 N. Country Club Rd., tel. 502/526–5555 or 800/331–3131, fax 602/527–0328. 78 studios, 24 2-bedroom suites. Facilities: Heated pool, spa, sports court, exercise room, grocery-shopping service, complimentary airport shuttle, coin-op laundry, pets permitted. AE, D, DC, MC, V. $$$*

Howard Johnson's. Just off I–40, this three-story motel is a typical Howard Johnson's, with functional modern furniture. But the guest rooms are in an attractive ski-lodge-style building, and some suites have fireplaces. The small, heated indoor pool and a 24-hour coffee shop are pluses, and a courtesy van transports guests to the airport, train, or bus station. *2200 E. Butler Ave., 86004, tel. 602/779–6944 or 800/654–2000, fax 602/779–6944, ext. 341. 100 rooms with bath. Facilities: indoor pool, sauna, restaurant, lounge. AE, D, DC, MC, V. $$*

Little America of Flagstaff. This is the biggest motel in town, and a deservedly popular place. It's far enough from the tracks to allow visitors to sleep undisturbed as the trains roar through town, the grounds are surrounded by evergreen forests, and it's one of the few places in Flagstaff that offers room service. Rooms are surprisingly plush: All have brass chandeliers, comfortable sitting areas with French Provincial–style furniture, phones in the bathrooms, and large stereo TVs; king rooms have small refrigerators, too. *2515 E. Butler Ave. (Box 3900), 86004, tel. 602/779–2741 or 800/352–4386, fax 602/779–7983. 248 rooms* *with bath. Facilities: pool, kitchenettes, restaurant, cocktail lounge, 24-hour coffee shop, hiking trail, laundry service, gift shop, courtesy van, service station/garage. AE, D, DC, MC, V. $$*

Monte Vista Hotel. Built in 1926, many Hollywood stars have stayed at this historic downtown hotel over the years—the guest rooms come by the glamorous names attached to them honestly. The restored Southwestern deco lobby, with its shoe-shine stand and curved archways, is appealing, and rates are low, but rooms and hallways are somewhat dark, and the men buying racing forms who hang out at the front desk make this an iffy choice for female travelers. *100 N. San Francisco St., 86001, tel. 602/779-6971, fax 602/779-2904. 45 rooms with bath. Facilities: restaurant, cocktail lounge, gift shop. AE, D, DC, MC, V. $-$$*

Highland Country Inn. Near ASU, this is one of the few nonchain motels in town that's consistently clean and reliable. The accommodations are nothing out of the ordinary, but they have cable TV with free HBO. No-smoking rooms are available. *223 S. Milton Rd., 86001, tel. 602/774-5041, fax 602/774-5043. 42 rooms with bath. Facilities: heated outdoor pool, complimentary coffee, guest laundry. AE, D, MC, V. $*

Bed-and-Breakfast
★

Inn at Four Ten. B&Bs are a nice alternative to the chain motels in Flagstaff, and this one offers a quiet but convenient downtown setting. Most of the accommodations in the beautifully restored 1907 structure are spacious suites, with private bath, private entrance, and minikitchen. The full breakfast might include crepes, blueberry pancakes, or quiche. There's no smoking inside. *410 N. Leroux St., 86001, tel. 602/774-0088. 6 suites with bath, 2 rooms share bath, 1 room with bath accessible to travelers with disabilities. AE, MC, V. $-$$*

Jerome

Dining **House of Joy.** Situated in a former bordello, this now respectable restaurant attracts patrons from all over the region—perhaps as much for its legendary setting as its food. Two small dining rooms are dimly lighted and strung with red lights, but the stuffed animals and dolls on display (and for sale) offset any air of luridness. Book a table several weeks in advance as this popular restaurant is open only on weekends and only for dinner. Classic Continental dishes such as chicken Kiev and veal cordon bleu are well prepared. The hot muffins, home-baked breads, and desserts, all of which vary from day to day, are highlights. *Hull Ave., just off Main St., tel. 602/634-5339. Reservations required. Dress: casual but neat. No credit cards; personal checks accepted. Closed weekdays and weekend lunch. $$$*

Lodging **Jerome Inn.** The style is Victorian in this creaky but characterful old hotel left over from Jerome's heyday almost 100 years ago. The bar and restaurant downstairs can be noisy, especially on Saturday night; walls are thin; and most rooms share a bath, but it's hard to beat the prices. Try to book the Montana room—it's one of the hotel's largest, and it offers a lovely view of the mountains and downtown as well as a firm mattress. *Main St., Box 36, 86331, tel. 602/634–5094. 7 rooms, 1 with private bath. Facilities: library, restaurant. DC, MC, V. $*

Bed-and- **The Cottage Inn.** A 1917 porch-fronted house off the main road
Breakfasts (in a neighborhood known as Upper Hogback), this B&B offers beautiful views of Verde Valley. The two bedrooms have a private entrance and share a bath; the sitting room, which can accommodate two on a pullout bed, is used when a party of six rents the entire house. A full breakfast is served upstairs in the dining room. *747 East Ave., Box 823, 86331, tel. 602/634–0701. AE, D, MC, V. $$.*

Hillside House. Another B&B in a historic house (this one built in 1904), the Hillside House also has outstanding views of the Verde Valley. The rooms are done in a rather unattractive mishmash of styles—mostly 1960s furniture, kitschy animal pictures, and ruffled bedspreads—and share a bath; one room has a double bed and the other has a sleeping loft large enough for one fairly thin person. Breakfast is Continental. The rate is lowered if only one person occupies the suite. *687 Main St., Box 305, 86331, tel. 602/634–5667. 2-room suite, one bath. Facilities: refrigerator in room. MC, V. $$*

Sedona–Oak Creek Canyon

Dining **L'Auberge de Sedona.** This highly regarded French restaurant has been playing musical chefs recently, but the current king of the kitchen, John Harrings, has a good deal of haute-cuisine experience. One of the most romantic dining spots in Arizona, L'Auberge is done in Country French–style with Pierre Deux–type fabrics. The cuisine takes advantage of both classic and nouvelle styles, with light, subtle sauces, somewhat modest portions, and fresh ingredients. The six-course fixed-price menu ($49) might include smoked Scottish salmon, wild game consommé with duck ravioli, and filet mignon with foie gras, wild mushrooms, and truffle sauce; an à la carte menu is also available. Ask for a table overlooking the stream, preferably in the smaller room near the entrance. *L'Auberge La., tel. 602/ 282–1667. Reservations strongly suggested. Jacket required. AE, D, DC, MC, V. $$$$*

Pietro's. A savvy entrepreneur from New York's garment district has managed to pull together the ingredients for a successful Sedona restaurant: good northern Italian cuisine; a friendly, attentive staff; and a lively, casual atmosphere (which sometimes feels crowded). Among the popular dishes are osso buco and duck ravioli; the eggplant and ricotta appetizer is a good starter. Such desserts as amaretto cheesecake, *tiramisù*, and zabaglione will destroy whatever's left of your diet. *2445 W. Hwy. 89A, tel. 602/282–2525. Reservations advised. Dress: casual. D, MC, V. Dinner only. $$$*

Sedona Swiss. It's hard to go wrong with a chef who's used to pleasing Swiss embassy diplomats in Washington—and this very gemütlich European restaurant doesn't. The breakfast pastry in the adjoining café is light and buttery, and such classic dinner entrées as beef Stroganoff or rack of lamb Provençale are delicately seasoned and well prepared; lighter alternatives such as pasta with fresh salmon are also available. The low-priced buffet lunch draws in the tour-bus crowd (the restaurant sits on a street just off the main Uptown drag), but in the evening the pretty chalet-style dining room is suitably sedate and romantic. French, Italian, and German are spoken here. *350 Jordan Rd., tel. 602/282–7959. Reservations advised. Dress: casual for breakfast and lunch, casual but neat at dinner. MC, V. No dinner Wed. $$$*

★ **Heartline Cafe.** Attention to detail—fresh flowers on the tables, house salads without a leaf of iceberg—and outstanding, innovative cuisine make this attractive café stand out in a town that's beginning to form a high yuppie-restaurant profile. The menu is American with a Southwestern flavor: Dinner entrées might include oak-grilled salmon marinated in tequila and lime, or duck with pears and green peppercorns. A too-temptingly priced sampler for two allows you and your companion to try all the luscious desserts on the menu. Meals are served in a plant-filled, light wood-beamed dining room or, on fine days, on a rosebush-lined terrace. *1610 W. Hwy. 89A, tel. 602/282–0785. Reservations advised. Dress: casual but neat. AE, D, MC, V. No lunch Sun. $$–$$$*

The Atrium. New owners—one the former executive chef at the acclaimed El Tovar in the Grand Canyon—have given a tired Tlaquepaque restaurant a chic new bistro menu and an attractive new look. The restaurant is still going through some growing pains, but prices are so reasonable it's worth taking a chance. The place is pretty in pink at dinnertime, when such appetizers as sweet-potato ravioli might precede pan-seared salmon with horseradish mashed potatoes or roast duck with sun-dried cherries in a Port wine sauce. Or come in for a comforting breakfast of hot Irish oatmeal or brioche French toast. *Tlaquepaque, AZ 179 at the bridge, tel. 602/282–5060. Reservations advised. Dress: casual. No credit cards; personal checks accepted. $$*

Rincon del Tlaquepaque. This lovely Spanish-style restaurant nestled in the upscale Tlaquepaque mall serves Sonoran Mexican food and some Native American–inspired items such as Navajo tacos and pizzas. Towering sycamores shade the outdoor patio, where diners can watch shoppers stroll through the flower-filled and stone-sidewalked shopping area. Try the margaritas and chimichangas. *Tlaquepaque, AZ 179 at the bridge, tel. 602/282–4648. Reservations advised. Dress: casual. AE, MC, V. Closed Mon. $$*

Shugrue's Restaurant Bakery & Bar. A combination coffee shop and upscale restaurant (one room has vinyl booths, another pink tablecloths and a fireplace), Shugrue's in West Sedona attracts a loyal following of locals who come for safe food and large portions rather than for culinary adventure. Omelets, salads, and burgers are on the menu, along with Mexican fare and, at dinnertime, steaks and seafood. Shugrue's Hillside branch has a more ambitious, more expensive, and more inconsistent menu, as well as a lovely setting overlooking Sedona's red rocks. *2250 W. Hwy. 89A, tel. 602/282–2943;671 AZ 179 (Hillside Shopping*

Center), tel. 602/282–5200. Dress: casual. Reservations suggested. AE, MC, V. $–$$

Mandarin House. Its name notwithstanding, the Mandarin House serves everything from standard Cantonese to Szechuan fare, with dishes ranging from the exotic (shark-fin salad) to the old standbys (egg foo yong). Well-priced lunch specials include crispy egg rolls made on the premises. Dark green tablecloths, carved chairs, and dark-wood furnishings lend this restaurant, just down the road from the Oak Creek Factory Stores, a certain elegance. *6486 Hwy. 179, Suite 114, tel. 602/284–9088. Reservations accepted. Dress: casual. AE, MC, V. $*

Lodging **Enchantment Resort.** Designed as a tennis resort, Enchantment has excellent sports facilities, but it's the stunning setting
★ of Boynton Canyon that makes it unique. The rooms, decorated in vibrant Southwestern patterns, are set in 56 pueblo-style casitas; all have dazzling views, and many offer fireplaces and kitchenettes. Fresh-squeezed orange juice and a newspaper are delivered to rooms each morning, and an upscale restaurant serves fine Continental cuisine. One drawback: Although flashlights are provided, it's difficult to find one's way around the largely unlighted premises at night; less-than-intrepid guests can call the front desk for golf-cart transport. *525 Boynton Canyon Rd., 86336, tel. 602/282–2900 or 800/826–4180, fax 602/282–9249. 162 rooms with bath. Facilities: 6 outdoor pools, 12 tennis courts, pitch-and-putt golf course, fitness center, health center, aerobics, croquet, children's programs, guided hikes, bicycling, kitchenettes, restaurant, lounge, gift shop. AE, D, DC, MC, V. $$$$*

Garland's Oak Creek Lodge. In the heart of Oak Creek Canyon, this lodge was built in the 1930s and bought by its current owners, Gary and Mary Garland, in the 1960s. Fifteen comfortably furnished cabins, some including fireplaces and pullout beds for extra guests, share 17 acres of beautiful land (at an elevation of 5,000 feet) with an organic apple orchard. Accommodations look out over the canyon itself or the rugged cliffs surrounding it. The lodge is operated on a modified American plan, with excellent breakfasts and dinners included in the room price, along with afternoon tea. Garland's is usually booked solid months in advance—it's open only from April 1–November 15—but it's worth a phone call to check. *Hwy. 89A, 8 mi north of Sedona (Box 152), 86336, tel. 602/282–3343. 15 cabins with bath. Facilities: restaurant, volleyball court, croquet, tennis court, swimming hole. MC, V. $$$$*

★ **Los Abrigados.** This place really sparkles at Christmas, when half a million tiny lights illuminate the grounds, but it's a dazzler year-round. All the spacious suite accommodations, attractively decorated in shades of plum and teal or rust and salmon, have microwaves, minibars stocked with microwavable items, and coffeemakers, as well as two TVs and two phones; in addition, some have private spas and fireplaces. A state-of-the-art health club, offering such extras as massages and facials, will help burn off the calories picked up at the Canyon Rose restaurant, which serves excellent Southwestern fare. Guests can also picnic at

Oak Creek, which runs through the grounds of this 20-acre, tree-lined property. The shops of Tlaquepaque are right next door. *160 Portal La., 86336, tel. 602/282–1777 or 800/521–3131, fax 602/282–2614. 175 suites. Facilities: 2 restaurants; jazz lounge; health club with sauna, steam room, whirlpool, tanning, and fitness classes; heated outdoor pool; 3 tennis courts; volleyball court; children's programs and baby-sitting. AE, D, DC, MC, V. $$$$*

L'Auberge de Sedona Resort. This resort consists of a central building and—the major attraction—a number of sweet, secluded cabins in a wooded setting along a stream. Phoenix couples flock to those romantic, Country French hideaways and dine in the first-class French restaurant (*see* Dining, *above*). There's a small heated pool for summertime swimming. *L'Auberge La. (Box B), 86336, tel. 602/282–1661 or 800/272–6777, fax 602/282–2885. 96 rooms, 34 cottages, all with bath. Facilities: 2 restaurants, gift shop, pool, spa. AE, D, DC, MC, V. $$$–$$$$*

Bell Rock Inn. Just down the road from Oak Creek's factory-outlet stores, a few miles south of Sedona, this motel offers rooms nicely furnished in Southwestern pastels; many have red-rock views. About 50 new units, many of them suites, were added in the spring and summer of 1994. *6246 AZ 179, 86336, tel. 602/282–4161. 97 rooms and suites with bath. Facilities: restaurant, lounge, pool, Jacuzzi. AE, MC, V. $$–$$$*

★ **Sky Ranch Lodge.** There may be no better vantage point in town from which to view Sedona's red-rock canyons than the private patios or balconies at Sky Ranch Lodge, perched near the top of Airport Mesa. Some rooms have stone fireplaces, some have kitchenettes; all are well decorated in dark blues and beiges with ceramic tile trim. Paths on the grounds wind around fountains and, in summer, through colorful flower gardens. This is an excellent value choice. *Airport Rd. (Box 2579), 86336, tel. 602/282–6400, fax 602/282–7682. 92 rooms, 2 cottages, all with bath; 20 rooms with kitchenette. Facilities: pool, whirlpool. MC, V. $–$$$.*

Bed-and- **Briar Patch Inn.** Set in a wonderfully verdant canyon with a
Breakfasts rushing creek, this B&B has accommodations to match. All the
★ hewn-wood cabins (in Native American and Mexican styles) have kitchenettes; some offer decks overlooking Oak Creek, and many feature fireplaces. On summer mornings you can sit outside and enjoy home-baked breads and fresh egg dishes while listening to classical music performed live. New Age and crafts workshops are held on the premises at various times. *Star Rte. 3, off Hwy. 89A 3 mi north of Sedona, Box 1002, 86336, tel. 602/282–2342. 11 2-person cabins, 4 4-person cabins. Facilities: fishing hole, library, masseuse. MC, V. $$$–$$$$*

Casa Sedona. You can have all the modern amenities—Jacuzzi tub for two, and air-conditioning and heating units—and still be able to commune with nature at this appealing B&B. A large redwood deck, where a full breakfast is served when the weather is fine, has stunning red-rock views, also enjoyed by all of the rooms. The rooms, which all have gas-run fireplaces, are done in an eclectic style with differing Southwestern themes; one is done in deep blues, burgundies and tans with a Native American-print bedspread, another in shades of peach and sea green with a light oak closet. *55 Hozoni Dr., 86336, tel. 602/282–2938 or 800/525–3756. 11 double rooms with bath. Facilities: Large-screen TV/VCR, music center in living room, catered dinners. D, MC, V. $$–$$$$*

The Lodge at Sedona. A first-class operation—breakfast, for example, is often prepared by a chef from a local resort—The Lodge still manages to feel intimate and friendly. Rooms in this rambling wood-and-stone house are individually decorated in every style from romantic Renaissance to cowboy kitsch; some have fireplaces and/or redwood decks. Of the five public areas where guests can mingle, perhaps the best is the lace-curtained breakfast nook, shaded by trees and looking out onto the red rocks in the distance. *125 Kallof Pl., 86336, tel. 602/204–1942 or 800/619–4467. 11 rooms, 2 suites, all with bath. AE, MC, V. Facilities: library, meeting room. $$–$$$$*

The Arts and Nightlife

The Arts

Flagstaff Between the **Flagstaff Symphony Orchestra** (tel. 602/774–5107), **Theatrikos Community Theater** (11 W. Cherry Ave., tel. 602/774–1662), and Northern Arizona University's **School of Performing Arts** (tel. 602/523–3731), there's bound to be something cultural going on in Flagstaff when you visit. This is especially true in summer: From early June through the first week in August, the **Flagstaff Festival of the Arts** (403 N. Agassiz St., tel. 602/774–7750 or 800/266–7740) offers everything from art, films, plays, and dance to sunset jazz dinners and a Mexican fiesta.

Other annual events that reflect the area's culture and crafts include the **All Indian Powwow** and **The Native Arts Fair,** both held the weekend before the Fourth of July; contact the Flagstaff Visitors Center (*see* Important Addresses and Numbers in Essential Information, *above*) for details. **Festival in the Pines,** sponsored annually during the first weekend of August by the Mill Avenue Merchants' Association (tel. 602/967–4877), features an arts-and-crafts fair. The **Coconino Center for the Arts** (2300 N. Fort Valley Rd., U.S. 180 N, tel. 602/779–6921) hosts a **Festival of Native American Arts** each summer from late June through early August; the center also sponsors the **Trappings of the American West** from mid-May to early June, which focuses on cowboy art—everything from painting and sculpture to cowboy poetry readings. Sales shows of artwork by Zuni, Hopi, and Navajo tribes are held at the **Museum of Northern Arizona** (3001 N. Fort Valley Rd., tel. 602/774–5211), a judged event that runs from late May through early August. Classic cars and '50s nostalgia are the draws at the **Route 66 Festival** (tel. 602/833–7150), held along the famous thoroughfare in early June. Flagstaff's observatories help make the late September/early October **Festival of Science** (tel. 602/523–3719) a stellar attraction.

Jerome   Jerome's annual music festival has been canceled, but the **Chili Cookoff** in February and **Arizona's Oldest Home Tour** in May are worth checking out. Contact the Jerome Chamber of Commerce (Box K, 86331, tel. 602/634–2900) for details.

Sedona   Find out about cultural events in Sedona at **The Book Loft** (175 AZ 179, just south of the "Y," tel. 602/282–5173), which often hosts poetry readings, theatrical readings, and lectures. The Sedona **Jazz on the Rocks Festival** (tel. 602/282–1985), held every September, always attracts a sellout crowd that fills the town to capacity; at jazz-festival time it's even more important than usual to book ahead for rooms. The **Sedona Heritage Day Festival,** sponsored by the Sedona Historical Society (tel. 602/282–2186), is celebrated in late June; it includes such activities as cake- and pie-baking contests and the reenactment of horseback mail delivery. The **Sedona Arts Center** (tel. 602/282–3809) sponsors events ranging from classical concerts to plays; phone for information about upcoming programs.

Nightlife

A university town, **Flagstaff** has a number of places where the college crowd gathers after dark. The misleadingly named **Museum Club** (3404 E. Route 66, tel. 602/526–9434) is a tourist-friendly cowboy honky-tonk, housed in an old barnlike structure with a dance floor; there's usually a country-swing band. For live entertainment nightly—everything from bluegrass to jazz and rock—in a sociable atmosphere, try the **Main Street Bar and Grill** (4 S. San Francisco St., tel. 602/774–1519); the food's good, too, so come early for dinner. **Charly's** (23 N. Leroux St., tel. 602/779–1919), in the lobby of the historic Weatherford Hotel, attracts a loyal local following to its late-night jazz and blues bands. In 1994, two microbreweries started things hopping (as it were) in town: the **Beaver Street Brewery and Whistlestop Café** (11 S. Beaver St., tel. 602/779–0079) and the **Flagstaff Brewing Company** (16 E. Rte. 66, tel. 602/773–1442).

The nightlife in Sedona, geared toward a resort crowd, tends to be a bit more sedate. **On the Rocks,** the lounge at Canyon Rose at Los Abrigados (160 Portal La., tel. 602/281–1777), hosts bands nightly, mostly of the swing and jazz variety. **Enchantment Resort** (525 Boynton Canyon Rd., tel. 602/282–2900) has an attractive bar where live piano music keeps the beautiful people entertained. **Cups Bistro & Gallery** (1670 W. Hwy. 89A, tel. 602/282–2531), a comfy coffeehouse, often features live jazz or blues in the evening, and **Heartline Cafe** (*see* Dining, *above*) sometimes puts on dinner theater or opera nights. The closest you'll come to a rollicking cowboy bar in town is **Rainbow's End** (3235 W. Hwy. 89A, tel. 602/282–1593), a steak house with a large dance floor and live country-western bands.

Fun-seeking Sedonans often head over to Jerome on the weekend for the live music and livelier scene at the **Spirit Room** (tel.

602/634-5792) on Main Street. Just down the block, **Paul & Jerry's Saloon** (tel. 602/634-2603) also attracts a rowdy crowd to its two pool tables and old wooden bar.

6 Phoenix and Central Arizona

By Mark Hein

In central Arizona, one of the world's great deserts meets one of its great mountain ranges, providing a stunning variety of natural environments for the visitor to enjoy within easy touring distance. Central Arizona also combines some of the oldest human dwellings in the Western Hemisphere with the homes of contemporary Native American tribes and America's newest, fastest-growing major urban center, metropolitan Phoenix.

At the center of central Arizona lies the Valley of the Sun, named for its 330-plus days of sunshine each year. This 1,000-square-mile valley is the northern tip of the Sonoran Desert, a surprisingly fertile, rolling expanse of prehistoric seabed that stretches from central Arizona deep into northwestern Mexico.

The valley is studded with cacti and creosote bushes, crusted with hard-baked clay and rock, and scorched by summer temperatures that can stay above 100°F for weeks at a time. But its dry skin responds magically to the touch of rainwater. Spring is a miracle of poppies strewn among the flower-crowned saguaros, of ruby, ivory, and gold blossoms bursting from the dry spikes of the ocotillo and the thorny beaver-tail pads of the nopal. And, as the Hohokam discovered, this miracle can be augmented by human hands. From 300 BC to AD 1450, their tilled, rowed, and irrigated fields yielded cotton, corn, and beans. Then, for reasons neither archaeology nor Native American lore has yet revealed, these skillful, energetic people suddenly abandoned their homes.

From the time the Hohokam left until the American Civil War, the once-fertile Salt River valley lay forgotten, used only by occasional small bands of Pima and Maricopa peoples. Then in 1865, the U.S. Army established Fort McDowell in the mountains to the east, where the Verde River flows into the Salt. To feed the men and the horses stationed there, Jack Swilling, a former Confederate army officer, had the idea of reopening the Hohokam canals in 1867. Within a year fields bright with barley and pumpkins earned the area the name of Punkinsville. But by 1870, when the town site was plotted, the 300 inhabitants had decided that their new city would rise "like a phoenix" from the ashes of a vanished civilization.

Phoenix indeed grew steadily. Within 20 years, it had become large enough—at about 3,000 people—to wrest the title of territorial capital from Prescott. It got a high school in 1895, and at statehood, in 1912, the area, irrigated by the brand-new Roosevelt Dam and Salt River Project, had a burgeoning cotton industry. Copper and cattle were mined and raised elsewhere but were banked and traded in Phoenix, and the cattle were slaughtered and packed here, in the largest stockyards outside Chicago.

Meanwhile climate, so long a crippling liability, became an asset. Desert air was the prescribed therapy for respiratory ills rampant in the sooty, factory-filled East; Scottsdale began in 1901 as "30-odd tents and a half-dozen adobe houses" put up by health-seekers. By 1930, visitors seeking warm winter recreation rather than a cure were filling the elegant San Marcos Hotel in Chandler and the new Arizona Biltmore, first of the many luxury resorts for which the area is known worldwide today.

When low-cost air-conditioning made its summer heat manageable, the Sun Belt boom began. From 1950 to 1990, the Phoenix urban area more than quadrupled in population, catapulting real estate and home-building into two of the state's biggest industries. Cities planted around Phoenix have become its suburbs, and fields that for decades grew cotton and citrus now grow microchips and homes. Glendale and Peoria on the west side, and Tempe, Mesa, and Chandler on the east, make up the nation's third-largest Silicon Valley.

The Valley of the Sun is ringed by mountains. Squaw Peak is situated within Phoenix, just north of downtown, and the Papago Peaks are local landmarks between Phoenix and Scottsdale. East of Phoenix, past Tempe and Mesa, stand the barren peaks of the Superstition Mountains, named for their eerie habit of seeming just a few miles away and luring unwary prospectors to a dusty death. Beyond the Superstitions, central Arizona is mountains all the way into New Mexico. South of Phoenix, easily visible from the airport, rise the much less lofty peaks of South Mountain Park. Not 5 miles from downtown, this 12-mile-wide chain of dry mountains divides the valley from the rest of the Sonora Desert. West of Phoenix, past Glendale and Tolleson, the formidable, barren-seeming White Tank Mountains separate the valley from the empty lands that slope steadily downward toward the Colorado River and the Mojave Desert of California on the other side.

But north of Phoenix, behind the dusty Hieroglyphic Mountains (misnamed for Hohokam petroglyphs found there), rises the gigantic Mogollon Rim. This shelf of land, almost as wide as Arizona, was thrust 2,000 to 5,000 feet into the air back in the Mesozoic age; it got its name for posing an overwhelming *mogollon* (obstruction) to Spanish-speaking explorers probing northward. These slopes are green with pine trees, and the alpine meadows are lush with grasses and aspens. Here, after gold was found in the early 1860s, President Lincoln sent the Arizona Territory's first governor to found the capital at Prescott and secure the mineral riches for the Union.

Today, the northern mountains serve as a cool, green refuge for valley dwellers. The bumpy wagon roads up the Black Canyon toward Prescott and Flagstaff were key summer escape routes 100 years ago, and their dramatically engineered successor, the four-lane split-level I–17, leads tens of thousands on exodus every weekend from May to September.

Phoenix and central Arizona are places in which to take it easy, go slow, and dress informally. As the old desert hands say, you don't begin to see the desert until you've looked at it long enough to see the colors; and you aren't ready to get up and move until you've seen the sun go down.

Essential Information

Important Addresses and Numbers

Tourist Information
The **Phoenix and Valley of the Sun Convention and Visitors Bureau** (1 Arizona Center, Suite 600, tel. 602/254–6500) has a satellite office in the Hyatt Regency Phoenix (2nd and Adams Sts., tel. 602/254–6500). The **Phoenix Chamber of Commerce** (34 W. Monroe St., tel. 602/254–5521) is in the heart of downtown.

Emergencies
For **police, fire, ambulance** or **highway** emergencies dial 911.

Hospitals
Samaritan Health Service (tel. 602/230–CARE) has four valley hospitals—Good Samaritan (downtown), Desert Samaritan (east), Maryvale Samaritan (southwest), and Thunderbird Samaritan (northwest)—and a Deer Valley (north) urgent-care clinic; all share a 24-hour hot line. **Scottsdale Memorial Hospital** (tel. 602/481–4411) has three campuses in the northeastern valley. **Maricopa County Medical Center** (tel. 602/267–5011) has been rated one of the nation's best public hospitals.

Doctors
The **Maricopa County Medical Society** (tel. 602/252–2844) and the **Arizona Osteopathic Medical Association** (tel. 602/840–0460) offer referrals during business hours on weekdays.

Dentists
The **American Dental Association Valley** chapter (tel. 602/957–4864) has a 24-hour referral hot line.

Late-Night Pharmacies
Walgreen's has eight 24-hour locations throughout the valley—in east Phoenix (38th St. and Thomas Rd., tel. 602/275–7507), north Phoenix (7th St. and Bell Rd., tel. 602/375–0093), and west Phoenix (5127 W. Indian School Rd., tel. 602/247–1014); in the eastern suburbs of Tempe (1719 E. Southern Ave., Tempe, tel. 602/838–3642), Chandler (1986 N. Alma School Rd., Chandler, tel. 602/899–6713), and Mesa (330 E. Brown Rd., Mesa, tel. 602/898–8025; Main St. and Recker Rd., Mesa, tel. 602/985–0155); and in the western suburb of Peoria (6815 W. Peoria Rd., Peoria, tel. 602/878–7998). **Osco Drugs** has five 24-hour outlets, in central Phoenix (3320 N. 7th Ave., tel. 602/266–5501), west Phoenix (35th Ave. and Glendale Ave., tel. 602/841–7861), north Phoenix (Cactus Rd. and Tatum Rd., tel. 602/996–7320), Scottsdale (Scottsdale Rd. and Shea Rd., tel. 602/998–3500) and Mesa (1836 W. Baseline Rd., tel. 602/831–0212).

Weather
Pressline (tel. 602/271–5656, then press 3333) gives up-to-date valley conditions and three-day forecasts, as does the **U.S. National Weather Service** (tel. 602/265–5550).

Arriving and Departing

By Plane
Most air travelers visiting Arizona fly into Sky Harbor International Airport (tel. 602/273–3300). Just 3 miles east of downtown Phoenix, it is surrounded by freeways linking it to almost every part of the metro area. Although it is one of the nation's half-dozen busiest airports, it is also one of the most compact.

Sky Harbor has three commercial terminals, each with rental luggage carts, taxi stands, car-rental booths, ATM banking, and courtesy telephones. Terminals 3 and 4 (there is no longer a Terminal 1) also have several shops and restaurants, and 24-hour car-rental booths.

Answers & Apples passenger service desks at all three terminals (tel. 602/267–7964 or 602/267–7994) offer fax, notary, and insurance services; the airport chaplain's office (tel. 602/244–1346) aids travelers in distress.

Airlines Sky Harbor is the home airport of **America West** (tel. 800/235–9292) and a hub for **Southwest** (tel. 800/435–9792). Other airlines with frequent flights to Sky Harbor are **Alaska** (tel. 800/426–0333), **American** (tel. 800/433–7300), **Continental** (tel. 800/525–0280), **Delta** (tel. 800/221–1212), **TWA** (tel. 800/221–2000), **United** (tel. 800/241–6522), and **USAir** (tel. 800/428–4322).

For flights to the Grand Canyon, Page, Lake Powell, Lake Havasu, and other Arizona points, try **America West** (tel. 800/235–9292) and commuter **Skywest** (tel. 800/453–9417).

Between the It's easy access to downtown Phoenix, and Tempe (3 miles away
Airport and to the west and east, respectively) is one of Sky Harbor's strong
Downtown points. It's also only 15 minutes by freeway from Glendale (to the west) and Mesa (to the east).

Unfortunately, two favorite tourist areas, Scottsdale (to the northeast) and Sun City (to the northwest) are harder to reach—each takes 30–45 minutes by car and requires using surface roads for all or part of the trip.

Sky Harbor has limited bus service, ample taxi service, and very good shuttle service to points throughout the metro area. Very few hotels offer a complimentary limo or shuttle, but most resorts do. You will probably want to rent a car, either at the airport or from wherever you are staying (most rental firms will deliver).

These companies have airport booths or free pickup from nearby lots: **Alamo** (tel. 800/327–9633), **Avis** (tel. 800/331–1212), **Budget** (tel. 800/527–0700), **Hertz** (tel. 800/654–3131), **Thrifty** (tel. 800/367–2277), and, if you care more about your wallet than about appearances, **Rent-A-Wreck** (tel. 602/254–1000).

By Bus **Phoenix Transit** buses (tel. 602/253–5000) will get you directly from Terminal 2, 3, or 4 to downtown Phoenix's outdoor bus terminal (1st and Washington Sts.) or downtown Tempe (Mill and University Aves.) in about 20 minutes for $1. Senior citizens and children ages 6–12 pay half-fare; children 5 and under ride free.

The **Red Line** runs westbound to Phoenix every half-hour from about 6 AM until after 9 PM weekdays (Saturday, you take Bus 13 and transfer at Central Avenue to Bus 0 north; there is no Sunday service). The Red Line runs eastbound to Tempe every half-hour from 4 AM to 7 PM weekdays (no weekend service); in another 25 minutes, it takes you to downtown Mesa (Center and Main streets).

With free transfers, Phoenix Transit can take you from the airport to most other valley cities (Glendale, Sun City, Scottsdale, etc.), but the trip is likely to be slow unless you manage to catch an express line.

By Taxi Only three firms—and one specializing in transporting handicapped travelers—are licensed to pick up at Sky Harbor's commercial terminals. All add a $1 surcharge for airport pickups, do not charge for luggage, and are available 24 hours a day. A trip to downtown Phoenix can range from $4 to $12, or $13.75 for a wheelchair-lift van. The fare to downtown Scottsdale averages around $15–$16.

AAA Cab (tel. 602/253–8294), **Checker/Yellow Cab** (tel. 602/252–5252), and **Courier Cab** (tel. 602/232–2222) all charge around $2 for the first mile and $1.30 per mile thereafter. **American HTS** (tel. 602/272–7211) offers wheelchair and stretcher service, the former at a $15 pickup fee ($20 evenings and weekends) and $1.25 per mile. All expect tips.

The blue vans of **Supershuttle** (tel. 602/244–9000) also cruise Sky Harbor, each taking up to seven passengers to their individual destinations, with no luggage fee or airport surcharge. Fares range from competitive with the cheapest taxi for a short run, such as downtown Phoenix or Tempe, to 25% or more below the best taxi fares on longer trips. You can reserve a Supershuttle back to the airport (call ahead to schedule pickup, and allow one hour at the airport before your flight). Wheelchair vans are also available. Drivers expect tips.

By Limousine A few limousine firms are allowed to cruise Sky Harbor, and many more provide airport pickups by reservation. All of these are on 24-hour call. **La Limousine** (tel. 602/242–3094) charges $15–$50, depending on distance. **Classic Limousine** (tel. 602/252–LIMO) will take up to six riders (by reservation only) for $30–$50, depending on how far you're going. **Scottsdale Limousine** (tel. 602/946–8446) also requires reservations but offers a toll-free number (tel. 800/747–8234) and complimentary soft drinks; it costs from $40 to $70, plus tip.

By Car If you're coming to Phoenix from the west, you'll probably come on I–10—this transcontinental superhighway's last link was joined in 1990 in a tunnel under downtown Phoenix. The trip from the Los Angeles basin, via Palm Springs, takes five to eight hours, depending on where you start and how many rest stops you make. The older I–40 runs along old Route 66, entering Arizona in the northwest, near Kingman; U.S. 93 traverses from there to Phoenix, for a total journey of 10–12 hours. From San Diego, I–8 slices across low desert to Yuma and on toward the valley on what the Spanish called El Camino del Diablo (the Devil's Highway); at Gila Bend, take AZ 85 up to I–10. The trip takes a total of 8–10 hours.

From the east, **I–10** takes you from El Paso, across southern New Mexico, and through Chiricahua Apache country into Tucson, then north to Phoenix (a total of about 9–11 hours). The northeastern route, **I–40** from Albuquerque, crosses Hopi and

Navajo historic lands to Flagstaff, where I–17 takes you south to Phoenix, also a 9- to 11-hour journey. For a scenic shortcut, take AZ 377 south at Holbrook, across Petrified Forest country to Heber, in the pines of the Mogollon Rim; then take AZ 260 down the 2,000-foot drop to Payson, and AZ 87 through saguaro cactus forests to Phoenix.

By Train **Amtrak** (tel. 800/872–7245) has only one connection, the former Southern Pacific line between New Orleans and Los Angeles, that passes through Phoenix (eastbound, 8:25 AM Monday, Wednesday, and Saturday; westbound, 11:30 PM Tuesday, Thursday and Sunday). It stops at the downtown terminal (4th Ave. and Harrison St., tel. 602/253–0121) in what is now the industrial part of town, and you may have to phone for a taxi. The much more heavily used former Santa Fe line between Los Angeles and Chicago runs through Flagstaff, 150 miles north of the valley; an Amtrak bus leaves Sky Harbor International Airport daily at 5:40 PM.

By Bus **Greyhound Lines** (tel. 602/271–7425 or 800/231–2222) has statewide and nationwide routes from its main terminal in the heart of downtown (525 E. Washington St.), sandwiched between the Civic Plaza complex and the new America West Phoenix Suns Arena.

Getting Around

If you plan to see anything, *you will need a car.* The metro area developed in the automobile era, and only a few downtowns (Phoenix, Scottsdale, Tempe) are pedestrian-friendly. There is no mass transit beyond a bus system that does not even run seven days a week.

By Car Driving is easy in the Valley of the Sun: Rain is rare, fog makes headlines, and it never snows. Most metro-area streets are well marked and well lighted, and the freeway system (not funded until the late 1980s and still being built) has made dramatic strides in linking most of the valley together. Arizona requires seat belts on front-seat passengers and children 16 and under. (For car-rental firms, *see* Between the Airport and Downtown, *above.*)

Around downtown Phoenix, AZ 202 (Papago Freeway), AZ 143 (Hohokam Freeway) and I–10 (Maricopa Freeway) make an elongated east–west loop, embracing the state capitol area on the west and the airport on the east. At mid-loop, AZ 51 (Squaw Peak Freeway) runs north into Paradise Valley. And from the loop's east end, I–10 runs south to Tucson, 100 miles away, while US 60 (Superstition Freeway) branches east to Tempe and Mesa.

Driving in the valley presents one major challenge: Phoenix and all its suburbs are laid out on a single, 800-square-mile grid of horizontal and vertical streets. Even the freeways all run north–south and east–west. (Grand Avenue, running about 20 miles from downtown northwest to Sun City, is the *only* diagonal.) This makes places easy to find but means you must allow generous driving time to get from point A to point B, since you have to trace two legs of a right triangle to do it.

By Bus **Phoenix Transit** (tel. 602/253–5000) is a good rudimentary bus system, with 20 express lines and 42 regular routes that reach most of the valley suburbs. But there are no 24-hour routes; only a skeletal few lines run between sundown and 10:30 PM or on Saturday; and there is no Sunday service. Fares are $1, with free transfers; senior citizens and children 6–18 pay half-fare, and children 5 and under ride free. Phoenix Transit also runs a 25¢ **Downtown Area Shuttle** (DASH), with purple minibuses circling the area between the renovated east end of downtown and the state capitol, on the west end, at 10-minute intervals. The system also serves major thoroughfares in several suburbs—Glendale, Scottsdale, Tempe, and Mesa. In addition, **Dial-A-Ride** services (tel. 602/253–4000) are available throughout the valley.

By Taxi Taxi fares are unregulated in Phoenix, except at the airport. (For a listing of leading firms and their fares, *see* Between the Airport and Downtown, *above*.) The 800-square-mile metro area is so large that one-way fares of $30–$50 are not uncommon; you might want to ask what the damages will be before you get in. Except within a compact area, such as central Phoenix, travel by taxi is not recommended.

Guided Tours

Reservations for tours are a must all year, with seats often filling up quickly in the busy season, October–April. All tours provide pickup services at area resorts, but some offer lower prices if you drive to the tour's point of origin.

Orientation Tours **Gray Line Tours** (P.O. Box 21126, Phoenix 85036, tel. 602/495–9100 or 800/732–0327) offers a seasonal, three-hour narrated drive through Phoenix and Scottsdale for $27, touring downtown Phoenix, the Arizona Biltmore hotel, Camelback Mountain, mansions in Paradise Valley, Arizona State University, Papago Park, and Scottsdale's 5th Avenue. For $30, **Vaughan's Southwest Custom Tours** (Box 31312, Phoenix 85046, tel. 602/971–1381) offers a four-hour trip for 11 or fewer passengers in custom vans, stopping at the Heard Museum, the Arizona Biltmore, and the state capitol building. Vaughan's will also take visitors east of Phoenix on the Apache Trail, a scenic route that passes through old mining towns and includes a narrated boat ride on **Dolly's Steamboat Cruises** at Canyon Lake. The cost is $55, with the tour available September through May, weather permitting.

Special-Interest Tours If you prefer to see the desert country from a four-wheel-drive vehicle, you'll find plenty of options. For example, **Carefree Jeep Adventures** (Box 5423, Carefree 85377, tel. 602/488–0023 or 800/294–JEEP) travels into the Tonto National Forest on old stage and mining roads, where you can see petroglyphs and rock carvings, taste the fruit of cholla cactus, and hold target practice with tin cans and .22 rifles. That three-hour journey costs $45–$60, as does a sunset tour; children 12 and under are half-price.

Arizona Scenic Tours (3116 E. Shea Blvd., Phoenix 85028, tel. 602/971–3601) heads past Pinnacle Peak toward the Verde River on dirt desert roads. Two people can expect to pay $50 each (beverages included) for four hours, but the price drops to $45 per person if more than two make the trip.

For a longer trip into the Sonoran Desert north of the valley, **Explorer Desert Tours** (3310 W. Bell Rd., Phoenix 85023, tel. 602/938–1302) takes group tours only, in 15-person vans to nature trails, gold mines, and a mountain steak house on the six-hour "Sundowner" tour, at $67 per person.

If you'd rather hike than ride, **The Open Road Tours** (1622 E. Gardenia Ave., Phoenix 85020, tel. 602/997–6474 or 800/766–7117) takes hikers to the Squaw Peak Mountain Preserve or South Mountain Park for $35 per half-day. Three- to five-day hikes can be arranged.

Cimarron Adventures and River Co. (7714 E. Catalina Dr., Scottsdale 85251, tel. 602/994–1199) arranges half-day float trips and moonlight dinner cruises down the Salt, Verde, and Gila rivers. Day trips cost about $55 per person, with the night cruise about $70. Multiday wilderness tours are available on the Upper Gila River and the scenic Upper Verde River.

Want to tour Phoenix from above? Check out the many hot-air-balloon ascents. **Naturally High Balloon Co.** (4845 E. Desert View Dr., Phoenix 85044, tel. 602/252–6766 or 800/23–TO–FLY) flies daily all year at $100–$110 per person, depending on the season. The cost includes either Continental breakfast or an afternoon snack and a champagne ceremony at the end of the 60- to 90-minute ride, with bubbly, balloon history and a souvenir certificate. *See also* Hot-Air Ballooning in Sports and the Outdoors, *below.*

At the Estrella Sailport, **Arizona Soaring Inc.** (Box 858, Maricopa 85239, tel. 602/568–2318) offers sailplane rides in a basic trainer or high-performance plane for prices ranging from $48 to $90. The adventuresome can opt for a wild 15-minute acrobatic flight for $80.

If you prefer a less dizzying option, **Wagonmasters** (34015 N. Cave Creek Rd., Cave Creek 85331, tel. 602/488–4479 or 602/501–3239) leads 15-minute to one-hour horse-drawn-carriage tours around Old Scottsdale for $20–$70. They are also available for weddings, birthdays, and other special events.

One of the most interesting guided tours in town explores **Taliesin West** (13201 N. 108th St., Scottsdale 85259, tel. 602/860–2700), winter headquarters of the Frank Lloyd Wright Foundation. With its redwood-and-rock design set at the base of the McDowell Mountains, Wright's winter home typifies his concept of blending function with nature. Hour-long guided tours cost $10; a weekly three-hour tour goes behind the scenes and talks with Wright associates working and studying at the site. The cost is $25.

Walking Tour A 45-minute self-guided walking tour of **Old Scottsdale** takes visitors to 14 historic sites in the area. Maps showing the route can be picked up in the **Scottsdale Chamber of Commerce** office (7343 E. Scottsdale Mall, Scottsdale 85251, tel. 602/945–8481 or 800/877–1117) weekdays 8:30–5, Saturdays 10–5, and Sundays 11–5.

Opening and Closing Times

Generally, banks are open Monday–Thursday 9–4, Friday 9–6. Selected banks have Saturday morning hours, and a few large grocery stores have bank windows that stay open until 9 PM.

Most enclosed shopping malls are open weekdays 10–9, Saturday 10–6, and Sunday noon–5; some of the major centers (*see* Shopping, *below*) are open later on weekends.

Many grocery stores are open 7 AM–9 PM, but several stores within major chains throughout the valley are open 24 hours.

Radio Stations

AM **KTAR 620:** News, talk, sports; **KIDR 740:** Children; **KFYI 910:** News, talk; **KPHX 1480:** Spanish-language.

FM **KBAQ 89.5:** Classical; **KJZZ 91.5:** Jazz, National Public Radio; **KKFR 92.3:** Top 40; **KUPD 97.9:** Rock; **KNIX 102.5:** Country; **KVVA 107.1:** Spanish-language.

Exploring

Highlights for First-Time Visitors

Casa Grande (*see* Tour 4)
Downtown Scottsdale (*see* Tour 3)
Heard Museum (*see* Tour 2)
Heritage Square, The Mercado, and **Arizona Center** (*see* Tour 1)

Tour 1: A Walking Tour of Downtown Phoenix

Numbers in the margin correspond to points of interest on the Phoenix: Tours 1 and 2 map.

A stroll through the renovated east end of downtown gives you a look at Phoenix's past and present, as well as a peek at its future. In moderate weather, it's a pleasant walking day; from late May to mid-October, it's best to break it up over two days. And be sure to take advantage of the 25¢ DASH (Downtown Area Shuttle)—*see* By Bus in Getting Around in Essential Information, *above*.

You'll notice a number of Time Out options in this and the tours that follow—in the warm months, it's best to allow a half-hour of sitting indoors, sipping a tall, cool drink (not alcohol; it speeds dehydration) for every hour of walking or shopping.

① Begin your tour at **Heritage Square,** from 6th to 7th streets between Monroe and Adams, a city-owned block of renovated turn-of-the-century homes in a parklike setting. (There's ample parking in adjacent lots, and it's free if you get your ticket stamped by a merchant along the walking tour.)

To the east, across 7th Street, you'll see the ornate brick bulk of Monroe School; built in 1914, it now houses part of the U.S. Department of Defense Analysis. Just south of it are the graceful modern copper-roofed condos of Renaissance Square, a pioneering urban project built on city-donated land.

The queen of Heritage Square itself is the **Rosson House,** an 1895 gingerbread Victorian in the Eastlake style (made famous in San Francisco). Built by a physician who served a brief term as mayor, it is the sole survivor of the fewer than two dozen Victorians erected in Phoenix. It was bought and restored by the city in 1974. A 30-minute tour of this classic is worth the modest price. *6th and Monroe Sts., tel. 602/262–5071. Admission: $3 adults, $2 senior citizens and students, $1 children 6–12. Open Wed.–Sat. 10–3:30, Sun. noon–3:30.*

On the south side of the square, along Adams Street, stand four houses built between 1899 and 1901 on sites bought from the Rossons. The Midwestern-style **Stevens House** holds the **Arizona Doll and Toy Museum** (602 E. Adams St., tel. 602/253–9337); next to it, in the California-style **Stevens-Haustgen House,** is the handiwork of **Craftsmen's Gallery** (604 E. Adams St., tel. 602/253–7770). The fourth dwelling is the **Silva House,** a mail-order 1900 bungalow restored by the Salt River Project (one of the valley's two major power companies and its largest irrigator) that includes a room devoted to Phoenix history and one with rotating displays on water and electricity in the valley. Two houses on the south side of Adams Street are still being restored.

Time Out The third house in the row, the Bouvier–Teeter House, offers elegant refreshment—afternoon high teas at the **Heart in Hand Tea Room** (622 E. Adams St., tel. 602/256–7572), served Tuesday through Saturday from 10 to 6, Sunday from noon to 5. Or, for more casual fare in one of the square's two restored carriage houses, just north of the Heart in Hand Tea Room, **Jack and Jenny's Barn and Grill** (618 E. Adams St., tel. 602/255–0213) makes sandwiches to order and has a wide array of fruit, juices, soft drinks, and sweets.

② **The Mercado** (542 E. Monroe St., tel. 602/256–6322), a bright-colored, neo-Aztec fantasy built in 1990, occupies two blocks immediately north of Heritage Square, just across Monroe Street, from 5th to 7th streets. Spend some time at the **Museo Chicano** on the second story. It supports the work of modern Hispano-American artists in the United States and Mexico, and its exhibits portray the range of Hispanic culture, classic and modern. Its gift shop also offers some terrific bargains. *641 E. Van Buren St., tel. 602/257–5536. Admission: $2 adults, $1 senior citizens and students. Open Wed.–Sat. 10–3.*

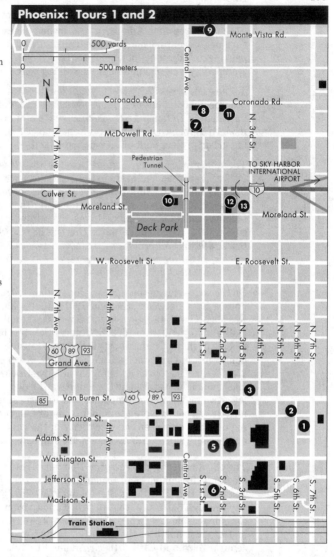

America West Phoenix Suns Arena, **6**

Arizona Center, **3**

Arizona Museum of Science and Technology, **5**

Ellis-Shackelford House, **10**

Heard Museum, **9**

Herberger Theater Center, **4**

Heritage Square, **1**

The Mercado, **2**

Phoenix Art Museum, **8**

Phoenix Central Library, **7**

Phoenix Little Theatre, **11**

Phoenix Performing Arts Building, **13**

Phoenix Visual Arts Building, **12**

From The Mercado, cross 5th and Van Buren streets. On your right, you'll see the imposing buildings of old Phoenix Union High School, Greek Revival–style buildings that served as the city's first secondary school in 1900 and were abandoned three-quarters of a century later. With their shells preserved and their interiors remodeled, they are now home to several city and county offices.

On the northwest corner of the intersection, you'll see two glass-clad office towers with a lane of royal palms between them. Follow the palm trees: They lead to the **Arizona Center's** dramatic sunken garden and fountains (see how many giant bronze frogs you can find). Opened in 1991, this multiuse complex provides downtown's premier spot for cool, shaded outdoor sitting and wandering, even in the heat of summer.

On the other side of the ponds stands the curved, double-deck open structure of the city's newest downtown shopping mall. There are a variety of chain and specialty stores, from men's and women's clothing to Southwestern art and '50s collectibles, and a host of clever cart merchants. And there's usually live music (including top valley jazz artists) in the courtyard. In addition to hosting several good eateries, Arizona Center is the home of the state's biggest sports bar—would you believe eight restaurant-size spaces spread over two stories, indoors and out?

Time Out The most restful refreshment spot in the center is **Amalfi** (455 N. 3rd St., tel. 602/257–0605), a real Italian sidewalk café that does Caesar salads, great sandwiches and desserts, as well as Italian sodas and steamed coffees.

Leaving the Arizona Center at Amalfi, head south to 3rd and Van Buren streets. You can catch the 25¢ DASH shuttle here, or you can stroll a block south to Monroe, with the mission-style adobe of **St. Mary's Basilica** on your left, then a block west between the dramatic modern facades of the **Herberger Theater Center** (on your right) and **Symphony Hall** (on your left), facing each other across the fountain- and sculpture-dotted Phoenix Civic Plaza courtyard. One more block, south along 2nd Street past the Hyatt Regency Phoenix to Adams, takes you to the next stop.

Here, amid the splendor and dignity of downtown, is a building with children's paintings all over its windows. It's the **Arizona Museum of Science and Technology,** a hands-on exploratorium for children of every age. Permanent displays include exercises in gravity, centrifugal force, and optical illusions. *80 N. 2nd St., tel. 602/256–9388. Admission: $4.50 adults, $3.50 senior citizens and children 4–12. Open Mon.–Sat. 9–5, Sun. noon–5.*

Finally, if you're really an indefatigable walker and an avid sports fan, another two blocks down 2nd Street will take you to the site of the **America West Phoenix Suns Arena** (2nd and Jefferson Sts., tel. 602/379–2000). This multifacility sports palace is almost a mall in itself, with cafés, an athletic club, and shops, in addition to the basketball-and-hockey stadium and team offices. It's an interesting tour even when there's no game on.

From the arena (or from Symphony Hall, across from the science museum, if you skip the arena), you can catch the DASH northbound for The Mercado and walk back to your car.

Tour 2: Cultural Center Walking Tour

The heart of Phoenix's new downtown cultural center is the rolling greensward of **Deck Park.** Begun in 1991 atop the I–10 tunnel under Central Avenue, it spreads a mile from 3rd Avenue on the west to 3rd Street on the east, and a quarter mile from Portland Street north to Culver. Completed in 1993, it is the city's second-largest downtown park (the largest is half-century-old Encanto Park, 2 miles northwest).

Gathered around Deck Park, mostly to the north, are museums, theaters, an art center, and the central library. Seeing all of them makes a comfortable day tour in moderate weather; in the warm months, it is too much for one day. Bus 0 runs up and down Central Avenue every 10 minutes on weekdays (at half-fare from 9 to 3) and every 20 minutes on weekends.

❼ Start at the **Phoenix Central Library** (12 E. McDowell Rd., tel. 602/262–4636), on the northeast corner of McDowell Road and Central Avenue. It's easy to find, and its palm-lined parking area has no time limit.

Immediately north of the library, in the same complex and sharing a courtyard, is the **Phoenix Art Museum.** It is particularly **❽** noteworthy for its clothing and costume collection, fine Asian art, 19th-century European paintings and drawings, and the American West collection, featuring painters from Frederic Remington to Georgia O'Keeffe. *1625 N. Central Ave., tel. 602/ 257–1222. Admission: $4 adults, $3 senior citizens over 65, $1.50 students, children 5 and under free. Admission free on Wed. Tours free. Open Tues. and Thurs.–Sat. 10–5, Wed. 10–9, Sun. noon–5.*

Two blocks north, cross Monte Vista and turn right 100 yards to **❾** the **Heard Museum.** In 1928 Dwight and Maie Heard donated their classic Arizona adobe home and their impressive Southwestern art collection to found what has become the nation's leading museum of Native American art and culture. Orient yourself with the multimedia show, then see the award-winning "Native Peoples of the Southwest" display; don't miss the kachina doll room (anchored by the Barry Goldwater collection). Modern Native American arts, interactive art-making exhibits for children, and live demonstrations by artisans are always on hand. In the spring, you may catch the annual Native American Arts & Crafts Show; call and ask, because its dates vary. *22 E. Monte Vista Rd., tel. 602/252–8840. Admission: $5 adults, $4 students and senior citizens, $3 juniors 13–18, $1 children 4–12, Native Americans free. Admission free Wed. after 5. Open Mon.–Sat. 9:30–5, Wed. 9:30–9, Sun. noon–5.*

If your day hasn't unaccountably disappeared in the museums, go back to Central Avenue, cross the street, and catch a No. 0 bus heading south. (Or walk, if it's below 90°F and you're hardy.)

At Culver Street, a long block south of McDowell Road, is the northern edge of Deck Park. The stately brick home with the **❿** gabled roof on the southwest corner is the **Ellis–Shackelford House** (1242 N. Central Ave., tel. 602/261–8699). One of Phoenix's first mansions, it was long the home of the Arizona Historical Society Museum (now in Papago Park, near the Phoenix Zoo). It houses the Phoenix Historic Preservation Office

Compliments of the American Express® Card and Red Lion Hotels.

Maui Book

TRAVEL GUIDE

and, in back, the restored railcars of the **Phoenix Street Railway** (tel. 602/254–0307 to arrange a visit).

Time Out   Halfway back to McDowell Road are two places that offer both rest and nourishment. At the **Spaghetti Company** (1418 N. Central Ave., tel. 602/257–0380) you can have lunch, spinach salad and wine, any of countless pasta dishes or other dinners, any day of the week. Across the street at **The Blue Fin** (1401 N. Central Ave., tel. 602/254–3171), the atmosphere is quick and informal, and the Japanese fast food is light and pleasant.

Now you have a choice: You can head back to the library complex, where you haven't yet seen the **Phoenix Little Theatre** (25 E. Coronado Rd., tel. 602/254–2151), just east of the museum and north of the library. Here the city's leading community theater group and its adjunct, the PLT Cookie Company, present plays and musicals for adults and children; you might end your day by catching a show.

If you're not ready to head back, you can go into Deck Park at the Ellis-Shackelford House, through the pedestrian tunnel under Central Avenue (with I–10 roaring beneath your feet), and walk 2½ blocks east to the **City Arts Center** (3rd and Moreland Sts., tel. 602/262–6583). In the **Phoenix Visual Arts Building,** valley professional and amateur artists do class and studio work in graphics, ceramics, sculpture, photography, and other media; check for current exhibits and sales. Adjacent is the **Phoenix Performing Arts Building,** a venue for small, experimental dance and theater groups. A performance here is a fine way to spend an evening after a day spent walking the city's cultural paths.

Tour 3: Scottsdale Walking Tour

Numbers in the margin correspond to points of interest on the Scottsdale map.

Historic sites, nationally known art galleries, and lots of clever boutiques fill downtown Scottsdale, easily turning a walking tour into several hours if you browse. Historic Old Scottsdale features the look of the Old West, while fashionable 5th Avenue is known for its shopping. Cross onto Main Street and enter a world frequented by the international art set; discover more galleries and interior-design shops on Marshall Way and Craftsman Court. This tour offers an overview of the area; *see* the Shopping section, *below*, for some specific recommendations.

While your tour can easily be completed on foot, a trolley (cost: $2 in summer, free the rest of the year) runs through the 5th Avenue area; the Ollie Trolley tours all of Scottsdale and charges $3 for an all-day pass. For information about both, call 602/941–2957. Also look for the horse-drawn Heritage Carriages (tel. 602/941–0369), which provide romantic transportation after dark and are usually found where Brown Avenue intersects Main Street.

Begin your tour by parking in the free public lot on the north-west corner of 2nd Street and Wells Fargo Avenue east of Scottsdale Road. A portion of the garage is signed for a three-hour limit; go to upper levels that don't carry time restraints, as enforcement is strict.

1 Head north on the brick-paved sidewalks leading to **Scottsdale Mall.** This tree-shaded setting has plenty of benches and grassy areas for restful contemplation. To your right, paths lead to a sculpture- and fountain-filled plaza around Scottsdale's **city hall, public library,** and **Center for the Arts** (7383 E. Scottsdale Mall, tel. 602/994–2301). The center presents a full schedule of concerts, and exhibits are changed frequently. Its gift shop, **The Artspot,** has unusual jewelry as well as posters and art books.

2 After circling the plaza, head west to the redbrick **Scottsdale Chamber of Commerce** building (7343 Scottsdale Mall, tel. 602/945–8481), constructed in 1910 as Scottsdale's first schoolhouse. Inside, shopping maps and helpful tips are provided if you're looking for something special. Ask for the walking-tour map of Old Scottsdale so you can note historic buildings as you go.

3 Continue west into **Old Scottsdale** on Main Street. Billed as "The West's Most Western Town," this area features rustic store-fronts and wooden sidewalks; it's touristy, but it's also the genu-ine item, giving visitors a taste of life here 80 years ago. Stores carry kitschy souvenirs, but you'll also find some nicer jewelry, pots, and Mexican imports.

Head north on Brown Avenue and turn left on 1st Avenue to continue sightseeing in Old Scottsdale.

Time Out The southeast corner of 1st Avenue and Scottsdale Road marks **4** a landmark of sorts: the candy pink-and-white **Sugar Bowl Ice Cream Parlor** (4005 N. Scottsdale Rd., tel. 602/946–0051), run by a local family since 1958 and frequented from its beginning by Paradise Valley cartoonist Bil Keane (the menu carries his "Family Circus" work). Although sandwiches, soups, and salads are available, you're missing the point if you don't indulge in the gooey sundaes, floats, and parfaits.

For an entirely different milieu, walk south on Scottsdale Road **5** and turn right onto **Main Street.** This block is literally filled with art galleries that contain artwork done in a variety of styles, in-cluding contemporary, Western realism, Native American, and traditional. With very few exceptions, casual visitors are made welcome in the galleries, although children may be bored. An-other option for viewing the galleries is the seasonal **Art Walk,** held from 7 to 9 PM each Thursday, October through May. The street takes on a party atmosphere during the evening hours when everyone is browsing.

Continue on Main Street across Marshall Way for several antiques shops, where specialties include elegant porcelains and china, fine antique jewelry, and Oriental rugs.

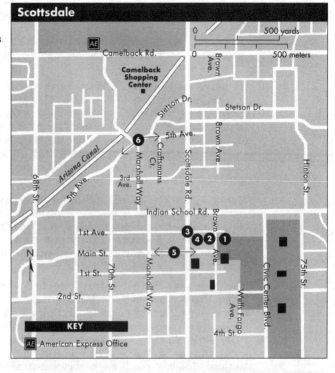

Scottsdale

KEY

AE American Express Office

Time Out   For a cool drink or light meal after daytime gallery-hopping, try **Arcadia Farms** (7014 E. 1st Ave., tel. 602/941–5665), where such eclectic sandwiches as rosemary-seasoned *focaccia* with chicken, roasted eggplant, and feta cheese are brought out to diners on a tree-shaded patio. Desserts are exceptional, so leave room. Open 8 AM to 3 PM Monday through Saturday; lunch reservations recommended.

If you walk north on 70th Street and cross Indian School Road, you'll discover another niche of galleries, upscale gift and jewelry stores, and several specialty boutiques. Farther north on Marshall Way across 3rd Avenue, the street is filled with more art galleries and creative stores with a Southwestern flair.

When you reach the fountain with the prancing horses, you're on **5th Avenue,** a 40-year-old stretch that is a shopping tradition in Phoenix. Whether you're seeking cacti or casual clothing, fine art or handmade Native American jewelry, you'll find it here.

Off 5th Avenue, Stetson Drive has a few interesting stores carrying original Native American artifacts, as well as books on Arizona and the Southwest; here you'll find **O'Brien's Art Emporium** (7122 E. Stetson Dr., tel. 602/945–1082), the oldest art gallery in Arizona.

Tour 4: Casa Grande Ruins National Monument and Florence

Numbers in the margin correspond to points of interest on the Around Phoenix map.

An hour's drive south of Phoenix takes visitors back to prehistoric times and the site of Arizona's first known civilization, as well as one of its major pioneer western towns. The Casa Grande Ruins National Monument, 1 mile north of Coolidge, captures some vivid reminders of the Hohokam Indians, who began farming in this area more than 1,500 years ago. Florence, one of central Arizona's first cities, is rich in examples of Territorial architecture.

Start your tour by heading southeast on I–10 leaving Phoenix. You'll pass Exit 160, which leads to **Williams Air Force Base,** site of the largest pilot-training facility in NATO but recommended for closure soon. The same exit is the closest freeway access to **Compadre Stadium,** spring-training home of the Milwaukee Brewers each February and March.

1 Soon you'll see a sign noting that you've entered the **Gila River Indian Reservation.** On the right, Exit 162A indicates **Firebird International Raceway** (20000 S. Maricopa Rd., tel. 602/268–0200), site of the Arizona National drag-racing finals each February and local Friday-night races; **Firebird Lake** (20000 S. Maricopa Rd., tel. 602/268–0200), a boat-racing site where the World Hydroplane Finals are held each November; and **Compton Terrace** (20000 S. Maricopa Rd., tel. 602/796–0511), one of the valley's largest outdoor concert venues.

The landscape changes to desert scrub, and the sun can become intense, so make use of sunscreen, hats, and drinking water. Large, strangely shaped saguaro cacti next begin to dominate **2** the landscape, covering a hillside as you cross the **Gila River**.

Time Out Thirty-seven miles south of Phoenix off I–10 is a disabled-accessible **rest area** with covered picnic tables. It's the last available stop until you reach your destination 20 miles later.

Take Exit 185 east off I–10 and follow the signs a short way to AZ 387. It's a two-lane road flanked by saguaros, and the spring landscape features brilliant red-tipped ocotillo cacti and yellow and purple wildflowers. Halfway into this 7-mile stretch, you'll climb a rise and see the Gila River valley spread out below. Four miles later, turn right onto AZ 87 and head 7½ miles to the ruins.

3 The **Casa Grande Ruins National Monument,** established in 1918, provides a close look at a structure first seen by European explorers in the 17th century. Allow an hour to inspect the site, longer if park rangers are giving a talk at the interpretive ramada or leading a tour.

Start at the visitor center, where a small museum features artifacts and information on the Hohokam, who lived here and

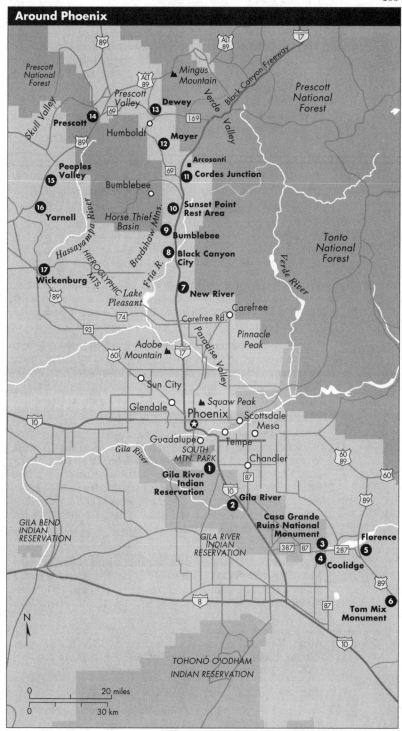

farmed irrigated cotton fields until they vanished mysteriously in about AD 1450. Step outside and begin your self-guided tour with an inspection of the 35-foot-tall Casa Grande (Big House), built around 1350 and still close to its original size. It's covered by a modern roof for protection from the sun and wind. Neighboring structures are much smaller, and only a bit of the 7-foot wall around the compound is still in evidence. The original purpose of Casa Grande still puzzles archaeologists; some think it was an ancient astronomical observatory.

Cross the parking lot by the covered picnic grounds and climb the platform for a view of an unexcavated ball court, said to date from the 1100s. Although only a few prehistoric sites can be viewed, more than 60 are included in the monument area.

A small gift shop in the lobby of the visitor center sells books about early Native American civilizations and other aspects of Arizona history. *1 mi north of Coolidge on AZ 87, tel. 602/723–3172. Admission: $2 adults, children under 16 and senior citizens over 62 free (with Golden Age Passport). Open daily 7–6.*

If traipsing among the ruins has given you an appetite, it's a
❹ short trip to **Coolidge,** 1 mile south on AZ 87, where you'll find fast-food hamburgers, chicken, and pizza. A public park with a children's playground is at 4th and Central avenues.

Take AZ 287 another 9 miles east from the monument to
❺ **Florence,** an old Western town distinguished by an American Victorian courthouse and more than 150 other sites listed on the National Register of Historic Places. An annual walking tour of historic Florence is held on the first Saturday in February.

The **Pinal County Visitor Center** (912 N. Pinal St., tel. 602/868–4331) answers questions and provides brochures weekdays from 9 to 5 September through May and 10–2 June through August. Two attractions are the **Pinal County Historical Museum** (715 S. Main St., tel. 602/868–4382), which displays furnishings from early 1900s homes and Native American crafts and tools, and the **McFarland Historical State Park,** where the 1878-era Pinal County Courthouse (Main and Ruggles Sts., tel. 602/868–5216) houses memorabilia of former Governor and U.S. Senator Ernest W. McFarland.

Several attractive shops and restaurants are found on Florence's Main Street, including the turn-of-the-century **Florence General Store** (1218 N. Main St., tel. 602/868–5748) and **Old Pueblo Restaurant** (505 S. Main St., tel. 602/868–4784), serving good Mexican food.

Time Out At **Jim-Bob's Auld Tyme Ice Cream Parlor** (913 N. Main St., tel. 602/868–9392), ice cream and hard-packed frozen yogurt are made on the circa-1886 adobe-walled premises.

Fans of Western-movie hero Tom Mix may want to drive 18 miles
❻ south on U.S. 89 to the **Tom Mix Monument,** at the site of his fatal automobile accident in 1940. Pack some soft drinks; it's low

desert (in fact, a showplace of dry-land vegetation), and no refreshments are on hand.

From Florence, retrace your route to Phoenix via AZ 287, 87, and 387 to link up with I–10 north and the 40-minute drive back to the Valley of the Sun.

Tour 5: Prescott and Wickenburg

Just over two hours north of Phoenix, after one of the most scenic drives in a state renowned for breathtaking vistas, you disappear into the tall pine country of Arizona's territorial capital. A slight westward jog on the way back leads you through legendary gold country and past modern dude ranches.

Start your tour by getting on I–17 (Black Canyon Freeway) and heading north. The sunken freeway is accessible from most major east–west arteries from Washington Street north. Between Van Buren Street and McDowell Road, it also connects with I–10 in a tall "stack" interchange.

Traveling north, you'll pass off-ramps for **Metrocenter,** the western valley's giant shopping-mall complex (*see* Shopping, *below*), and **Turf Paradise** (at Bell Road), the valley's popular Thoroughbred-horse track.

Abruptly, the developed areas thin out, and within 5 miles, as you pass the dark volcanic rubble of Adobe Mountain on your left, you are in open desert. Another half-dozen miles, just past Carefree Road (AZ 74), and you start climbing into foothills, where you'll see huge, spiky saguaro cacti; thick-leaved creosote bushes; and thin, spiny cholla cacti.

7 **New River,** spread out in the dry valley under which the Fria River's south fork flows, has service stations and several modest eating places.

Another 10 miles up the road is your last chance to be sure you're ready for the 2,000-foot ascent of the Mogollon Rim. On the way, the scenery shifts to classic desert mountainscape: exposed granite jutting up, covered with broken rock and scrappy vegetation; saguaros and creosote; and tall, lacy, green-limbed paloverde trees standing in the dry, flat washes. You may spot hawks or even eagles circling on the thermal currents, watching for prey.

8 At **Black Canyon City,** you enter Yavapai County and begin the climb up the rim. It's a beautifully graded modern highway, four lanes and completely divided, but it's a challenge—and an unfair one to an undercooled engine—so be sure to top out your car's fluids (and your own, if you don't want a half-hour wait).

Time Out Almost out of town, Exit 244 takes you east to the **Squaw Peak Buffalo Steakhouse** (Dog Track Rd., Black Canyon City, tel. 602/374–9247 or 602/395–9913). Besides big steaks, burgers, Canyon City Chicken sandwiches (served with sautéed mushrooms, onions, Swiss cheese and bacon), and homemade pie, a family of buffalo (not on the menu) linger just outside in a half-acre pen. Also on the site are a gas station and souvenir shop.

As you make the dramatic climb up the Mogollon Rim, you can see the geologic strata of the upthrust earth neatly laid out in the roadside rock—rust and pink, black and purple—and feel the air temperature drop rapidly. And in 6 miles, almost at the summit, you'll see the exit for **Bumblebee** and the **Horse Thief Basin.** The former, about 10 miles away, is a mining ghost town in the cleft of the Black Canyon to your left; the latter, some 20 miles farther along, is a beautiful wilderness area high in the Bradshaw Mountains on the other side. But go only if you've got good shoes and tires: 100 yards from the freeway, the paved road turns to dirt.

Three more miles and you suddenly reach the top—a wide, flat, grass-covered mesa, like a huge chunk of Nebraska pastureland stuck in the middle of purple mountaintops (and dotted with the clustered beaver-tails of nopal cacti). In fact, this semidesert plateau at about 4,000 feet *is* cattle-grazing land; you'll probably see some of the herds. At **Sunset Point Rest Area,** you can also see the spectacular view off the mesa and across the Black Canyon.

In 10 more miles, you come to the edge of the plateau, and for a moment you see the breathtaking sweep of the Verde Valley from above; then you swoop down a steep incline, at the bottom of which is the **Cordes Junction** turnoff, AZ 69. Here, you leave I–17 and head northwest to Prescott.

But first, about a mile down a partly paved road northeast from the gas stations and cafés, is one of the world's architectural wonders—**Arcosanti.** This evolving community, masterminded by Italian architect Paolo Soleri, is being built by its residents as a totally energy-independent town. It looks almost like a huge playground or modern-art theme park, with its desert-rock retaining walls and festive forms in earth-cast concrete. But it's full of ideas for dramatic design and ecologically sensitive living; it's worth taking an hour out for a tour, eating at the café, and bringing home one of the hand-cast wind-bells. *I–17 at Cordes Junction, Mayer 86333, tel. 602/632–7135. Admission free. Open daily 9–5. Tours: $5, hourly 10–4.*

Back on AZ 69, you're in the Valley of Big Bug Creek (you can see its course by looking for the willows south of the road). In 7 miles, after crossing the Big Bug a couple of times, you'll reach **Mayer,** a provisioning center for the gold hunters who scoured the area in the last century. The tall stack of its long-silent smelter peers over a hill, and some enchanting historic buildings still stand on Main Street, a mile or so off the road.

Another 12 miles through the rolling chaparral hills (highlighted by white datura blossoms and fiery Native American paintbrush in the fall), past Mayer's sister mining town of Humboldt, is **Dewey.**

Time Out Right on the edge of town, take AZ 169 east toward the looming 7,000-foot shoulders of Mingus Mountain; after 100 yards, pull in at **Young's Farm** (AZ 169, tel. 602/632–7272). This family-run, 47-year-old farm with its 25-year-old store has become a beloved purveyor of potpies and pumpkins, sweet corn and cider, hayrides, and honey and fresh bread. The Farm Kitchen coffee shop and bakery is open daily, 7 AM to 4 PM.

As you leave Dewey, AZ 69 widens to five lanes (the "Arizona lane" in the middle is for left turns only), and the landscape turns to scrub pines. In about 6 miles, you pass through **Prescott Valley,** a strip of mobile-home lots and fast-food stores that sprouted in the absence of zoning laws (watch your speed—they do have traffic laws), and then the pine trees and the hills suddenly grow taller.

⑭ Eight miles later, you enter **Prescott,** with the sandstone red Sheraton standing atop a butte in the foreground and Thumb Butte towering a few miles in the background. In a forested bowl at 5,300 feet above sea level, this lovely site was the first capital of the Arizona Territory and remains first choice for summer refuge among Phoenix-area desert dwellers.

As soon as you see the Sheraton, get into the left lane: For some reason, at the junction with U.S. 89, most lanes take you back out of town to the north. But the left lane becomes **Gurley Street,** the city's main drag. Immediately, you have a choice of motels, including the historic Mission Inn, now the **American Motel** (1211 E. Gurley St., 86301 tel. 602/778–0787), and the venerable **Senator Inn,** famous for its themed rooms (1117 E. Gurley St., 86301, tel. 602/445–1440).

Heading into town, you'll notice the many Victorian frame houses. Prescott was proclaimed capital by President Lincoln and settled by Yankees to ensure that gold-rich northern Arizona would be a Union resource—Tucson and southern Arizona were strongly pro-Confederacy. Despite a devastating downtown fire in July 1900, Prescott remains the Southwest's richest store of late-19th-century New England–style architecture (some wags say that long before Scottsdale declared itself "The West's Most Western Town," Prescott was "The West's Most Eastern Town").

About 1½ miles along Gurley is **Courthouse Plaza,** between Cortez and Montezuma streets. This is the heart of the city, where the old Yavapai County Courthouse stands, guarded by an equestrian bronze of turn-of-the-century journalist and lawmaker Bucky O'Neill, who died while charging San Juan Hill with Teddy Roosevelt. A block east of Courthouse Plaza, the historic **Hassayampa Inn** (122 E. Gurley St., 86301, tel. 602/778–9434) was recently restored to its classic 1927 splendor; it's priced like a Phoenix hotel but delivers memorable Southwestern elegance for the money.

The quickest way to get oriented is to find the south end of the plaza. There, across from the courthouse's rear entrance,

stands the **Chamber of Commerce** (117 W. Goodwin St., tel. 602/
445–2000). Among the many maps and brochures here are two
gems—"Historic Downtown Prescott: Walking Tour Guide" and
"Prescott's Driving Tour Guide." Either of these will have you
feeling like a local in a half-hour.

Flanking the plaza's west side, Montezuma Street, is **Whiskey
Row,** named for a string of brawling pioneer taverns; some still
stand, though the social activity here is very subdued. Upgrad-
ing one end of Whiskey Row is the mahogany-paneled **Hotel St.
Michael** (205 W. Gurley St., tel. 602/776–1999), reopened in
1988 as a very modestly priced hostelry with a café and two
floors of shops, one a gaslighted turn-of-the-century underground "mall." Near the middle of Whiskey Row is **Maude's** (146
S. Montezuma St., tel. 602/778–3080), an always full, fresh-
scrubbed breakfast and lunch spot that would be at home in
Mendocino or Santa Fe. And at the row's south end, the **Gallop-
ing Goose** (162 S. Montezuma St., tel. 602/778–7600) is a former
gas station filled with lots of kitschy cowboy and Native American crafts alongside stunning collections of kachina dolls and
jewelry by some of the Southwest's best Native American artists.

Farther south on Montezuma is a good place to look for more
lodging options. Four blocks from Whiskey Row is the **Prescott
Country Inn** (503 S. Montezuma St., 86303, tel. 602/445–7991), a
1940s motor court transformed into a cozy bed-and-breakfast;
about 2 miles farther, after Montezuma changes names (to
White Spar and then Copper Basin Road), there is a mile-long
stretch with seven hotels and motels in the pines and four restaurants strategically set among them.

Fun eating places are all over town. On the plaza's east side is
the playful restored '50s experience of **Kendall's Burgers** (113 S.
Cortez St., tel. 602/778–3568), complete with soda fountain; up
the street a block or so is **Chris' New York Deli** (125 N. Cortez
St., tel. 602/778–2472), a lively hole-in-the-wall with noshes
that taste like Brooklyn's. Farther north is the fern-and-brass of
Murphy's (201 N. Cortez St., tel. 602/445–4044), with a 60-beer
pub and an award-winning kitchen that turns out prime rib,
pasta, a dozen seafood dishes, and some sharp appetizers (how
about bay-shrimp nachos?). Back south to Gurley Street and
west past Montezuma Street is **Nolaz** (216 W. Gurley St., tel.
602/445–3765), where Cajun dishes get tender treatment.

Time Out   For unforgettable tortillas, go one block west of the plaza on
Gurley Street, turn right on McCormick for half a block, and
swing left into the curved driveway under the big apple tree.
The little building beside the white house is **Angel's Food Products** (120½ S. McCormick, no phone). Try a tortilla hot from the
oven.

Antiques and collectibles have become such an extensive part of
the Prescott scene that the best bet is to stop at the first shop
you see and ask for a brochure. The local dealers' group has put

together a clear map of more than two dozen shops, noting their specialties and hours.

Lovers of the past won't want to miss the **Sharlot Hall Museum,** a remarkable two-square-block re-creation of territorial Arizona, including the original log mansion of the governor, just two blocks west of Courthouse Square. Besides the mansion and museum, the parklike setting holds three other fully restored period homes, a working blacksmith shop, and the first territorial jail. It's easy to spend half or all of a day in this place. *415 W. Gurley St., tel. 602/445-3122. Admission free; donation requested. Open Apr.-Oct., Tues.-Sat. 10-5; Nov.-Mar., Tues.-Sat. 10-4, Sun. 1-5; closed Mon.*

Prescott is also home to the **Bead Museum** (140 S. Montezuma St., tel. 602/445-2431), an international collection, with beads from 3,000 BC to modern times; the much-respected **Phippen Museum of Western Art** (4701 Hwy. 89 N, about 5 mi north of the entrance to town, tel. 602/778-1385); and the **Smoki Museum** of Native American artifacts (100 N. Arizona, tel. 602/445-1230).

If you make Prescott a day trip, you'll probably find you've stayed a little longer than you expected. Your best bet is to end the day by retracing your route along Gurley Street, back onto AZ 69, and then south on I-17. The trip, from Courthouse Square to downtown Phoenix, can be done comfortably in 2½ hours, including a rest stop.

If you decide to spend a night or two in Prescott, you'll have some time to view another part of Arizona and its past on the way back to Phoenix. To do that, take Montezuma Street south out of town; in about 4 miles, it enters the **Prescott National Forest** and winds through the forested tops of the northern Bradshaw Mountain range (you saw the south end of these mountains across Black Canyon on the way up).

Then the road drops and winds about 15 miles to the lush mead-
⓯ ows of **Peeples Valley,** named for the rancher who started a gold rush there by finding nuggets in Antelope Creek. Another 8
⓰ miles and you're at **Yarnell,** dropping below the timberline and into the desert.

Here you'll enter the watershed of the elusive Hassayampa River, whose furtive habits (traveling below the surface most of the year, then bursting into flood in winter or spring) gave the reputation of liars to locals who swore they lived on a river.

⓱ About 25 miles along the way is **Wickenburg,** home of dude ranches and tall tales. This city is named for Henry Wickenburg, whose nearby Vulture Mine was the richest gold strike in the Arizona Territory. On the main drag are the **Hassayampa Bridge,** the nearby **Jail Tree** (where prisoners were chained, the desert heat sometimes finishing them off before their sentences were served), and the **Gold Nugget** (222 E. Wickenburg Way, tel. 602/684-2858), a Western-style eating place perfect for easy refueling for your journey. Half a block north on Valentine Street is **Anita's Cocina** (62 N. Valentine St., tel. 602/684-5777), which offers authentic Mexican fare. If you have time, the **Dessert Caballeros** (21 N. Frontier St., tel. 602/684–7075), a local charitable equestrian group, maintains a fine museum of Hassayampa lore. If you opt for a longer stay in Wickenburg, there are plenty of dude ranches to accommodate you (*see* Lodging, *below*).

About 10 miles out of Wickenburg, you can save yourself considerable time by taking AZ 74 east (it's the Carefree Road you passed going north). In just 30 miles, it reaches I–17, leaving you with a 15-minute trip into downtown, whereas if you stay on U.S. 89, you'll angle into the urban area through every suburb on the west side before reaching downtown.

Tour 6: The White Mountains

Numbers in the margin correspond to points of interest on The White Mountains map.

The drive into eastern Arizona's White Mountains offers a representative tour of the state's many climates and striking vistas. This trip can be completed as either of two loops, depending on which scenery proves most appealing. Most of the year, it's a demanding but entirely possible day trip. Still, the beauty of the mountains and meadows makes at least one overnight stay all but irresistible. If you're going in the winter or early spring, you may need chains—and you'll probably want to take ski clothes and equipment as well, and make at least a weekend of it.

❶ From Phoenix, take I–10 and then U.S. 60 (the Superstition Freeway) east through the suburbs of Tempe, Mesa, and Apache Junction. The massive escarpment of the **Superstition Mountains** heaves into view and slides by to the north, as the Phoenix metro area gives way to cactus- and creosote-dotted desert. The Superstitions are supposedly home to the legendary **Lost Dutchman Mine,** the location—not to mention the existence—of which has been hotly debated since pioneer days.

❷ About 7 miles east of Apache Junction off U.S. 60 is the Peralta Trail Road, a bumpy route to the Peralta Trail. The trail winds up a small valley for a spectacular view of **Weaver's Needle,** a monolithic rock formation that is one of Arizona's more famous sights. This is about a two-hour side trip, including the medium-difficulty hike.

At Florence Junction, the four-lane freeway becomes a two-lane highway and starts rising steadily into the foothills of the Mescal Mountains.

Time Out Be sure to stop at the **Boyce Thompson Southwestern Arboretum,**
❸ about a dozen miles beyond Florence Junction. Its compact, informative walking tour takes in exhibits of Arizona's exotic desert flora, and it's a shady spot to break for a picnic lunch (*see* What to See and Do with Children, *below*).

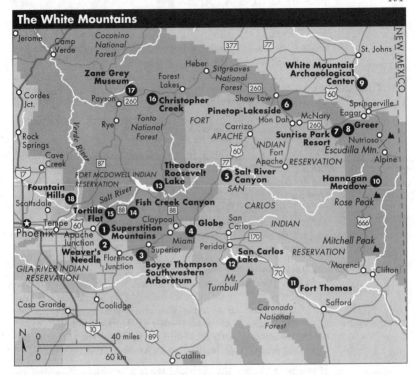

The White Mountains

Only a half-dozen miles farther on is **Superior,** the first of several modest mining towns and the launching point for a dramatic winding ascent through the Mescals to a 4,195-foot pass affording panoramic views of this copper-rich range and its huge, eerily dormant open-pit mines. Collectors will want to watch for antiques shops through these hills, but be forewarned: The quality varies considerably. The descent is just as quick into **Miami** and **Claypool,** once-thriving boom towns that have carried on quietly since major-corporation mining ground to a halt in the 1970s. The working-class buildings are dwarfed by the mountainous piles of copper tailings to the north.

❹ Dotted with majestic cypress trees, **Globe,** in the southern reaches of Tonto National Forest, is the last and most cosmopolitan of these mining towns. This is a good place to eat and fill the gas tank if necessary, because it's the last appreciable town for about 90 miles of mostly mountainous country. **Jerry's Restaurant** (669 E. Ash St., Globe, tel. 602/425–5282) is a humble café offering standard American and Mexican eats at reasonable prices.

After Globe, follow U.S. 60 north (don't continue east on U.S. 70), and the terrain immediately changes to the Tonto's ponderosa pine forests as the highway begins climbing through rolling ❺ hills. The highlight of this stretch is the magnificent **Salt River Canyon,** about 40 miles past Globe. After entering the San Carlos Indian Reservation, U.S. 60 drops from the Natanes Plateau into a vast gorge, making a series of hairpin turns, to cross the Salt River and then climb out again along the canyon's northern cliffs. This is a truly spectacular chasm, unfairly overlooked in a state full of world-famous gorges.

Time Out	Stop before crossing the bridge to stretch your legs and wander along the banks of the Salt, enjoying its rock-strewn rapids. On hot Arizona days you can slip your shoes off and dip your feet into the chilly water for a cool respite.

The road out of the Salt River Canyon offers several breath-taking overlooks worth stopping to enjoy. The highway continues to climb to the **Mogollon Rim**—a huge geologic upthrust that bisects Arizona from northwest to southeast—and its cool upland pinewoods. **Show Low,** in the Apache Sitgreaves National Forest, is a crossing point for east–west traffic along the rim and traffic headed for Holbrook and points north.

At Show Low, turn right onto AZ 260, and soon you'll find yourself in the newer tourist/retirement community of **Pinetop–Lakeside** (the two towns joined in 1984 but still have separate post offices). It's a lengthy succession of shopping malls, restaurants, and motels, more numerous than appealing. But the slowly curving highway through these twin towns is usually dotted on the weekends with fruit-and-vegetable stands, purveying modestly priced, wonderfully fresh Arizona produce.

If you plan to stay the night, there is a good mix of hostelries worth considering, among them **Bartram's Bed and Breakfast** (Rte. 1, Box 1014, Lakeside 85929, tel. 800/257–0211); **Coldstream B&B** (Box 2616, Pinetop 85935, tel. 602/369–0115); and the cottages (with boats available) at **Spring Hill on Rainbow Lake** (Box 1040, Lakeside 85929, tel. 602/368–8688).

After Pinetop–Lakeside, the road dips into the Fort Apache Indian Reservation. At the tiny crossroads town of **Hon Dah,** AZ 260 swings east again. **McNary** is next, a ramshackle Native American community built among the pines—but don't hurry through if you see a tent and a sign advertising Indian fry bread. Try this doughy fried dish with honey or other fillings for a taste of Native American cuisine.

Already more than a mile above sea level, the highway continues its gradual but steady climb after McNary into the White Mountains, leaving the reservation for the Apache National Forest. Get a breath of the thin, pine-scented air; it tends to be cool even in the middle of a summer day.

At AZ 273 winter and early spring visitors will want to turn right to **Sunrise Park Resort,** the state's largest ski area, with five day lodges, 11 lifts, and 65 trails on three mountains rising to 11,000 feet. Operated by the White Mountain Apaches, the resort is one of the most successful Native American business enterprises in the United States. The recently remodeled **Sunrise Ski Lodge** offers modern accommodations and solid American dining at reasonable prices. The tribe also operates a modest outdoor-sports center, which rents a variety of equipment, from cross-country skis to mountain bikes. *Sunrise Park Resort, Greer 85927, tel. 800/772–SNOW or 602/735–7676 for skiing reports. Open year-round.*

❽ Down AZ 260 another five minutes is the turnoff summer and fall tourists won't want to miss—AZ 373 for **Greer,** a tiny, charming community built around a meadow and trout ponds. Here are numerous lodges and resorts of varying quality and price. **Greer Lodge** offers huge and hearty meals, with cozy overnight accommodations in a rustic log cabin; the friendly help keeps a fire stoked and roaring through the cool alpine evenings. *Greer Lodge, Box 244, Greer 85927, tel. 602/735–7515. Open year-round.*

This area of gently sloping national forest land is dotted with meadows, lakes, and small reservoirs and dominated by 11,590-foot Baldy Peak. It's a wonderland for outdoor activities: hunting, fishing, horseback riding, hiking, boating, camping. Much of it remains under the control of the Apache nation, so visitors must take care to respect the land as they do and to honor their wishes.

Another 10 minutes east on AZ 260 are the twin towns of **Springerville** and **Eagar,** in Round Valley. The region, hard against the New Mexico border, brims with Old West lore. This is where William Bonney (aka Billy the Kid) herded livestock before turning outlaw. Many of the towns were founded by Mormon pioneers and there is a big Mormon church between the two towns, but they are dominated by their high school's domed stadium, testament to the residents' love of sports and to the sometimes harsh winter weather.

❾ For a pleasant stop and a step back 1,000 years, head north on AZ 666 about 12 miles from Springerville to the **White Mountain Archaeological Center.** At Raven Site Ruin, on a former cattle ranch, James and Carol Cunkle lead amateurs, students, and professionals in unearthing evidence of a pottery-making Native American culture that flourished from about AD 1000 to 1450. Half-day hikes visit nearby petroglyphs; day-long programs add hands-on training in ruin-sifting. Longer stays include accommodations at a restored 19th-century bunkhouse. The tiny museum is a marvel. *White Mountain Archaeological Center, HC 30, St. Johns 85936, tel. 602/333–5857. Admission: $3 adults, $2 children 12–17 and senior citizens, with guided 1-hour tour; children under 12 free. Open May 1–Oct. 15, daily 10–5.*

Springerville is a decision point: Should you head south or west on the return trip to Phoenix? At Springerville, AZ 260 joins U.S. 60, which continues east into New Mexico, and the so-called "Devil's Highway" (AZ 666), surely one of the world's curviest roads, coming down from the Painted Desert.

If you decide to head south from Springerville on AZ 666, this lonely highway passes through **Nutrioso** under 10,912-foot
❿ Escudilla Mountain and eventually rises to **Hannagan Meadow,**

one of Arizona's most splendid camping areas. Lush and isolated, it provides a home to elk, deer, and range cattle. Don't miss the splendid overlooks on the way.

Time Out | Waiting by the roadside in the middle of the meadow is the log-built **Hannagan Meadow Lodge,** where you can enjoy a meal or a month in a setting of unparalleled peace and beauty, with people who have true appreciation for life outside the city, but not without amenities. *Hannagan Meadow Lodge, HC61 Box 335, Alpine 85920, tel. 602/339–4370. Open year-round.*

From Hannagan Meadow, the road south twists and turns as it descends into a huge wilderness devoid, for the most part, of humans, and passes under Rose and Mitchell peaks (there is camping near the latter).

Eventually passing through the mining towns of **Morenci** and **Clifton,** AZ 666 then swings back west, links up with U.S. 70, and provides a fairly straight shot through **Safford** and across ⑪ rather uninteresting desert to Globe. As you near **Fort Thomas,** keep your eyes peeled—$28,000 in gold pieces, meant to pay the soldiers there, was stolen back in May 1889 and still hasn't been found. About 12 miles farther along, on your left, you'll see towering 8,282-foot Mt. Turnbull, then the spreading expanse of ⑫ **San Carlos Lake,** a reservoir behind Coolidge Dam. (Dedicating it in 1927, Will Rogers observed, "If that was my lake, I'd mow it.") At Peridot, if you turn north on AZ 170, 4 miles brings you to the town of San Carlos: It used to be Rice, until the dam put the original San Carlos underwater.

Once you reach Globe, you can retrace your original route back along U.S. 60 to Phoenix. Or if you prefer, **The Apache Trail** (AZ 88) departs from Claypool to the north, passing several ranches ⑬ en route to the massive **Theodore Roosevelt Lake** reservoir, a favorite aquatic recreational area flanked by the desolate Mazatzal and Sierra Anchas mountain ranges. The Apache Trail eventually winds its way back to Apache Junction via the mag- ⑭ nificent, bronze-hued **Fish Creek Canyon.**

Time Out | Close to the end of the Apache Trail are the old-time restaurant, ⑮ bar, and country store at **Tortilla Flat.** This is a fun place to stop for a well-earned rest and refreshment—miner- and cowboy-style grub, of course—before heading back the last 20 miles to civilization. *1678 W. Superstition Blvd., Apache Junction, tel. 602/984–1776. Open year-round weekdays 9–6, weekends 8–7.*

Back at Springerville, your other homeward option is to follow U.S. 60 west along the forested Mogollon Rim, enjoying its thrilling overlooks. From Show Low, take AZ 260 west along the Rim through a variety of small retirement and ranching communities. After **Forest Lakes,** the road dives off the Rim, hugging sheer cliffs for a 2,000-foot drop to the broad, verdant **Tonto Basin.**

Time Out Below the rim, in the Tonto Basin, is **Christopher Creek,** a primi-
⓰ tive community with a humble but decent restaurant, the **Creekside Steak House & Tavern** (HCR Box 146, Payson, tel. 602/478–
4389). **The Christopher Creek Lodge** (Star Route Box 119,
Payson 85541, tel. 602/478–4300) offers no-frills log-cabin
accommodations.

West of Christopher Creek a huge forest fire charred much of
the terrain several summers ago, destroying (along with millions of trees) the antiques-filled **Zane Grey Cabin,** once the
home of the novelist whose popular tales—many of which were
made into films—colorfully documented the rough-and-tumble
life of this corner of the Old West. Now Mel and Beth Counseller
recall his life and career a dozen miles down the road with photo-
⓱ graphs, videos, art, and new mementos at the modest **Zane Grey
Museum.** *408 W. Main St., Suite 8, Payson 85547, tel. 602/478–
4243. Open year-round, daily 9–5.*

You're back to civilization in **Payson,** a bustling vacation town
with an interesting, unpretentious municipal golf course and a
good supply of antiques shops. Turn south on U.S. 87 for the last
hour-long dash across the ridges of the Mazatzals.

Descending into a saguaro-studded basin, you reach the Salt
River again, this time on the Fort McDowell Mohave–Apache
Reservation, whose residents have outlasted the fort where the
U.S. Army based its northern campaign against the Apaches.
⓲ When you see the 140-foot spray of the **Fountain Hills** fountain,
get ready to turn right at Shea Boulevard and head back, via
Scottsdale, into Phoenix.

What to See and Do with Children

Aimed at children of elementary-school age, the **Arizona Museum for Youth** displays fine arts in a manner accessible to youngsters. Hands-on exhibits allow children to make crafts or
participate as they go through the museum. A tour takes about
1–1½ hours. *35 N. Robson St., Mesa, tel. 602/644–2468. Admission: $2. Open Tues.–Fri. 1–5, Sat. 10–5, Sun. 1–5.*

Arizona Museum of Science and Technology (*see* Tour 1, *above*).

About an hour east of Phoenix on U.S. 60, the **Boyce Thompson
Southwestern Arboretum** is one of the treasures of the Sonoran
Desert. From the visitor center, well-marked, self-guided trails
traverse 35 acres, winding through all of the desert's varied
habitats—from gravelly open desert to lush creekside glades—
rich with native flora and wildlife. The **Smith Interpretive Center,** a National Historic Site, houses displays on such topics as
geology and mining plus two greenhouses with cacti and other
succulents. The arboretum is a wonderful place to stop for a picnic on your way to the mining towns of Superior and Miami. *Box
AB, Superior 85273, tel. 602/689–2811. Admission: $4 adults,
$2 children 5–12. Open daily 8–5. Closed Christmas.*

Great Arizona Puppet Theatre (3302 N. 7th St., Phoenix 85011, tel. 602/277–1275) mounts a yearlong cycle of inventive puppet productions, mostly original, in a converted church; it also offers classes in puppet making and operation.

At the **Hall of Flame,** retired firefighters lead tours past more than 100 restored fire engines and more than 3,000 helmets, badges, and other fire fighting–related articles. *6101 E. Van Buren St. (in Papago Park), tel. 602/275–3473. Admission: $4 adults, $1.50 children 6–17, children 6 and under free. Open Mon.–Sat. 9–5, Sun. 12–4.*

Model-train displays, stores with railway memorabilia and items for the train hobbyist, and a restored Pullman car fill the popular **McCormick Railroad Park.** For $1, children can ride the miniature train or the 1929 merry-go-round. *7301 E. Indian Bend Rd., tel. 602/994–2312. Admission free. Call for hours.*

At the foot of South Mountain, **Mystery Castle,** hand-built out of found desert rocks, is chock-full of oddities that will fascinate everyone in the family. There are 18 rooms with 13 fireplaces, 90 bottle-glass portholes, a downstairs grotto, and a roll-away bed with a mining railcar as its frame. *800 E. Mineral Rd. (at south end of 7th St.) tel. 602/268–1581. Admission: $3 adults, $1 children 5–15. Open Tues.–Sun. 11–4.*

Phoenix Children's Theatre (1202 N. 3rd St., tel. 602/265–4142) stages a full season, usually adaptations of fairy tales and children's books, at the city's Performing Arts Building.

At the **Phoenix Zoo,** a new 21,000-square-foot Baboon Kingdom exhibit brings together more than 1,300 animals, grouped by continent of origin. Native American and African elephants (including one that produces artwork sold in galleries!) and a rare Sumatran tiger are among the attractions. A 30-minute narrated tour on the safari train costs $1 and gives a good overview of the park. *5810 E. Van Buren St. (in Papago Park), tel. 602/273–7771. Admission: $6 adults, $5 senior citizens over 62, $3 children 4–12. Open daily 9–5, except Christmas.*

Original and reconstructed buildings from all over Arizona set the stage for the **Pioneer Arizona Museum.** Guides in the blacksmith shop, print shop, schoolhouse, and homes demonstrate daily activities from the past. *Pioneer Rd. exit off I–17, tel. 602/993–0212. Admission: $5.75 adults, $5.25 senior citizens and students, $4 children 4–12, children 3 and under free. Open daily 9–5, closed July 4–Oct. 1.*

The false fronts on **Rawhide**'s dusty Main Street house saloons, gift shops, old-time photo studios, and craftspeople as well as opportunities to take a stagecoach ride or to pan for gold. Hayrides travel a short distance into the desert for a cookout under the stars on weekends. *23023 N. Scottsdale Rd., Scottsdale, tel. 602/563–1880. Admission $2 (rebate with dinner); separate charges for shops, restaurants, attractions. Open Mon.–Thurs. 5–10 PM, Fri.–Sun. 11–10.*

Similar to Rawhide, but a better deal because the price of entry is all-inclusive, **Rockin' R Ranch** includes a petting zoo, a reenactment of a wild shoot-out, and—the main attraction—a nightly cookout with a Western stage show. Browse the shops until the chow—beef, beans, and biscuits—is served, followed by music and entertainment. Reservations are required. *6136 E. Baseline Rd., Mesa, tel. 602/832–1539. Admission (includes meal and show): $14.95 adults, $8.50 children 3–12. Open year-round; call for hours.*

The **Sunrise Preschool** (642 E. Monroe St., tel. 602/253–0381) at the east end of The Mercado (*see* Tour 1, *above*) offers high-quality child care with drop-in rates, 24 hours a day.

Shopping

Since its resorts began multiplying in the 1930s and 1940s, Phoenix has acquired a healthy share of high-style clothiers and leisure-wear boutiques. But well before that, Western clothes were dominant here—jeans and boots, cotton shirts and dresses, 10-gallon hats and bola ties (the state's official neckwear). They still are. Plain or designer, cowboy or vaquero, with rivets or silver *conchos* or diamonds, Western is always in style, and outfitters abound.

In the past decade, Sun Belt awareness has brought a tide of interest in Southwestern furnishing styles as well, from the pastels of the desert mountains and skies to the handmade lodgepole furniture of the pueblo and rancho. These—as well as Mexican tiles and tinware, wrought iron and copper work, courtyard fountains and paper flowers—have never died out here. Always an essential part of the way southwesterners shape their homes, work spaces, and public places, these crafts have flourished in the current revival.

At the same time, the drivers of many a wagon train in the past century and many a U-Haul in this one have headed west and ended up unloading here. As a result, the shops and auctions of Phoenix and its suburbs contain an unexpectedly wide array of antiques and collectibles.

On the scene long before any of these, of course, were the fine and powerful arts of the Southwest's true natives—Navajo weavers, sand painters, and silversmiths; Hopi weavers and kachina-doll carvers; Pima and Papago basket makers and potters; and many more.

Inspired by the region's rich cultural traditions, contemporary artists have flourished here as well, making Phoenix—and in particular, Scottsdale, a city with more art galleries than gas stations—one of the Southwest's two great art centers (alongside Santa Fe, New Mexico).

Most of the valley's power shopping is concentrated in central Phoenix and downtown Scottsdale. But auctions and antiques shops cluster in odd places—and as treasure hunters know, you've always got to have an eye open.

Malls   The open-air **Park Central Mall** (Central Ave. and Earll Dr., tel. 602/264–5575) is the oldest and closest to downtown, amid the high rises of Central Avenue. Anchored by a **Dillard's** department store (3033 N. 3rd Ave., tel. 602/277–0564) that sells all the seasonal clearance items from the other stores in the Dillard's chain, Park Central also has the popular **Limited Express** (55 Park Central Mall, tel. 602/266–3450); the **Miracle Mile Deli** (9 Park Central Mall, tel. 602/277–4783), a traditional favorite with downtown shoppers; and **Leonard's Luggage** (Park Central Mall, tel. 602/264–3591), the valley's oldest purveyor of luxury leather goods and accessories.

Metrocenter (I–17 and Peoria Ave., tel. 602/997–2641), on the west side of Phoenix, is an enclosed double-deck mall, the state's largest. The adjacent **Castles N Coasters** (9445 N. Metro Pkwy. E, tel. 602/997–7575), a miniature-golf park and video-game palace, and the in-mall **Metro Midway** (13615 N. 35th Ave., tel. 602/395–9915), an array of rides and games, make Metro the valley's best mall for teens and younger children. Inside, its anchor department stores include **Robinson's** (9700 N. Metro Pkwy. E, tel. 602/943–2351). Metrocenter has nearly every store Park Central has and many more, but in a Muzak-filled, disinfected, deodorized environment that might as easily be in St. Louis or Seattle or Secaucus.

Fiesta Mall (AZ 360 and Alma School Rd., Mesa, tel. 602/833–5450) and the new **Superstition Springs Mall,** a dozen miles farther east (AZ 360 and Superstition Springs Rd., Mesa, tel. 602/832–0212), provide slightly smaller copies, without the youth attractions, for the eastern valley—though the latter does boast a handsome indoor carousel and a pleasant outdoor cactus garden to stroll in. The somewhat older but just expanded **Paradise Valley Mall** (Cactus and Tatum Rds., tel. 602/996–8840) does likewise for northeastern Phoenix.

Scottsdale Fashion Square (Scottsdale and Camelback Rds., Scottsdale, tel. 602/990–7800) is a definite step up. Besides Robinson's and Dillard's, it is anchored by **Bullock's** (6900 E. Camelback Rd., Scottsdale, tel. 602/994–3111), and its mix of stores runs more to specialty shops; children will want everything in the **Disney Store** (7014 E. Camelback Rd., Scottsdale, tel. 602/423–5008) and **Warner Bros. Studio Store** (7014 E. Camelback Rd., Scottsdale, tel. 602/423–1663).

Biltmore Fashion Park (24th St. and Camelback Rd., tel. 602/955–8400), about 8 miles west in Phoenix, is yet another step up. **I. Magnin** (2400 E. Camelback Rd., tel. 602/955–7200) and **Saks Fifth Avenue** (2500 E. Camelback Rd., tel. 602/955–8000) are its anchors, and designer boutiques are its stock-in-trade—**Banana Republic** (2582 E. Camelback Rd., tel. 602/955–9108), **Beaton's** (2480 E. Camelback Rd., tel. 602/955–5061), **Bruno Magli** (2542 E. Camelback Rd., tel. 602/956–6661), **Gucci** (2504 E. Camelback Rd., tel. 602/957–8710), and **Polo by Ralph**

Lauren (2580 E. Camelback Rd., tel. 602/952–0155) are among them. Grown-up toy shops include **The Sharper Image** (2596 E. Camelback Rd., tel. 602/956–8077) and **Williams-Sonoma** (2450 E. Camelback Rd., tel. 602/957–0430). **Borders Books and Music** (2402 E. Camelback Rd., tel. 602/957–6660) is a great family place, complete with coffee shop; the new outpost of **Planet Hollywood** (2402 E. Camelback Rd., tel. 602/954–7827) seasons its menu with the hope of spotting one or more of its movie-star owners. Biltmore Fashion Park also has more fine eating in a small compass than anywhere else in Arizona; *see* the reviews of **Roxsand, Steamers, Oscar Taylor's,** and **Christopher's** in the Dining section, *below.*

The Borgata (6166 N. Scottsdale Rd., tel. 602/998–1822), a recreation of a medieval Italian walled village, may slip into pretentiousness, but it offers a pleasant enough selection of boutiques and galleries. **Dos Cabezas** (tel. 602/991–7004) has won a well-deserved following as a creative source of Southwestern interior and apparel design, and **Laise Adzer** (tel. 602/948–1528) is a byword for eclectic high fashion.

Markets and Auctions | **Guadalupe Farmer's Market** (9210 S. Avenida del Yaqui, Guadalupe, tel. 602/730–1945) has all the fresh ingredients of Mexican cuisine that you'd find in a rural Mexican market—tomatillos, many varieties of chili peppers (fresh and dried), fresh-ground *masa* (cornmeal) for tortillas, cumin and cilantro, and on and on. **Mercado Mexico** (8212 S. Avenida del Yaqui, Guadalupe, tel. 602/831–5925), about six blocks north, sells childhood treats Mexican adults remember fondly, from *cajetas* (goat's milk candy) to cocoa blocks and sweet powders in paper tubes. The rest of the shop is shelf after shelf of ceramic, paper, tin, and lacquerware, at unbeatable prices.

John Brunk & Sons Auctions (4001 N. 7th St., tel. 602/264–3204) moves a barnful of cast-off furnishings, appliances, tools—and often several decent antiques or collectibles—twice each Wednesday, at 9 AM and from 7 PM until the last lot is gone. **Ron Brunk Inc. Auction** has a warehouse auction Sunday at noon in the western valley, not far from Sun City (11001 N. 99th Ave., Peoria, tel. 602/933–7748). **Hudson & Associates** (3602 N. 35th Ave., tel. 602/269–8662) gavels off a diverse gathering of goods starting at 7 PM each Friday, as does **Ware's Auction** (38th Ave. at Indian School Rd., tel. 602/278–0489) at 7 PM Monday.

Barrett & Jackson Classic Car Auction (5530 E. Washington St., tel. 602/273–0791) is a nationally recognized dealer in rare and antique autos, and the annual January mega-auction draws collectors from around the world.

Southwestern Arts and Crafts | The **Heard Museum** (22 E. Monte Vista Rd., tel. 602/252–8848) sells the finest selection of Southwestern Native American arts and crafts in the valley—both traditional and modern—at its gift shop. The museum is also the ideal place for learning about whatever medium or art form interests you and to see Native American artists and artisans at work almost every day.

Herman Atkinson's Indian Trading Post (3957 N. Brown Ave., Scottsdale, tel. 602/949–9750) is another fine—but eclectic— source for Native American and especially Mexican work, from silver to lacquer goods to boots and paper flowers. Mixed in is a good deal of inexpensive (but often pretty good) tourist ware, and even an intriguing roomful of African carvings.

Godber's Jewelry (7542 E. Main St., Scottsdale, tel. 602/949– 1133) is one of the oldest, most reliable Native American-jewelry outlets in central Arizona. Begun 60 years ago by a reservation trading-post family, it's a fine place for learning the many styles of Southwestern jewelry and discovering your own preferences.

Gilbert Ortega (7229 E. Main St., Scottsdale, tel. 602/947–2805) began as a reliable trader, then mushroomed into an industry with nine Scottsdale locations (including two at The Borgata), four in Phoenix, and one each in Tempe, Sun City, and Carefree. Only a fairly experienced Native American–jewelry buyer should shop here.

Folklórico (7216 E. Main St., Scottsdale, tel. 602/947–0758) is a fine purveyor of Southwestern folk arts and crafts.

Finally, don't forget the gift shop at the **Museo Chicano** (641 E. Van Buren St., tel. 602/257–5536), on **The Mercado**'s second floor. It's open Tues.–Fri., 10 AM–3 PM.

Sports and the Outdoors

Participant Sports

When participating in outdoor sports in Phoenix, be aware that the desert heat imposes its particular restraints on activities. From May 1 to October 1, do not jog or hike from one hour after sunrise until a half-hour before sunset. During those times, the air is so hot and dry that your body will lose moisture—and burn calories—at a dangerous, potentially lethal rate. Don't head out to desert areas at night, however, to jog or hike in the summer; that's when rattlesnakes and scorpions are out hunting. Hikers and bicyclists should wear lightweight but opaque clothes, strong sunscreen (rated 15 or higher), high UV-rated sunglasses, a hat or visor, and should carry a water supply of one quart per person for each hour of activity, even in winter.

Bicycling Although the relatively level terrain is great, the desert makes special demands on cyclists: *See* the advice on hours and clothing, *above*. Be sure to have a helmet and a mirror when riding in the streets: There are few adequate bike lanes in the valley.

Scottsdale's Indian Bend Wash (along Hayden Rd., from Shea Blvd. south to Indian School Rd.) has bikeable paths winding among its golf courses and ponds. **Pinnacle Peak**, about 25 miles northeast of downtown Phoenix, is a popular place to take bikes for the ride north to Carefree and Cave Creek, or east and south over the mountain pass and down to the Verde River, toward

Fountain Hills. **Cave Creek** and **Carefree**, in the foothills about 30 miles northeast of Phoenix, offer pleasant riding with a wide range of stopover options. **South Mountain Park** (*see* Hiking, *below*) is the prime site for mountain bikers, with its 40-plus miles of trails—some of them with challenging ascents, and all of them quiet and scenic.

For rentals, contact **Landis Cyclery** (712 W. Indian School Rd., tel. 602/264–5681; 2180 E. Southern Ave., Tempe, tel. 602/839–9383; 10417 N. Scottsdale Rd., Scottsdale, tel. 602/948–9280) or **Tempe Bicycle** (330 W. University Dr., Tempe, tel. 602/966–6896; 9180 E. Indian Bend Rd., Scottsdale, tel. 602/998–2219; 267 E. Bell Rd., tel. 602/375–1515).

To get in touch with fellow bike enthusiasts and find out about regular and special-event rides, contact the **Arizona Bicycle Club** (Gene or Sylvia Berlatsky, tel. 602/264–5478), the state's largest group, or the **Greater Arizona Bicycle Association** (Mike Gerads, tel. 602/496–0303).

Golf The Valley of the Sun is the valley of year-round golf par excellence. More than 100 courses, from par-3 to PGA championship links, are available (some lighted at night), and the PGA's Southwest section headquarters here. For a detailed listing, contact the **Arizona Golf Association** (*see* Chapter 1, Essential Information).

One of the newer, upscale courses, **Ahwatukee Country Club** (12432 S. 48th St., tel. 602/893–1161), set along the edge of South Mountain Park, is semiprivate but also has a public driving range. The **Arizona Biltmore** (24th St. and Missouri Ave., tel. 602/955–9655), the granddaddy of Phoenix golf courses, offers two 18-hole PGA championship courses, lessons, and clinics. Two low-price public courses, both in scenic city settings, are **Encanto Park** (2705 N. 15th Ave., tel. 602/253–3963) and **Papago Golf Course** (5595 E. Moreland St., tel. 602/275–8428). If you're in the Superstition Mountains area, try the desert course at **Gold Canyon Golf Club** (6100 S. Kings Ranch Rd., Apache Junction, tel. 602/982–9449). The best course in the Sun Cities, **Hillcrest Golf Club** (20002 N. Star Ridge, Sun City West, tel. 602/975–1000), is a PGA Senior Tour site. Take the children along to **PGA Tour Family Golf Center** (8111 E. McDonald Dr., Scottsdale, tel. 602/948–2551), which combines goofy golf, a driving range, and lessons at all levels. For big, sweeping views of the city, **Thunderbird Country Club** (701 E. Thunderbird Trail, Phoenix, tel. 602/243–1262) has 18 holes of championship-rated play on the north slopes of South Mountain. **Tournament Players Club at Scottsdale** (17020 N. Hayden Rd., Scottsdale, tel. 602/585–3600), a 36-hole course created by Tom Weiskopf and Jay Morrish, is the site of the PGA Phoenix Open.

Health Clubs The **Arizona Athletic Club** (1425 W. 14th St., Tempe, tel. 602/894–2281), near the airport at the border between Tempe and Scottsdale, is the valley's largest facility. It offers nonmember visitors a day rate of less than $15.

Jazzercise (tel. 602/420–1006) has 36 franchised sites in the valley, where people who are already on a program can keep on course while on vacation.

Life Centers of Arizona (4041 N. Central Ave., tel. 602/265–5472), in central Phoenix, is geared to the working man and woman, so it offers nonmembers both reasonable day rates ($5–$15) and a variety of quick workout options.

Naturally Women (2827 W. Peoria Ave., tel. 602/678–4000; 3320 S. Price Rd., Tempe, tel. 602/838–8800; 7750 E. McDowell Rd., tel. 602/947–8300) focuses on women, from its health profiles to its diet and exercise programs; it offers one free visitor's day, then a day rate of about $10 afterward.

Hiking The valley boasts some of the best desert mountain hiking in the world—the **Phoenix Mountain Preserve System,** in the mountains that surround the city, even has its own park rangers, who can help you select and plan your hikes. For information and group hiking reservations, call the South Zone Rangers' Office (tel. 602/495–0222).

Squaw Peak (2701 E. Squaw Peak Dr., just north of Lincoln, tel. 602/262–7901) is a favorite two-hour hike that ascends the landmark mountain from a well-equipped park in the North Mountains Preserve. Children can handle this one if the adults take it slowly. The rangers also lead a fine, easy hike through the park, introducing desert geology, flora, and fauna.

Camelback Mountain (north of Camelback Rd. on 48th St., tel. 602/256–3220), another landmark hike, has no park, and the trails are noticeably more difficult. This is for intermediate to experienced hikers.

The soft sandstone **Papago Peaks** (Van Buren St. and Galvin Pkwy., tel. 602/256–3220) were sacred sites for the Tohono O'odham tribe and probably the Hohokam before them; now they provide accessible caves, some petroglyphs, and splendid views all around the valley. This is another good spot for family hikes. The Phoenix Zoo, the Desert Botanical Garden, and the new Arizona Historical Society Museum are on the site.

South Mountain Park (10919 S. Central Ave., tel. 602/495–0222) is the jewel of the city's Mountain Park Preserves. At 16,000 acres, it is the nation's largest city park, and its mountains and arroyos contain more than 40 miles of marked and maintained trails—all multiuse, for hiking, horseback riding, and mountain biking. It also has three auto-accessible lookout points, with 65-mile sightlines. The rangers can help you plan hikes to see some of the 200 petroglyph sites located so far.

Horseback Riding More than two dozen stables and equestrian tour outfitters in the valley attest to the saddle's enduring importance in Arizona—even in this auto-dominated metropolis.

All Western Stables (10220 S. Central Ave., tel. 602/276–5862), one of several stables at the entrance to South Mountain Park, offers rentals, guided rides, hayrides, and at the end of the trail, steak fries.

The two **Hole-in-the-Wall Stables** (7677 N. 16th St., tel. 602/997–1466; 7777 Pointe Pkwy., tel. 602/431–0817) are both near large parts of the Phoenix Mountain Preserve System and have guided solo and group, hourly, and overnight options.

Adjacent to the Phoenix North Mountains Preserve, **North Side Stables** (25251 N. 19th Ave., tel. 602/581–0103) offers everything from pony rides to pack trips—even stagecoach rentals.

Old MacDonald's Ranch (26540 N. Scottsdale Rd., Scottsdale, tel. 602/585–0239) provides guided trail rides, hayrides, and catered cookouts.

Superstition Stables (Windsong and Meridian Rds., Apache Junction, tel. 602/982–6353) is licensed to lead tours throughout the entire Superstition Mountains area for more experienced riders; easier rides are also available.

Hot-Air Ballooning Another unusual sport that has soared in the desert air is hot-air ballooning. The following are a few of the three dozen companies that offer uplifting experiences; all use pilots who are certified by the Federal Aviation Administration: **An Aeronautical Adventure** (tel. 602/991–4260) has daily flights and will sell you a balloon if the bug really bites. **Hot Air Expeditions** (tel. 602/788–5555 or 800/831–7610) features a champagne flight and free pickup and return at local resorts. **Naturally High** (tel. 602/252–6766) offers not only ascents with trained pilots, among them recent state champions, but also training for aspiring crew members.

Jogging Phoenix's unique 200-mile network of canals provides a naturally cooled (and often landscaped) scenic track throughout the metro area. Two other popular jogging areas are Phoenix's **Encanto Park,** 3 miles northwest of Civic Plaza, and Scottsdale's **Indian Bend Wash,** which runs for more than 5 miles along Hayden Road—both have lagoons and tree-shaded greens.

Tennis At **Hole-in-the-Wall Racquet Club** (7677 N. 16th St., Pointe Hilton at Squaw Peak Resort, tel. 602/997–2543), eight paved courts are available for same-day reservation for $15/hour; at the affiliated **Watering Hole Racquet Club** (11111 N. 7th St., Pointe Hilton at Tapatio Cliffs Resort, tel. 602/997–7237) the 15 courts are hard and lighted for night games. **Mountain View Tennis Center** (1104 E. Grovers St., tel. 602/788–6088), just north of Bell Road, is a Phoenix city facility with 20 lighted courts that can be reserved for $2.50 for 90 minutes of singles. For the same price you can play at **Phoenix Tennis Center** (6330 N. 21st Ave., tel. 602/249–3712), another city facility with 22 lighted hard courts. **The Pointe Hilton at South Mountain Tennis Club** (7777 S. Pointe Pkwy., tel. 602/438–9000) has 10 lighted hard courts for $20/hour.

Tubing In a region not known for water, one indigenous aquatic sport has developed. Tubing—riding an inner tube down calm water and mild rapids—has become a very popular tradition on the

Salt and Verde rivers. Outfitters that rent tubes include **Saguaro Lake Ranch Tube & Raft Rental** (13020 N. Bush Hwy., Mesa, tel. 602/984–2194), right on the way into the McDowell Mountains, where the river action is (they also offer bed-and-breakfast accommodations), and **Salt River Recreation Tube Rental & Shuttle** (Bush Hwy., Mesa, tel. 602/984–3305), conveniently located and offering transportation to and from your starting point.

Spectator Sports

Auto Racing **Phoenix International Raceway** (7602 S. 115th Ave., Avondale 85323, tel. 602/252–3833), the valley's NASCAR track, is the site of a Winston Cup 500 each November and the Indy car Slick 50 race each April.

Balloon Racing **The Thunderbird Hot-Air-Balloon Classic** (tel. 602/978–7208) has grown into a schedule of festivities surrounding the national invitational balloon race, held each November.

Baseball *See* Chapter 1, Essential Information, for information on **Cactus League** spring training.

Basketball **The Phoenix Suns** (2nd and Jefferson Sts., tel. 602/379–SUNS) have been NBA playoff regulars for several years. Their new America West Phoenix Suns Arena is almost as exciting as their game.

Golf **The Phoenix Open** (tel. 602/585–4334), played each January at the Tournament Players Club in Scottsdale, is a $1 million event on the PGA Tour. In March, the women compete for the $550,000 purse in **Standard Register PING Tournament** (tel. 602/942–0000), held at the Moon valley Country Club.

Rodeos **The Parada del Sol,** held each year by the Scottsdale Jaycees (3515 N. 75th St., Scottsdale, tel. 602/990–3179), includes a rodeo, a lavish parade famed for its silver-studded tack, and a 400-mile daredevil ride from Holbrook down the Mogollon Rim to Phoenix by the Hashknife Riders.

The Rodeo of Rodeos, sponsored by the Phoenix Jaycees (4133 N. 7th St., tel. 602/263–8671), has one of the Southwest's oldest and best parades.

The World's Oldest Rodeo (Box 2037, Prescott 86302, tel. 800/358–1888), held each July as part of Frontier Days, gives the Phoenix rodeos a run for their money.

Dining

Phoenix's food traditions arose from a unique blend of Old West and New West cultures. In the mid-19th century, the north Mexican rancho cooking that had been in Arizona for 150 years was joined by the Anglo-European food of American settlers. Arizona Territory was also an outpost of the West's cattle-ranching boom, and the railroads brought a significant early influx of Chinese settlers.

By the mid-20th century, the valley was rich in Mexican food, mostly in the style of the adjoining Mexican state of Sonora; steak houses, from cowboy to fancy (Phoenix was a major stockyard center until the 1970s); and Chinese restaurants, mostly Cantonese. There was plenty of good family eating, but not much haute cuisine; when Phoenicians wanted to get fussy, the men put on bola ties and the women donned silver-and-turquoise jewelry, and they paid someone to pour "Continental" sauces on their steaks.

Then, during the 1970s, things took off. Southeast Asian refugees brought peppery Oriental dishes that were instantly welcome in a city used to salsa and sweet-and-sour. Immigrants from Central America and the Middle East brought more variations on familiar themes, as well as new approaches. Soon, "Southwestern international" was born—and by the late '80s, it had taken hold of America's culinary imagination. Today, as innovative chefs and restaurateurs create new offshoots, this vibrant and inventive cuisine continues to thrive.

Few restaurants require men to wear jackets and ties; in any situation, a bola tie will always suffice. The *guayabera* (Mexican wedding shirt) is also an appropriate warm-weather option in all but the fanciest places. Similarly, slacks or a simple dress are welcome almost everywhere for women; the fanciest places expect a dress or pantsuit. (Restaurants are open daily, unless otherwise noted.)

Highly recommended restaurants are indicated by a star ★.

Category	Cost*
$$$$	over $40
$$$	$20–$40
$$	$10–$20
$	under $10

per person, excluding drinks, service, and sales tax (6%–7%)

American **Ruth's Chris Steakhouse.** Most meat fanciers agree that steak seldom gets better handling than at this New Orleans–based chain. Amid brass, wood, and glass (and great views, in the Scottsdale location), you can get thick, juicy lamb or pork chops, but planks of beef are this restaurant's business. Calorie- and cardiac-watchers, beware: Portions are massive, and everything—even the broiled shrimp—comes swimming in the house butter bath. *2201 E. Camelback Rd., tel. 602/957–9600; 7001 N. Scottsdale Rd., Scottsdale, tel. 602/991–5988. Reservations required. Jacket suggested. AE, MC, V. $$$*

Steamers. Watching the chefs at work in the open kitchen is one of the main attractions of this bright and spacious seafood house. Another is the attentive, knowledgeable service staff; yet another is the wonderful array of New England–style standards, from chowders to halibut to lobster. (Don't stray into the fancy nouvelle part of the menu; simplicity is the strong point here.) *2576 E. Camelback Rd., tel. 602/956–3631. Reservations advised. Dress: casual. AE, MC, V. $$$*

★ **Top of the Market.** This smaller, slightly costlier annex upstairs from the larger, noisier Fish Market (itself a popular place) has captured the atmosphere of a San Francisco wharf restaurant. Its menu would stand up well in the City by the Bay. Everything from charbroiled orange roughy to whole Dungeness crab is skillfully handled and imaginatively seasoned; the handmade pastas are terrific, too. Try flan or strawberries for dessert. *1720 E. Camelback Rd., tel. 602/277–3474. Reservations required. Dress: casual. AE, DC, MC, V. $$$*

American Grill. The decor is leather, brass, ferns, and etched glass; a large bar at the entry and a lounge with cozy tables and soft, live jazz add to the classic San Francisco pub ambience. But the action is in the glassed-in exhibition kitchen and the booths, where regional varieties of American cuisine (notably Cajun and Southwestern) are prepared and consumed. The N'awlins Barbecued Shrimp is a fine appetizer; chowder in a bowl of sourdough bread can't be beat. Powerful desserts, too. *1233 S. Alma School Rd., Mesa, tel. 602/844–1918. Reservations advised. Dress: casual. AE, D, DC, MC, V. $$*

Durant's. This old downtown standby in black leather and red wallpaper hasn't changed since the '50s, and neither has its popularity (even its prices are refreshingly out-of-date). It has a front door, but everyone enters through the kitchen from the parking lot. With its crowded bar and open booths, Durant's is one of Phoenix's prime see-and-be-seen places. On the menu, steaks and chops are prominent, but check out the steamed clams or the chicken livers. *2611 N. Central Ave., tel. 602/264–5967. Reservations advised for dinner. Dress: casual. AE, D, DC, MC, V. $$*

★ **Landmark.** After 50 years as a Mormon church and a brief turn as a college, this massive brick Victorian became a restaurant. It's done in lush carpeting, rose-patterned wallpaper, and wall-to-wall antiques; expect to wait a half-hour downstairs in the small lounge, surrounded by historical photos. Upstairs, you start at the huge salad bar of well-made Americana, from garden marinade to seafood salad and thick, rich soups. A sauerbraten-sauced pot roast with heavenly mashed potatoes leads the entrées; and finally, the Landmark pie is a must for fudge lovers. *809 W. Main St., Mesa, tel. 602/962–4652. No reservations. Dress: casual. AE, DC, MC, V. $$*

Oscar Taylor's. Another favorite with the meat-and-potatoes crowd, this Chicago-style '20s steak house combines a cozy atmosphere, brisk service, and beautiful cuts of meat. The prime rib is a house specialty; the ribs are, too. But the best-kept secret is a huge, delicately simple veal chop. *2420 E. Camelback Rd., tel. 602/956–5705. Reservations advised. Dress: casual. AE, DC, MC, V. $$*

Rose's. Comfortably elegant in blue and burgundy tones, and conveniently located on the northern edge of downtown, the restaurant at the Best Western Executive Park hotel is a quiet, tony haven of American-Continental cuisine with some nice Southwestern edges. Regional pasta dishes are a house specialty, as is the chicken quesadilla. *1100 N. Central Ave., tel. 602/ 252–2100. Reservations required. Dress: casual. AE, D, DC, MC, V. $$*

★ **Rustler's Rooste.** The Johnny-come-lately among the Valley's western restaurants is the biggest and nearest to town—and the most fun. It's at the east end of South Mountain Park just off I–10 (take the Baseline exit west), in the theme-park atmosphere of The Pointe Hilton on South Mountain, Arizona's largest resort. Decorated in a playful miner-cowpoke style, complete with a slide from the bar down to the dining rooms, it offers excellent steaks, juicy barbecued pork ribs and chicken, hefty Mexican-style shrimp, and homemade ice cream. The Cowboy Stuff Platter ($16) puts a sample of almost everything the restaurant serves (except rattlesnake) on your plate. *7777 S. Pointe Pkwy., tel. 602/431–6474. Reservations advised. Dress: casual or Western. AE, D, DC, MC, V. $$*

★ **The Stockyards.** When Arizona had cattle barons, they cut their deals and steaks here. The feedlots and barons are gone, but the restaurant remains, a landmark just a half-mile east of Sky Harbor Airport. Its ornate Victorian interior retains the original brass-trimmed bar and three salons—the black-leather Cattleman's Room, the gold-papered Gold Coast Room, and the mural-walled Rose Room. The menu features beef handled with respect, from massive prime rib and steaks to succulent calves' liver and calf fries (Rocky Mountain oysters). *5001 E. Washington St., tel. 602/273–7378. Reservations advised. Dress: casual. AE, DC, MC, V. $$*

T-Bone Steakhouse. You drive south on 19th Avenue past the end of the pavement a ways, and there, on the slopes of South Mountain, is a big outdoor barbecue in a parking lot. Inside the rustic wooden building are wooden benches at oilcloth-covered tables; steaks and chicken come to you, cooked to match the splendid, sweeping vistas of the desert sunset or the valley lit up at night. Salad and beans, giant slices of toast, and fresh hot baked potatoes are always on hand, and Fridays and Saturdays, amateur Western musicians take the microphone. *10037 S. 19th Ave., tel. 602/276–0945. No reservations. Dress: casual or Western. AE, MC, V. $$*

★ **Bev's Kitchen.** Some folks call it country, some call it soul food, and some just call it home. Whatever you call it, you may have to wait in line a bit to enjoy it. This handsome downtown diner (which started life beside an auto lot on the south side) contains gracious staff and great food—hand-pounded chicken-fried steak, crumbling moist catfish, lively hot links, and potatoes and greens and corn and cabbage and yams done by people who love their vegetables (boiled down some, of course). What's your reward for finishing all that? Bev's pies. *7 W. Monroe St., tel. 602/ 252–1455. No reservations. Dress: casual. No credit cards. $*

Ed Debevic's. This brash, noisy place adjacent to Marriott's Camelback Courtyard hotel is to restaurants what "Happy Days" was to TV—a nostalgic, half-accurate, but wholly entertaining revision of the '50s. It has red-leather dinettes, a working jukebox with Elvis and Tessy Brewer and dozens more, gum-snapping waitresses—and terrific burgers, malts, and

Adrian's, **44**
American Grill, **72**
Bahía San Carlos, **45**
Bev's Kitchen, **52**
Byblos, **67**
Char's, **65**
Chianti, **32**
China Doll, **48**
China Gate, **5, 63, 70**
Chompies, **4**
Christo's, **15**
Christopher's, **26**
Compass Room, **54**
Los Dos Molinos, **59, 73**
Durant's, **47**
Ed Debevic's, **29**
Eddie's Grill, **22**
The Eggery (Good Egg), **2, 7, 11, 17, 21, 35, 36**
Eliana's, **43**
Giuseppe's, **28**
Golden Moon Palace, **49**
Goldie's 1895 House, **51**
Gourmet of Hong Kong, **46**
Greekfest, **25**
Greektown, **14**
La Hacienda, **10**
Havana Café, **34**
Indian Delhi Palace, **62**
Jasmine Café, **68**
Korean Garden, **66**
Landmark, **74**
La Pila, **41**
Lone Star Steak House, **20**
Lucky Restaurant, **40**
Macayo, **3, 12, 23, 39, 64, 69**
Marquesa, **10**
Matador, **53**
Mediterranean House, **18**
Mint Thai, **76**
Mrs. White's Golden Rule Café, **55**
Munch a Bagel, **16**
The Olive Garden, **1, 6, 9, 71**

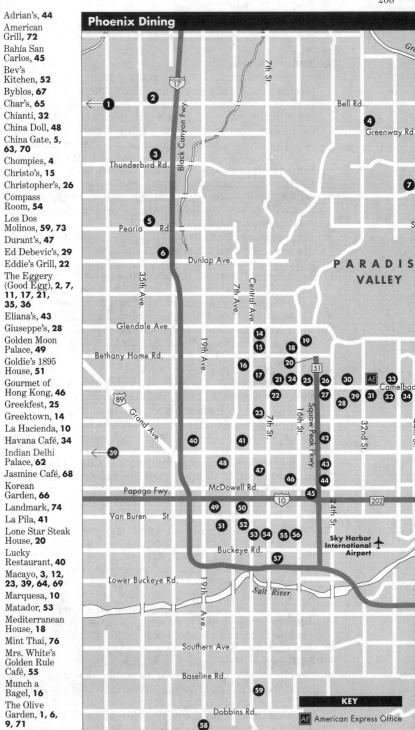

Phoenix Dining

fries. Blue-plate specials, from chili to meat loaf and gravy, are a tasty hoot. With prodding, "Cookie" and the girls (and the waiters, led by a guest-kissing nerd) will provide tableside diversions. Forty-plus diners blush to remember, but children love it. *2102 E. Highland Ave., tel. 602/956–2760. Reservations advised on weekends. Dress: casual. MC, V. $*

The Eggery/The Good Egg. Cute decor (more airy and Southwestern at Eggery outlets, more cluttered country at Good Eggs) and a lengthy menu mark this cheerful, comfy breakfast-brunch chain. Besides an array of cleverly named egg creations, from scrambler skillets to frittatas, as well as pancakes and waffles, there are welcome light options such as yogurt, granola, and fruit dishes. Service is brisk and friendly, children are welcome, and there's no rush despite the crowds. *5109 N. 44th St., tel. 602/840–5734; 4326 E. Cactus Rd. (at Paradise valley Mall), tel. 602/953–2342; 2957 W. Bell Rd. (northwest), tel. 602/ 993–2797; 2 E. Camelback Rd., tel. 602/263–8534; 906 E. Camelback Rd, tel. 602/274–5393; 6149 N. Scottsdale Rd., Scottsdale, tel. 602/991–5416; 14046 N. Scottsdale Rd., Scottsdale, tel. 602/483–1090. No reservations. Dress: casual. AE, MC, V. $*

Lone Star Steak House. Tucked in an uptown corner mall, this noisy and crowded spot cluttered with Texas and country-western items does simple, effective things with steaks (including a classic chicken-fried) and serves up some of the best mashed potatoes you've had since you were a youngster. On the steaks, ask them to hold the lemon butter; the meat's better by itself. *6003 N. 16th St., tel. 602/248–STAR. Reservations accepted for groups of 5 or more. Dress: casual. AE, MC, V. $*

Mrs. White's Golden Rule Café. This little downtown, down-home lunch spot brings smiles to those who love liver and boiled cabbage, as well as to fanciers of such standard American fare as fried chicken, corn on the cob, and yams. The food is cooked with a light, loving touch, service is friendly, prices are low, and the payin' is honor system. *808 E. Jefferson St., tel. 602/262–9256. No reservations. Dress: casual. No credit cards. Lunch only. $*

Unique Foods & Services. For snappy barbecue and soul classics done simply and with authority, this handsome little downtown café across the street from the restored Booker T. Washington School (now home to the *New Times* alternative newspaper) is the place to be. Breakfasts are hearty; for lunch or dinner, hot links and ribs are memorable, and the delicate catfish and fried chicken reflect chef Wazir Karim's scrupulous concern for healthful, flavor-rich cooking. Greens and gumbo are cooked with love, and don't forget about the bean pie. Good local jazz, too. *1153 E. Jefferson St., tel. 602/257–0701. No reservations. Dress: casual. No credit cards. $*

Asian **China Doll.** The venerable ancestor of valley Cantonese restau-
Chinese rants still is *the* place for family and association banquets and Chinese New Year's feasts. Its dinners—including ginger fish, for which you select your own tilapia swimming in the lobby tank—are reliably executed classics. And its dim sum is some of the best in town. Annie White is a gracious, witty hostess. *3336*

N. 7th Ave., tel. 602/264-0538. Reservations advised. Dress: casual. AE, DC, MC, V. $$

★ **China Gate.** Seldom do chain restaurants rise so high or remain so consistent in quality—not to mention this chain's breadth of cuisines, from Mongolian to Cantonese, Beijing to spicy Szechuan. Mandarin ribs are a special experience, as is the combination of shrimp and sea cucumber. Decor is striking, and layout emphasizes privacy amid open space. *3033 W. Peoria Ave., tel. 602/944-1982; 7820 E. McDowell Rd., Scottsdale, tel. 602/946-0720; 2050 W. Guadalupe Rd., Mesa, tel. 602/897-0607. Reservations advised for dinner. Dress: casual. AE, D, DC, MC, V. $$*

Golden Moon Palace. A modest place in the somewhat seedy area just north of the state capitol mall, Golden Moon has been serving very fine food for a very long time. Half is simply decorated with red-leather booths and lanterns; the other half is a banquet room where local families celebrate and entertain guests. Service is genteel and attentive. The egg rolls are sweet and stuffed with fresh veggies, the garlic chicken is a masterpiece, and the fried rice is a meal in itself. *1408 W. Van Buren St., tel. 602/254-9229. Reservations advised for dinner. Dress: casual. AE, D, DC, MC, V. Closes 9 PM. $*

Gourmet of Hong Kong. Here are the bustling sounds and incomparable flavors of Hong Kong, nestled in this tiny downtown establishment. Staff and owners rush in and out of the narrow, steamy open kitchen to take your order and serve you; to-go diners stand between the tables, eagerly waiting. The house plate is a succulent, satisfying sampler; hot-sour chicken wings, Peking duck, lobster, and garlic pork are delightful. *1438 E. McDowell Rd., tel. 602/253-4859. Reservations advised. Dress: casual. MC, V. $*

Lucky Restaurant. Lucky you, if you look past the unpromising exterior, skip the buffet, and try something from the menu or the chalkboard. A little nerve and you'll have a rewarding adventure. If beef with bitter melons is available, don't miss it. The soft-shell crabs in black-bean sauce are unforgettable, too. *3317 N. 19th Ave., tel. 602/274-9477. No reservations. Dress: casual. No credit cards. $*

Indian **Indian Delhi Palace.** Midway between downtown and Tempe, right across from Motorola's semiconductor plant, you'll step through the door of a double storefront and into India. Attentive service and delightful flavors enhance the illusion. Sip tea and nibble home-baked *naan* and *kalcha* breads while perusing the lengthy menu. The tandoori chicken and the yogurt lamb are two of many wonderful dishes, but the best bet is the inclusive dinner. The lunch buffet is another fun way to tour India's kitchens. *5050 E. McDowell Rd., tel. 602/244-8181. No reservations. Dress: casual. MC, V. $$*

Japanese **Shogun.** In this small converted tavern, the cheerful staff offers ★ the best all-around Japanese experience in the valley, starting with an outstanding sushi bar. At the tables there are both finely turned standards such as teriyaki and tempura and adventures into such unfamiliar areas as fish marinated in rice wine.

Children are welcome here, too. *12615 N. Tatum Blvd., tel. 602/ 953–3264. Reservations advised. Dress: casual. DC, MC, V. $$*

Yamakasa. Simple and serene in decor and service, this family-run restaurant offers excellent sushi and a menu that focuses on tempura- and teriyaki-style cooking. No dazzle, but calm consistency makes this a refreshing place in which to enjoy an unhurried evening in the shadow of Fuji. *9301 E. Shea Blvd., Scottsdale, tel. 602/860–5605. Reservations advised. Dress: casual. AE, DC, MC, V. $$*

Korean **Korean Garden.** Simple in decor and menu, this well-staffed, friendly place provides both familiar fare, such as *bulgoki* (grilled, marinated beef strips), and exotic treats such as *bibim bab* (a bowl of assorted vegetables and beef, with hot sauce, topped with a fried egg) and *jap chae* (pan-fried clear noodles with vegetables and beef). And each of the many kinds of *kimchi* (hot, marinated chopped cabbage) is a fiery treat. *1324 S. Rural Rd., Tempe, tel. 602/967–1133. No reservations. Dress: casual. MC, V. $*

Thai **Mint Thai.** A tiny, graceful place that started out remarkable
★ and has never wavered, Mint Thai offers the broadest menu of the valley's Thai restaurants—and if you find a dish not prepared with delicacy and power, it'll be a first. Soups range from the subtly simple *tom ka gai* (hot-sour in coconut milk) to the spectacular *Thai suki* (a beef-pork-chicken-squid-shrimp extravaganza); curries are gentler than those of north India, with deep flavors; the *rama* beef in peanut sauce is amazing. And you've never had sweet-and-sour like this before. Even the tea stands out. *1111 N. Gilbert Rd., Gilbert, tel. 602/497–5366. Reservations advised on weekends. Dress: casual. AE, MC, V. $$*

Char's. This austerely simple restaurant gave birth to Phoenix's brood of Thai houses, and Grandpa Char still oversees things here. Meals are carefully prepared and courteously served, from the snappy skewered-chicken *satay* appetizer to the *tom yum gai* (hot-sour soup) and *yum yai* salad (chicken and shrimp salad with peanut dressing) to a noodle-rich *pad Thai* or a belly-warming curry. Tell your server if you want the pepper meter set on low; Thai like it hot. *927 E. University Dr., Tempe, tel. 602/967–6013. Reservations advised for large groups. Dress: casual. AE, MC, V. $*

Pan-Asian **Jasmine Café.** This bright eastern valley spot, done in a California clutter of neon and ferns and collectibles, allows you to taste virtually all the Far East's cuisines in one sitting. The menu embraces Chinese, Japanese, Thai, Korean, and a little poetic license in a fun, endlessly varied array that's served in small portions—you can fill your table with experiments and share. The service is a bit uneven, but the food is worth it. *1805 E. Elliott Rd., Tempe, tel. 602/491–0797. No reservations. Dress: casual. DC, MC, V. $*

Deli **Chompie's.** In a north Phoenix corner mall not far from Paradise
★ Valley Mall sits a cheerful New York deli. Big breakfasts—from blintzes to home fries to hefty omelets—give way to high-piled

sandwiches on fresh-baked bread and rolls at lunchtime (all with pickles, the way lunch was meant to be served). Not only do they make their own bagels, but the huge bakery case is a trip to Vienna, with its stunning array of traditional European treats and American inventions. Take a number! *3202 E. Greenway Rd., tel. 602/971–8010. Reservations recommended for 6 or more. Dress: casual. MC, V. $–$$*

★ **Munch a Bagel.** Just north of Camelback, on one of the main morning routes into downtown, sits one of Phoenix's most popular reasons to leave home early or get to work a little late. A quick breakfast special of eggs, onion-tossed potatoes and a fresh bagel is worth stopping for; so is a more leisurely linger over one of the huge omelets (try the No. 3 with tongue or pastrami) and a frothy cappuccino or café latté. Any deli sandwich you order for lunch is guaranteed to send you home with a smile and a doggie bag. *5114 N. Seventh St., tel. 602/264–1975. Reservations recommended for 6 or more. Dress: casual. AE, D, DC, MC, V. $*

European **Christopher's.** Christopher Gross, one of the valley's lead-
French ing chef-entrepreneurs, has re-created a bistro worthy of
★ the Champs-Elysées and, adjacent to it, an elegant, mono-grammed-linen-and-silver modern restaurant. They share an open kitchen. Classic fish, veal, and chicken are flawlessly cooked, sauced, and presented—with surprising Southwestern touches. *2398 E. Camelback Rd., tel. 602/957–3214. Reservations required. Jacket and tie advised. AE, DC, MC, V. $$$$*

Voltaire. The valley's most consistent classical French cuisine makes its home in a residential Scottsdale neighborhood. Nothing nouvelle here; there may not be a recipe that's less than 100 years old. But when you have the urge to cap off a drive through the desert with escargots, onion soup *gratinée*, and perfectly handled rack of lamb, this is the place. Then there's the hard work: Crepes suzette, cherries jubilee, or the exquisite crème caramel? *8340 E. McDonald Dr., Scottsdale, tel. 602/948–1005. Reservations required. Jacket and tie advised. AE, MC, V. Closed Sun. and Mon. $$$*

German **Zur Kate.** Outside, you're in a corner mall on a busy Mesa thoroughfare; inside, you're in a friendly, family inn in Bavaria. Steins and Tyrolean caps belonging to regulars line the walls; the soups are hearty and good, the sauerbraten, *kassler ripchen* (smoked pork loin), dumplings, and tiny spätzle noodles are wonderful. Not to mention the wursts and the fresh apple strudel. Music and gemütlich service complete the pleasures. *4815 E. Main St., Mesa, tel. 602/830–4244. Reservations accepted. Dress: casual. MC, V. Closed Sun. $$*

Greek **Greekfest.** Here, Greek cooking meets haute cuisine. In a taste-
★ ful Athenian taverna, with painted vines and racked wines on the whitewashed walls, classic dishes are handled exquisitely. Greekfest offers a quietly festive evening with the feather-light spanakopita appetizers; the sweet, succulent lamb; the fresh, tart dolmades stuffed to bursting and sour-light avgolemono as

both soup and sauce. *1940 E. Camelback Rd., tel. 602/265–2990. Reservations advised. Dress: casual. DC, MC, V. $$*

Greektown. At this warm family operation cheered by posters and murals, Papa greets, Mama cooks, and Son seats. The combo appetizer offers a pick of the Greek islands; lamb stew and seafood are good bets. When it's time for dessert, there are honey, nuts, and phyllo dough aplenty—and Mama's rice pudding. Wash it down with good, thick coffee. *539 E. Glendale Ave., tel. 602/279–9677. Reservations advised. Dress: casual. AE, MC, V. $$*

Italian **Giuseppe's.** In a tiny, noisy storefront in a corner mall, the
★ Carotenuto family has hidden a treasure: Savory pastas and homemade sauces, exquisitely creamy stuffed eggplant and zucchini, drop-off-the-bone ribs and rich, moist meatballs—plus sinfully sweet desserts, from *tiramisù* to hard-shelled ice cream *tartuffos*. All this and checkered tablecloths, too. (Bring your own wine.) *2824 E. Indian School Rd., tel. 602/381–1237. Reservations recommended for 5 or more. AE, MC, V. Closed Sun. $–$$$*

Chianti. This charming little poster-hung restaurant stays crowded, but the unusually alert service neither forgets nor flusters you. The antipasto salad is a crisp overture of clear, tangy flavors, the pastas are well handled and sauced. Espresso or cappuccino, with perhaps a gelato or spumoni, ends a delightful meal. *3943 E. Camelback Rd., tel. 602/957–9840. Reservations advised. Dress: casual. AE, MC, V. $*

The Olive Garden. Plant-filled rooms, cleverly chopped into private nooks on varied levels, create a pleasing atmosphere. The food does more justice to the range of Italian cuisine than you would expect from a chain—from the garlicky bread sticks to a fine pesto and very creditable sauces (Alfredo and marinara are both consistently successful). A good place to go beyond spaghetti and pizza, and a nonthreatening "grown-up" setting for the young. *10223 N. Metro Pkwy. E (at Metrocenter mall), tel. 602/943–4573; 9805 W. Bell Rd., Sun City, tel. 602/977–8378; 1261 W. Southern Ave. (at Fiesta Mall), Mesa, tel. 602/890–0440; 4868 E. Cactus Rd., Scottsdale, tel. 602/494–4327. No reservations. Dress: casual. DC, MC, V. $*

Spanish **Marquesa.** Two soft-hued, intimate rooms at the Scottsdale
★ Princess are accented with huge glass jars of jewel-like vegetables and fruits and graceful giant clay olive-oil urns. Here, Catalan food gets an exciting Southwestern interpretation. The stunning presentations match the flavors—duck-breast fillets in fruit sauce; pimentos stuffed with crab; a rich chowder of mussels, scallops, and spicy chorizo sausage; and huge shrimp in almond sauce, to name a few. Service is gracious, wines well chosen, desserts inspired. *7575 E. Princess Dr., Scottsdale, tel. 602/585–4848. Reservations required. Jacket and tie advised. AE, DC, MC, V. $$$$*

Tapas Papa Frita. Master chef Joseph Gutiérrez (the genius who created Marquesa) opened his own place here, in honor of his Spanish parents. The traditional tapas are the basis of the menu—such exotic nibbles as fried squid in garlic mayonnaise, mushroom- and herb-stuffed little turnovers, countless escargot treatments. But magnificent Spanish entrées, such as sweet, spit-roasted pig and tender, heartily sauced oxtails, are not to be missed. Nor is the flamenco dancing, Thursday through Saturday evenings. *3213 E. Camelback Rd., tel. 602/381–0474. Reservations advised. Dress: casual. AE, DC, MC, V. $$$*

Mexican and Latin American ★ **La Hacienda.** About 20 miles northeast of downtown in the chi-chi Scottsdale Princess Resort, this tile-roofed hacienda filled with carved tables and chairs and huge clay *ollas* (water jars) shows what happens when Sonoran food goes haute cuisine. It ranges from a quesadilla stuffed with crab to the tableside drama of *cochinillo asado* (roast stuffed suckling pig), from a chili relleno filled with pork loin and nuts to the sea-sweet *cabrilla rellena de salpicón* (crab-stuffed bass in lime mayonnaise). *7575 E. Princess Dr. (1 mi north of Bell Rd.), Scottsdale, tel. 602/585–4848. Reservations required. Dress: casual. AE, DC, MC, V. $$$–$$$$*

★ **La Pila.** For more than a decade, chef Norman Fierros has been elaborating his "Nueva Mexicana" fantasies, based on fresh Sonoran peasant dishes and inventive seasonings and presentations. Fans have followed him happily. At his latest restaurant, tucked amid ferns and fountains (*pilas*) beneath a midtown high rise, he creates flowerlike six-inch tortilla chips for warm-hearted brown *chipotle* salsa, a shrimp-and-lime ceviche so light it floats, meltingly tender grilled chicken buds in a fiery mole sauce (quench it in the custardlike rice), and his signature fish tacos with cilantro pesto. If you're coming for lunch, skip breakfast; if you're coming for dinner, fast. *2020 N. Central Ave., tel. 602/252–7007. Reservations recommended for 5 or more. Dress: casual. MC, V. Lunch and dinner Mon.–Sat., brunch only Sun. $$–$$$$*

★ **Havana Café.** At this clean, cozy café in black and gray, you'll likely have to wait; try Arriba, the tapas bar upstairs, for Spanish-style snacks and sherry. Cuban cuisine, surprisingly, shows more European than Latin American influence. Pork becomes a moist, marinated, garlic-laden roast; tamales are moist and sweet, with meat mixed throughout the masa, not wrapped in it. Hot sauces are unheard of, and *papas fritas* (french fries) are much in evidence. Talk about a sweet tooth—try the desserts, but have a cup of espresso at hand. *4225 E. Camelback Rd., tel. 602/952–1991. No reservations. Dress: casual. AE, MC, V. Closed Sun. $$*

Macayo. This family-run chain has been a valley standby for half a century, and its six colorful outlets provide well-prepared Sonoran dishes in a romantic setting of folk-art decor: tacos, tostadas, tamales (especially the sweet green corn), chili relleno, *huevos rancheros* (fried eggs rancho style, atop corn tortillas and slathered with fresh salsa), refried beans—and creamy flan or honey-filled *sopapillas* (puffy tortillas) for dessert. It's a great place for introducing children to Mexican food. *4001 N. Central Ave., tel. 602/264–6141; 7829 W. Thomas Rd., tel. 602/873–0313; 1909 W. Thunderbird Rd., tel. 602/866–7034; 11107 N. Scottsdale Rd., Scottsdale, tel. 602/596–1181; 300 S.*

Ash Ave., Tempe, tel. 602/966–6677; 1920 S. Dobson Rd., Mesa, tel. 602/820–0237. Reservations advised for dinner. Dress: casual. AE, D, DC, MC, V. $$

Richardson's. Loose-cushioned, Santa Fe adobe booths surround a lively small sports bar; the open kitchen turns out that fiery fugue of flavors known as New Mexican style. *Zozobra* toast (a Southwestern foccacia) or blue, red and yellow corn chips with two salsas start things off. The green chile stew is to die for—or from, if you're not used to pepper heat. *Carne adovada* (pork roast in red chile sauce) and an angel-hair pasta made of red chilies are scrumptious; the Chimayo chicken (stuffed with spinach, dried tomatoes, poblano chilies and Asiago cheese) is also memorable. *1582 E. Bethany Home Rd., tel. 602/265–5886. Reservations recommended. Dress: casual. AE, DC, MC, V. $$*

★ **Such Is Life.** In an intimate corner of a small office building, chef-owner Moises Treves creates a cuisine worthy of Guadalajara's famed Tapatío district. Squeeze in and start with *nopal polanco* (broiled prickly pear cactus—no thorns); move on to a soup (the black bean sings), then choose a signature salad or an entrée: fillets done in peppers or *chipotle* sauce, stunning garlic shrimp, chicken Maya (shredded in anise-hinted *achiote* sauce) or *poblano* (in chili chocolate sauce) or meltingly tender pork any of three ways. *3602 N. 24th St., tel. 602/955–7822. Reservations recommended. Dress: casual. AE, D, DC, MC, V. $$*

Adrian's. This modest, creek-rock building with wrought-iron grilles and a tiny outdoor patio transports you in food and decor a little farther south than Sonora, to the coastal towns of Sinaloa on the Sea of Cortés (Anglos call it the Gulf of California). Many dishes are similar to Sonoran rancho fare, and Adrian does them well, especially pork with *nopalitos* (sliced cactus pads); but local Hispanic families keep coming for such treats as *Vuelve a la Vida* (Return to Life)—a cocktail of shrimp, abalone, oyster, and crab—or garlicky broiled whole pike over which you squeeze tiny, sweet Mexican limes. *2234 E. McDowell Rd., tel. 602/273–7957. No reservations. Dress: casual. No credit cards. $*

Bahía San Carlos. In the shadow of the Squaw Peak Parkway, just down the street from Adrian's, is that restaurant's best competitor in the *mariscos* (seafood) category. This popular, noisy little place is hung with huge posters of Mexico's palm-shaded beaches and serves almost nothing but seafood. Tostadas piled with sweet-tangy *salpicón* (lime-soaked, seasoned, shredded crab) make a splendid appetizer; the *Caldo Siete Mares* (Seven Seas Soup) is a wonderful sampler of fish, squid, shrimp, crab, and more. *19th St. and McDowell Rd., tel. 602/340–0892. No reservations. Dress: casual. No credit cards. $*

Los Dos Molinos. One is a standard storefront in Mesa; the other is a large white hostelry in south Phoenix. Both house pure, hot New Mexico–style cooking—Victoria Chávez and her daughters turn out delicious *barbacoa* (spicy rancho barbecue), multitextured *chilaquiles* (layered tortillas, cheeses, and homemade chili sauce), and other delights with a humor as lively as the seasonings. It keeps the handful of tables and booths full.

Beware: The hot sauce can rip your lips off. *260 S. Alma School Rd., Mesa, tel. 602/835–5356, both closed Sun.; 8646 S. Central Ave., tel. 602/243–9113, closed Mon. No reservations. Dress: casual. No credit cards. $*

Eliana's. Salvadoran food is an interesting variation on the staple themes of Latin American fare, and this family-run storefront has plenty of heart and hearty food. You know tacos and burritos; now meet *papusas*, crisp crosses between tortillas and puffy pita pockets, stuffed with meat, cheese, and sauces. From tamales, it's a short but tasty leap to these veggie-filled varieties with their soft, creamy *masa* (cornmeal) wrappings. And the *sopas* (soups) are an adventure. *1627 N. 24th St., tel. 602/ 225–2925. No reservations. Dress: casual. No credit cards. $*

Matador. This downtown tradition, across from the Hyatt Regency Phoenix in a tastefully Mayan-modern setting, is a fine way to meet Mexican food in general and Sonoran cuisine in particular. Dishes are reliable, authentic, and well spiced without burning and range from the familiar (tacos, enchiladas, quesadillas) to the adventurous (*menudo*, or tripe soup; *burros de lengua*, or beef-tongue burritos). It's also a perennially popular breakfast spot where civic leaders and groups gather before the workday hits high gear. *125 E. Adams St., tel. 602/254– 7563. Reservations advised for large parties. Dress: casual. AE, D, DC, MC, V. $*

Middle Eastern ★ **Mediterranean House.** On a dozen white-clothed tables in a corner-mall storefront, a Korean family serves an array of fine Mediterranean standards. The appetizer platter introduces hummus and *baba ghanoush* (eggplant dip) with pita triangles for dipping, plus spicy falafel balls (herbed, deep-fried hummus). Not to be missed are the chicken entrées—lemon-garlic Egyptian, rolled in sesame flour; creamy herbed Moroccan, in a yogurt sauce; and ambrosial Olympic, in a secret marinade with black-olive sauce. Leading the half-dozen vegetarian main dishes is fettuccine in creamed spinach. *1588 E. Bethany Home Rd., tel. 602/248–8460. Reservations. Dress: casual. Closed Sun. $$*

Byblos. This Lebanese standby in Tempe is not heavy on ambience, but care is taken with the food, and the staff usually dines at one of the tables, inquiring regularly as to how you're doing. The appetizers are a good introduction, from the nutty hummus to the complex flavors of falafel in pita-bread pockets. But save room for the main courses, well-sampled via the mixed grill, which includes three kinds of shish kebab. *3332 S. Mill Ave., Tempe, tel. 602/894–1945. No reservations. Dress: casual. AE, MC, V. $*

Samyra's Lebanese Cuisine. In this modest, out-of-the-way spot 2 miles south of downtown, Samyra Sopp has been cooking and serving friendly Lebanese lunches for 16 years. Scoop hummus *bitahini* (hummus-and-sesame paste) and baba ghanoush into chunks of her fresh-baked bread, then dig into tangy *yabrak* (lamb and rice rolled in grape leaves) or, if she has made any, some *koosa* (lamb-stuffed squash) or *fasoulia* (a lamb-lima bean stew). The delicate strains of Arabic music lull you all the way to the honeyed baklava. *713 E. Mohave St., tel. 602/252–9644. Reservations recommended for 6 or more. No credit cards. Dress: casual. Open 11–2 Mon.–Fri. $*

Southwestern International ★ **Vincent's on Camelback.** Vincent Guerithault is acknowledged to be among the West's master chefs extraordinaire; this is where people come to experience his art. One of the handful of Southwestern cuisine's originators, he joined his classical country-French training with Mexican traditions to create duck tacos, crab cakes in avocado salsa, lobster with smoky *chipotle* chili pasta, and so on. Racks of lamb and symphonic pâtés are here, too, as are a heart-smart menu and an intelligent wine list. Desserts aren't heart-smart, but they are luscious. *3930 E. Camelback Rd., tel. 602/224–0225. Reservations advised. Dress: casual but neat. AE, DC, MC, V. $$$$*

★ **Compass Room.** Spectacular views have always made the Hyatt Regency Phoenix's rotating crown room an attraction. Since 1989, chef Mark Ching has given it food to match. In fact, it's become one of the most exciting galleries for Southwestern culinary art. Consider this dinner: smoky eggplant soup, a salad of peppered lamb slivers and greens, a choice of fiery Southwestern cioppino or beef tenderloin in jalapeño-jus reduction and cilantro-lime hollandaise. Whatever else you have, try the "Cajun croutons," crusty fried oysters in a red-pepper mayonnaise, as a side or in the Caesar salad. While the room rotates another 90 degrees, try one of Ching's cobblers or his chocolate pâté. *122 N. 2nd St., tel. 602/252–1234. Reservations required. Jacket and tie suggested. AE, D, DC, MC, V. $$$*

★ **Eddie's Grill.** Its look and location are upscale—a modern office complex 4 miles north of downtown, black-trimmed art deco furniture, fine handmade ceramics on the tables. Its cuisine, as eclectic as the decor, makes this one of Phoenix's hottest half-dozen. Chef-owner Eddie Matney's "Ameriterranean" is a playful, shifting blend of Southwestern and North African. Try succulent Mo' Rockin' Shrimp in *chermoula* sauce (lime juice, olive oil, four kinds of pepper, cilantro, and mustard) or baked goat cheese with black beans and pita chips for starters. There's a Southwestern Tower (mixed greens and margarita chicken with peppers and jack-cheese dressing, layered in corn tortillas); and steak wrapped in herbed mashed potatoes—and Eddie loves to feed you. *4747 N. 7th St., tel. 602/241–1188. Reservations advised. Dress: casual. AE, MC, V. $$$*

★ **RoxSand.** Chef-owners RoxSand Suarez and Spyros Scocos have woven together Greek, Asian, Continental, and Caribbean influences (among others) to create a unique trans-Continental cuisine. Eclectic is the word in this trendy but very friendly café-restaurant, where a solo snacker is as welcome as a hungry foursome. Be on the lookout for such surprises as sea-scallop salad, salmon with piroshki and cabbage roll, Jamaican jerked rabbit, and an ever-changing array of handmade desserts. This is a meal for adventurers. RoxSand shares Biltmore Fashion Park mall's casual elegance, adding its own zest. *2594 E. Camelback Rd., tel. 602/381–0444. Reservations advised. Dress: casual. AE, DC, MC, V. $$$*

Christo's. The sign says "Ristorante," and the northern Italian food is finely done. But Christo and Connie Panagiotakapoulos have reached throughout the Mediterranean for their cuisine, offering pastas, lamb dishes, calamari, and other regional specialties in a variety of accents. The decor and ambience are crisply contemporary, the service adroit. *6327 N. 7th St., tel. 602/264–1784. Reservations advised. Dress: casual. AE, MC, V. Closed Sun. $$–$$$*

Goldie's 1895 House. This charmingly restored downtown Victorian would fit right in on California's Mendocino coast. There's always soft music (live jazz, classical guitar) and an art gallery and museum that change shows regularly. Standards get subtle extra touches—a hot turkey sandwich on sourdough under a light dill sauce, or baked orange roughy in Parmesan-scallion butter—and there are surprises, such as roast duck in pomegranate sauce. There's also a new high-health menu and, in 1995, a yearlong centennial celebration. Plan ahead: The hours are as compact as the rooms (lunch weekdays 11–2; dinner; Mon.–Thurs. 5–9, Fri.–Sat. 5–10, Sun. 3:30–10; the Attic Dinner Theater performs 7 PM Thurs.–Sun.). *362 N. 2nd Ave., tel. 602/254–0338. Reservations advised. Dress: casual. AE, DC, MC, V. $$*

Timothy's. In this cozy cottage north of Camelback Road, chef-owner Tim Johnson offers a double treat—French-influenced Southwestern cuisine and live jazz. He does jambalaya, steak au poivre, and veal; like the music, the food gets hottest when the voices blend, as in Cajun prime rib, or salmon in phyllo dough with chili hollandaise. It's not always quiet, but service is brisk and dinner is served until midnight. *6335 N. 16th St., tel. 602/ 277–7634. Reservations advised. Dress: casual. AE, D, DC, MC, V. $$*

Lodging

Metro Phoenix has a considerable array of lodging options, from world-class resorts and dude ranches to roadside motels, from luxury and executive hotels to no-frills business suites and family-style operations where you can do your own cooking.

Resorts are usually far from the heart of town—too far to be convenient if your interests are in Phoenix proper. The exceptions: the historic Arizona Biltmore, unthinkably far out when it was built and now handily close in; the gigantic Pointe Hilton on South Mountain, less than 3 miles from the airport; and its two sister Pointe resorts, each within 7 miles of downtown. Most of the others are in Scottsdale, a self-contained, very tourist-friendly suburb; a few are scattered 20 to 30 miles out of town. And the dude ranches cluster around Wickenburg, 60 miles northwest.

Business and family hotels are closer to town—and to the average vacation budget. Until 20 years ago, families drove in from the west on Grand Avenue or from the east on Van Buren Street and pulled into any of dozens of courtyard motels with mission-style adobe facades. That is no longer a safe option, as the neighborhood is seedy; but aside from the airport, no single hotel district has emerged, so offerings are scattered throughout Phoenix and its suburbs.

Travelers flee snow and ice to bask in the Valley of the Sun. As a result, winter is the high season, peaking in January through March, and summer is giveaway time, when weekend packages at the fanciest resorts cost less than a winter night at a midrange hotel.

The rise of suite hotels in recent years—with kitchenettes for in-room meal preparation—is rapidly making room service obsolete in all but luxury or resort-class hotels. In its place, such complimentary services as a made-to-order breakfast, poolside or lounge happy hour, and a morning newspaper are becoming standard. Where room service is not noted below, expect some combination of these.

Highly recommended lodgings are indicated by a star ★.

Category	Cost*
$$$$	over $160
$$$	$110–$160
$$	$60–$110
$	under $60

All prices are for a standard double room, excluding 6½% state tax, 1% city tax, and 15% service charge.

Central Phoenix **$$$$** **Hyatt Regency Phoenix.** This landmark faces Civic Plaza like a giant kachina figure, its disk-shaped rotating restaurant atop 24 floors of dark sandstone. Desert- and Indian-style decor dominate, blended together with Hyatt's trademark atrium design and sky-view elevators. Shops, meeting rooms, and an on-site branch of the visitors bureau attest to the focus on conventions, which crowd the hotel in spring. Rooms are comfortable, utilitarian, and modestly sized; there are balcony rooms on floors 3–7, poolside rooms on 3 (the atrium roof blocks east views on 8–10). The Theater Terrace Café's Southwestern food and themed seasonal menus are a cut above standard hotel fare; the rooftop Compass Room's meals match its splendid views (*see* Southwestern International in Dining, *above*). *122 N. 2nd St., Phoenix 85004, tel. 602/252–1234 or 800/233–1234, fax 602/254–9472. 711 rooms. Facilities: pool, health club, shops, meeting rooms, 2 restaurants, bar-lounge, "gold passport" floors (6–8), concierge, covered parking. AE, D, DC, MC, V.*

$$$ **Embassy Suites.** Just 5 miles from downtown, this 19-year-old, four-story open-courtyard hotel was overhauled in 1990. Lush palms and olive trees hide bubbling fountains and a huge sunken pool, while four glass-walled elevators lift you to your floor. Free breakfast and evening social hour are shared in the spacious clubhouse at café tables, by a large sunken fireplace/conversation pit, and in front of a wide-screen TV off in a corner.

Suites are compact but dramatic, with emerald carpets and drapes, Santa Fe geometric wallpaper and bedspreads. The tiny kitchenette has a microwave, sink, and bar refrigerator. The White Buffalo offers lunch and dinner with wonderful views. *2333 E. Thomas Rd., Phoenix 85016, tel. 602/957–1910 or 800/ EMBASSY, fax 602/955–2861. 183 suites. Facilities: pool, sauna, shop, restaurant, meeting rooms, free airport limo, parking. AE, D, DC, MC, V.*

★ **Hilton Suites.** A model of excellent design within tight limits, this 11-story atrium opened in 1990. A more luxurious version of the frequent-traveler suites concept, it sits off Central Avenue, 2 miles north of downtown amid the Phoenix plaza cluster of office towers. The marble-floored, pillared lobby with giant urns opens into the atrium, with fountains, palms, and the lantern-lighted New Orleans–style restaurant. Modern fauvist art hangs on the walls; thematic colors are sand and bright teal blue, and Navajo-inspired motifs mark carpets and borders. Suites continue the bold design, with bleached wood furniture and rough-cut custom metal chandeliers. Each large bathroom opens to both living room and bedroom, which have two windows apiece (one that opens), and every couch is a sofa bed. Each room also has a microwave (the gift shop sells snacks and offers free VCR movies). This practical and popular property is likely to become a classic. *10 E. Thomas Rd., Phoenix 85012, tel. 602/ 222–1111 or 800/HILTONS, fax 602/265–4841. 226 rooms. Facilities: pool, exercise room, sauna, shop, restaurant, bar, business center, covered parking. AE, D, DC, MC, V.*

Holiday Inn Crowne Plaza. After a huge fire decades ago, total rebuilding, and a series of owners, the historic Adams Hotel is just a memory. In its place stands a 19-story modern shell cleverly crafted for the desert, with sand-colored walls, arcaded sidewalks, and scooped arches shading each window. A 1994 renovation brought the tired inside back to life, healing several years of neglect. Soft green carpeted halls lead to compact rooms in desert shades, with rose and stone-blue carpeting; tables, desks, and lamps are marble, glass, and bronze and patinated copper. The young staff is gracious, and the scale and services are those of a major hotel, including the revitalized shops and restaurants. *111 N. Central Ave., Phoenix 85004, tel. 602/257–1525 or 800/465–4329, fax 602/253–9755. 534 rooms. Facilities: pool, health club, sauna, outdoor jogging track, shops, meeting rooms, 2 restaurants, bar-lounge, concierge, limo-tour desk, covered parking. AE, D, DC, MC, V.*

$$ **Best Western Executive Park.** One of downtown's hidden jewels,
★ this small eight-story facility sits on Central Avenue at the new Deck Park (beneath which I–10 passes under the heart of the city). Simple and elegant, the rooms are brightened by peach-and-sand color walls and prints by Southwestern masters. Moderate-size rooms have comfortable beds and large, well-lighted desks, compact brass-trimmed bathrooms with coffeemakers, and (above the second floor) commanding city views. The eighth-floor suites are dramatic, with ample balconies and sitting rooms; off the drape-swathed bedroom is a vast dressing

Phoenix Lodging

Ambassador Inn, **16**

Arizona Biltmore, **6**

Best Western Executive Park, **20**

The Boulders, **13**

The Buttes, **28**

Camelback Courtyard by Marriott, **9**

Comfort Inn Airport, **24**

Crescent Hotel, **5**

Doubletree Suites, **26**

Embassy Suites, **18**

Flying E Ranch, **1**

Hilton Pavilion, **31**

Hilton Suites, **19**

Holiday Inn Crowne Plaza, **21**

Hotel Westcourt, **4**

Hyatt Regency Phoenix, **23**

Hyatt Regency Scottsdale at Gainey Ranch, **11**

InnSuites Phoenix/Central, **17**

Kay El Bar Ranch, **2**

Lexington Hotel, **7**

Marriott's Camelback Inn, **10**

Mesa Travelodge, **30**

Motel 6 Scottsdale, **14**

The Phoenician, **15**

The Pointe Hilton on South Mountain, **29**

Quality Inn Airport, **25**

Radisson Tempe, **27**

Rancho de los Caballeros, **3**

Ritz-Carlton, **8**

San Carlos Hotel, **22**

Scottsdale Princess, **12**

KEY

AE American Express Office

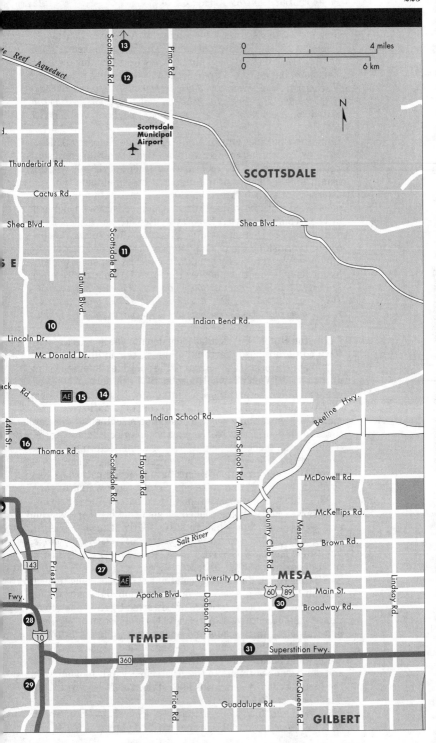

room with Roman tub, plus a standard bathroom with shower. Rose's restaurant does a nice array of American-Continental dishes, with Southwestern accents. The Heard Museum, Phoenix Art Museum, and main library are within walking distance. This hotel has charm, a great location—and great prices. *1100 N. Central Ave., Phoenix 85004, tel. 602/252–2100 or 800/528–1234, fax 602/340–1989. 107 rooms. Facilities: pool, health club, sauna, meeting rooms, restaurant, bar, parking. AE, D, DC, MC, V.*

InnSuites Phoenix/Central. A mile east of the Embassy Suites is an older, cozier, and cheaper version of the open-courtyard suite hotel. Under its red-tile roofs are apartment-style suites dating from the mid-1960s, with orange and brown outside trim and discreet but stylish furnishings (rose carpet with a light Japanese floral motif in wall art, drapes, and bedspreads) and half-kitchen, complete with refrigerator, utensils, and dishes. Front suites hear 32nd Street's traffic; 24 second-story suites have balconies overlooking the pool and densely landscaped garden. An 8-by-10 nook serves daily breakfast, a second dispenses poolside happy hour, and a third houses the four-station exercise room. *3101 N. 32nd St., Phoenix 85018, tel. 602/956–4900 or 800/950–1688, fax 602/957–6122. 76 suites. Facilities: pool, exercise room, meeting rooms, free airport limo, parking. AE, D, DC, MC, V.*

Lexington Hotel. Only 3 miles from downtown, in a nest of midtown corporate-headquarters buildings, this is Phoenix's best bet for sports lovers. Carved out of the poolside conference wing of the old Del Webb TowneHouse in 1987 (the former hotel became an office tower), the Lexington now houses a sports bar (noisy and crowded), 11 racquetball courts (a national tournament site), an aerobics room, a 40-station machine workout center, a full indoor basketball court, and a large outdoor waterfall pool. The ambience is bright, modern, and informal. Rooms range in size from moderate (in the cabana wing, where baths have bidets and first-floor rooms have poolside patios) to very small (tower wing) and were completely redecorated in early 1993. In the locker rooms, no amenity is spared. And the restaurant serves hefty, home-cooked meals. This is where visiting pro teams—and fans—like to stay. *100 W. Clarendon Ave., Phoenix 85013, tel. 602/279–9811; fax 602/631–9358. 167 rooms. Facilities: pool, health club, sauna, shops, restaurant, 2 bars, covered parking. AE, D, DC, MC, V.*

San Carlos Hotel. Phoenix's second-oldest hotel is being reborn. Built in 1927, it was a popular downtown hub and landmark for decades; now, its seven stories are dwarfed by the Valley Bank Center and other skyscrapers. A 1990 refurbishment put deep blue carpeting in the halls and added new wallpaper, drapes, and spreads in the 120 snug rooms and suites (whose 3-inch concrete walls ensure quiet). Fixtures—from the pedestal sinks and old-fashioned toilets to the Austrian crystal chandeliers in the lobby—echo '30s and '40s high style. *202 N. Central Ave., Phoenix 85004, tel. 602/253–4121 or 800/528–5446; fax 602/253–4121, ext. 209. 105 rooms. Facilities: pool, shops, restaurant, deli, pub, meeting rooms, covered parking. AE, D, DC, MC, V.*

Airport
$$–$$$$
★

The Buttes. Two miles east of Sky Harbor, nestled in desert buttes at I–10 and AZ 360, is Phoenix's best hotel buy. Built in 1986 and redecorated in 1993, it joins dramatic architecture (the lobby's back wall is the volcanic rock itself), classic Southwest design (pine and saguaro-rib furniture, original works by major regional artists), and stunning valley views. Rooms are moderate in size and comfortable, with a compact bath and half-closet; decor includes desert colors and live cactus. "Radial" rooms are largest, with the widest views; inside rooms face the huge free-form pool in its rock amphitheater, with waterfall, Jacuzzis, and cantina. Concierge-floor amenities are well worth the nominal added fee. The elegant Top of the Rock restaurant and the quiet luxury of the dawn-to-midnight Market Café are definite pluses. *2000 Westcourt Way, Tempe 85282, tel. 602/225–9000 or 800/843–1986, fax 602/438–8622. 353 rooms. Facilities: pool, health club, saunas, 5 tennis courts, jogging and hiking trails, shops, 2 restaurants, 3 bars, business center, meeting rooms, concierge floor, parking (with lot shuttle), AE, D, DC, MC, V.*

Doubletree Suites. In the Gateway Center, just a mile north of the airport, this striking hotel is the best of a dozen choices for the traveler who wants to get off the plane and into a comfortable room. Past the lobby full of modernist regional art lies a honeycomb of six-story towers, linked by mazes of walkways and richly landscaped gardens. The modest-size rooms are rose, blue-gray, and Navajo white with comfy furniture. The kitchenettes have microwaves. Topper's, a pleasantly intimate restaurant, offers a relaxed wine bar. Business and sports facilities are extensive; the casual elegance and easy access attract visiting celebrities. *320 N. 44th St., Phoenix 85008, tel. 602/225–0500 or 800/528–0444, fax 602/225–0957. 242 suites. Facilities: pool, health club, sauna, 2 tennis courts, shops, restaurant, bar-lounge, meeting rooms, free airport shuttle, parking. AE, D, DC, MC, V.*

★ **The Pointe Hilton on South Mountain.** The Southwest's largest resort (950 suites on 1,000 acres), this Mexican-Mediterranean extravaganza opened in 1987 alongside the nation's largest city park (South Mountain, a 16,000-acre desert preserve). Of all the valley's luxury resorts, this is the most convenient—3 miles from the airport, about 7 miles from downtown Phoenix or the eastern valley. Three lavishly designed and decorated suite hotels (one set on winding hillside streets like a coastal village), a four-story sports center, and four separate restaurants are linked by landscaped walkways and roads; carts and drivers are on 24-hour call. Spacious, high-ceilinged suites combine undyed fabrics, whitewashed timbers, and lodge fireplaces with dark-wood–accent furniture, cinnamon carpets, and Mexican handicrafts. Golf, tennis, riding, and several pools are among the amenities. *7777 S. Pointe Pkwy., Phoenix 85044, tel. 602/438–9000 or 800/876–4683, fax 602/431–6535. 950 suites. Facilities: lake, 3 pools, health center, saunas, 100-horse stable, 10 tennis courts, 18-hole golf course, jogging and hiking trails, shops, 4 restaurants, 3 lounges, meeting rooms, parking. AE, D, DC, MC, V.*

$ **Ambassador Inn.** The scenic enclosed courtyard with flowers, fountain, and bubbling stream sets the tone for this 170-room property 4 miles north of Sky Harbor International Airport. The blue-and-brown traditionally styled rooms have refrigerators and electric stove tops. A small weight room with exercise bikes as well as a cheerful pink coffee shop and a brass-trimmed bar are on the premises. Less than a mile away are shopping, golf, tennis, and an indoor ice rink. Rates are adjusted for room location, with those nearest the pool costing more than those on the street side, but all are bargains. *4727 E. Thomas Rd., Phoenix 85018, tel. 602/840–7500 or 800/624–6759, fax 602/840–5078. 170 rooms. Facilities: exercise room, pool, whirlpool spa, restaurant, bar, banquet and meeting room, free airport shuttle, parking. AE, D, DC, MC, V.*

Comfort Inn Airport. The location isn't scenic but it's convenient: This Spanish-style motel is 4 miles from downtown Phoenix and 2 miles north of Sky Harbor International Airport. A red-tile roof and Mexican-tile accents give character to the premises; where rich greenery surrounds the pool. The 49 traditional rooms are dark and small but include a table and two chairs. There's no restaurant, but Bill Johnson's Big Apple three blocks west has good biscuits, grits, and barbecue. *4120 E. Van Buren St., Phoenix 85008, tel. 602/275–5746 or 800/228–5150. 49 rooms. Facilities: pool, parking. AE, D, DC, MC, V.*

Quality Inn Airport. Even though downtown Phoenix and the airport are only five minutes away, guests can retreat to a quiet garden at this modest two-story motel. Thick oleander hedges separate the parking lot from the well-tended courtyard and pool, which are surrounded on three sides by 90 rooms. First-floor accommodations have patios that open onto the tropical greenery and flower beds. The orange-carpeted and dark-wood rooms are basic but large; the tiled baths have separate dressing areas. *3541 E. Van Buren St., Phoenix 85008, tel. 602/273–7121 or 800/221–2222, fax 602/231–0973. 90 rooms, 2 suites. Facilities: pool, coffee shop, lounge, parking. AE, D, DC, MC, V.*

Biltmore–
Scottsdale
$$$$

Arizona Biltmore. After a summer '91 face-lift, the grande dame of Arizona resorts is as lively and lovely as ever. Designed by Frank Lloyd Wright's colleague Albert Chase McArthur, it has been a masterpiece among world-class resorts since it opened in 1929. The lobby has stained-glass skylights and wrought-iron pilasters. Rooms feature gold-foil ceilings, handmade teak furnishings, and brown-and-pink marble baths. Outdoors there are lush flower gardens and stunning views. Restaurants—all very good—range from casual to late-night elegant, with a soda fountain open till 10. *24th St. and Missouri Ave., Phoenix 85016, tel. 602/955–6600 or 800/950–0086, fax 602/381–7600. 502 rooms. Facilities: 3 pools, 12 lighted tennis courts, 2 PGA golf courses, health club, jogging paths, bike rental, 3 restaurants, 3 lounges, concierge, shopping limo, parking. AE, D, DC, MC, V.*

The Boulders. A dozen miles north of The Princess on Scottsdale Road, the valley's most dramatic luxury resort hides among hill-size granite boulders in the foothills town of Carefree. Opened in 1984, The Boulders offers adobe casitas (and patio homes for long-term rental) in a graceful desert landscape; golf courses stretch like carpeting between the giant stones, and a stunning main lodge by the architect Robert Bacon blends beautifully with its surroundings. Remodeled in 1992, the casitas are compact but comfortable, with curving, pueblo-style half-walls and shelves; each has a patio with a view, miniature kiva fireplace, stocked wet bar, and a spacious bath and dressing area with a deep tub and adobe vanity. The modified American plan features breakfast at The Latilla (the lodge's main restaurant) or at The Club on the green, and dinner at either The Latilla or the Palo Verde. The Latilla is Californian in style, the Palo Verde Southwest international. The nearby el Pedregal center, a dramatic twin to the resort, has shopping and more eating options; and Carefree multiplies these many times over. *34631 N. Tom Darlington Dr., Carefree 85377, tel. 602/488–9009 or 800/553–1717, fax 602/488–4118. 136 casitas, 22 patio homes. Facilities: fitness center, 2 pools, 6 tennis courts, 2 18-hole golf courses, jogging and hiking paths, horseback riding, Jeep and balloon rides, llama treks, room service, meeting rooms, parking. AE, D, DC, MC, V.*

Marriott's Camelback Inn. Begun in the mid-'30s as a posh "by invitation only" resort, the Camelback Inn was bought and expanded in the late '60s by J. W. Marriott, who recouped his investment by selling the 423 casitas and suites as condos in 1970–72. (Owners are guaranteed four weeks a year.) The inn "Where Time Stands Still," as its adobe clock-tower entrance still proclaims, is an oasis of comfortable predictability in the gorgeous valley between Camelback and Mummy Mountains. The lobby, a classic of early Southwestern design, is a high point; so is the young, helpful staff and the airy, calm, and clean 25,000-square-foot spa. The casita rooms are big on windows and amenities but small in size, and their architecture and decor are dull and embarrassingly motel-like. The Chaparral Room serves standard Continental fare, and the Navajo Room offers American and Southwestern dishes; neither shows much imagination. The Camelback is content to rest on its laurels, and a steady stream of guests are, too. *5402 E. Lincoln Dr., Scottsdale 85253, tel. 602/948–1700 or 800/24CAMEL, fax 602/951–8469. 400 rooms, 23 suites. Facilities: spa, 3 pools, 10 tennis courts, 2 18-hole golf courses, hiking paths, horseback riding, Jeep and balloon rides, 5 restaurants, 2 lounges, room service, meeting rooms, parking. AE, D, DC, MC, V.*

The Phoenician. Before the Arizona financier Charles Keating was otherwise distracted, he and his wife devoted a lot of time to this resort, now Kuwaiti-owned. You may question the suitability of the lobby's French provincial decor and its authentic Dutch master paintings for a desert locale, but there's no question that a great deal of attention was paid to details. It's the highest-priced property in town, and you wouldn't want to stay here if you didn't have lots of money (or were not on an expense account)—for example, unless you shell out for valet parking each time, you have to wander around a labyrinthine underground garage to fetch your car. But if this type of petty concern never crosses your mind, relax and enjoy the superb service and luxurious facilities, which include a pool fully inlaid with mother-of-pearl. *6000 E. Camelback Rd., Scottsdale 85251, tel. 602/941–8200 or 800/888–8234. 442 rooms, 107 casitas, 31 suites. Facilities: 4 restaurants, boutiques, golf course, 11 tennis courts, 7 swimming pools, health club, sauna, steam room, beauty salon, barbershop, archery, badminton, croquet, volleyball, basketball, jogging trails, supervised children's programs. AE, D, DC, MC, V.*

★ **Scottsdale Princess.** The most tasteful of the Scottsdale resorts, the Princess can accommodate large groups—such as those who come to play in the PGA Tour Phoenix Open, held here every year—without seeming crowded. Rooms in the red-tile-roofed main building and the casitas, spread out over 450 beautifully landscaped acres, are furnished in Spanish style, with large, carved pieces, but sand-colored rugs and bedspreads contribute to an overall airy effect; each casita has three telephones, an oversize tub, and such extras as an iron and an ironing board. The Marquesa Restaurant (*see* Dining, *above*) has been consistently rated one of the best in the state. *7575 E. Princess Dr., Scottsdale 85255, tel. 602/585–4848 or 800/344–4758, fax 602/585–0091. 400 rooms in main building, 125 casitas, 75 villas. Facilities: 5 restaurants, bar, nightclub, horseback riding, 2 18-hole golf courses, 9 tennis courts, 3 pools, health club, spa, racquetball, squash, steam bath, saunas, boutiques and pro shops, hairdresser. AE, D, DC, MC, V.*

$$$–$$$$ **Hyatt Regency Scottsdale at Gainey Ranch.** A fun place for families, with its complex of pools, fountains, water slides, and lagoons plied by gondolas, this resort has a bit of a Disneyland ambience. At night the palm trees are lit up in bright shades of green and orange, and the public areas tend to be crowded. Rooms, which are comfortably, if predictably, furnished in contemporary style, offer all the expected amenities. A standout is The Golden Swan Restaurant, serving Southwestern cooking at its best—light and wonderfully tasty. Three 9-hole courses offer golfers a choice of terrains—dunes, arroyo, or lakes—depending on whether you fancy sand traps or water traps. *7500 E. Doubletree Ranch Rd., Scottsdale 85258, tel. 602/991–3388 or 800/233–1234, fax 602/483–5550. 493 rooms. Facilities: 10 pools, lagoons, 9 tennis courts, 3 9-hole golf courses, health club, 3 restaurants, 2 lounges, concierge floor, parking. AE, D, DC, MC, V.*

★ **Ritz-Carlton.** Like an 11-story false front, this sand-colored neo-Federal mid-rise facing Biltmore Fashion Square mall hides a graceful, well-appointed luxury hotel that pampers the traveler. Built in 1988, it has large public rooms decorated with 18th- and 19th-century European paintings and handsomely displayed china collections. Rooms are moderately spacious with an armoire closeting a TV and refrigerator (stocked), a small closet with a safe, and a marble bath well supplied with amenities. Because the hotel is business-oriented, rates go down on the weekend. The compact, elegant health club and the daily high tea are highlights, and a modestly named The Restaurant is among the valley's best at Southwest-flavored Continental.

2401 E. Camelback Rd., Phoenix 85016, tel. 602/468–0700 or 800/241–3333, fax 602/957–6076. 267 rooms, 14 suites. Facilities: health club, pool, 2 saunas, tennis court, concierge, concierge floor, business center, outdoor meeting pavilion, shop, covered valet parking, 2 restaurants, 2 bars. AE, D, DC, MC, V.

$$ **Camelback Courtyard by Marriott.** This four-story hostelry, which opened in 1990, delivers compact elegance in its public areas and no-frills comfort in its rooms and suites. A medium-size lap pool and whirlpool fill the courtyard, landscaped with granite boulders and palms. Standard doubles are handsomely carpeted and draped while suites are done in gray with rose accents. The considerable savings are achieved by dropping such "hotel" features as 24-hour room service (it's available from 5 to 10 PM) and relying on the attached Town and Country mall for gift and grooming shops, travel services, and the like. *2101 E. Camelback Rd., Phoenix 85016, tel. 602/955–5200 or 800/321–2211, fax 602/955–1101. 143 rooms, 12 suites. Facilities: health club, pool, whirlpool, spa, restaurant, bar, parking. AE, D, DC, MC, V.*

$ **Motel 6 Scottsdale.** The best bargain in Scottsdale lodging is easy to miss, but it's worth hunting for the sign along Camelback Road. Just steps away from the newly renovated Scottsdale Fashion Square and Camelview Plaza, this motel is also close to the specialty shops of 5th Avenue and Scottsdale's Civic Plaza. Amenities aren't a priority here, but the price is remarkable considering the stylish and much more expensive resorts found close by. Rooms are small and spare with brown carpets and print bedspreads, but the well-landscaped pool offers a pleasant outdoor respite under the palms. *6848 E. Camelback Rd., Scottsdale 85251, tel. 602/949–7583. 122 rooms. Facilities: pool, hot tub, parking. AE, D, DC, MC, V.*

East Valley **Hilton Pavilion.** The Pavilion's ambience is defined by etched
$$–$$$ glass and brass, tropical greenery, and art deco–style furniture; the staff is young and eager to help. Rooms are moderately spacious and darkly earth-toned, with small baths and closets and a large lighted table; corner suites and the top two floors have unstocked minibars and the best views. This eight-floor atrium hotel in the heart of the East valley, just off AZ 360. The east valley's largest shopping mall, Fiesta Mall, is almost next door, and downtown Phoenix is 18 miles away. *1011 W. Holmes Ave., Mesa 85210, tel. 602/833–5555 or 800/445–8667, fax 602/649–1886. 263 rooms, 57 suites. Facilities: pool, whirlpool spa, weight room, restaurant, 2 bars, gift shop, parking. AE, D, DC, MC, V.*

Radisson Tempe. Set snugly between the Arizona State University campus and Old Town Tempe, this informal courtyard hotel is handy to the East valley and downtown Phoenix. The tone is set by the spacious adobe-and-verdigris lobby and the young, polo-shirted staff. Many visitors come for ASU sports and the pro-football Cardinals (the stadium is virtually next door); Tempe's Chamber of Commerce and visitor's bureau are both headquartered here. Rooms are bright, simple Southwestern and comfortable. The hotel has a pleasant, quiet sports bar, and a creditable restaurant (The Arches); guests also have Old Town Tempe's wide array of restaurants, shops, and clubs at their feet. *60 E. 5th St., Tempe 85281, tel. 602/894–1400 or 800/547–8705; fax 602/968–7677. 303 rooms. Facilities: pool, exercise club, sauna, 3 tennis courts, shops, 2 restaurants, bar-lounge, meeting rooms, parking. AE, D, DC, MC, V.*

$ **Mesa Travelodge.** Rooms are newly refurbished at this small, plain motel three blocks west of Mesa's downtown center: New blue carpet, cream wallpaper, and bedspreads and art prints in Southwestern motifs, brighten the 38 rooms overlooking a small pool. The motel's busy corner spot can mean continual street noise, but low prices help compensate. *22 S. Country Club Dr., Mesa 85210, tel. 602/964–5694 or 800/578–7878, fax 602/964–5697. 38 rooms. Facilities: pool, parking. AE, D, DC, MC, V.*

West Valley and Metrocenter **$$$** **Crescent Hotel.** This eight-story, terraced white concrete hostelry across I–17 from Metrocenter, the state's largest shopping mall, was built in 1987 by financier Charles Keating. In 1989 it was taken over by the federal government, and it was purchased in 1991 by Kuwaiti investors. They appear to have made the Crescent a viable upper-end hotel. Mrs. Keating's "Southwestern imperial" decor remains—vast public rooms with massive stone arches and concrete columns, terra-cotta tile floors and bleached-wood paneling, with rose carpets in the hallways. The sizable rooms have deep rose carpeting, mauve bedspreads and drapes, and pale-toned furnishings. The full-size pool and tennis courts, and the compact health club are all well appointed. Charlie's restaurant is pricey and uneven, but there are ample eating options nearby. *2620 W. Dunlap Ave., Phoenix 85021, tel. 602/943–8200 or 800/423–4126, fax 602/371–2856. 332 rooms, 12 suites. Facilities: health club, pool, 2 saunas, whirlpool spa, tennis court, squash courts, putting green, volleyball court, concierge, concierge floor, business center, shop, restaurant, bar, parking. AE, D, DC, MC, V.*

Hotel Westcourt. This undistinguished-looking brown block sits on the outer circle of the huge Metrocenter shopping mall, but in a small space it packs 284 rooms around a large central pool. Modest-size rooms (identical to those in its stunning sister hotel, The Buttes) are done in muted Southwestern colors, with bentwood chairs, small refrigerators, and compact baths. The concierge floor charges only a minimal additional fee; lobby-suite sitting rooms overlook the atrium; poolside junior suites (carved from regular-size rooms) are like elegant little cabanas. Breakfast and luncheon buffets are available in Trumps Bar and Grill, as is menu service through the evening. Other dining options abound within a short walk. *10220 N. Metro Pkwy. E, Phoenix 85051, tel. 602/997–5900 or 800/858–1033, fax 602/997–1034. 269 rooms, 15 suites. Facilities: health club, pool, sauna, whirlpool spa, tennis court, concierge, concierge floor, business center, shop, 2 restaurants, bar, parking. AE, D, DC, MC, V.*

Wickenburg **$$$$** **Rancho de los Caballeros.** Now more of a luxury resort than a dusty dude ranch, this 20,000-acre spread began with 320 acres in 1947 and gradually evolved to include an exclusive housing development, a championship golf course, and a 5,000-square-foot conference center. Trail rides are still a popular feature here, and the annual weeklong Desert Caballeros Trail Ride, starting downtown, is a major event among southwestern horse folk. In the huge main lodge, the original *sala* (living room) has been remodeled; surrounding the copper fireplace now is bright, neo-Mexican decor, and adjacent are game rooms. The American-plan (15% tips included) meals are provided in the bright dining room (breakfast and dinner, restaurant style) and poolside from a half-dozen buffet carts. Rooms—from the original brick Sun Terrace duplexes to the recently built Bradshaw Suites (with optional kitchenette and sitting room)—are spacious and done in low-key Southwestern decor; the baths do not have luxury amenities. *1551 S. Vulture Mine Rd., Wickenburg 85390, tel. 602/684–5484, fax 602/684–2267. 73 rooms. Facilities: pool, horseback riding, 4 tennis courts, 18-hole golf course, skeet and trap shooting range, parking. Closed June–Sept. No credit cards.*

$$$ **Flying E Ranch.** This vast spread, on a breeze-swept rise with a 400-square-mile view, typifies the modern dude ranch. About 4 miles west of town to the site of the Wickenburg Massacre and then a mile back from the highway, the 21,000-acre ranch was established in 1946. Most of the rooms have grand views, the original knotty pine walls and whitewashed pine and leather furniture; bathrooms are clean and modern. Minirefrigerators and wet bars are unstocked, as is the lounge (which does have mixers for the sundown cocktail hour); bring your own spirits. But the staff's spirits are high and infectious; city slickers adore the morning, lunch, and evening cookout rides and the occasional "dudeos," in which Flying E greenhorns ride and rope against dudes from other spreads; and the weekly barn dance is not to be missed. American-plan meals are family style on gingham-checked oilcloth over trestle tables, with Western music playing in the background. Rides cost extra. *Box EEE, Wickenburg 85358, tel. 602/684–2690 or 602/684–2173, fax 602/684–5304. 16 rooms. Facilities: pool and whirlpool, horseback riding, weight room, tennis court, basketball court, outdoor chess, lounge, parking. Closed May–Oct. No credit cards.*

Kay El Bar Ranch. Tucked into a hollow beside the Hassayampa River just 3 miles north of town, this is what dude ranches used to be—homey, comfy, and away from it all, with more horses than people, but not too many of either. This National Historic Site, opened as a dude ranch in 1925, was revived in 1980 by two sisters from the East, Jane Nash and Jan Martin. Immense old salt cedars tower over fat saguaros and some of the biggest mesquite trees in Arizona, all shading the 10-room adobe bunkhouse with its family-style lodge room; the two-bedroom, two-bath cottage (built in 1914); and the brightly decorated cookhouse, where eating is family style. Rooms are compact and clean, with small, modern bathrooms, and decor is down-home Western. The American-plan rates include three hearty meals a day (some outdoors by the corral) and horseback rides. *Box 2480,*

Wickenburg 85358, tel. 602/684–7593. 10 rooms, 1 cottage. Facilities: pool, library, horseback riding, volleyball, golf privileges, lodge room, parking. Closed May–mid-Oct. MC, V.

The Arts and Nightlife

The Arts

Phoenix performing-arts groups have grown rapidly in number and sophistication, especially in the past two decades. Completion of the downtown **Symphony Hall** (225 E. Adams St., tel. 602/262–7272) and **Herberger Theater Center** (222 E. Monroe St., tel. 602/252–TIXS), which face each other across the Civic Plaza mall, has given many groups a state-of-the-art permanent home amid spiffy surroundings; the developing "cultural district" just 2 miles north, around Deck Park, houses several more.

The most comprehensive ticket agencies are **Dillard's** (13 locations including all Dillard's department stores and Phoenix Civic Plaza, tel. 602/678–2222) and the **Arizona State University ticket office** (Gammage Center, Tempe, tel. 602/965–3434).

Theater **Actors Theatre of Phoenix** (320 N. Central Ave., Suite 104, tel. 602/254–3475) is the resident theater troupe at the Herberger. Besides a full season of drama, comedy, and musical theater, it presents original one-act plays in its lunchtime Brown Bag series Tuesday through Thursday.

Arizona Theatre Company (Herberger Theater Center, 222 E. Monroe St., tel. 602/256–6995), Arizona's only full Equity company, splits its season between Tucson and Phoenix, where it performs at the Herberger. Its playbill usually includes four popular plays and two lesser-known works.

Black Theater Troupe (333 E. Portland St., tel. 602/258–8128) performs at the Herberger and at its own house, the Helen K. Mason Center, a half-block from the city's Performing Arts Building on Deck Park. It presents original and contemporary dramas and musical revues, as well as adventurous adaptations, such as its recent version of *Steel Magnolias*.

Dinner **Copper State Dinner Theatre** (6727 N. 47th Ave., Glendale, tel. *Theater* 602/937–1671), the valley's oldest dinner troupe, stages light comedy at Max's, a West valley sports bar.

Murder Ink (4130 N. Goldwater Blvd., Scottsdale, tel. 602/423–8737 or 800/255–4440) presents audience-participation whodunits at the Impeccable Pig restaurant and antiques/crafts shop in Scottsdale and other valley locations.

Classical **Arizona Opera** (Symphony Hall, 225 E. Adams St., tel. 602/266– **Music** 7464), one of the nation's most highly respected regional companies, stages a four-opera season, primarily classical, in Tucson and Phoenix.

Phoenix Symphony Orchestra (3707 N. 7th St., tel. 602/264–6363), the resident company at Symphony Hall, has reached the first rank of American regional symphonies. Its rich season includes orchestral works from classical and contemporary literature, a chamber series, composer festivals, and outdoor pops concerts.

Dance **A. Ludwig Co.** (tel. 602/965–3914), the valley's foremost modern dance troupe, includes the choreography of founder-director Ann Ludwig of the Arizona State University faculty in its repertoire of contemporary works.

Ballet Arizona (3645 E. Indian School Rd., tel. 602/381–0184), the state's professional ballet company, presents full seasons of classical and contemporary works (including commissioned pieces for the company) in both Tucson and Phoenix, where it is the resident dance company at the Herberger Theater Center.

Film Harkins Theaters, a locally owned chain, is the only one in the valley that shows anything but mass-market movies. Its **Cine Capri** (2323 E. Camelback Rd., tel. 602/956–4200), a classic wide-screen, superstereo theater from the '60s, occasionally offers giant-screen revivals such as *Dr. Zhivago* and *Spartacus*. At **Camelview 5** (70th St. and Camelback Rd., tel. 602/423–9900), one screen usually shows a major foreign release or domestic art film.

Galleries The gallery scene in Phoenix and Scottsdale is so extensive that your best bet is to consult the Friday and Sunday listings in *The Arizona Republic* or the Marquee section in Saturday's *Phoenix Gazette*. Southwestern art—from traditional to avant-garde Native American, from the Cowboy Artists of America to performance art—is varied and abundant. Photography also enjoys a strong tradition in Arizona.

Nightlife

Downtown Phoenix used to close up at sunset—until the advent of the Arizona Center. The heart of town at last has nightclubs, restaurants, and upscale bars that compete with livelier resorts and clubs in Scottsdale, along Camelback Road in north-central Phoenix, and elsewhere around the valley.

Among music and dancing styles, country-western has the longest tradition here; jazz, surprisingly, runs a close second. Rock clubs and hotel lounges are also numerous and varied. At its major and minor venues, the valley attracts a steady stream of pop and rock acts; for concert tickets, try **Dillard's** (13 valley locations, including Phoenix Civic Plaza, tel. 602/267–1246).

The best listings and reviews are in the weekly *New Times* tabloid newspaper, distributed Wednesday; the Friday and Sunday Life & Leisure sections of *The Arizona Republic*; and the Marquee section of Saturday's *Phoenix Gazette*.

Bars and Lounges **The Plaza Bar** on the mezzanine of the Hyatt Regency Phoenix (122 N. 2nd St., tel. 602/252–1234) offers a quiet getaway with a sparkling downtown view.

A lively (during happy hour, noisy) upscale crowd takes advantage of the city's most spectacular view at **Top of the Rock Bar,** the lounge in Top of the Rock restaurant (2000 W. Westcourt Way, Tempe, tel. 602/225–9000) at The Buttes.

An elegant uptown spot, **Top of Central** (8525 N. Central Ave., tel. 602/861–2437) has soft music and room for larger groups.

Comedy **The Last Laugh** (8041 N. Black Canyon Hwy., tel. 602/995–5653) is the valley's oldest successful comedy club.

The Improv (930 E. University Dr., Tempe, tel. 602/921–9877), part of a national chain, books better-known talent.

Country and Western **Cheyenne Cattle Co.** (455 N. 3rd St., tel. 602/253–6225), in the Arizona Center downtown, is the newest country-and-western dance spot in town.

At **Mr. Lucky's** (3660 W. Grand Ave., tel. 602/246–0686), the granddaddy of Phoenix western clubs, you can dance the two-step all night (or learn it, if you haven't before).

Toolie's Country (4231 W. Thomas Rd., tel. 602/272–3100) books the best national acts.

Jazz **American Bar & Grill** (1233 S. Alma School Rd., Mesa, tel. 602/844–1918) books easy-listening artists for Wednesday–Saturday gigs that fit its San Francisco–style lounges. (Good neo–New Orleans and Southwestern food are featured, too.)

At **Unique Foods and Services** (1153 W. Jefferson St., tel. 602/257–0701), a fine jazz sextet accompanies the barbecue and greens Friday nights till 11 PM (and via closed-circuit radio the rest of the week) in a smoke- and alcohol-free environment youngsters can enjoy.

Timothy's (6335 N. 16th St., tel. 602/277–7634) is yet one more venerable venue that joins top jazz performances with fine French-influenced Southwestern cuisine.

Frisco's (7575 N. 16th St., tel. 602/997-2424), a recent offspring of Timothy's, offers outstanding local jazz artists, an open Sunday night jam session, and daring Southwestern takes on classic San Francisco menus.

Rock and Blues A small club, **Anderson's Fifth Estate** (6820 E. 5th Ave., Scottsdale, tel. 602/994–4168) mixes DJ nights, local bands, and occasional touring rock and country/folk acts.

Mason Jar (2303 E. Indian School Rd., tel. 602/956–6271) hosts regular alternative rock nights and occasional blues and rock oldies.

Warsaw Wally's (2547 E. Indian School Rd., tel. 602/955–0881) is the top valley blues club, but its poolroom draws rough trade.

Singles With 36 TVs and five giant screens, as well as an outdoor volley-ball court, **America's Original Sports Bar** (455 N. 3rd St., tel. 602/252–2112) in The Arizona Center is big and boisterous.

At the popular **Denim & Diamonds** (3905 E. Thomas Rd., tel. 602/225–0182), folks turn up dressed in anything from casual to glam for drinking and dancing.

In the Arizona Center, **Hooters** (455 N. 3rd St., tel. 602/257–0000) draws crowds with its T-shirted, short-shorted wait-resses, its beer and burgers and potato-skins menu, and its in-door-outdoor visibility.

Macayo's Depot Cantina (300 S. Ash Ave., Tempe, tel. 602/966–6677) combines a lively "meet market," frequented by students from the nearby ASU campus, with a very creditable Mexican restaurant.

Studebaker's (705 S. Rural Rd., Tempe, tel. 602/829–8495) joins bar, buffet, and dancing with live DJs for a noisy place to meet friends Tuesday–Saturday nights.

7 Tucson and Southern Arizona

American Express offers Travelers Cheques built for two.

Cheques *for Two*℠ from American Express are the Travelers Cheques that allow either of you to use them because both of you have signed them. And only one of you needs to be present to purchase them.

Cheques *for Two* are accepted anywhere regular American Express Travelers Cheques are, which is just about everywhere. So stop by your bank, AAA* or any American Express Travel Service Office and ask for Cheques *for Two*.

Travelers Cheques

Pack light.
Take the one number you need for any kind of call, anywhere you travel.

Checking in with your family back home? Calling for a tow truck? When you're on the road, the phone you use might not accept your calling card. Or you might get overcharged by an unknown telephone company. Here's the solution: dial 1 800 CALL ATT.[sm] You'll get flawless AT&T service, competitive calling card prices, and the lowest prices for collect calls from any phone, anywhere. Travel light. Just bring along this one simple number: 1 800 CALL ATT.

By Edie Jarolim and Trudy Thompson Rice

A treasure of mountains, deserts, canyons, and dusty little cowboy towns, southern Arizona remains undiscovered, for the most part, by visitors; the vast majority of the state's tourists head north for the Grand Canyon, often neglecting the southern half of the state. But it would be a pity to miss southern Arizona. It's uncrowded, the weather is usually mild, and there is plenty to see and do. Among the area's myriad attractions are historic Tombstone, Yuma, and Bisbee, where you can indulge in Old West fantasies galore; the huge, oddly shaped cacti of Saguaro National Monument; the eerily towering rock formations of Chiricahua National Monument; the lively shops and restaurants in Nogales, across the Mexican border; and, of course, Tucson. A gateway to southern Arizona, Tucson offers the traveler everything from culture to sports, from ballet, symphony, and the University of Arizona's photography museum, which has one of the largest modern collections in the country, to golf, tennis, and Hi-Corbett Field, where the Colorado Rockies compete with seven other major-league baseball teams during spring training.

Although it is Arizona's second-largest city, Tucson feels like a small town, albeit one enriched by its deep Mexican and Old West roots. It is at once a bustling center of business and a kicked-back university and resort town. Metropolitan Tucson has some 665,000 year-round residents—making it second in population to the state's capital, Phoenix—but the population swells in the winter, when "snowbirds" come to the area to enjoy the warm sun that shines on the city more than 320 days every year. Winter temperatures hover around 65°F during the day and 38°F at night. Summers are unquestionably hot—with July averaging 101°F during the day and 73°F at night—but not as hot as in Phoenix: Although it is 100 miles to the south and both cities lie in desert valleys created by surrounding mountains, Tucson is cooler in the summer because it's higher in altitude (2,400 feet, compared with Phoenix's 1,100 feet). And because Tucson averages only 11 inches of rain a year (more than half of which falls from July to September), the low humidity makes even July's heat feel far more comfortable than one would expect.

In a part of the world where everything seems new and buildings more than 50 years old are known as historic places, Tucson is an exception. Historians have dated Tucson's earliest citizens to AD 100, when the Hohokam Indians made their home in the fertile farming valley. During the 1500s, Spanish explorers arrived to find Pima Indians enjoying the mild weather and growing crops.

The name Tucson came from the Indian word *stjukshon* (pronounced "STOOK-shahn"), meaning "spring at the foot of a black mountain." (The springs at the foot of Sentinel Peak, made of black volcanic rock, are now dry.) The name became Tucson (originally pronounced "TUK-son") in the mouths of the Spanish explorers who built the *presidio* (walled city) of San Augustin del Tuguison in 1776 to keep Native Americans from reclaiming the city. The walled city was affectionately called the Old Pueblo by its early settlers, and the nickname has stuck till this day.

Father Eusebio Francisco Kino, a Jesuit missionary, first visited the village in 1687 and returned a few years later to build missions in the area. His influence is still strongly felt throughout the region; especially noteworthy is the Mission San Xavier del Bac, just south of Tucson.

Four flags have flown over Tucson—those of Spain, Mexico, the U.S. Confederacy, and the Union. Arizona didn't become a state until 1912, so its colorful days as a territory are still very much a part of the area's lore. The Butterfield stage line was extended to Tucson in the 1850s, bringing in adventurers, a few settlers, and more than a handful of outlaws. Much of the city's growth was shaped by the University of Arizona, opened in 1891 on land "donated" by two gamblers and a saloon keeper (their benevolence was reputed to have been inspired by a bad hand of cards).

Tucson's growth really took off during World War II, thanks to Davis-Monthan Air Force Base. It was also around this time that air-conditioning made the desert hospitable to visitors and residents alike. Today the city's economy relies heavily on tourism, the university, and some high-tech industries. The resident population is now almost one-quarter Hispanic, and some of the best Mexican food north of the border can be found in restaurants here. The influence of Spanish and Mexican settlers is also strongly felt in the city's architecture and culture.

Tucson is a good jumping-off point for a visit to southern Arizona. Several day trips can be coordinated from the city, but to get the full flavor of such towns as Bisbee, Douglas, and Ajo, plan on an overnight stay. As you might expect, the desert areas are popular in winter, and the cooler mountain areas are more heavily visited in summer months.

Check plane fares carefully when you're planning your trip. Though you may not want to spend time in Phoenix, sometimes it's cheaper to fly into that city and then take a scenic 2½-hour drive down the Pinal Pioneer Parkway (U.S. 79), or a speedier trip on I–10, to Tucson.

Essential Information

Important Addresses and Numbers

Tourist Information
The **Metropolitan Tucson Convention and Visitors Bureau** (130 S. Scott Ave., 85701, tel. 602/624–1817 or 800/638–8350), located downtown, is open weekdays 8–5 and weekends 9–4.

Emergencies
For the **police, ambulance, fire department,** dial 911, a free call from public pay phones.

Doctors and Dentists
The Pima County Medical Society (tel. 602/795–7985) will refer visitors to Tucson physicians; the Arizona State Dental Association (tel. 602/881–7237) can recommend a dentist in the area.

Hospitals **El Dorado Hospital and Medical Center** (1400 N. Wilmot Rd., tel. 602/886–6361), **Northwest Hospital** (6200 N. La Cholla Blvd., tel. 602/742–9000), **St. Joseph's Hospital** (350 N. Wilmot Rd., tel. 602/296–3211), **Tucson General Hospital** (3838 N. Campbell Ave., tel. 602/327–5431), **Tucson Medical Center** (5301 E. Grant Rd., tel. 602/327–5461), **University Medical Center** (1501 N. Campbell Ave., tel. 602/694–0111).

Late-Night Pharmacies Six **Walgreen's** drugstores in the city have 24-hour prescription service; for the location nearest you, call 800/WALGREENS (800/925–4733). A number of Osco Drug stores also offer 24-hour prescription service; if you phone 800/654–OSCO and give the zip code of the place where you're staying, you'll be referred to the closest open pharmacy.

Other Useful Numbers Chamber of Commerce (tel. 602/792–1212); local and state road conditions (tel. 602/573–7623); Tucson Parks and Recreation Department (tel. 602/791–4873); weather (tel. 602/881–3333).

Arriving and Departing by Plane

Tucson International Airport (tel. 602/573–8000) is 8½ miles south of downtown, west of I–10 off the Valencia exit. Carriers include **Aeromexico** and its subsidiary, **Aerolitoral** (tel. 800/237–6639), **American** and its subsidiary, **American Eagle** (tel. 800/433–7300), **America West** (tel. 800/235–9292), **Arizona Airways** (tel. 800/274–0662), **Continental** (tel. 800/525–0280), **Delta** (tel. 800/221–1212), **Morris Air** (tel. 800/444–5660), **Northwest** (tel. 800/225–2525), **Reno Air** (tel. 800/736–6247), and **United** (tel. 800/241–6522).

Between the Airport and Downtown In addition to the modes of transportation listed below, many hotels provide courtesy airport shuttle service; inquire when making reservations.

By Car It makes sense to rent at the airport. Parking is not a problem in most parts of town. Rental-car agencies at the airport include **Budget** (tel. 602/889–8800 or 800/527–0700) and **National Inter-rent** (tel. 602/573–8050 or 800/227–7368). The driving time from the airport to downtown varies, but it's usually less than half an hour; add 20 minutes during rush hours (7:30–9 AM and 4:30–6 PM).

By Taxi Taxi rates vary widely; they are unregulated in Arizona. It's always wise to inquire about the cost of a trip before getting into a cab. You shouldn't pay much more than $16 from the airport to the heart of downtown. A few of the more reliable cab companies are **Yellow Cab** (tel. 602/624–6611), **Checker Cab** (tel. 602/623–1133), and **Fiesta Taxi** (tel. 602/622–7777), whose drivers speak both English and Spanish.

By Van or Bus **Arizona Stagecoach** (tel. 602/889–1000), with an office at the airport, takes groups and individuals to all parts of Tucson for $8.50 to $26, depending on the location.

If you're traveling light and aren't in a hurry, you can take a city **Sun Tran** (tel. 602/792–9222) bus to central Tucson for only 75¢.

Bus 11, which leaves every ½ hour from a stop at the left of the lower level as you come out of the terminal, goes north on Alvernon Way, and you can transfer to most of the east–west bus lines from this main north–south road; ask the bus driver which one would take you closest to the location you need. You can also transfer to a variety of lines from Bus 25, which leaves less frequently from the same airport location and heads to the Roy Laos center at the south of town. You must have exact change, but transfers are free.

Arriving and Departing by Car, Bus, and Train

By Car From Phoenix, 111 miles northwest, I–10 east is the road that will take you to Tucson. Also the main traffic artery through town, I–10 has well-marked exits all along the route. At Casa Grande, 70 miles north of Tucson, I–8 connects with I–10, bringing travelers into the area from the west. From Nogales, 63 miles south on the Mexican border, take I–19 into Tucson.

By Bus Buses to Los Angeles, El Paso, Phoenix, Flagstaff, Douglas, and Nogales depart and arrive regularly from Tucson's **Greyhound Lines** terminal (2 S. 4th Ave. at E. Broadway, tel. 800/231–2222). For travel to Phoenix, **Arizona Shuttle Service, Inc.** (tel. 602/795–6771) runs express service from three locations in Tucson every hour on the hour, 4 AM–8 PM (9 PM in the busy winter season) every day; the trip takes approximately 2½ hours. One-way fares are $19 for adults, $10 for children under 12. Call 24 hours in advance for reservations.

By Train **Amtrak** serves the city with westbound and eastbound trains three times a week; the station is downtown at 400 East Toole Street (tel. 800/872–7245).

Getting Around

A car is almost a requirement if you're really going to explore Tucson and southern Arizona. You can get around downtown on foot and by bus or taxi, but getting to know the area requires a road trip or two.

By Car Much of the year, traffic in Tucson isn't especially heavy, but during the busiest winter months (December through March) streets in the central area of town can get congested. There's a seat-belt law in the state, as well as one that requires children under the age of four to ride in a secure child-restraint seat. Don't even think of drinking and driving; if you do, you'll spend your vacation in jail. Arizona's strict laws against driving under the influence are strongly enforced.

If you haven't rented a car at the airport (*see* Between the Airport and Downtown, *above*), you might try **U-Save Auto Rental** (tel. 602/790–8847 or 602/745–2119), **Enterprise** (tel. 602/747–9700 or 602/881–9400) or **Rent-A-Ride** (tel. 602/750–1900) in the city center. In addition, **Carefree Rent-A-Car** (tel. 602/790–2655) offers reliable used cars at good rates.

By Bus and Trolley Within the city limits, public transportation is available through **Sun Tran** (tel. 602/792–9222), Tucson's bus system. On weekdays, buses start running at around 6 AM; some lines operate until 10 PM, but most only go until 7 or 8 PM. Service is more limited on weekends. A one-way ride costs 75¢ (transfers are free); those with valid Medicare cards can ride for 25¢. The **Sun Tran Trolley** runs between downtown and the University of Arizona, Monday–Saturday, for 25¢ each way. Call for information on Sun Tran bus and trolley routes and costs.

The city-run **Van Tran** (tel. 602/620–1234) offers transportation in specially outfitted vans for riders with disabilities. Call for information and reservations.

Guided Tours

Orientation Tours **Great Western Tours** (tel. 602/721–0980) and **Tucson Tour Company** (tel. 602/297–2911 or 602/544–2664) take individuals and groups to such popular sights as Old Tucson, Sabino Canyon, and the Arizona–Sonora Desert Museum and also offer in-depth tours of the city and its neighborhoods. **Old Pueblo Tours** (tel. 602/575–1175), with a slightly different itinerary—including "A" Mountain and San Xavier del Bac Mission—provides a fine historical overview of the area. Many tour operators are on limited schedules during the summer, but **Off the Beaten Path Tours** (tel. 602/296–0909) has excellent customized excursions year-round. **Sunshine Jeep Tours** (tel. 602/742–1943) and **Trail Dust Jeep Tours** (602/747–0323) both offer trips to the Sonoran Desert in open-air four-wheel-drive vehicles.

Special-Interest Tours In the spring and fall, those interested in visiting the area's historic missions can contact **Kino Mission Tours** (tel. 602/628–1269), which has professional historians and bilingual guides on staff. If you've always wanted to star in a western and you're feeling flush, contact the folks at **Cowboy Movie Fantasy Camp** (tel. 602/745–8221): The day of filming is fun, and you'll end up with a video in which you appear to be doing dangerous cowboy stunts. **Stage Stop Tours** (tel. 602/394–2211) depart from Patagonia (*see* Off the Beaten Track in Exploring, *below*) to a number of ghost towns in southern Arizona.

Walking Tours For an easy-to-follow self-guided tour of historic downtown Tucson, head for the **Visitors Bureau** (130 S. Scott Ave., tel. 602/624–1817 or 800/638–8350). The friendly, knowledgeable docents of the **Arizona Historical Society** (tel. 602/622–0956) conduct walking tours of the El Presidio neighborhood every Saturday at 10 AM from October through April (price: $4 for adults). **Old Pueblo Walking Tours** (tel. 602/323–9290) gears its weekend strolls around historic neighborhoods to visitors' interests—for example, architecture or photography; the cost is $10.

Out-of-Town Tours Several tour companies offer bus or van excursions to points throughout southern Arizona. **Gray Line Tours** (Box 1991, Tucson 85702, tel. 602/622–8811) takes groups or individuals to such destinations as Bisbee, Tubac, and Nogales; **Tumbleweed Tours**

& Trips (tel. 602/749–3034) specializes in smaller groups and more imaginative tours of the area. **Ajo Stage Line** (tel. 602/387–6559 or 800/942–1981) departs from Ajo (*see* Southwestern Arizona, *below*) to Rocky Point and the Pinacote volcanoes in northern Mexico.

Opening and Closing Times

The majority of central-city businesses, including shops and some restaurants, close at the end of the office workday, sometimes as early as 5:30 or 6. Malls have more extended hours; most stores are open weekdays 10–9, weekends 10–6. Banking hours vary widely; most Tucson banks are open weekdays 9–4 (inside lobby services) and 9–5 (drive-in service); on Saturday some lobbies are open 8–2. Almost all banks have automated teller machines (ATMs), so customers with a banking network card can get cash when the banks are closed.

Radio Stations

AM **KNST 790:** News, talk; **KTKT 990:** Sports Entertainment Network; **KJYK 1490:** Top 40; **KUAT 1550:** National Public Radio, jazz.

FM **KUAT 89.1:** National Public Radio, jazz; **KUAZ 90.5:** Classical; **KXCI 91.3:** Alternative rock, folk, blues; **KLPX 96.1:** Rock; **KIIM 99.5:** Country.

Exploring Tucson

Tucson covers more than 500 square miles in a valley ringed by mountains; for tours of the area it's necessary to have a car. The central part of town, where most of the shops, restaurants, and businesses are located, is roughly bounded by Wilmot Road on the east, Oracle Road on the west, River Road to the north, and 22nd Street to the south. The older downtown section, accessible just east of I–10 off the Broadway–Congress exit, is much smaller and easy to navigate on foot. (Streets there don't run true to any sort of grid, however, so it's best to get a good, detailed map.) If you're out walking in the hot weather, stop for frequent breaks to drink fluids: Tucson's dryness can dehydrate visitors quickly, especially if they are accustomed to living in a high-humidity area. Avoid alcohol because it aggravates dehydration, and wear sunscreen and a hat (even in the winter months if you're sun-sensitive).

Highlights for First-Time Visitors

Arizona–Sonora Desert Museum (*see* Tour 3)
El Presidio District (*see* Tour 1)
Kitt Peak National Observatory (*see* Off the Beaten Track)
Mission San Xavier del Bac (*see* Tour 5)
Mt. Lemmon (*see* Tour 4)
Sabino Canyon (*see* Off the Beaten Track)

Saguaro National Monument (*see* Tour 3)
Tubac (see Tour 5)
University of Arizona (*see* Tour 2)

Tour 1: El Presidio District

Numbers in the margin correspond to points of interest on the Tucson: Tours 1 and 2 map.

Originally the center of town, the downtown area is home to three historic districts: Barrio Historico, Armory Park, and El Presidio. The first two, somewhat spread out, are best toured by car; a map available from the Metropolitan Tucson Convention and Visitors Bureau (*see* Tourist Information, *above*) marks a number of noteworthy sites. The El Presidio district, which has the greatest concentration of historical structures, can easily be explored on foot.

The area bounded by Franklin and Pennington streets on the north and south and by Church and Main avenues on the east and west encompasses more than 130 years of the city's architectural history, and dates from the original walled El Presidio del Tucson, a Spanish fortress built in 1776, when Arizona was still part of New Spain. The largest plaza in this historical area is now called **El Presidio Park**; it's bordered on the south side by several modern high-rise government buildings and on the east side by the mosaic-domed **Pima County Courthouse.** This Spanish Colonial–style structure, perhaps Tucson's most beautiful historic building, was built in 1927 on the site of the original single-story adobe court of 1869; a portion of the old Presidio wall can be seen on the courthouse's second floor, and another section of the fort was recently discovered in front of the building. The park itself, an attractive open area with a large modern sculpture in the center, is shared by a combination of city workers and homeless people.

Head north and cross Alameda Street to the Tucson Museum of Art and Historic Block. You can walk around the area on your own, but it's worth asking at the museum for one of the free docent tours. The five historic buildings on this block are listed in the National Register of Historic Places and include La Casa Cordova, the Fish House, and the Stevens Home (*see below*). The other two residences, the **Romero House,** believed to incorporate another section of the Presidio wall, and the **Corbett House,** occupied for 56 years by the influential Tucson family for whom Hi-Corbett Field is named, are not open to the public. In the center of the museum complex is the **Plaza of the Pioneers,** honoring Tucson's early citizens.

If you're ready to go inside, the **Tucson Museum of Art** houses a collection of pre-Columbian art, as well as a permanent display of 20th-century art depicting the West—some wonderful, some less than inspiring—and hosts some interesting traveling shows. The museum's gift shop features a fine variety of works (jewelry, silk scarves, weavings, ceramics) by local artisans. *140 N. Main Ave., tel. 602/624–2333. Admission: $2 adults, $1 se-*

Tucson: Tours 1 and 2

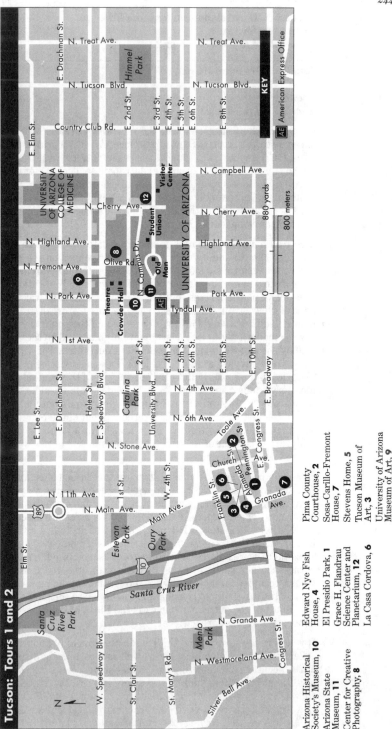

N. Treat Ave.
E. Drachman St.
N. Treat Ave.

Himmel Park

N. Tucson Blvd.
N. Tucson Blvd.

E. Elm St.
Country Club Rd.
E. 2nd St.
E. 3rd St.
E. 4th St.
E. 5th St.
E. 6th St.
E. 8th St.

E. Elm St.

UNIVERSITY OF ARIZONA COLLEGE OF MEDICINE

N. Campbell Ave.

■ Visitor Center
N. Cherry Ave.
N. Cherry Ave.
⑫

■ Student Union
N. Highland Ave.
Highland Ave.

⑧
N. Fremont Ave.
Olive Rd.

⑨
Old Main
N. Park Ave.
UNIVERSITY OF ARIZONA
Park Ave.

Theatre ■
⑪
Crowder Hall ■
⑩
AE
Tyndall Ave.

N. 1st Ave.

E. Drachman St.
Helen St.
E. Speedway Blvd.
Catalina Park
E. 2nd St.
E. 4th St.
E. 5th St.
E. 6th St.
E. 8th St.
E. 10th St.

E. Lee St.
University Blvd.
N. 4th Ave.
E. Broadway

N. 6th Ave.

N. Stone Ave.
N. 4th Ave.

Toole Ave.
E. Congress St.

N. 11th Ave.
1st St.
Church St.
② ①
E. Pennington St.
⑥ Alameda
⑤ ④ ①
89
N. Main Ave.
Franklin St.
③
⑦
Granada Ave.

Estevan Park
Oury Park
Elm St.

10
Santa Cruz River
Santa Cruz River Park

W. Speedway Blvd.
St. Clair St.
St. Mary's Rd.
Menlo Park
N. Grande Ave.
N. Westmoreland Ave.
Silver Bell Ave.
Congress St.

N ←

880 yards
800 meters

0 | 0

Arizona Historical
Society's Museum, **10**

Arizona State
Museum, **11**

Center for Creative
Photography, **8**

Edward Nye Fish
House, **4**

El Presidio Park, **1**

Grace H. Flandrau
Science Center and
Planetarium, **12**

La Casa Cordova, **6**

Pima County
Courthouse, **2**

Sosa-Carillo-Fremont
House, **7**

Stevens Home, **5**

Tucson Museum of
Art, **3**

University of Arizona
Museum of Art, **9**

*nior citizens and students, children under 12 free; Tues. free.
Free docent tours available upon request. Open Mon.–Sat. 10–
4, Sun. noon–4. Closed national holidays.*

When you leave the museum, walk down Main Avenue to the
❹ corner of Alameda (less than a block away) to the **Edward Nye
Fish House,** built in 1868 of adobe by the early Tucson merchant
for whom it is named. Fish, a merchant, entrepreneur, and poli-
tician, and his wife, Maria Wakefield Fish, a prominent educa-
tor, shaped much of early Tucson history; they hosted such
visitors as President and Mrs. Rutherford B. Hayes here. Their
residence, notable for its 15-foot beamed ceilings and saguaro-
cactus-rib supports, now houses the El Presidio art gallery,
which sells contemporary and traditional Southwestern oils,
watercolors, bronzes, and ceramics. *120 N. Main Ave., tel. 602/
884–7379. Admission free. Open Mon.–Sat. 10–5, Sun. 1–4.
Closed Sun. June–Aug.*

Also on Main Avenue, just north of the Fish House and architec-
❺ turally similar, is the 1865 **Stevens Home.** Here wealthy politi-
cian and cattle rancher Hiram Stevens and his Mexican wife,
Petra Santa Cruz, entertained many of Tucson's leaders—including Edward and Maria Fish—during the 1800s. A drought
brought the Stevenses' cattle ranching to a halt in 1893, and Stevens killed himself—having unsuccessfully attempted to kill his
wife—in despair. The house was restored in 1980 and now hosts
one of Tucson's best restaurants, Janos (*see* Dining, *below*).

For one of the best examples of simple but elegant adobe archi-
❻ tecture, head across the Plaza of the Pioneers to **La Casa Cordova.** One of the oldest buildings in Tucson, with the original part
built in about 1848, it is now home to the Mexican Heritage Museum. When you enter La Casa Cordova through the double
doors on Meyer Avenue, the room on your right has an exhibit of
the history of the Presidio; three rooms off the patio display furnishings of the Indian and pioneer settlers of the period. If you
are lucky enough to be here from November through March,
don't miss the Naciemento, a traditional Christmas display filling an entire room with miniatures arranged in elaborate scenes
from the Old and New Testaments and from Mexican rural life.
When you visit the museum, you'll understand why adobe—
brick made of mud and straw, cured in the hot sun—was so
widely used in early Tucson. It offers a natural insulation from
the heat and cold, and it is durable in Tucson's dry climate. In
some cases the woody cactus ribs built into the walls and ceilings
for extra support poke through the hard-packed adobe. *175 N.
Meyer Ave., tel. 602/624–2333. Admission free. Open Sept.–
Apr. Mon.–Sat. 10–4, Sun. noon–4. Closed Mon. June–Aug.
and on national holidays.*

Time Out **Old Town Artisans,** across Meyer Avenue from Casa Cordova, is
a 13-room marketplace set in a 19th-century adobe building,
with a focus on Southwestern and Mexican crafts. The pretty
Courtyard Café (186 N. Meyer Ave., tel. 602/622–0351) on the

patio, mist-cooled in summer, is a fine place to enjoy a salad or a sandwich.

❼ Sosa-Carillo-Fremont House is worth a short detour south. The only building spared when the surrounding barrio was torn down to build the Tucson Convention Center, this is one of Tucson's oldest adobe residences. Originally purchased by José Maria Sosa in 1860, it was owned by the Carillo family for 80 years; Arizona's territorial governor, John C. Fremont, may have spent a night or two here when the place was briefly rented out to his daughter in 1880. The restored house, now a branch of the Arizona Historical Society, is furnished in 1880s fashion and has rotating displays of territorial life. *Convention Center Complex, between the Music Hall and the Arena (parking at 151 S. Granada Ave.), tel. 602/622-0956. Admission free. Walking tours of the Presidio and Tucson Historic District are given Oct.–Apr., Sat. at 10; $4 adults, children under 7 free. Open Wed.–Sat. 10–4.*

Tour 2: University of Arizona Neighborhood

A university—especially in the Southwest—might not seem to be the most likely spot for a vacation visit, but this one is unusual. Not only is the institution itself of historical importance, but it also hosts museums for special interests ranging from photography to mineralogy. Parking in the university area is a hassle, so it's best either to leave your car elsewhere or take extra care to park it legally in a university lot. Although there are several lots throughout the campus, they're often crowded, so it's a good idea to park in the first legal spot you find. Read and heed all the signs: They mean business.

The U of A, as the University of Arizona is known locally (versus ASU, its rival state university in Phoenix), covers 325 acres and is a major economic influence on the city. More than 35,000 students attend graduate and undergraduate classes here. The original land for the university was "donated" by a couple of gamblers and a saloon owner in 1891, and $25,000 of territorial money was used to build Old Main (the original building) and hire six faculty members. The money ran out before the Old Main's roof was placed, but a few enlightened local citizens pitched in with the funds to finish it. Most of the city's populace was less enthusiastic about the institution: They were disgruntled when the 13th Territorial Legislature granted the University of Arizona to Tucson and awarded rival Phoenix with what they considered to be the real prize—an insane asylum and a prison.

Note: For all of the university's institutions, it's best to call ahead and verify opening and closing hours; budget cuts have caused schedule changes in a number of cases. The *Tucson Official Visitors Guide*, available from the Tucson Convention and Visitors Bureau (*see* Tourist Information, *above*) includes a detailed map of the campus.

Start your tour on the northwestern corner of campus, at the junction of Speedway Boulevard and Park Avenue, where you'll find a large parking garage. A pedestrian underpass leads to the
❽ Center for Creative Photography, located in a gray concrete building on the left. Set up to house the university's extensive Ansel Adams holdings, this is one of the world's largest collections of 20th-century photography, including works by such artists as Paul Strand, W. Eugene Smith, and Edward Weston. Changing exhibits in the main gallery highlight various holdings of the collection, but if you'd like to spend an hour looking at the pictures of a particular photographer in the center's archives, call to arrange an appointment. *1030 N. Olive Rd., tel. 602/621–7968. Admission free. Open Mon.–Fri. 11–5, Sun. noon–5. Closed Sat., national and state holidays.*

Catercorner from the center on the right-hand side is the small
❾ University of Arizona Museum of Art, with a wide-ranging collection of European paintings from the Renaissance through the 17th century. A collection of bronze and plaster sculptures by Jacques Lipschitz is a highlight of the museum. *Fine Arts Complex, Bldg. 2, tel. 602/621–7567. Admission free. Open Sept.–mid-May, weekdays 9–5, Sun. noon–4; mid-May–Aug., weekdays 10–3:30, Sun. noon–4. Closed Sat., national and state holidays.*

Head directly south two blocks on Park Avenue and then go east
❿ on 2nd Street to reach the Arizona Historical Society's Museum. (If you're driving and this is your first stop, park your car in the lot at the corner of 2nd and Euclid streets and then inquire at the museum about the token system.) Well-displayed exhibits transport the visitor through Arizona history, starting with the Hohokam Indians and Spanish explorers and highlighting important influences such as mining and cattle ranching. Children are welcome, and several exhibits are geared to the interests of older young people. The museum's gift shop focuses on items from the late 1800s; many are reproductions, but there are a number of antiques as well. Unusual souvenirs are also available at the library, which houses an extensive collection of historical Arizona photographs and sells reprints of most of them for a small fee. *949 E. 2nd St., tel. 602/628–5774. Admission free (donations appreciated). Open Mon.–Sat. 10–4, Sun. noon–4. Closed national and state holidays.*

One block to the south on University Boulevard, just inside the
⓫ main gate of the university, is the Arizona State Museum, the oldest in the state, dating from territorial days (1893). Phase I of the $1.7 million "Paths of Life: American Indians of the Southwest" exhibit, occupying some 10,000 square feet in the museum's north building, opened in late 1993. The cultural traditions, origins, and contemporary lives of native tribes of Arizona and Sonora, Mexico, are explored through a variety of displays and video programs. *Park Ave., tel. 602/621–6302. Admission free. Open Mon.–Sat. 10–5, Sun. noon–5. Closed national holidays.*

Time Out Just outside the campus gate, University Boulevard is lined with student-oriented eateries. You won't find sophisticated fare, but portions tend to be hearty and prices low. **Geronimoz** (800 E. University Blvd. at Euclid, tel. 602/623–1711) stands out for its good burgers and salads and large selection of beers.

Back on campus, as you head east, University Boulevard turns into the grassy University Mall; continue on to Cherry Avenue to reach the **Grace H. Flandrau Science Center and Planetarium.** Tucson is a major center for astronomy; lighting ordinances have been designed here to allow viewing of the usually clear desert skies at night, even in the center city. Planetarium attractions include a 16-inch public telescope, the impressive Star Theatre, where a multimedia show brings astronomy to life, and an interactive meteor exhibit. Laser light shows are held here at night. Take your camera; special adapters allow you to take pictures through the telescopes. *Cherry Ave. and University Blvd., tel. 602/621–4515. Theater admission: $4.50 adults, $4 senior citizens and students, $2.50 children 3–13, children under 3 not admitted; laser light shows: $5. Open Mon. 9–5, Tues.–Thurs. 9–5 and 7–9:30, Fri. 9–5 and 7–midnight, Sat. 1–5 and 7–midnight, Sun. 1–5. Show times vary; call 602/621–7827 for recorded message. Telescope hours during the summer are Tues.– Sat. 8–10 PM; in winter, Tues.–Sat. 7–10 PM.*

The basement of the Flandrau Science Center now hosts the **Mineral Museum,** which exhibits more than 2,000 samples. Although the stress is on Arizona-area minerals—for example, those found at such mines as Bisbee and Tiger—you can see specimens here from all over the world. The collection includes many gemstones and excellent displays of meteorites and radioactive rocks. *Tel. 602/621–4227. Admission free. Open weekdays 8–5, Sat. 1–5. Closed university holidays.*

Tour 3: Tucson Mountain Park and Saguaro National Monument West

Numbers in the margin correspond to points of interest on the Tucson: Tours 3–5 map.

If you have a car at your disposal and are interested in getting to know the flora and fauna of the Sonora Desert—as well as some of its depictions in the cinema—this is an ideal trip for you. If you don't drive, at least consider taking one of the many tours to the Arizona–Sonora Desert Museum (*see* Guided Tours in Essential Information, *above*) in the 17,000-acre **Tucson Mountain Park.** Also within the boundaries of the park, which is just south of Saguaro National Monument West, is the Old Tucson Studios theme park. Your best plan is to head out early in the morning to Saguaro National Monument, the farthest of the three and the one without shaded areas for you to duck into. Then spend the rest of the morning at the Arizona–Sonora Desert Museum, and at lunchtime go over to Old Tucson, which offers the best choice of eateries. Most of the shows featured in Old Tucson don't start until noon, in any case. If you're not going to visit Old Tucson, consider taking lunch along; there are lots of picnic and barbecue areas in Saguaro National Monument, or you can dine on the terrace of the Desert Museum's new restaurant.

From Tucson, take Speedway Boulevard west to where it joins Anklam Road and becomes Gates Pass Road; here you will see signs for Old Tucson Studios. At this juncture Gates Pass Road becomes Kinney Road; continue on for about 12 miles (passing signs for the Arizona–Sonora Desert Museum) until you come to
⑬ **Saguaro National Monument West.** The two portions of the Saguaro National Monument are separated by the city of Tucson: The eastern portion covers more than 62,000 acres and climbs through five climate zones; the smaller western portion, the one explored on this tour, has more than 21,000 acres, all approximately at the same elevation. Both sections of the park are forested by the huge saguaro (pronounced "suh-WAR-oh") cactus, which is native to the Sonora Desert and known for its towering height (often 50 feet) and arms that reach out in weird configurations. The cactus is ribbed vertically with accordionlike pleats that expand to store water gathered through its shallow roots during the infrequent desert rain showers. In the springtime (usually April or May), the giant succulent sports a tiny party hat of white blooms. At any time of year, the sight of these kings of the desert ruling over their quiet domain is awe-inspiring.

The slow-growing cacti (they can take up to 15 years to grow 1 foot) are protected by state and federal laws, so enjoy but don't disturb them. In recent years, they have suffered a decline because a decrease in the coyote population has led to an abundant rabbit population. Rabbits and other small animals nibble at the base of the young saguaro, gathering nutrients and water for survival and thereby hindering or halting the cactus's slow growth.

You'll see the most wildlife if you go through the park early in the morning, when the animals are at their liveliest. Desert critters such as snakes and scorpions aren't necessarily hostile unless you crowd them, so just watch your step and respect their habitat.

Before you venture into the desert, it's worth stopping in at the large new visitor center that opened at Saguaro National Monument West in 1994. A sophisticated slide show in the auditorium ends with a spectacular look at the landscape outside the window; an extremely lifelike display simulates the flora and fauna of the region; and an expanded sales area carries a large array of books and maps. Walkways from the side of the center lead out onto short nature trails, and you can get information about longer hiking trails that wind through the park. Ask how to get to Signal Hill, where you can explore petroglyphs (rock drawings) left by the Hohokam Indians centuries ago. *Tel. 602/883–6366. Admission free. Open daily 8–5.*

About another half-mile south of the visitor center, on Kinney
⑭ Road, the **Arizona–Sonora Desert Museum** is not to be missed.

The name "museum" is misleading for this site, which is more like a beautifully planned zoo. In this microcosm of a desert environment, hummingbirds, cactus wrens, rattlesnakes, scorpions, bighorn sheep, and prairie dogs all busy themselves in natural habitats ingeniously planned to allow the visitor to look on without disturbing them. Besides the wildlife exhibits, there is also the Earth Sciences Center, which features a damp limestone cave and meteor and mineral displays that encourage visitors to feel the texture of the stones and inspect them under magnifying glasses. Exhibits and interactive programs change with the season. For example, during the spring visitors are invited to help identify local wildflowers.

Allow at least two hours for your visit to the museum, longer if you have some real nature lovers with you. You'll be outdoors most of the time, so take a jacket if you're visiting in winter and take frequent water breaks if you're visiting in summer; it can get really hot and dry here. The new Ironwood Terrace restaurant, near the hummingbird exhibit, offers a variety of hot and cold sandwiches, along with burgers, soups, salads, and Mexican entrées. Wheelchairs and strollers are available at the museum, but pets aren't allowed in, so don't take them along on hot days; they can suffer heat stroke if they are confined to the car. *2021 N. Kinney Rd., tel. 602/883–2702. Admission: $7.95 adults, $1.50 children 6–12. Open Mar.–Sept., daily 7:30–6; Oct.–Feb., daily 8:30–5. Ticket sales stop 1 hr before closing. MC, V.*

⑮ Go another 2 miles south on Kinney Road to get to **Old Tucson Studios.** Signs all along the way from town will direct you to this film set-cum-theme park, which will look familiar to you if you've seen even one old western flick. More than 250 westerns have been shot here during the last 50 years, including *Gunfight at the OK Corral, Rio Lobo,* and *The Last Outpost,* starring Ronald Reagan. The TV series "High Chaparral," "Little House on the Prairie," and, more recently, "The Young Riders" have all used the frontier and adobe buildings of Old Tucson as a backdrop.

Time Out   Enjoy Lilly's Red Dog Revue, a corny but fun cancan show, while having a burger or ribs at the **Red Dog Palace Saloon** at Old Tucson. There are also a half-dozen other places in the complex where you can have a snack or a drink.

Young children may be frightened by the loud gunfights staged in the streets, but the older ones will love them. Sheriff's deputies constantly run after bad guys (all local actors), and willing visitors are enlisted to take part in the chase through the park. Less energetic guests can sit down to view some of the films shot on location here. Other attractions include magic shows, stunt shows, a petting farm, stagecoach rides—and, as you might imagine, souvenir shops galore. The admission price now includes a short pony ride for children. *201 S. Kinney Rd. (inside Tucson Mountain Park), tel. 602/883–6457. Admission: $11.95 adults, $7.95 children 4–11; after 5 PM $7.95 adults and children. Open daily 9–9.*

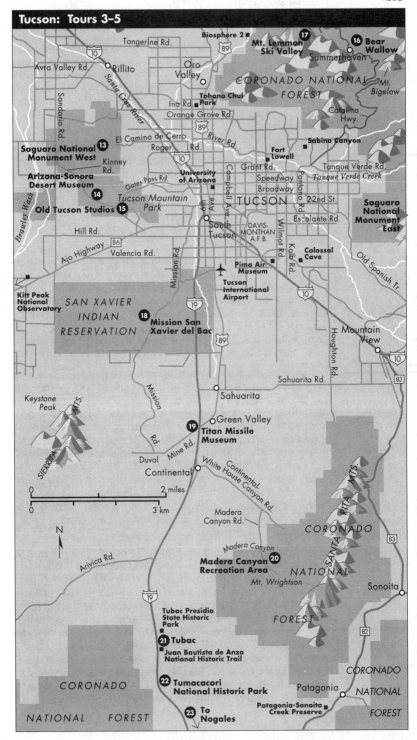

Tucson: Tours 3–5

Tour 4: Mt. Lemmon

This tour takes you to the southernmost ski slope of the continental United States, but you don't have to be a skier to visit; during the warm months, you can enjoy hiking and picnicking in this lovely area. In summer, the mountain's 9,157-foot elevation brings welcome relief from the heat, and in the winter, the craggy old mountain often sports a cap of snow that draws all levels of enthusiasts.

Mt. Lemmon is one of the Santa Catalina Mountains, which stand guard at the northern rim of the valley that is Tucson. Every 1,000 feet of elevation in these mountains is equivalent to traveling 300 miles north—thus the vegetation at the top of Mt. Lemmon is similar to that found in southern Canada. Standing in a forest of pines blanketed by snow, you might have trouble remembering that there's a desert with cacti and wildflowers less than 35 miles away.

If you're making the trip in the winter, check road conditions by calling 602/741–4991; throughout the year, it's also a good idea to call the Mt. Lemmon Construction Hot Line (tel. 602/749–3329) to check whether ongoing road repairs will interfere with your drive. On temperate days, consider packing a picnic lunch. Wear layers of clothing so you can cool or warm yourself as you change elevation. And be sure to fill up the tank before you leave town, because there are no gas stations on Mt. Lemmon Highway.

If all's clear, take Grant Road to the east side of town, where you can pick up Tanque Verde Road. Follow that until you reach Catalina Highway, which becomes Mt. Lemmon Highway as you head north. Drive this road for 30 twisting, climbing miles until you come to Mt. Lemmon Ski Valley—unless the heat inspires you to turn off a little side road to the cool, charming village of Summerhaven. It's not a good idea to take trailers and recreational vehicles on this mountain road, and it's best for all drivers to travel during daylight hours. Safety aside, it would be a pity to miss seeing the rock formations along the way; they look as though they were carefully balanced against one another by architects from another planet.

Hikers can take any number of side trips on this tour. There are some 150 miles of well-marked and well-maintained trails in the Mt. Lemmon area, for all levels of expertise. Of the several trails around Rose Canyon Lake, a good one for beginners is the **Green Mountain Trail,** which starts ½ mile past the Rose Canyon turn-off from Mt. Lemmon Highway. The route takes you 4 miles (one-way) from San Pedro Vista—with lovely mountain views to the east—to General Hitchcock Campground. More experienced hikers will enjoy the ½-mile trek, ascending more than 600 feet, to the top of **Mt. Bigelow** from the Palisades ranger station; coming down is the hard part. The Santa Catalina Ranger District (tel. 602/749–8700) can give you current information on hiking trails.

⓰ If you've brought your lunch, watch for **Bear Wallow** just after milepost 22 on Mt. Lemmon Highway. There are picnic areas and plenty of room to stretch out under a tree for a siesta. You probably won't see any bears, but the variety of birds is astounding—watch for electric-blue Steller's jays and an assortment of hummingbirds.

⓱ Mt. Lemmon Highway ends at **Mt. Lemmon Ski Valley** (tel. 602/576–1321, or 602/576–1400 for a recorded snow report). Skiing here depends on natural conditions—there's no artificial snow—so call ahead for information; some winters there's plenty of powder, and others it's rather scarce. There are 16 runs, open daily, ranging from beginner to advanced. Lift tickets cost $25 for an all-day pass and $20 for a half-day (starting at 1 PM); children 12 and under ski for $10. Ski equipment can be rented, and private instruction starts at $30 an hour. A $36 first-time skier's package includes equipment rental, a lesson, and a lift pass upon completion of the lesson. Even in off-season, visitors will enjoy a ride on the double-chair lift that whisks them to the top of the slope—some 9,100 feet. The cost is $4.50 for adults and $2 for children under 12. Many hikers ride the lift and then head out on one of several trails that crisscross the summit.

Time Out The **Iron Door** (tel. 602/576–1321) in Mt. Lemmon Ski Valley is open weekends 9:30–5:30, weekdays 10–5. In winter, the focus is on burgers, chili, corn bread, and soups; in warmer weather, lots of salads turn up on the menu. This place is popular on the weekends—parking can be tough.

Tour 5: Along I-19

There's something for everyone en route from Tucson to Nogales along I–19—history buffs, bird-watchers, hikers, Mexican-food lovers, and folks whose idea of heaven is to shop until they drop. The tour roughly follows the Camino Real (King's Road) that the conquistadors and missionaries took from Mexico up to what was once the northernmost portion of New Spain.

Drive southwest on I–19 from Tucson about 9 miles and get off on San Xavier Road; about three-quarters of a mile west, you'll
⓲ come to the shining White Dove of the Desert, or **Mission San Xavier del Bac** (tel. 602/294–2624). The oldest Catholic church in the United States still serving the community for which it was built, San Xavier was founded in 1692 by Father Eusebio Francisco Kino, who established 22 missions in northern Mexico and southern Arizona; it was constructed out of native materials by Franciscan missionaries between 1777 and 1797. Today it is owned by the Tohonó O'odham Indian tribe (the name means "Desert People Who Have Come from the Earth").

The beauty of the mission, with elements of Spanish, Baroque, and *mudejar* (Spanish Islamic) architectural styles, is highlighted by the stark desert landscape against which it is set. Inside, there's a wealth of painted statues, carvings, and frescoes;

the mission has been called the Sistine Chapel of the United States by Paul Schwartzbaum, who worked on restoring Michelangelo's masterwork in Rome and is helping to supervise the restoration, which began in 1992, of the mission's artwork. A visitor center in the front part of San Xavier del Bac offers displays of the history and architecture of the church; it's adjoined by a gift shop, open 9–5.

Across the parking lot from the mission, San Xavier Plaza has a number of shops that sell fine Native American crafts. Look especially for jewelry, pottery, and baskets featuring man-in-the-maze designs, and for friendship bowls, both particular to the Tohonó O'odham tribe. Works of the northern Arizona Hopi and Navajo are also represented.

Time Out For wonderful Indian fry bread—large, round pieces of dough brought up fresh from the hot oil and topped with all sorts of delicious possibilities—stop in **The Wa:k Snack Shop** (tel. 602/573–9191) at the back of the plaza. You can also have breakfast or a Mexican lunch here.

Mass is celebrated daily at San Xavier; on Sundays and religious holidays, there's often a mariachi band—one of the many Mexican influences in evidence here. Call ahead for information about special celebrations.

Get back on I–19 and drive south some 20 miles; at exit 69 you'll **⑲** come to the **Titan Missile Museum**, site of the only one of 54 Titan II missiles left intact when the Salt II treaty with the Soviet Union was signed. Visitors can descend into the command post where a ground crew of four lived, and look at the 114-foot, 165-ton, two-stage liquid-fuel rocket. Now empty, it originally held a nuclear payload with 214 times the explosive power of the bomb that destroyed Hiroshima. *1580 W. Duval Mine Rd., tel. 602/791–2929. $5 adults, $4 senior citizens and active military personnel, $3 juniors 10–17. Open Nov.–Apr., daily 9–5; May–Oct. Wed.–Sun., 9–5. Closed Christmas.*

Bird-watchers and hikers will want to get off I–19 at exit 63 and drive along White House Canyon Road, which turns into Madera Canyon Road; it veers south into Coronado National Forest and the Santa Rita Mountains—among them Mt. Wrightson, the highest peak in southern Arizona at 9,453 feet. With approxi- **⑳** mately 200 miles of scenic trails, the **Madera Canyon Recreation Area** (tel. 602/281–2296 in Nogales, 602/670–5464 in Tucson) is a favorite destination for hikers; the higher elevations and thick pine cover make it especially popular in summer with Tucsonans looking to escape the heat. Birders flock here year-round; about 400 avian species have been spotted in the area. As you enter the recreation area, you'll see a small visitor center, open only on weekends and operated by the volunteer Friends of Madera Canyon. Nearby, the Box Springs campground has 13 sites with toilets, potable water, and grills, available on a first-come, first-served basis (cost: $5 per vehicle per night).

㉑ Forty-five miles south of Tucson at exit 34 you'll come to **Tubac**, site of the first European settlement in Arizona in 1726. A year after the Pima Indian uprising in 1851, a military garrison was established here to protect early Spanish settlers, missionaries, and peaceful Indian converts of the nearby Tumacacori Mission (*see below*) from further attack. It was from here that Juan Bautista de Anza led the expedition of 240 colonists across the desert that resulted in the founding of San Francisco in 1776. Arizona's first newspaper, *The Weekly Arizonian*, was printed here in 1859, and in 1860 Tubac was the largest town in Arizona. Today, the quiet little town is a popular art colony; the crafts sold in the more than 70 shops here—mostly staffed by the artists who make the goods sold in them—range from carved wooden furniture and hand-thrown pottery to delicately painted tiles and silk-screened fabrics. The annual **Tubac Festival of the Arts** has been held in February for more than 30 years; for exact dates, contact the Tubac Chamber of Commerce (tel. 602/398–2704).

There's an archeological display of portions of the original 1752 fort at the **Tubac Presidio State Historic Park and Museum** in the center of town. In addition to the visitor center, which has an exhibit area detailing the history of the early colony, the park includes Tubac's 1885 schoolhouse and a pleasant picnic area. *Presidio Dr., tel. 602/398–2252. Admission: $2 adults, $1 children 12–17. Open daily 8–5. Closed Christmas Day.*

Time Out Just north of Tubac on the road paralleling I–19, the **Tubac Country Market** (410 E. Frontage Rd., tel. 602/398–9532 or 602/884–1514 in Tucson) has a patio where you can enjoy a tasty breakfast or lunch and a stunning vista; reasonably priced gourmet dinners are offered by reservation only. A large gift shop carries well-priced crafts from Arizona and Mexico; there's also a deli and a grocery.

You can take the same route that the conquistadors used to get to the next site: The first 4½ miles of the de Anza National Historic Trail from Tumacacori to Tubac were dedicated in 1992. You'll have to cross the Santa Cruz River (which is usually pretty low) three times in order to complete the hike, and the path is rather sandy, but it's a pleasant journey along the tree-shaded banks of the river.

㉒ Another option is to drive 3 miles south along the east frontage road of I–19 to reach **Tumacacori National Historic Park**. The site was visited by missionary Father Eusebio Francisco Kino in 1691, but the Jesuits didn't build a church here until 1751. Visitors can still see some ruins of this simple structure, but the main attraction is the mission of San José de Tumacacori, built by the Franciscans around 1799–1803. A combination of circumstances—Apache attacks, a bad winter, and Mexico's withdrawal of funds and priests—caused the friars to flee in 1848, and persistent rumors of wealth left behind by both the Franciscans and the Jesuits led treasure-seekers to unsuccessfully pillage the site. It was finally protected in 1908, when it became a national monument.

You can pick up a pamphlet with a self-guided tour of the grounds and of the de Anza trail from the visitor center; guided tours are also offered daily. A small museum displays some of the mission's original artifacts, and the patio garden boasts a variety of native plants. In 1990, when Tumacacori became a national historic park, two mission ruins were added, both about 15 miles to the southwest; they are currently being excavated, however, and are not open to the public. In addition to a Christmas Eve service, costumed historical high masses are held at Tumacacori in spring and fall. An annual fiesta held here in the first week of December features arts and crafts and food booths. *Exit 29 off I–19, tel. 602/398–2341. Admission: $2 adults 17 and older, under 17 and Golden Age, Golden Eagle, and Golden Access cardholders free. Open daily 8–5. Closed Thanksgiving and Christmas.*

Those who want a glimpse of present-day Hispanic culture can ㉓ continue on to **Nogales,** a bustling border town. It can get fairly rowdy on weekends, when underage Tucsonans head south to drink, but it offers some good restaurants and fine-quality crafts and furnishings in addition to the usual border schlock. If you're just coming for the day, it's best to park on the Arizona side of the border (you'll see many guarded lots that cost about $4 for the day) and walk across. Practically all the good shopping is within easy strolling distance of the border.

The shopping area centers mainly around Avenida Obregón, which begins a few blocks west of the border entrance and runs north–south; just follow the crowds. You'll find a wide selection of handicrafts, furnishings, and jewelry here; except at shops that indicate otherwise, bargaining is not only acceptable but expected. **El Zarape Curios** (Av. Obregón 161) specializes in sterling-silver jewelry and designer clothing. For upscale imports, particularly French perfumes, try **Mickey's** (Av. Obregón 128), **Via Veneto** (Aves. Obregón and Aguirre), and **Versailles** (Av. Obregón 111). **Continental Curios** (Av. Obregón 98) is a large department store with a wide selection of rebozos (shawls), appliquéd and embroidered clothing, hand-blown glassware, and leather huaraches. **El Changarro** (Calle Elías 93) specializes in high-quality furniture, antiques, pottery, and handwoven rugs. Most of the good restaurants near the border are also on Obregón. Take this street as far south as you like; you'll know you have entered workaday Mexico when the shops are no longer fronted by smiling, English-speaking men trying to hustle you in the door ("Take a look! Good prices!").

Time Out Large, friendly **Elvira** (Av. Obregón 1, tel. 631/2–47–73) has long been a favorite for day-trippers to Mexico. It's been cleaned up and expanded in recent years, but a free shot of tequila still comes with each meal. Try any of the excellent fish dishes, the chicken mole, or the chile rellenos.

What to See and Do with Children

There are plenty of things to occupy children in Tucson and southern Arizona. Besides the activities listed here, a number are cited in Participant Sports, *below*. (Remember, however, that when you take children outdoors, their skin is especially prone to sunburn and windburn. Protect them with hats and sunscreen, and offer liquids frequently to prevent dehydration.) Many resorts also have activities designed to entertain children while their parents sightsee. Inquire when you make reservations.

Arizona–Sonora Desert Museum (*see* Tour 3, *above*).

Biosphere 2. This is a trip for school-age children; little ones will enjoy being outdoors but won't really appreciate the tour. (*See* Off the Beaten Track, *below*.)

The dry limestone **Colossal Cave,** 20 miles east of Tucson and 6 miles north of I–10, is filled with stalagmites and stalactites. The cave has never been fully explored, and legend has it that gold is hidden in the dark recesses. *Old Spanish Trail Rd., tel. 602/647–7275. Admission: $6.50 adults, $5 children 11–16, $3.50 children 6–10. Open Oct.–mid-Mar., Mon.–Sat. 9–5, Sun. and holidays 9–6; mid-Mar.–Sept., Mon.–Sat. 8–6, Sun. and holidays 8–7.*

Children love the old-fashioned melodramas at the **Gaslight Theatre** (7010 E. Broadway, tel. 602/886–9428), where hissing the villain and cheering the hero are part of the audience's duty. Tickets are $12 for adults, $10 for students and senior citizens, and $6 for children under 13. There is free popcorn, and beer, wine, and soft drinks are available.

At **Golf 'n' Stuff Family Fun Centers,** children can play video games and miniature golf, ride bumper boats, and drive little race cars. *6503 E. Tanque Verde Rd., tel. 602/296–2366. No admission fee; each attraction priced separately. Open Sun.–Thurs. 10 AM–10 PM, Fri.–Sat. 10 AM–1 AM.*

International Wildlife Museum allows youngsters to touch and feel different animal skins, and teaches them many other things about more than 200 species of birds and mammals from all over the world via interactive computers. There's a theater that shows wildlife films, a gift shop, and a small restaurant that serves buffalo burgers. *4800 W. Gates Pass Rd., tel. 602/624–4024. Admission: $5 adults, $3.75 senior citizens, students, and military personnel, $1.50 children 6–12. Open daily 9–5. Closed major holidays.*

Kids interested in aerospace technology will enjoy the walk through U.S. aviation history at the **Pima Air Museum.** The huge collection of historic aircraft includes a full-scale replica of the Wright brothers' 1903 Wright Flyer and a mock-up of the X-15, the world's fastest aircraft. *6000 E. Valencia Rd., tel. 602/574–9658. Admission: $5 adults, $4 military personnel and* *senior citizens over 62, $3 children 10–17. Open daily 9–5 (no one admitted after 4). Closed Christmas.*

The small but well-designed **Reid Park Zoo** won't tax the children's—or your—patience. If you're visiting in the summertime, go early in the day when the animals are active. *Lake Shore Lane, off 2nd St. between Alvernon Way and Country Club Rd., tel. 602/881–4753. Admission: $3 adults, $2 senior citizens over 62, 75¢ children 5–14. Open daily 9–4. Closed Christmas.*

At **Tucson Children's Museum,** kids are encouraged to touch and explore the exhibits, which are oriented toward science, language, and history. *200 S. 6th Ave., tel. 602/884–7511. Admission: $3 adults, $1.50 senior citizens and children 3–14. Open Sat. 10–5, Sun. 1–5; call for weekday hours.*

Off the Beaten Track

It sounds a bit like the stuff of science fiction: In order to study how human beings can live in harmony with their environment, eight persons set up housekeeping for two years in an enclosed 3-acre environment. But this exercise in recycling on a grand scale is part of an ongoing experiment taking place about 45 minutes from downtown Tucson at **Biosphere 2,** the first and most dramatic of a series of enclosures scheduled to take place over the next 100 years. The privately funded project is being watched with interest—as well as some skepticism—by scientists all over the world.

The miniature world created within Biosphere includes tropical rain forest, savanna, desert, thorn scrub, marsh, ocean, and agricultural areas as well as a living area for the humans who inhabit the sphere—along with 3,800 plant and animal species. Guided walking tours, which last about an hour, don't enter the sealed sphere, but a film explains the project, and visitors are able to look at the human and animal residents through observation areas. The Biosphere Café, overlooking the Santa Catalina Mountains, offers meals and snacks. Reasonably priced hotel rooms with excellent views are available on Biosphere's premises. No cameras or camcorders are allowed inside, and pets and picnicking are not permitted on the site. *Hwy. 77, mile marker 96.5, tel. 602/825–6200. Admission: $12.95 adults, $10.95 senior citizens, $6 children 5–17. Open daily 9–5; guided tours given every hour on the hour 11–3. Closed Christmas.*

On the way back into town from Biosphere, you might want to stop off at **Tohono Chul Park,** which is making its own effort to preserve our environment—specifically the desert region. On its 35 acres, a demonstration garden, greenhouse, geology wall, and other exhibits educate visitors about the unique area, while shady nooks and nature trails allow for leisurely sitting or strolling. Two gift shops, a small art gallery, a tearoom (*see* Dining, *below*), and the Haunted Bookshop (*see* Shopping, *below*) are additional reasons to visit this lovely landscaped setting. *7366 Paseo del Norte, tel. 602/742–6455. Admission: $2 donation*

suggested. Park open daily 7 AM–sunset; building open Mon.–
Sat. 9:30–5, Sun. 11–5.

All year round, but especially during summer, locals flock to **Sabino Canyon** in the northeast corner of town. Part of the Coronado National Forest but filled with saguaros and other desert flora and fauna, this is a good spot for hiking, picnicking, or enjoying the waterfalls, streams, natural swimming holes, and shade trees that provide a respite from the heat. No cars are allowed; a narrated tram ride (45 minutes round-trip) takes you to the top of the canyon; you can get off and on at any of the nine stops. There's also a tram ride to adjacent Bear Canyon. When there's a full moon, nighttime tram tours are offered. *Sabino Canyon Rd. in the Santa Catalina foothills, tel. 602/749–2861 (recorded tram information) or 602/749–8700 (visitor center). Tram fare: $5 adults, $2 children 3–12.; Bear Canyon tram fare: $3 adults, $1.25 children. Call for schedules, which change throughout the year. Visitor center open weekdays 8–4:30, weekends 8:30–4:30.*

Funded by the National Science Foundation and managed by a group of more than 20 universities, **Kitt Peak National Observatory** is part of the Tohonó O'odham reservation. After much discussion back in the late 1950s, tribal leaders agreed to share their 4,400 square miles with the observatory's 19 telescopes. Among these is the McMath, the world's largest solar telescope, which is cooled by piped-in coolant. From a visitors' gallery, you can see into the telescope's light-path tunnel, which goes down hundreds of feet into the mountain. In addition to the vital research into aspects of the sun carried out here, Kitt Peak scientists have also observed distant galaxies. The scientists and staff are friendly and knowledgeable and keen to share their enthusiasm for astronomy.

The museum's visitor center has exhibits on astronomy and information about the telescopes at the facility; tapes, mostly about the cosmos, run continuously in a minitheater. Free guided tours, which take about an hour, depart from the center weekdays at 11, 1, and 2:30; on weekends, an additional tour is given at 9:30 AM if enough people show up. Complimentary brochures enable you to take self-guided tours. A gift shop sells excellent examples of Tohonó O'odham handiwork as well as astronomy-related items. To reach Kitt Peak from Tucson, take I–10 to I–19 south, exit at Ajo Hwy/AZ 86. Take AZ 86 44 miles to the AZ 386 junction; turn left and follow the winding mountain road up to the observatory. (In inclement weather, it's a good idea to contact the highway department to confirm that the road is open.) There's a picnic area about 1½ miles below the observatory; aside from vending machines in the observatory buildings, there's no place to get food or gas within 20 miles of Kitt Peak. *Kitt Peak National Observatory, tel. 602/322–3426 or 602/322–3350 for recorded message. Suggested donation: $2. Open daily 9–4. Closed major holidays.*

Art galleries and boutiques coexist with real Western saloons in **Patagonia,** a tiny, tree-lined town some 82 miles southeast of

Tucson, surrounded by rolling hills and choice cattle-grazing land. For the most scenic route here, take I–10 to AZ 83 south, and then pick up AZ 83 in Sonoita. The cheerful Ovens of Patagonia (corner 3rd Ave. and Naugle St., tel. 602/394–2483) is a pleasant place to stop for a light lunch or snack, and the Mesquite Grove Gallery (371 McKeown Ave., tel. 602/394–2358) carries an appealing variety of local crafts; both are in the center of town. At the Patagonia–Sonoita Creek Preserve (tel. 602/394–2400), 750 acres of riparian habitat are protected along the Patagonia–Sonoita Creek. More than 260 bird species have been sighted here, along with deer, javelina, coatimundi, desert tortoise, snakes, and more. To get here, make a right on 4th Avenue, which comes to a dead end, and then make a left; this paved road soon becomes dirt and leads to the preserve in about ¾ of a mile. Patagonia is also a good jumping-off point for a tour of southern Arizona's wineries (*see below*).

Wineries   Wyatt Earp might have been hooted out of town if he had swaggered up to a bar and ordered a glass of cabernet, but wine is in these days in cowboy country. Connoisseurs debate the merits of the various wineries that have sprung up in this area since 1974, but if you want to decide for yourself, you might start a tour with **R.W. Webb** (13605 E. Benson Hwy., tel. 602/762–5777); take I–10 east about 12 miles, and get off at Vail, exit 279. Most of the other growers are in the area where Routes 82 and 83 intersect: Get back on I–10 for two more exits, then drive south on Route 83 for 24 miles to Sonoita. Growers in the scenic ranching region nearby include the kosher **Santa Cruz Winery** (lower Elgin Rd., Elgin, tel. 602/455–5373); **Sonoita Vineyards** (3 mi southeast of Elgin, tel. 602/455–5893), and **Arizona Vineyards** (1830 Patagonia Hwy., 3 mi north of Nogales on Rte. 82, tel. 602/287–7972). Most of them give tours and tastings Thursday through Sunday; call for hours. Tiny Elgin hosts two surprisingly sophisticated but reasonably priced restaurants. **Karen's Wine Country Cafe** (tel. 602/455–5282) could be straight out of Sonoma, California, with its Country French–style patio and innovative menu focusing on salads and pasta dishes—and of course a good selection of wines by the glass. **Er Pastaro** (tel. 602/455–5821), a homey, low-key place established by a former manager of Regine's in New York, offers a variety of sauces for its pastas, as well as a nice selection of Italian wines. Hours at both restaurants are limited; call ahead.

Casinos   After a long struggle with the state of Arizona, two Indian tribes now operate casinos on their Tucson-area reservations. The Pascua Yaqui tribe runs the **Casino of the Sun** (7406 S. Camino de Oeste, tel. 602/883–1700 or 800/344–9435), which has lots of slot and video-gambling machines, as well as a bingo game; keno will probably be added by the time you read this. The Tohonó O'odham tribe's **Desert Diamond Bingo and Casino** (7350 S. Old Nogales Hwy., tel. 602/295–9790) offers 500 one-armed bandits and live keno in addition to bingo. No alcohol is sold or permitted at either casino.

Tucson for Free

De Grazia's Gallery in the Sun is the museum, gallery, work-shop, former home, and grave site of the Arizonan artist Ted De Grazia, who depicted southwest Indian and Mexican life. Built by the artist himself with the help of Native American friends, the sprawling, spacious single-story museum utilizes only natu-ral material from the surrounding desert. None of De Grazia's original oil paintings, sculptures, or watercolors are for sale, but the museum's gift shop offers a wide selection of cards, prints, lithographs, ceramics, and books by and about the color-ful artist. *6300 N. Swan Rd., tel. 602/299–9191. Admission free. Open daily 10–4.*

Fort Lowell Park and Museum, now a city park, was once the site of a Hohokam Indian village and, many centuries later, a fort. At a small museum run by the Arizona Historical Society, the reconstructed commanding officers' quarters gives visitors a glimpse of military life in territorial days. There are also rotat-ing exhibits of photographs and frontier artifacts. *2900 N. Craycroft Rd., tel. 602/885–3832. Admission free. Open Wed.–Sat. 10–4.*

Shopping

There are a lot of special gifts and souvenirs to be found in the Tucson area. Native American crafts range from exquisite jew-elry and basketry to the more pedestrian (but still authentic) tourist items. You'll see an abundance of both varieties in shops and even in some department stores; **San Xavier Plaza**, across from San Xavier mission, carries the work of a variety of native peoples, including the Tohonó upon whose reservation the church is located. Those looking for work by other regional art-ists might drive down to **Tubac,** a community 45 miles south of Tucson. Hard-core bargain hunters usually continue south to the Mexican border and **Nogales.** *See* Tour 5 in Exploring, *above,* for details on all three areas.

In Tucson itself, much of the retail activity is focused around malls, but you'll find shops with more character in two areas. The **downtown** district hosts a number of art galleries, antiques shops, and crafts stores; Congress Street is a particularly good block to browse, and the Old Town Artisans complex (186 N. Meyer Ave., tel. 602/623–6024), near the Tucson Museum of Art, has a large selection of Southwestern wares. The adjoining **4th Avenue** neighborhood, near the University of Arizona, is also fertile ground for unusual items. The Fourth Avenue Merchants Association (347 E. 4th St. at 4th Ave., tel. 602/624–5004) repre-sents the many artsy boutiques and restaurants that line 4th Avenue between 2nd and 9th streets.

Malls **Tucson Mall** (4500 N. Oracle Rd. at Wetmore Rd., tel. 602/293–7330) is probably the most heavily shopped mall in town, serving both the sophisticated and the family shopper with two floors of stores, including Dillard's, Broadway Southwest, Sears, JC

Penney, and almost 200 specialty shops. For tasteful Southwestern T-shirts, belts, jewelry, and posters, try Señor Coyote, on the second floor of the mall.

El Con Mall (3601 E. Broadway at Alvernon Way, tel. 602/327–8767) is Tucson's oldest mall and has more than 130 stores, including J C Penney, Foley's, and Montgomery Ward. Possibly its most popular store is a huge House of Fabrics, headquarters for craftspeople and needleworkers of all persuasions.

Park Mall (5870 E. Broadway at Wilmot Rd., tel. 602/748–1222) is a family shopping mecca, one of those utilitarian places where you can get all that practical stuff checked off your list in one trip. It has more than 120 stores, including Sears, Dillard's, and Broadway Southwest.

Foothills Mall (7401 N. La Cholla Blvd. at Ina Rd., tel. 602/742–7191), the most upscale of the malls, isn't usually very crowded. In addition to such department stores as Dillard's and Foley's, it features a variety of tony boutiques. If you're experiencing shopper's fatigue, a cup of the good coffee at the Java House might perk you up.

Specialty Shops Check the **Cabat Studio** (627 N. 4th Ave., tel. 602/622–6362) for exceptional Southwestern paintings and ceramics by Erni and Rose Cabat. **Impressions II, Ltd.** (2990 N. Swan Rd., Suite 147, tel. 602/323–3320) features work by R. C. Gorman and many other internationally known artists, as well as art by several talented but well-kept local secrets. The more cutting-edge downtown galleries include **Etherton/Stern** (135 S. 6th Ave., tel. 602/624–7370) and Dinnerware (135 E. Congress St., tel. 602/792–4503). **Art Life** (Box 36777, Tucson 85740, tel. 602/797–1271), published twice a year, lists local galleries and artists.

Art Galleries

Books **Tohono Chul Park** (*see* Off the Beaten Track, *above*) is home to the **Haunted Bookshop** (tel. 602/297–4843), with its outstanding selection for bibliophiles of all ages. There's a coffeepot on the porch in the wintertime, plenty of nooks for a quiet read, and a tunnel for children to crawl through.

In the downtown area, **Book Arts Gallery** (49 N. Scott St., tel. 602/884–5501) features beautiful handmade books as well as rare editions of more conventionally published work. Near the University of Arizona, the **Audubon Nature Shop** (300 E. University Blvd., tel. 602/629–0510) carries hiking maps, field guides, and binoculars, along with a wide range of natural history books. Also in the neighborhood is **Books West Southwest** (2452 N. Campbell Ave., tel. 602/326–6661), focusing on regional works, and **Settlers West Books & Prints** (6420 N. Campbell Ave., tel. 602/577–8749), which has a large collection of Western and wildlife prints, some of them limited editions. Pick up your topographical maps and specialty guides to Arizona at **Tucson's Map and Flag Center** (3239 1st Ave., tel. 602/887–4234).

Cacti You won't need to stick a cactus in your suitcase, if you want to take back a spiny souvenir (it's illegal anyway): **B&B Cactus Farm** (11550 E. Speedway Blvd., tel. 602/721–4687), on the far eastern side of town, has a huge selection of desert plants and will ship all over the country.

Gifts **Desert House Crafts** (2837 N. Campbell Ave., tel. 602/323–2132) has been part of the Tucson art scene for more than 40 years. Designs are inspired, and execution is flawless. **Sangin** (300 N. 6th Ave., tel. 602/882–9334) is set in a historic warehouse filled with baskets, home furnishings, dried flower arrangements, and jewelry—some imported, some made by local artists. The one-way street system downtown makes the store a bit hard to find, but the chili-pepper baskets and twined-branch cacti are worth searching for.

Native **Bahti Indian Arts** (St. Philip's Plaza, 4300 N. Campbell Ave.,
American tel. 602/577–0290) specializes in Native American art, including
Arts and high-quality jewelry, pottery, baskets, and more. **Huntington**
Crafts **Trading Co.** (111 E. Congress, tel. 602/628–8578) carries masks and pottery made by the Yaqui and Tarahumara Indians. The **Kaibab Shops** (2841 N. Campbell Ave., tel. 602/795–6905) have been selling a wide variety of Native American crafts in Tucson for more than 40 years.

Western Wear **Corral Western Wear** (4525 E. Broadway Blvd., tel. 602/322–6001), with a large array of shirts, hats, belts, jewelry, and boots, caters to both urban and authentic cowboys and cowgirls. **Stewart Boot Manufacturing** (30 W. 28th St., South Tucson., tel. 602/622–2706) has been making handmade leather boots for more than 50 years; factory imperfects are available.

Sports and the Outdoors

Participant Sports

Ballooning What better way to take advantage of Arizona's mild winter months than to take a quiet hot-air-balloon ride in the early morning hours and get a bird's-eye view of the frisky desert wildlife down below? Two reputable companies in the region are **Balloon America** (Box 31255, Tucson 85751, tel. 602/299–7744; Oct.–June only) and **Southern Arizona Balloon Excursions** (Box 5265, Tucson 85703, tel. 602/624–3599). Both welcome individuals and groups and offer champagne celebrations and daily flights by pilots who are licensed by the Federal Aviation Administration (FAA). Prices range from $115 to $250 per person, depending on the season and the length of the flight.

Bicycling Tucson has designated bikeways, routes, lanes, and paths for bikers all over the city. You can cycle through rugged terrain, up and down winding roads, or even along frequently used byways in the Tucson area. If you want even more isolated and scenic locations, try some of the mapped biking tours for the southern part of Arizona; contact the **Metropolitan Tucson Convention and Visitors Bureau** (130 S. Scott Ave., tel. 602/624–1817 or 800/638–8350) for additional information.

Reliable and centrally located places for bike rentals include **The Bike Shack** (940 E. University Ave., tel. 602/624–3663) and **Full Cycle** (3232 E. Speedway Blvd., tel. 602/327–3232). **Sunrise Bicycle** (4772 E. Sunrise Dr., tel. 602/577–2292) will deliver and pick up bikes without charge, and includes a helmet in the price of the rental.

There are a number of cyclists' clubs in Tucson, and many of them offer tours throughout southern Arizona. Write ahead to **La Touristas** (3450 N. Stone Ave., No. 171, Tucson 85705) and **Tucson Wheelmen** (1016 Chauncey St., Tucson 85719)—neither has an official telephone number—for information about upcoming tours. Or call the **Greater Arizona Bicycling Association's** (Box 43273, Tucson 85733, tel. 602/885–8807) week-by-week recorded news line of rides in the Tucson area; they're for all ages and levels, and visiting cyclists are welcome to participate.

Bird-Watching In the Huachuca Mountains, the 300-acre **Ramsey Canyon Preserve** (90 mi southeast of Tucson, off AZ 92, tel. 602/378–2785) is home to more than 170 species of birds, as well as dozens of species of butterflies, deer, snakes, frogs, and mountain lions. Even closer to Tucson, in the nearby Santa Rita Mountains, **Madera Canyon** (*see* Tour 5 in Exploring, *above*) is another bird-lovers' haven. **The Wild Bird Store** (3522 E. Grant Rd., tel. 602/322–9466) offers free naturalist-guided bird walks nearly every Sunday year-round.

Camping There are at least 100 camping areas scattered throughout the southern region of Arizona; though it can get very chilly at night in the desert, the weather's usually good enough year-round to make sleeping out under the vast, starry night sky an appealing option. Summertime is the time to camp in the state's cooler higher-altitude campgrounds.

The closest public campground to Tucson is probably at **Catalina State Park,** about 9 miles north of town on U.S. 89 (11570 N. Oracle Rd., tel. 602/628–5798). Located in the desert foothills of the Santa Catalinas, the campground accommodates tents as well as RVs. It fills up quickly in good weather because it's close to town; unfortunately, there is no reservation system.

Recreational vehicles can park in any number of facilities around town; the **Metropolitan Tucson Convention and Visitors Bureau** (130 S. Scott Ave., tel. 602/624–1889 or 800/638–8350) can provide information about specific locations.

Golf You can easily dedicate a vacation to golf in Tucson, which has some of the best desert courses in the country and more than 320 days of sunshine in which to play them. *The Tucson & Southern Arizona Golf Guide*, published by Tucson Guide Quarterly, Inc. (Box 42915, Tucson 85733, tel. 602/322–0895), describes and rates all the local courses; send $1 for a copy. For a golf package based on your budget, interests, and experience, you might contact **Tee Time Arrangers** (6286 E. Grant Rd., tel. 602/298–4800 or 800/742–9939). If you're planning to stay a week or more, **Tucson's Resort Golf Card** (6286 E. Grant Rd., Tucson 85712, tel. 602/886–8800), offering year-round discounts at seven of the area's best courses, is a good deal; write or call for information.

Resorts Many avid golfers check into one of the tony local resorts (described in more detail in Lodging, *below*) and do nothing but tee off for a week. Golf vacation specialists include **Tucson National Golf & Conference Resort** (2727 W. Club Dr., tel. 602/297–2271), home of the Northern Telecom Open, with 27 holes; **Westin La Paloma,** which has a 27-hole layout designed by Jack Nicklaus (rated among the top 75 resort courses by *Golf Digest*); **Sheraton El Conquistador,** its 45 holes in the Santa Catalina foothills affording 360° views of the city; and the 36-hole Tom Fazio–designed **Loews Ventana Canyon** course. Those who don't mind getting up early to beat the heat will find some excellent golf packages at these places in the summer. In high season (Jan. 15– Apr. 15) only guests can play the courses, but the rest of the year all but Westin's La Paloma course are open to the public.

Municipal The flagship of the five low-priced municipal golf courses within
Courses the city of Tucson (Randolph North, Randolph South, El Rio, Fred Enke, and Silverbell) is **Randolph North,** which hosted the PGA and LPGA Tour for many years. For details about these city-operated courses, contact the Tucson Parks and Recreation Department (tel. 602/791–4336); call a week in advance for weekday reservations at any of the courses.

Public In Tucson the Arnold Palmer–managed **Starr Pass Golf Club**
Courses (3645 W. 22nd St., tel. 602/622–6060) was developed as a Tournament Player's Course; a co-host of the Northern Telecom Open with Tucson National (*see* Resorts, *above*), it offers 18 highly rated holes. Two executive courses, **Cliff Valley** (5910 N. Oracle Rd., tel. 602/887–6161) and **Dorado Country Club** (6601 E. Speedway, tel. 602/885–6751), are good for those who just want to play a few short rounds.

South of Tucson, near Nogales, **Rio Rico Resort and Country Club** (1550 Camino a la Posada, tel. 602/281–8567) was designed by Robert Trent Jones, Jr.; an excellent 18-hole course, it's one of Arizona's biggest sleepers. In Green Valley **San Ignacio Golf Club** (4201 S. Camino del Sol, tel. 602/648–3468), designed by Arthur Hills, is a challenging desert course in a beautiful setting; nearby **Canoa Hills** (1401 W. Calle Urbano, tel. 602/791– 2049) is a good choice for the average golfer.

Hiking Tucson is a wonderful place for hiking; there are many desert trails to explore in the winter, and in summer the nearby mountain ranges offer cooler trekking options. The Exploring section (*see* Tours 3, 4, and 5, and Off the Beaten Track, *above*) offers some options for day trips that include good hiking opportunities: **Tucson Mountain Park, Mt. Lemmon, Madera Canyon, and Kitt Peak. Sabino Canyon** (*see* Off the Beaten Track, *above*) has a variety of trails closer to town. In addition, for hiking inside Tucson city limits, you might test your skills climbing trails up Sentinel Peak, generally called **"A" Mountain** (it sports a huge *A* first painted on it by fans of a victorious university football team in 1915). State and city parks in the area also offer a variety of hiking experiences; there are literally hundreds of trails in the immediate Tucson area. **Catalina State Park** (11570 N. Oracle Rd. [U.S. 89], tel. 602/628–5798), less than 10 miles north of town, is crisscrossed by hiking trails.

If you want to go a bit farther afield, head south past the Huachuca Mountain range, where you can wander in and out of old **ghost towns** such as Fort Duquesne, Pearce, and Washington Camp in the Patagonia Mountains. To the east of Tucson, beyond the Rincons and the Whetstone Mountains, the Dragoon Mountains are both beautiful and of historical interest; located here is **Cochise's Stronghold,** where the Apache chief hid out with his people during 11 years of battle with U. S. troops. Farther east, **Chiricahua National Monument** (*see* Southeastern Arizona, *below*) offers a number of well-marked trails in a striking setting.

The local chapter of the **Sierra Club** (738 N. 5th Ave., Suite 214, Tucson 85705, tel. 602/620–6401) welcomes out-of-town visitors on their weekend hikes around the area; there's a $2 suggested donation per person for nonmembers. For hiking on your own, a good source of information is **Summit Hut** (5045 E. Speedway Blvd., tel. 602/325–1554), which has an excellent collection of hiking reference materials and a friendly staff who will help you plan and outfit your trip; packs, tents, bags, shoes, and skis can be rented here.

Horseback Riding What's a trip to the Southwest without at least one ride on the back of a horse? **Desert-High Country Stables** (6501 W. Ina Rd., tel. 602/744–3789) offers trail rides, hayrides, and cookouts. **Pantano Stables** (4450 S. Houghton Rd., tel. 602/298–9076) holds special holiday and birthday rides—and even Western weddings—in addition to regular trail rides. **Pusch Ridge Stables** (13700 N. Oracle Rd., tel. 602/297–6908) is adjacent to Catalina State Park, and its riders may even see bighorn sheep in the Santa Catalina foothills.

Rockhounding If rockhounding interests you, write to the Arizona Office of Tourism (1100 W. Washington St., Phoenix 85007, tel. 602/542–8687) and ask for brochure RG/150M/8-89, which provides information about the best places in the area to visit. Amateur traders and buyers might consider joining the thousands of professionals who come to town in February for the huge **Tucson Gem and Mineral Show** (Box 42543, Tucson 85733, tel. 602/322–5773), the largest of its kind in the world. Many precious stones as well as affordable samples are displayed and sold here, and even if you don't buy a thing, it's fun to look at all the fascinating rocks and gems. If you do plan to attend, make reservations far in advance; in 1995 every hotel and car-rental agency in town is likely to be booked up from February 9 through February 12.

Tennis A number of the hotels and resorts in town have tennis facilities; many courts are at Loews Ventana Canyon, Sheraton El Conquistador, Westin La Paloma, Westward Look, and Canyon Ranch resorts (*see* Lodging, *below*). The **Randolph Tennis Center** (100 S. Randolph Way, tel. 602/791–4896) offers 24 courts, 11 lighted, at very reasonable rates. You might also check with the

Tucson Parks and Recreation Department (tel. 602/791–4873) to see if there are courts at one of the city parks near where you're staying.

Spectator Sports

Cactus League Baseball In 1993 Tucson's **Hi-Corbett Field** (900 S. Randolph Way) welcomed the Colorado Rockies to their inaugural season of Cactus League practice games (*see* Chapter 1, Essential Information); call 602/327–9467 for information about the team schedule and about tickets. Hi-Corbett Field is also home to the Tucson Toros (tel. 602/325–2621), a minor-league team. Picnickers and squirrels sit side by side in adjacent Randolph Park to enjoy the games of both teams. Inside the stadium, during the training games, beer is sold behind first and third bases. Parking isn't easy to come by in the area, so park in any of the Randolph Park lots west of Hi-Corbett Field and take a short, plcasant walk through the park to get to the stadium.

Greyhound Racing You can watch racing dogs compete at **Tucson Greyhound Park** (2601 S. 3rd Ave., corner of S. 4th Ave. and 36th St., tel. 602/884–7576), but pari-mutuel wagering is the real attraction. There are two betting areas, the concession and bar area on the main floor and the clubhouse restaurant and bar upstairs. The track is open Wednesday through Sunday; call ahead for the schedule. Admission to the clubhouse is $3, $1.25 for the concession area. Only persons 18 or older can bet.

Dining

Tucson's culinary reputation is growing, and there are restaurants in town to satisfy every appetite. Southwestern cuisine, naturally featured here, ranges from barbecue and cowboy steaks to light nouvelle recipes that use such innovative ingredients as cactus and blue corn.

Tucson's residents have long boasted about their city's Mexican food, some rather grandly proclaiming their town "Mexican Food Capital of the U.S." (a title regularly challenged by San Antonians and Phoenicians). Most of the Mexican food in Tucson is Sonoran style—that is, derived from the cooking native to the adjoining Mexican state of Sonora. It's the type that's familiar to most Americans, featuring cheese, mild peppers, corn tortillas, and beef or chicken. Although Sonoran Mexican food has a well-earned reputation for being high in calories and saturated fats, many restaurants in Tucson now feature authentically prepared *pescado* (fish) or *pollo* (chicken) dishes that are flavorful yet lower in cholesterol. (Note that the salsa served with baskets of tortilla chips may be spicier than what you are used to. Proceed with caution. Similarly, when you ask the staff whether a dish is "hot," remember that their definition may be quite different from yours.)

Dress is more casual in Tucson than in many cities its size. Very few restaurants request that men wear jackets to dinner. The issue of whether to wear a tie takes on a new slant here—there's at least one cowboy steak house where anyone caught wearing such formal neckwear will have it snipped off and added to the restaurant's collection of city-slicker garb.

Late fall, winter, and early spring make up the high season for travel here; it's a good idea to call ahead for reservations during these busy months. Some restaurants close for a portion of the summer, taking advantage of the slow time to make repairs or give staff vacations. Again, it's wise to call ahead, this time to ensure that your intended destination is open and hasn't altered its hours. Don't assume, incidentally, that you'll have to dine indoors in summer—many Tucson restaurants cool their outdoor patios with a misting system.

While Tucson's variety of restaurants is akin to that of its big-city cousins, the city doesn't offer much in the way of late-night dining; most restaurants in town are shuttered by 10 PM. Some spots that keep later hours are noted below. In addition, **Coffee, Etc.** (2830 N. Campbell Ave., tel. 602/881–8070), which has great coffee and a varied menu, is open 24 hours.

Category	Cost*
$$$$	over $35
$$$	$25–$35
$$	$15–$25
$	under $15

per person, excluding drinks, service, and 7% sales tax (5% state plus 2% city)

Highly recommended restaurants are indicated by a star ★.

American
$$$

Rancher's Club. The four wood grills on which most of the foods are prepared are the key to the success of this upscale Western-style restaurant—pink tablecloths contrast nicely with dark wood, mounted animal heads, and sidesaddles. As the friendly staff explains, different woods impart different flavors to foods, so diners must be ready to make a choice from two grills: mesquite wood is offered every day, and hickory, sassafras, and wild cherry alternate during the week. The lobster is especially good, and the steaks are excellent, too (a note on the menu advises "Our steaks are copious and we encourage you to share"). An array of sauces, butters, and condiments provides diners with interesting ways to flavor their food. *5151 E. Grant Rd., tel. 602/321–7621. Reservations advised. Dress: casual but neat. AE, DC, MC, V. Closed Sun., Sat. lunch.*

$$–$$$
★

The Kingfisher Grill. Opened in late 1993, the Kingfisher has drawn critical kudos and a loyal following for its fine regional American cuisine. The chic setting—low lighting, bright turquoise and neon contrasting with warm brick walls and comfy black banquettes—is matched by the innovative menu. Try the bacquetta ravioli, filled with a delicate mixture of chopped sea bass, spinach, and garlic; or the grilled ahi tuna with a honey-sesame glaze, done to a perfect turn. From 10 to midnight, a "lite" menu features soups, salads, burgers, and selections from the oyster bar. *2564 E. Grant Rd., tel. 602/323–7739. Reservations advised for dinner. Dress: casual but neat. AE, D, MC, V. Closed Sun. lunch.*

Cafés **Milagro.** Opened in early 1994, this combination bookstore and
$$$$ coffeehouse attracts the town's literati, who come to read out-of-town newspapers (even the British tabloids are sold here) over terrific cappuccino and espresso. A small menu that changes daily emphasizes light Italian specialties such as pesto pasta salad or a grilled eggplant sandwich with *aioli* (garlic mayonnaise). *3073 N. Campbell Ave., tel. 602/795–1700. No reservations. Dress: casual. V, MC. Closed Sun. dinner.*

$ **Bailey & Bailey.** With its high ceilings, local artwork, black-and-white tiles, and charcuterie-style counter, B&B (as it's known locally) is hip but homey at the same time. This downtown arts-district café, next door to the Etherton/Stern gallery, has a good selection of fancy open-faced sandwiches, platters, salads, and pâtés to go along with its array of designer water and coffee. *135 S. 6th Ave., tel. 602/792–2623. No reservations. Dress: casual. AE, MC, V. Closed Sun.*

Cajun **Jerome's.** It may seem strange to think of New Orleans special-
$$ ties in the desert, but at Jerome's the menu goes beyond the usual jambalaya and étouffée. This casual, comfortable eatery serves some of the best fresh fish in town. There's a raw bar complete with chilled Gulf oysters, cherrystone clams, Gulf-shrimp cocktail, and calamari ceviche. Buttermilk biscuits and bread pudding with bourbon sauce supply any calories saved by eating the excellent mesquite-grilled mahimahi. Sunday's champagne brunch is a well-priced indulgence. *6958 E. Tanque Verde Rd., tel. 602/721–0311. Reservations advised. Dress: casual. AE, D, DC, MC, V. Dinner only (except Sun. brunch).*

Continental **Ventana Room.** This lovely dining room in the Loews Ventana
$$$$ Canyon Resort is a triumph of understated elegance. Muted col-
★ ors and low ceilings don't compete with the spectacular views, either of the lights of Tucson or the towering waterfall on the resort property. The contemporary Continental menu, which changes seasonally, has a California-inspired emphasis on lower-fat, lower-cholesterol preparation and beautiful presentation. Daily specials might include medallions of venison with dried cherry sauce or mesquite-grilled Pacific Northwest sturgeon fillet with avocado salsa. The wine list meets the high standards of the menu, and service is impeccable without being overbearing. *7000 N. Resort Dr., tel. 602/299–2020. Reservations advised. Jacket and tie advised. AE, D, DC, MC, V. Dinner only.*

$$$ **Anthony's.** This is an elegant yet comfortable place for a tasty meal and a lovely view of the city. Pink linen, stemmed crystal, and pink-rimmed china lend a light, festive look to the dining room. On a nice day, sit out on the patio for a cocktail. Lamb Wellington, Norwegian salmon sautéed lightly in a tomato-basil

Tucson Dining and Lodging

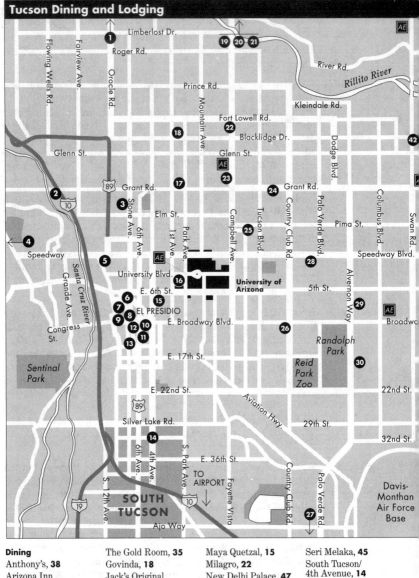

Dining

Anthony's, **38**

Arizona Inn
Restaurant, **25**

Bailey & Bailey, **11**

Boccata, **41**

Café Poca Cosa, **12**

Café Terra Cotta, **19**

Daniel's, **20**

El Charro Café, **6**

El Minuto Café, **9**

The Gold Room, **35**

Govinda, **18**

Jack's Original
Bar-B-Q, **46**

Janos, **8**

Jerome's, **51**

The Kingfisher
Grill, **24**

The Landmark Cafe, **1**

Le Bistro, **23**

Li'l Abner's, **33**

Maya Quetzal, **15**

Milagro, **22**

New Delhi Palace, **47**

Olson's, **26**

Olive Tree, **50**

Pappy's, **13**

Penelope's, **42**

Pinnacle Peak
Steakhouse, **48**

Presidio Grill, **28**

Rancher's Club, **43**

Seri Melaka, **45**

South Tucson/
4th Avenue, **14**

The Tack Room, **52**

Tohono Chul Tea
Room, **34**

Ventana Room, **37**

Yamato, **17**

Lodging

Arizona Inn, **25**
Canyon Ranch, **54**
Casa Tierra, **4**
Doubletree Hotel, **30**
El Presidio Bed and
Breakfast Inn, **7**
Embassy Suites
Tucson-Broadway, **44**
Flamingo Sun Hotel, **3**
Holiday Inn Tucson
Airport Hotel and
Convention Center, **27**

Hotel Congress, **10**
Lazy K Bar Guest
Ranch, **31**
The Lodge on the
Desert, **29**
Loews Ventana
Canyon Resort, **37**
Park Inn/ Santa
Rita, **12**
Peppertrees, **16**
Ramada Downtown
Tucson, **5**

Ramada Inn
Foothills, **49**
Rodeway Inn Tucson
North, **2**
Sheraton Tucson El
Conquistador, **39**
The Suncatcher, **56**
Tanque Verde
Ranch, **55**
Triangle L Ranch Bed
& Breakfast, **36**
Tucson Hilton
East, **53**

Westin La Paloma, **40**
Westward Look
Resort, **35**
White Stallion
Ranch, **32**
The Windmill Inn, **21**

sauce, and bananas Foster are all good dinnertime choices; for lunch you might try the crisp-baked lemon chicken with potato pancakes. The wine list is the largest in Arizona, and a classical pianist plays from 7 PM nightly. *6440 N. Campbell Ave., tel. 602/ 299–1771. Reservations advised. Dress: casual but neat. AE, DC, MC, V. Closed Sun. lunch.*

$$$ Arizona Inn Restaurant. This confident, friendly establishment, a Tucson classic, welcomes old friends and new visitors alike. Sit out on the patio for a lovely view of the grounds of this historic adobe inn, or enjoy the view through huge windows in the dining room, a light, airy place with many 1930s Southwestern details. On chilly evenings there's a fire. Steamed fish of the day served with ginger and leeks is a specialty, and the seared venison medallions are also popular. For dessert, try a slice of the terrific apple or pecan pie. Breakfast here is also a treat. *2200 E. Elm St., tel. 602/325–1541. Reservations advised. Jacket and tie advised for dinner. AE, MC, V.*

$$$ The Gold Room. Located at the beautiful Westward Look Resort in the Santa Catalina foothills north of town, this rather upscale restaurant offers a panoramic view of Tucson sparkling in the sun (or twinkling at night) from its glassed-in dining room. The food is generally fine, but the restaurant has gone through a number of chefs in the last few years and can be somewhat inconsistent. Popular Continental dishes such as chateaubriand for two and veal scaloppine remain staples of the menu. *245 E. Ina Rd., tel. 602/297–1151. Reservations advised. Jacket advised for dinner. AE, D, DC, MC, V.*

$$$ The Landmark Cafe. Come to this pretty, intimate restaurant on the northwest side of town at dinnertime for the well-prepared Continental standards—flambé of roast duck, say, or chateaubriand for two—served tableside. Lunch is a more casual affair, with a variety of sandwiches, pizzas, and salads on offer along with well-priced specialty plates such as veal liver with bacon and onion or stuffed pork loin. Whenever you come, save room for dessert; the Landmark Cafe is a consistent winner of Tucson's annual Taste of Chocolate competition. *7117 N. Oracle Rd., tel. 602/575–9277. Reservations advised at dinner. Dress: casual but neat. AE, D, DC, MC, V.*

French Le Bistro. Set in a nondescript building on a busy road near the
$$$ university, Le Bistro is one of the prettiest restaurants in town: Towering palms preside over pink lace-covered tables, burgundy chairs, and Art Nouveau–style etched mirrors. The setting is matched by the creations of young chef/owner Laurent Reux; born in Brittany, he offers many fish and shellfish dishes inspired by the seascape of his native region, such as supreme of salmon in a ginger crust with lime butter. Another popular specialty is Long Island duck in a raspberry vinaigrette. A revolving glass dessert display at the entrance will leave you pondering throughout the meal whether to opt for the triple-chocolate mousse cake, say, or the Key-lime tart. Lunch prices are very reasonable. *2574 N. Campbell Ave., tel. 502/327–3086.*

Reservations advised on weekends. Dress: casual but neat. D, MC, V. Closed weekend lunch.

$$$ **Penelope's.** Devotees of Patricia Sparks' place on Speedway Boulevard were bereft when a street-widening project left the chef/owner temporarily without a restaurant, but she's back now and better than ever in a more spacious northeast location. Four dining rooms decorated in Country French–style make a lovely setting for the prix-fixe menus (four or six courses, with or without wine, ranging from $25 to $41). The selections change often, but soups might include cream of mushroom or onion, entrées filet mignon *au poivre* (with crushed peppercorns) or sauteed boneless chicken breast with green-grape sauce. Desserts are uniformly excellent. *3071 N. Swan Rd., tel. 602/ 325–5080. Dress: casual but neat. Reservations advised for dinner. AE, D, DC, MC, V. Closed Mon., weekend lunch.*

Greek **Olive Tree.** In an appealing Santa Fe–style building, the Olive
$$ Tree serves up fine versions of such Greek standards as moussaka, shish kebab, and stuffed grape leaves, but also includes more unusual dishes on its menu. The Lamb Bandit is baked in foil with two types of cheese, potatoes, and vegetables; the daily fresh-fish specials are broiled in garlic, oregano, and olive oil, and served with a well-prepared orzo. This is not light cuisine. If you don't have room for the supersweet baklava, a cup of strong Greek coffee makes for a satisfying finish. *7000 E. Tanque Verde Rd., tel. 602/298–1845. Reservations advised. Dress: casual but neat. AE, MC, V. Closed Sun. lunch.*

Guatemalan **Maya Quetzal.** This friendly, down-home restaurant on trendy
$ 4th Avenue is inexpensive enough to allow those unfamiliar with Guatemalan food—and who isn't?—to sample lots of different dishes. Try the vegetarian paches (potato-meal tamales topped with a mild red pepper sauce) or the pollo en jocón (chicken with cilantro-flavored green sauce). A large, brightly colored mural, Guatemalan crafts, and a pleasant patio all add to the cheerful atmosphere. *429 N. 4th Ave., tel. 602/622–8207. No reservations. Dress: casual. MC, V. Closed Wed.*

Indian **New Delhi Palace.** Vegetarians, carnivores, and seafood lovers
$–$$ will all find something to enjoy at this elegant Indian restaurant. The congenial staff is helpful in explaining the menu, which features a wide variety of tandoori dishes, curries, rice, and breads. The "heat" of each dish can be adjusted to individual preference by the chef. If you're undecided, a lunch buffet and complete dinners offer nice samplings of several dishes. The atmosphere is quiet, with Indian music played softly, and tasteful displays of Indian objets d'art. *6751 E. Broadway, tel. 602/296– 8585. Reservations advised. Dress: casual. DC, MC, V.*

Italian **Daniel's.** A fine northern Italian menu, an excellent wine and
$$$ beer list, the largest selection of single-malt Scotches in town, and service that is attentive but not overbearing draw a sophisticated crowd to this chic art deco–style restaurant. The grilled eggplant and mushroom appetizer, *spaghetti alla putanesca* with olives, capers, and tomatoes, and *bistecca alla florentina* (a

tender rib-eye steak marinated in olive oil and herbs) are among the many recommended dishes; for dessert, a heavenly rum tiramisù somehow manages to be light and rich at the same time. *St. Phillips Plaza, 4340 N. Campbell Ave., tel. 602/742–3200. Reservations advised. Jacket advised. AE, DC, MC, V. Dinner only.*

$$–$$$ **Boccata.** In a tasteful mall in the foothills of the Santa Catalina
★ Mountains, this pretty restaurant serves excellent northern Italian cuisine, with some southern French dishes for good measure. The flowered tablecloths match the delicate aubergine and Tuscan-yellow walls, and the artwork ranges from contemporary to Victorian whimsy. A good wine list complements such entrées as penne *ciao bella* (with grilled chicken and a delicate white wine and Gorgonzola sauce) and a veal chop topped with a porcini-mushroom sauce; the steamed mussel appetizer is plentiful. Save room for the chocolate pecan pudding, served warm with Frangelico crème anglaise. *5605 E. River Rd., tel. 602/577–9309. Reservations advised. Dress: casual but neat. AE, DC, MC, V. Closed Sat.–Thurs. lunch; open for Sun. brunch.*

$$ **Olson's.** Although the name and the rather eclectic Southwestern decor suggest otherwise, this is an Italian restaurant, owned by University of Arizona men's basketball coach Lute Olson and his son, Greg. Don't worry—the original owner, Joe Scordato, a bona fide Italian, still expertly oversees operations. There are a few American and Continental dishes on the menu, but the focus is southern Italian, with such specialties as *pesce alla griglia* (salmon or swordfish grilled in a lemon-and-white-wine butter) and *braciole con fettuccine* (beefsteak with stuffing served over pasta with tomato sauce). *3048 E. Broadway, tel. 602/323–3701. Reservations advised. Dress: casual. AE, D, DC, MC, V. Closed weekend lunch.*

$ **Pappy's.** Come here for huge portions of Italian standards served in a pleasant atmosphere—plush booths, white tablecloths, and a small, tree-shaded patio. You can order a variety of pastas with assorted chicken, seafood, meat, or vegetable toppings, or opt for the hearty lasagna or fettuccine Alfredo. Prices are generally very reasonable, and the cold pasta primavera with chicken is a serious bargain at $4.95. Just down the block from the Temple of Music and Art, Pappy's is ideal for a pre-theater dinner (just leave the garlic-redolent doggy bag in the car when you go to the show). *375 S. Stone Ave., tel. 602/882–8908. Reservations advised on weekends. Dress: casual. DC, MC, V. Call ahead for hours, which vary throughout the week and season.*

Japanese **Yamato.** Colorful paper lanterns line the walls of this modest
$$ eatery, tucked away in a strip mall near the university. A sushi bar serves fish flown in daily from California, and a number of combination dinners such as shrimp tempura and teriyaki chicken are available. *Yaki soba* (beef and vegetables heaped on wheat noodles) makes a tasty, hearty meal. Many of Yamato's Japanese patrons gather on Saturday night from 10 PM to 1 AM for laser karaoke sing-alongs. *857 E. Grant Rd., tel. 602/624–*

3377. Reservations advised for 5 or more. Dress: casual. AE, MC, V. Closed Sat. lunch, Sun.

Malaysian **Seri Melaka.** Malaysian food, like Thai, uses plenty of curry, co-
$ conut, and other tasty condiments in its sauces. This popular restaurant on the east side of town is an excellent place to try the cuisine, and to indulge in good versions of such dishes as *satay* (grilled meat on a skewer with peanut sauce) and *lemak* (shrimp or chicken with vegetables in a sweet curry sauce). An extensive selection of well-prepared Chinese dishes is also on the menu. There's a buffet at lunchtime. *6133 E. Broadway, tel. 602/747–7811. Reservations accepted. Dress: casual. D, MC, V.*

Mexican **Café Poca Cosa.** This is a marvelously colorful (hot pink, bright
$–$$ green, and tropical orange) and lively restaurant in an unlikely
★ spot: the downtown Park Inn. Locals caught on to this hip, friendly place before the tourists did. Though portions are generous, the Mexican dishes are not prepared in the usual cheese-saturated Sonoran style. The menu, which changes daily, might include *pollo á mole* (chicken in a spicy chocolate-based sauce) or pork *pibil* (made with a tangy Yucatan barbecue seasoning). Consider a breakfast of green-chili tamales on the outdoor patio when the weather is fine. The tiny original restaurant across the street (20 S. Scott Ave.), also a lively treat, is open for breakfast and lunch during the week. *88 E. Broadway, tel. 602/622–6400. Reservations advised for large parties. Dress: informal. MC, V. Closed Sun. dinner.*

$–$$ **El Charro Café.** Started by Monica Flin in 1922, and run by her grandniece and her grandniece's husband today, El Charro still serves excellent versions of the American-Mexican staples Flin claims to have originated—chimichangas (flour tortillas rolled around seasoned beef or chicken and deep-fried) and cheese crisps, most notably. Daily "fitness-fare" specials such as sea-food enchiladas are delicious as well as healthful. You can dine outside on the front porch or inside in one of the bright, cheerful dining rooms; a new lounge serves appetizers and drinks. Next door, a gift shop sells mementos of this Tucson classic. *311 N. Court Ave., tel. 602/622–1922. Reservations advised. Dress: casual (but no tank tops). AE, MC, V.*

$–$$ **El Minuto Café.** This brightly decorated, bustling restaurant in Tucson's historic barrio is a good bet for those seeking a late meal downtown; it's open until 2 AM Friday and Saturday, 11 PM the rest of the week. In business for more than 50 years, El Minuto serves up crispy chimichangas, huge burritos, and green corn tamales (in season) made just right. All the ingredients are fresh and the Mexican beer selection is large. *354 S. Main Ave., tel. 602/882–4145. Reservations not required. Dress: casual. AE, MC, V.*

$–$$ **South Tucson/4th Avenue.** Every Tucsonan you meet will argue the merits of a favorite "real" Mexican restaurant, but invaria-bly it's on or near 4th Avenue in South Tucson. Technically a separate city, South Tucson has a large Mexican-American pop-ulation and thus many authentic and inexpensive places to find good south-of-the-border cuisine. Among the most popular: **Crossroads** (2602 S. 4th Ave., tel. 602/624–0395); **Gran Guadalajara** (2527 S. 4th Ave., tel. 602/620–1321); **Guillermo's Double L** (1830 S. 4th Ave., tel. 602/792–1585); **La Hacienda** (4207 S. 6th Ave., tel. 602/889–6613); **Micha's** (2908 S. 4th Ave., tel. 602/ 623–5307); **Mi Nidito** (1813 S. 4th Ave., tel. 602/622–5081); and **Xochimilcho** (2702 S. 4th Ave., tel. 602/882–5636). You'd be hard-pressed to have a bad meal—or a bad time—at any of these friendly, informal places. Many have mariachi bands on the weekends. MC and V are accepted at most.

Southwestern **Janos.** Comfortably situated in the Hiram Stevens House, an
$$$–$$$$ adobe home built in 1855, this downtown restaurant—adjacent
★ to the Tucson Museum of Art—offers innovative and superlative Southwest menus created by chef/owner Janos Wilder. A series of small, flower-filled dining rooms create an intimate, elegant atmosphere. Typical offerings include chipotle roasted rack of lamb and grilled swordfish with tomato coulis. The summer and fall $12.95 dinner specials allow the less well-heeled to indulge in a meal here. *150 N. Main Ave., tel. 602/884–9426. Reservations advised. Dress: casual but neat. AE, DC, MC, V. Closed Sun. Nov.–mid-May; Sun. and Mon. late May–Nov.*

$$$–$$$$ **The Tack Room.** This restaurant has won many awards for its food, and the setting—in a rustic but elegant old adobe on the grounds of a former resort—is romantic, but the service is a tad overfussy and the menu a bit safer than those of other first-rate restaurants in town. That said, it's still worth coming here for a splurge. Dark-wood beams and furnishings and a blue-and-maroon color scheme are complemented by the lighter dusty-rose linen; walls are hung with Southwestern landscapes by local artists. Arizona four-pepper steak flavored with different chilies is a favorite, as is the rack of lamb for two, prepared with mesquite honey, cilantro, and Southwestern limes. *2800 N. Sabino Canyon Rd., tel. 602/722–2800. Reservations advised. Jacket advised. AE, D, DC, MC, V. Closed Mon. mid-May–mid-Dec., and first 2 weeks of July.*

$$–$$$ **Café Terra Cotta.** Everything about this restaurant says Southwest—from the decor, with its bright pastels and bleached woods, to the food, which features such contemporary Southwest specialties as prawns stuffed with herbed goat cheese, pork tenderloin with black beans, and pizzas with sun-dried tomatoes; the garlic-custard appetizer is superb. The place for native yupsters as well as their out-of-town guests, Café Terra Cotta offers an impressive by-the-glass California wine list and a tasty Sunday brunch. Note: This reviewer has never had a bad meal here but has received some mixed reports from others. *St. Philip's Plaza, 4310 N. Campbell Ave., tel. 602/577–8100. Reservations strongly advised for dinner. Dress: casual. AE, D, DC, MC, V.*

$$–$$$ **Presidio Grill.** If it weren't for the saguaro cactus flanking the window, you might at first think you were in one of New York's chic downtown haunts, with stylish black booths and art deco light fixtures. But the food is Southwestern all the way. Blue-

corn pancakes with prickly-pear syrup appear on the Sunday brunch menu; lunch and dinner entrées include chicken Santa Fe, served with black beans, flour tortillas, grilled scallions, and two types of salsa; and an eggplant, artichoke heart, onion, and sun-dried tomato pizza. In the University of Arizona area, this place is open unusually late (for Tucson) on weekends. A cabaret-style supper club is offered in the restaurant's banquet room every month or so, when four-course dinners are coordinated with such entertainment as flamenco, jazz, blues, or opera. *3352 E. Speedway Blvd., tel. 602/327–4667. Reservations advised for 5 or more; tickets available for supper club. Dress: casual but neat. AE, MC, V.*

$$ **Li'l Abner's.** This Old West institution in the Butterfield Express stagecoach rest stop, which dates from the early 1800s, draws locals, who go straight for the mesquite-broiled two-pound porterhouse steaks. There's nothing here for vegetarians, except for the salad, beans, and salsa that come with all the entrées. On weekends, you can chow down to the sounds of a live country band. It's about a 20-minute drive from downtown. *8500 N. Silverbell Rd., tel. 602/744–2800. Reservations advised. Dress: casual. MC, V. Closed for lunch.*

$$ **Pinnacle Peak Steakhouse.** No nouvelle-cuisine fans welcome here: Anybody caught eating fish tacos or cactus jelly would probably be hanged from the rafters—along with all the ties snipped from loco city slickers. This is a cowboy steak house that the tourists love. It's fun, it's Tucson, and the food ain't half bad, either, partner. The excellent mesquite-broiled steaks come with salad, baked potatoes, and pinto beans; if you can handle more after all that, try the hot apple cobbler with vanilla ice cream. The restaurant is part of Trail Dust Town, a re-creation of a turn-of-the-century town, complete with an "opera" house featuring cancan girls and a barbershop quartet, souvenir shops, and an old-time photographer's studio, where you can have your picture taken in Western garb. *6541 E. Tanque Verde Rd., tel. 602/296–0911. No reservations. Dress: casual. AE, D, DC, MC, V.*

$$ ★ **Tohono Chul Tea Room.** This is a good choice for anybody seeking a quiet cup of tea or glass of wine, a satisfying sandwich, a crunchy salad, or a tasty dessert. The setting is unique—the tearoom is nestled in a wildlife sanctuary and surrounded by a fantastic cactus garden. Although the tearoom is typically Southwestern, with lots of Mexican tile and light wood, the menu covers Southwestern, Mexican, and American dishes. House favorites include chicken enchiladas made with Monterey Jack cheese, corn, and green chilies, and a sliced-tomato-and-basil sandwich served on French sourdough bread. Sunday brunch is especially good. *7366 N. Paseo del Norte, tel. 602/797–1711. Reservations accepted for 8 or more Mon.–Sat., no reservations accepted Sun. Dress: casual. AE, MC, V. Closed for dinner.*

$ **Jack's Original Bar-B-Q.** For those who like their Southwest cuisine in big, messy portions, this is the place to come. Jack's ribs

are smoky, meaty, and without equal in these parts; the sauce is rich and subtly flavored. The beans are also a real treat. Jack's impresses through good, honest food, not atmosphere—the floor is linoleum; the chairs and flowers are plastic. *5250 E. 22nd St., tel. 602/750–1280. No reservations. Dress: casual. MC, V.*

Vegetarian **Govinda.** The only place in town with a strictly nonmeat menu, **$** this Hare Krishna–run restaurant offers reasonably priced all-you-can-eat lunch and dinner buffets that include vegan options. Selections of hot and cold dishes vary daily, but ingredients are consistently fresh and the food is tasty if not particularly spicy. The atmosphere in the pretty, light wood dining room is somewhat subdued—perhaps because no alcohol is served or permitted. *711 E. Blacklidge Dr., tel. 602/792–0630. No reservations. Dress: casual. MC, V. Closed Sun.–Tues.*

Lodging

In Tucson you can enjoy the luxury of a desert resort or the more basic accommodations offered by small motels. A number of guest ranches—some of them from the 1800s when they were real working cattle ranches—can be found on the outskirts of town. The mountains surrounding Tucson host a bountiful array of campsites and parks for recreational vehicles, offering a cool respite from the desert heat in summer (*see* Camping in Participant Sports, *above*).

There is also a variety of bed-and-breakfast establishments in the area, ranging from bedrooms in modest homes to private cottages nestled on wildlife preserves. The **Arizona Association of Bed and Breakfast Inns** (3101 N. Central Ave., Suite 560, Phoenix 85712, tel. 602/277–0775) can provide referrals to member inns in the area. Seven of the larger, more professionally run inns in town have formed **Premier Bed & Breakfast Inns of Tucson** (3661 N. Campbell Ave., Suite 237, 85719, tel. 602/628–1800); write or call for a brochure. **Old Pueblo HomeStays** (Box 13603, Tucson 85732, tel. 800/333–9776) specializes in smaller, more casual B&Bs in southern Arizona and northern Mexico but also lists a number of the larger inns.

Prices vary widely between seasons. Room rates in summer—generally defined as April 15 through October 1—are sometimes as much as 60% lower than those in the winter, and visitors who don't mind warm weather can get some real deals at resorts that are quite pricey during the busy time. Note: Unless you book months in advance, you'll be hard-pressed to find a hotel room at any price in Tucson the week before and during the huge gem and mineral show (February 9–12 in 1995).

Category	Cost*
$$$$	over $160
$$$	$110–$160

$$	$70–$110
$	under $70

All prices are for a standard double room, excluding room tax (9.5% in Tucson and 6.5% in Pima County). Prices given here are winter, or high-season, rates.

Highly recommended hotels are indicated by a star ★.

Hotels

$$$–$$$$ **Arizona Inn.** Although this landmark '30s-era inn is close to the
★ university and downtown, you feel as though you're away from it all on its 14 lushly landscaped acres. All rooms have patios and lovely period furnishings; many have fireplaces. Service is excellent—friendly but unobtrusive. The staff hosts small conferences beautifully, attending to the details without fuss. Locals as well as guests frequent the hotel's restaurant (*see* Dining, *above*) and its cocktail lounge, which often has a piano player. *2200 E. Elm St., 85719, tel. 602/325–1541, fax 602/881–5830. 80 rooms. Facilities: pool, 2 tennis courts, library, gift shop. AE, MC, V.*

$$$ **Doubletree Hotel.** Convenient to the airport and to the center of town, this comfortable, contemporary-style property is also across the road from the municipal golf course at Randolph Park, which hosts the LPGA tournament every year; most of the participants stay here. Rooms are large, and done in salmon or turquoise with Southwestern-style furnishings. The pretty Cactus Rose Restaurant serves excellent nouvelle Southwestern cuisine and the Javelina Cantina in the lobby is a fun place in which to have a beer. *445 S. Alvernon Way, tel. 602/881–4200 or 800/528–0444, fax 602/323–5225. 295 rooms. Facilities: bar, pool, Jacuzzi, tennis courts. AE, D, DC, MC, V.*

$$$ **Embassy Suites Tucson–Broadway.** This centrally located hotel is 10 miles from Tucson International Airport, 5 miles from downtown, and a bit less than 5 miles from the University of Arizona. Accommodations are two-room suites (with a kitchenette) opening onto an atrium full of plants. Furnishings are tasteful if not exciting. Among the extras are a free cooked-to-order breakfast every morning and complimentary happy hour every evening; transportation to the airport and parking are also on the house. *5335 E. Broadway, 85711, tel. 602/745–2700 or 800/ 363–2779, fax 602/790–9232. 142 suites. Facilities: outdoor heated pool, whirlpool, microwaves in rooms, coin-op laundry. AE, D, DC, MC, V.*

$$$ **Tucson Hilton East.** This east-side property is convenient to Sabino Canyon and Saguaro National Monument East as well as to Davis–Monthan Air Force Base. An airy glass-atrium lobby takes full advantage of the view of the Santa Catalina Mountains. Rooms are nicely furnished, with modern light-wood fittings, pastel carpeting, and subtly patterned pastel bedspreads. The Wine Bar features one of the most extensive selections in town. The VIP level offers extra service and luxuries such as complimentary hors d'oeuvres, deluxe Continental breakfast, and a library. *7600 E. Broadway, 85710, tel. 602/721–5600, fax 602/721–5696. 225 rooms. Facilities: pool, exercise room (VIP level only), restaurant, bar. AE, D, DC, MC, V.*

$$ Holiday Inn Tucson Airport Hotel and Convention Center. Favored by businesspeople, this property is five minutes from the airport and adjacent to I–10. The decor is a mix of Mexican and Spanish, with dark print bedspreads and carpets throughout. In contrast, the light, cheerful lobby has a plant-filled atrium with a waterfall; saltillo-tile floors and white stucco walls give it an open, Southwestern feel. There are free shuttles to the airport and to the large El Con shopping center. *4550 S. Palo Verde Blvd., 85714, tel. 602/746–1161 or 800/465–4329, fax 602/741–1170. 299 rooms. Facilities: 2 restaurants, pool, sauna, whirlpool, tennis court, exercise room, cocktail lounge. AE, D, DC, MC, V.*

$$ The Lodge on the Desert. Although the ambience is that of an exclusive inn, prices at this little hotel, established in 1936, are reasonable. The place has retained the old-fashioned feel of a Mexican hacienda: The adobe architecture is accented with hand-painted Mexican tile and open-beamed ceilings; fireplaces warm many of the rooms in the winter; and lush gardens make the patios feel cool and private. The property is convenient to the university, near two major shopping malls, and within a mile of golf, racquetball, and tennis facilities. However, with charm comes old plumbing, and both maintenance and service here seem to have slipped in recent years. *306 N. Alvernon Way, Box 42500, 85733, tel. 602/325–3366 or 800/456–5634, fax 602/327–5834. 40 rooms. Facilities: restaurant, library, pool, shuffleboard, ping-pong, croquet, cocktail lounge. AE, D, DC, MC, V.*

$$ Ramada Downtown Tucson. Convenient to the freeway and to downtown, this hotel has an attractive Spanish-style lobby and a cheerful restaurant and lounge. Rooms are standard motel style but well maintained. *475 N. Granada Ave., 85701, tel. 602/622–3000 or 800/228–2828, fax 602/623–8922. 300 rooms. Facilities: pool, restaurant, bar. AE, D, DC, MC, V.*

$$ Ramada Inn Foothills. Families as well as business travelers stay in this more upscale, and slightly more expensive, Ramada Inn on the northeastern side of town, close to restaurants, Sabino Canyon, and mall shopping. An attractive light stucco building with rounded corners, this property has the expected generic rooms, but they're fairly new and more than serviceable. A Continental breakfast is complimentary, as are cocktails. Free passes to a local health club are available, and golf and tennis facilities are nearby. *6944 E. Tanque Verde Rd., 85715, tel. 602/886–9595 or 800/228–2828, fax 602/721–8466. 113 rooms. Facilities: restaurant, pool and sauna, lounge. AE, D, DC, MC, V.*

$$ ★ The Windmill Inn at St. Phillip's Plaza. Located in a chic shopping plaza filled with glitzy boutiques and good restaurants— *see* Daniel's and Café Terra Cotta in Dining, *above*—this all-suites hotel, built in 1992, offers attractive, Southwest-contemporary accommodations. Each suite has a separate sitting area, microwave, minifridge, two TVs, and two telephones. A few dollars extra will buy you a view of the pool rather than the parking lot. Complimentary coffee, pastry, and a newspaper are delivered to your door. All in all, it's a good deal for the price. *4250 N. Campbell Ave., 85718, tel. 602/577–0007 or 800/547–4747, fax 602/577–0045. 122 rooms. Facilities: pool, laundry facilities, free local calls, lending library, guest bicycles. AE, D, DC, MC, V.*

$ **Flamingo Sun Hotel.** When the Flamingo was built in 1953, it was the closest thing to a resort in town: Bing Crosby and his brothers opened up an act at the lounge, and hotel guests included Gene Autry, John Wayne, and Elvis Presley. Reopened in early 1994 after massive renovation, the property now offers comfortable standard rooms with Southwestern-style furnishings; some suites have microwaves and coffeemakers. If it doesn't have the cachet of its earlier heyday, captured in photos lining the lobby, the hotel is convenient to both downtown and the university and sports the swell original neon sign. *1300 N. Stone Ave., 85705, tel. 602/770–1910 or 800/300–2533, fax 602/770–0750. 79 rooms. Facilities: heated pool and Jacuzzi, coin-operated laundry, free local calls. D, DC, MC, V.*

$ **Hotel Congress.** Loved by many for its idiosyncratic charm, this downtown hotel was built in 1919 and restored to its original western version of Art Deco style. The renovated rooms, which vary in size, are individually furnished: All have black-and-white tiled baths and the original iron beds; some have desks and tables. Some unrenovated rooms are available for rock-bottom rates, but they're pretty grim, with cracked walls and bathtubs that need recaulking. Near the Greyhound and Amtrak stations and the main Sun Tran terminal, and close to downtown art galleries and restaurants, this is an excellent choice for those who don't have a car. The downside of this convenient location is noise, compounded on weekend nights when music from the popular Club Congress filters up to the rooms. *311 E. Congress St., 85701, tel. 602/622–8848, fax 602/792–6366. 40 rooms. Facilities: restaurant, bar, TV lounge, hair salon, nightclub. AE, MC, V.*

$ **Park Inn/Santa Rita.** When this hotel became a Park Inn in 1991 (it had been a Days Inn during the late 1980s), it also reclaimed the name by which it had been known in Tucson for years—the Santa Rita. The property was spiffed up during the past decade—modern furnishings, hand-painted Mexican tile, and adobe walls brighten the lobby—but rooms are still rather dark and drab, and the place sometimes shows its age in the plumbing. Still, the price is right, and the hotel is conveniently located near the downtown arts district and across the street from the visitor center; it's also home to the excellent Café Poca Cosa (*see* Dining, *above*). A Continental breakfast and happy hour are complimentary. *88 E. Broadway, 85701, tel. 602/622–4000 or*

800/437–7275, fax 602/620–0376. 165 rooms. Facilities: restaurant, beauty parlor, pool, Jacuzzi, sauna, AE, D, DC, MC, V.

$ **Rodeway Inn Tucson North.** Near I–10, and in the university area, this hotel caters to business as well as leisure travelers. The basic boxy motel architecture has been adapted to local style—a stucco exterior is accented with tasteful, low-key stripes of turquoise and pink. The pool is in a nicely landscaped courtyard studded with umbrella-shaded tables. Rooms are nothing fancy, but they are adequate. *1365 W. Grant Rd., 85745, tel. 602/622–7791 or 800/228–2000, fax 602/629–0201. 146 rooms. Facilities: pool, restaurant, lounge, coin-operated laundry. AE, D, DC, MC, V.*

Bed-and-Breakfasts

$$$ **The Suncatcher.** The poshest B&B in Tucson, The Suncatcher rests on 5 acres of desert at the far east end of town, near Saguaro National Monument East; a garden boasts 30 varieties of roses. Each of the four luxurious guest rooms pays homage to one of the world's great hotels, and the attention to detail matches that of the famous hostelries: Accommodations come with fresh-cut flowers, a TV and VCR, fine linens, terry bathrobes, hair dryers, and expensive toiletries. Guests have a choice of hot or cold breakfast, and afternoon hors d'oeuvres are complimentary. *105 N. Avenida Javelina, 85748, tel. 602/885–0883 or 800/835–8012. 4 double rooms with bath. Facilities: pool, Jacuzzi, videotape library, lighted tennis court. AE, MC, V.*

$$–$$$ **Peppertrees.** This restored Victorian just off the University of Arizona campus allows guests their privacy along with the usual B&B camaraderie. Two lovely Southwestern-style guest houses in the back of the tree-shaded main house have full kitchens, washers and dryers, and individual patios; 1½ baths are shared by two bedrooms in each unit (a room in the main house has a bath across the hall). Host Marjorie Martin prepares elaborate morning repasts for her visitors; her buttery shortbread, served at afternoon tea, is sold at local markets. *724 E. University Blvd., 85719, tel. 602/622–7167. 1 room with bath, 2 2-bedroom duplex cottages. Facilities: landscaped patio. MC, V.*

$$ **Casa Tierra.** For a real desert experience, head out to this bed-
★ and-breakfast on 5 acres of land near the Arizona–Sonora Desert Museum and Saguaro National Monument West; for the last 1½ miles you'll be driving along a dirt road. This adobe house built by Lyle Hymer-Thompson in 1989 expressly to serve as a B&B has three guest rooms, all with private bath and kitchenettes; all look out onto a lovely central courtyard with a paloverde tree and other desert foliage. Each guest room has a private entrance from individual back patios. The Southwestern-style furnishings include Mexican *equipales* (chairs with pigskin seats), tiled floors, and viga-beamed ceilings. The delicious breakfasts prepared by Karen Hymer-Thompson might include blue-corn pancakes, breakfast burritos, or oatmeal apple waffles; there's always lots of fresh fruit and baked goods to

accompany them. *11155 W. Calle Pima, 85743, tel. 602/578–3058. 3 rooms with bath. Facilities: hot tub, in-room micro-waves, minifridges. No credit cards. Closed June–Aug.*

$$ **El Presidio Bed and Breakfast Inn.** This B&B in the historic El Presidio district offers four charming accommodations, two in a Victorian adobe home built more than 100 years ago and two in separate guest houses. The Carriage House, furnished with Eastlake antiques dating from the 1880s, and the Gatehouse, done in Country French–style, have private entrances off a beautiful old courtyard, and both have kitchenettes. Guest rooms come well-stocked with fruits and bottled water, and all have phones, TVs, and robes. Breakfasts are generous and excellent. *297 N. Main Ave., 85701, tel. 602/623–6151. 3 suites, 1 room, all with bath. Facilities: TV in sitting room; privileges at nearby health club. No credit cards.*

$–$$ **The Triangle L Ranch Bed & Breakfast.** Out near Biosphere 2, a 45-minute drive northeast of Tucson at an elevation of 4,500 feet, Triangle L offers four private cottages—all at least 75 years old and furnished with antiques—scattered about the property's 80 acres. Buffalo Bill was among the regular visitors to the ranch, which was built in the 1880s. Hiking and sitting on the porch are activities equally favored by visitors. A ranch breakfast of eggs, homemade breads, fresh fruit, and plenty of coffee is served daily. Smoking outdoors only. *2805 N. Triangle L Ranch Rd., Box 900, Oracle 85623, tel. 602/896–2804 or 800/266–2804. 2 private cottages with bath, 2 with bath and kitchen. D, MC, V.*

Guest Ranches

Note: Unless otherwise indicated, price categories for guest ranches include all meals and most activities.

$$$$ **Lazy K Bar Guest Ranch.** In the Tucson Mountains, 16 miles northwest of town at an altitude of 2,300 feet, this family-oriented guest ranch will please children as well as adults. Steak cookouts are held every Saturday night, and the daily fare in the community dining room is hearty and good. As you might expect, horseback riding is a focus, with mounts available for greenhorns as well as those with experience. Riders are entertained with tales of the Old West as they explore the Saguaro National Monument on horseback. There are 23 rooms, all with private bath, situated in eight *casitas*, or cottages. The older buildings are made of Mexican Indian stucco and contain rooms with fireplaces and wood-beam ceilings. Rooms in the newer, adobe-brick buildings are larger and more modern. Rates for children 17 and under are very reasonable. There's a three-day minimum stay. *8401 N. Scenic Dr., 85743, tel. 602/744–3050 or 800/321–7018, fax 602/744–7628. 23 rooms. Facilities: pool, library, large-screen TV in the main lodge, BYOB lounge. AE, MC, V. Closed June 15–Sept. 1.*

$$$$ **Tanque Verde Ranch.** One of the country's oldest guest ranches,
★ Tanque Verde sits on more than 600 beautiful acres in the Rincon

Mountains between Coronado National Forest and Saguaro National Monument. There's plenty to do, from guided nature walks and trail rides to tennis and swimming. Rooms in the main ranch house or in private casitas are all furnished in tasteful Southwestern style; most have patios and some have fireplaces. Service is relaxed but very attentive. Cookouts and indoor meals are delicious. Many of the guests have been coming here for years; it's not unusual for more than two generations of a family to visit together. *14301 E. Speedway Blvd., 85748, tel. 602/296–6275 or 800/234–DUDE, fax 602/721–9426. 65 rooms. Facilities: indoor and outdoor pools, 5 tennis courts (1 lighted for night use), spa, exercise room, basketball, volleyball, horseshoes, fishing, horseback riding. AE, D, MC, V.*

$$$$ **White Stallion Ranch.** If you feel as if this place is right out of the
★ film *High Chaparral*, you won't be imagining things. Many scenes from the movie were shot on the ranch, which sits on 3,000 acres of desert mountain land. The True family—Cynthia, Russell, and Michael—has run the White Stallion for almost 30 years, and it feels like a family place, where children are welcome and large groups are easily accommodated. Horseback rides, a weekend rodeo, and hikes along mountain trails are just a few of the activities offered. A herd of longhorn cattle and a wide variety of birds, desert cottontail rabbits, and peacocks make their home on the grounds. Children will enjoy the petting zoo, where sheep and tiny goats gently nuzzle their visitors. There are no phones or TVs in the spare but comfortable rooms. *9251 W. Twin Peaks Rd., 85743, tel. 602/297–0252 or 800/782–5546, fax 602/744–2786. 23 rooms. Facilities: bar, ping-pong, 2 pool tables, TV/VCR room with video library, pool, hot tub, 2 tennis courts, shuffleboard, basketball, volleyball, horseback riding. No credit cards. Closed May–Sept.*

Resorts

$$$$ **Canyon Ranch.** Mel and Enid Zuckerman opened Canyon Ranch in 1979 on the site of the old Double U Guest Ranch, set on 70 acres in the desert foothills north of Tucson. Two activity centers include a 62,000-square-foot spa complex and an 8,000-square-foot Health and Healing Center, where dietitians, exercise physiologists, behavioral-health professionals, and medical staff counsel guests on everything from kicking the smoking habit to losing weight. Guests are pampered while they're being shaped up. The food is unobtrusively healthful, satisfying—within reason—even big appetites. Rooms are luxuriously furnished in muted Southwestern tones. Be aware, however, that unless you're seriously rich, the benefits of the stress reduction programs may be wiped out when you get the bill: Almost all of the ranch's special services cost extra. *8600 E. Rockcliff Rd., 85715, tel. 602/749–9000 or 800/742–9000, fax 602/749–7755. 67 standard rooms, 45 deluxe rooms, 41 luxury suites. Facilities: 1 indoor and 3 outdoor pools, 8 tennis courts, basketball, squash, racquetball, extensive workout equipment. AE, D, MC, V.*

$$$$ Loews Ventana Canyon Resort. One of the newer desert resorts, Ventana Canyon is unquestionably luxurious, but also snootier than most Tucson properties. The setting is spectacular: Expect to see desert cottontails around the 93-acre grounds, along with hummingbirds, quail, and other birds; don't be surprised if you find yourself sharing the golf course with a cottontail or two. Rooms are modern and chic, furnished in soft pastels and light woods; each bath has a miniature TV. The center of this open, airy property is an 80-foot waterfall that cascades down the Catalina Mountains into a little lake. Four restaurants offer guests a choice of casual poolside snacks and elegant dining; the upscale Ventana Room (*see* Dining, *above*) serves first-rate Continental cuisine. *7000 N. Resort Dr., 85715, tel. 602/299–2020 or 800/234–5117, fax 602/299–6832. 398 rooms. Facilities: 2 pools, golf course, 10 tennis courts, spa, health club, gift shops, hairdresser, cocktail lounge, disco. AE, D, DC, MC, V.*

$$$$ Sheraton Tucson El Conquistador. You'll know you're in the
★ Southwest when you step into the cathedral-ceilinged lobby of this golf and tennis resort: It has a huge copper mural filled with cowboys and cacti, as well as a wide-window view of one of the pools set against a backdrop of the rugged Santa Catalina Mountains. This friendly, relaxing place draws families and out-of-town conventioneers as well as locals, who take advantage of summer rates for the Sheraton's excellent sports facilities. Rooms, either in private casitas or the main hotel building, feature stylish light-wood furniture with tinwork and pastel-toned spreads and curtains, as well as balconies or patios; some of the suites have kiva-shaped fireplaces. The White Dove, the resort's fine dining room, reopened in 1994 with a new chef and an innovative Southwestern menu. Biosphere 2 is just about a 10-minute drive up the road from here. *10000 N. Oracle Rd., 85737, tel. 602/742–7000 or 800/325–7832, fax 602/544–1228. 438 rooms. Facilities: 45 holes of golf, 31 lighted tennis courts, 11 indoor racquetball courts, riding stables, 3 outdoor pools, 2 fitness centers, sauna, Jacuzzi, bicycle rentals, volleyball, basketball, 5 restaurants, gift shops. AE, D, DC, MC, V.*

$$$$ Westin La Paloma. Vying with the Sheraton and Loews Ventana for convention business, this sprawling pink resort offers lots of options for individual and family relaxation. The resort's golf, fitness, and beauty centers are top-notch; a huge pool has the only swim-up bar in Tucson; and reasonably priced child care at a special play lounge helps both parents and kids enjoy their stay. Accommodations make tasteful use of Southwestern colors and copper tones; views from private balconies are of the city lights, golf course, or grounds. The casual Desert Garden restaurant affords wonderful views of the Santa Catalina Mountains, while the more upscale La Villa specializes in freshly imported seafood. *3800 E. Sunrise Dr., 85718, tel. 602/742–6000 or 800/876–3683, fax 602/577–5878. 487 rooms. Facilities: golf course, 12 lighted tennis courts, volleyball, croquet, racquetball, pool, 3 spas, aerobics, exercise and weight rooms, beauty center, jogging and cycling trails, bike rentals, 5 restaurants, 2 bars, shopping arcade, business center. AE, D, DC, MC, V.*

$$$ **Westward Look Resort.** Set on 80 acres in the Santa Catalina
★   foothills north of town, Westward Look is 45 years old but
was recently completely refurbished. Either a city or a moun-
tain view is available from the well-appointed rooms spread
across the landscaped grounds, traversed by golf carts driven
by hotel staff to transport guests. The resort is dimly but beau-
tifully lit at night, the better for guests to stargaze. In-room
hot-beverage makers, irons and ironing boards, and refrig-
erators are among the many special touches. The resort's
Gold Room restaurant is excellent (*see* Dining, *above*), and
the lobby lounge features live entertainment every night but
Monday. Although it offers a full range of facilities, Westward
Look is more intimate (and less expensive) than the other
Tucson resorts. It draws many repeat visitors. *245 E. Ina Rd.,
85704, tel. 602/297–1151 or 800/722–2500, fax 602/297–9023. 244
rooms with bath. Facilities: 3 heated pools, 3 spas, 8 tennis
courts (5 lighted), cocktail lounge, 2 restaurants. AE, D, DC,
MC, V.*

The Arts and Nightlife

The Arts

Tucson, known as the most cultured of Arizona's cities, is one of
only 14 cities in the United States that is home to a symphony as
well as to opera, theater, and ballet companies. Winter is the
high season for most of Tucson's cultural activities because
that's when most of the visitors come, but there's something go-
ing on all the time.

Summer is when **Downtown Saturday Night,** a year-round event,
really comes alive. On the first and third Saturday nights of each
month (around 7–10 PM), Tucson's downtown arts district opens
up its galleries, studios, and cafés. There's dancing in the street—
everything from calypso to square dancing—and musical perfor-
mances ranging from jazz to gospel. Most of the activity takes
place along Congress Street and Broadway (from 4th Avenue to
Stone Street) and along 5th and 6th avenues, but the action radi-
ates in all directions. For information about this event and about
festivals, free workshops and classes, and performances in the
downtown arts district, contact **The Tucson Partnership, Inc.** (tel.
602/624–9977); this organization also offers material on self-
guided gallery and historic district walking tours.

The cost of attending any cultural event in Tucson will be a
pleasant surprise to anyone who's accustomed to paying East or
West Coast prices—symphony tickets can be purchased for as
little as $5 for some concerts, and tickets to a touring Broadway
musical can often be had for $22. Parking is frequently free.
Most of the city's cultural activity takes place either downtown
in the arts district, where the **Tucson Convention Center** (260 S.
Church St., tel. 602/791–4266) complex and the El Presidio
neighborhood are, or at the University of Arizona. Tickets to

Tucson arts and entertainment events can often be purchased through **Dillard's Box Office** (tel. 800/638–4253).

The free *Tucson Weekly*, published every Wednesday and found in most supermarkets and convenience stores, and the Friday edition of *The Arizona Daily Star* both have complete listings of what's on in town.

Dance Tucson shares its professional ballet company, **Ballet Arizona** (tel. 602/882–5022), with Phoenix; performances, which range from classical to contemporary, are held at the Music Hall in the Tucson Convention Center (*see above*). The most established of the modern companies, **Orts Theatre of Dance** (930 N. Stone Ave., tel. 602/624–3799), schedules a variety of outdoor and indoor performances.

Music The **Tucson Symphony Orchestra** (443 S. Stone Ave., tel. 602/882–8585 [box office] or 602/792–9155 [main office]), part of Tucson's cultural scene for more than 60 years, holds concerts in the music hall in the Tucson Convention Center complex. A variety of concerts and recitals, many of them free, are offered by the **University of Arizona's School of Music** (tel. 602/621–3065); a chamber-music series is hosted by the **Arizona Friends of Music** (tel. 602/298–5806) at the Leo Rich Theater in the Tucson Convention Center from October through April. The **Arizona Opera Company** (tel. 602/293–4336), headquartered in Tucson, puts on four major productions each year at the Tucson Convention Center's Music Hall.

From late February through late June, the Tucson Parks and Recreation Department hosts a series of **free concerts**, most of them held on the weekend at the De Meester Outdoor Performance Center in Reid Park. The Tucson Pops Orchestra and the Arizona Symphonic Winds alternate performances much of the time, but there are also special events, such as concerts by the Old Time Fiddlers and the Civic Orchestra. It's smart to arrive at least an hour before the music starts (usually at 7:30) so that you can position your blanket exactly where you want it. Call 602/791–4079 for the schedule.

The **Southern Arizona Light Opera Co.** (1202 N. Main Ave., tel. 602/323–7888 [east-side ticket office] or 602/884–1212 [west-side ticket office]) is becoming increasingly popular.

Tucson's jazz scene encompasses everything from afternoon jam sessions in the park to Sunday jazz brunches at the resorts in the foothills. The **Tucson Jazz Society Hot Line** (tel. 602/743–3399) offers information about the many events around town.

Poetry The **Tucson Poetry Festival** is held in early spring. A large range of poets, some internationally acclaimed—Allen Ginsberg and Amiri Baraka have been participants—come to town for three days of readings and related events. Call 602/321–2163 or 602/881–3206 for details.

The **University of Arizona Poetry Center** (1216 N. Cherry Ave., tel. 602/321–7760) runs a free series open to the public. Phone during fall and spring semesters for information on scheduled readers.

Theater Theater groups in town include Arizona's state theater, the **Arizona Theatre Company** (tel. 602/884–8210), which performs everything from classical to contemporary drama at the Temple of Music and Art (330 S. Scott Ave., tel. 602/622–2823) from November through May; it's worth coming just to see the beautiful, newly restored Spanish Colonial/Moorish–style theater. The department of theater arts at the University of Arizona (tel. 602/621–1162) also offers productions of all styles and periods through the **Studio Theatre Series** and through the **University Theatre**. The **a.k.a. theatre** (125 E. Congress St., tel. 602/623–7852) specializes in avant-garde productions, and **Invisible Theatre** (1400 N. 1st Ave., tel. 602/882–9721) presents contemporary plays and musicals.

Nightlife

Although Tucson doesn't have the huge selection of bars and clubs available in some major cities, there's something here to suit nearly every taste. Even if you can't two-step, it's worth stopping into one of the many local country-western clubs; a number of them offer free dance lessons, and the crowd is friendly to city slickers and cowpokes alike. Most of the major resorts have night spots that offer late-night drinks and sometimes dancing.

Rock/Variety **Club Congress** (311 E. Congress St., tel. 602/622–8848) is the main venue in town for cutting-edge rock bands. **The Outback** (296 N. Stone Ave., tel. 602/622–4700) showcases performers like Maria Muldaur or Mick Fleetwood, who wouldn't fill the convention center but draw a good crowd. At the **Cushing Street Bar and Restaurant** (343 S. Meyer Ave., tel. 602/622–7984) the focus is on blues, though live jazz and rock acts are also booked. The **Chicago Bar** (5954 E. Speedway Blvd., tel. 602/748–8169) features reggae on Wednesday and Thursday nights, rocking blues on Friday and Saturday nights, and a variety of live bands the rest of the week. Nearby **Berky's** (5769 E. Speedway Blvd., tel. 602/296–1981) also has live music—R&B and rock 'n' roll—every night. The DJ at Loews Ventana Canyon resort's **Flying V Bar & Grill** (tel. 602/299–2020, ext. 5280) packs in a collegiate crowd on Friday and Saturday nights.

Jazz Of the various clubs around town, **Cafe Sweetwater** (340 E. 6th St., tel. 602/622–6464) is the most consistent in the quality of its jazz acts—and the food's pretty good, too.

Country and Western An excellent house band gets the crowd two-stepping nightly at the **Maverick** (4702 E. 22nd St., tel. 602/748–0456). On Sunday night the **Cactus Moon Cafe** (5470 E. Broadway Blvd., tel. 602/748–0049) has a terrific all-you-can-eat buffet for $2 and free dance lessons. It's worth a drive to the **Wild Wild West** (4385 W. Ina Rd., tel. 602/744–7744), the Southwest's largest country-and-western nightclub, with a rotating bar, two dance floors, pool tables, and video games.

Southeastern Arizona

The southeastern corner of Arizona is a mix of ghost towns, rugged rock formations, dense, deep forests, and mountain mining towns. It's the site of Chiricahua National Monument, one of Arizona's best-kept secrets, and a paradise for birders, hikers, and antiquers—and anyone who has an interest in frontier history. Many consider this to be Arizona's most scenic region.

Much of this area is part of **Cochise County,** named in 1881 in honor of the chief of the Chiricahua Apache. Cochise waged war against troops and settlers for 11 years, but he was respected by Indian and non-Indian alike for his integrity and leadership skills. Today Cochise County is dotted by small towns, many of them much smaller—and all much tamer—than they were in their heyday. It's hard to imagine now, but Tombstone, headquarters for most of the area's gamblers and gunfighters, was once bigger than San Francisco. These days it derives most of its revenue from tourism, and the wildest visitor is usually a six-year-old traveling with Granny and Gramps on a winter vacation from North Dakota.

The area's terrain ranges from the rugged forests of its mountains to the desert grasslands of Sierra Vista. Cochise County is home to six and part of the seventh—including the Huachucas, Mustangs, Whetstones, and Rincons—of the 12 mountain ranges that compose the 1.7-million-acre Coronado National Forest.

Essential Information

Tourist Information
Benson–San Pedro Valley Chamber of Commerce (363 W. Fourth St., Box 2255, Benson 85602, tel. 602/586–2842).

Bisbee Chamber of Commerce (7 Naco Rd., Box BA, Bisbee 85603, tel. 602/432–5421).

Douglas Chamber of Commerce (1125 Pan American, Douglas 85607, tel. 602/364–2477).

Tombstone Chamber of Commerce (Fremont and 4th Sts., Box 995, Tombstone 85638, tel. 602/457–3911).

Willcox Chamber of Commerce & Agriculture (1500 N. Circle I Rd., Willcox 85643, tel. 602/384–2272 or 800/200–2272).

Getting There
By Car
From Tuscon, take I–10 east to reach the southeast. When you reach the town of Benson, take U.S. 80 south (turn off at Benson) to reach Tombstone, Bisbee, and Douglas.

By Bus
Greyhound Lines (tel. 800/231–2222) has service from Tucson to Douglas and Bisbee; you'll need to book a tour if you want to take the bus to Tombstone.

By Train
Amtrak (tel. 800/872–7245) trains run three times a week from Tucson to Benson.

Guided Tours   For an in-depth look at historic sights in Tombstone and the surrounding areas, contact **Tombstone Western Tours** (4th and Allen Sts., tel. 602/457–3256 or 800/228–1224).

Exploring

The loop tour suggested below covers the highlights of the region and should take at least two days; three days would offer a more leisurely trip, perhaps with some hiking and an excursion across the border from Douglas to the pleasant town of Agua Prieta in Mexico. If your time is more limited, consider taking a day trip through Texas Canyon to Tombstone and Bisbee, or one via Willcox to Chiricahua National Monument.

Numbers in the margin correspond to points of interest on the Southeastern Arizona map.

From Tucson, head east on I–10 for approximately 63 miles, where you'll see signs telling you that you're entering **Texas Canyon.** The rock formations here are exceptional—the huge boulders appear to be delicately balanced against one another.

Texas Canyon is also the home of the **Amerind Foundation** (the name is derived from the contraction of the words "American" and "Indian"), founded by the amateur archaeologist William Fulton in 1937 to learn about Native American cultures. Take Exit 318 (Dragoon Road) off I–10 and continue southeast for 1 mile until you reach the turnoff to the Amerind Foundation, a research facility and museum housed in a beautiful Spanish-style structure built between 1930 and 1959.

Visitors to the museum are given an overview of Native American cultures of the Southwest and Mexico through well-designed rotating displays of archaeological materials, crafts, and photographs. The museum store is well-stocked with books on history and Native American cultures, as well as items created by Native American craftspeople. The adjacent Fulton–Hayden Memorial Art Gallery offers an eclectic but interesting assortment of art (mostly from the Southwest) collected by William Fulton. The beautiful natural setting and the quality of the exhibits at the foundation make a visit here a delightful as well as an educational experience. *Dragoon Rd., tel. 602/586–3666. Admission: $3 adults, $2 senior citizens and children 12–18. Open Sept.– May, daily 10–4; June–Aug., Wed.–Sun. 10–4. Closed national holidays.*

From the Amerind Foundation, return to I–10 and backtrack 12 miles to **Benson,** once the hub of the Southern Pacific Railroad and a stop on the Butterfield Stagecoach route, but now a fairly sleepy little town. As you go through Benson on I–10, watch for Ocotillo Avenue, Exit 304. It's worth a detour for the **Singing Wind Bookshop** (Ocotillo Ave., tel. 602/586–2425), located about 3 miles out of town on a ranch. It's good to call before you drive out here because the shop's proprietor runs it in her spare time (she runs the ranch, too) and doesn't always keep regular hours.

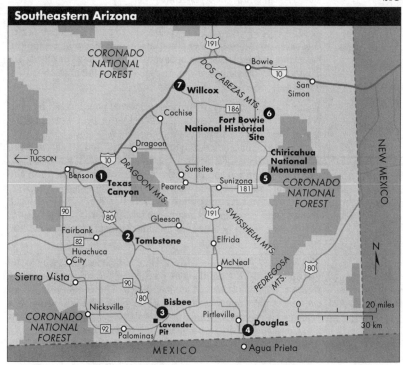

Southeastern Arizona

The unlikely location houses an excellent collection of books on Arizona wildlife, history, and geology.

Time Out   For a good green-chili burrito or a patty melt, stop in at the **Horseshoe Cafe** (154 E. 4th St., tel. 602/586–3303), which has occupied its current site on Benson's main street for more than 50 years. The neon horseshoe on the ceiling, the macramés of local cattle brands, and the large Wurlitzer jukebox all give this casual restaurant and lounge a unique Western character.

At Benson you'll pick up U.S. 80. Drive 24 miles south, through some rolling hills, to **Tombstone.** Headquarters of many of the West's rowdies in the late 1800s, Tombstone grew on the site of a wildly successful silver mine, which was discovered in 1877 by prospector Ed Schieffelin, who had been cautioned that "all you'll find there is your tombstone"—the area, originally called Goose Flats, was prone to Apache attack. He struck one of the West's richest veins of silver in the tough old hills and gave the town its name as an ironic "I told you so" to his detractors. The mine itself he called the Lucky Cuss, figuring that, indeed, he was one.

The promise of riches attracted all types of folks, including the outlaw type. Soon gambling halls, saloons, and houses of prostitution sprang up all along Allen Street. In 1881 the Earp family and Doc Holliday battled to the death with the Clanton boys at the famous shoot-out at the OK Corral. Over the past 100 years or so, scriptwriters and storytellers have done much to rewrite the exact details of the confrontation, but it's a fact that the town was indeed the scene of several gunfights in the 1880s. On Sundays, visitors are treated to replays of some of these on Allen Street.

Tombstone's rough-and-ready heyday was popularized by Hollywood in the 1930s and capitalized on by the local tourist industry in the decades that followed, but there's more to the town than the OK Corral, the souvenir shops on Allen Street, and the staged shoot-outs. "The town too tough to die" (it survived two major fires, an earthquake, the closing of the mines, and the moving of the county seat to Bisbee) was also a cultural center, and many of its original buildings remain intact. Check with the **Tombstone Chamber of Commerce** (*see* Essential Information, *above*) for a walking tour that includes several of the town's currently unmarked sights.

As you enter Tombstone, stop at **Boot Hill Graveyard,** where the victims of the OK Corral shoot-out are buried; it's on the northwestern corner of town, facing U.S. 80. The commercialism of the place may turn you off (you enter through a gift shop that sells novelty items in the shape of tombstones), but the site itself is interesting. Chinese names in one section bear testament to the laundry and restaurant workers who came from San Francisco during the height of Tombstone's mining fever. About a third of the more than 350 graves dug here from 1879 to 1974 are unmarked.

Once you've bought your tombstone-shaped yard sign, drive into town (less than 3 miles) on U.S. 80, which turns into Fremont Street. When you reach 3rd Street, head two blocks south to Toughnut Street, where the **Tombstone Courthouse State Historic Park** offers an excellent introduction to the town's—and the area's—past. The largest settlement between San Francisco and St. Louis in 1881, Tombstone was chosen as the seat of the newly established Cochise County; the courthouse built the next year was an expensive, stylish affair. Displays include a reconstruction of the original courtroom; numerous photographs of prominent—and notorious—town figures; and such area artifacts as the dozens of types of barbed wire used by local cattle ranchers. *Toughnut and 3rd Sts., tel. 602/457–3311. Admission: $2 adults, $1 children 12–17. Open daily 8–5. Closed Christmas.*

Go one block east on Toughnut and turn right onto 4th Street for the **Rose Tree Inn Museum.** Originally a boardinghouse for the Vizina Mining Company and later a popular hotel, this museum, with its 1880s period rooms and huge rose bush on the patio (listed in the Guinness Book of Records as the largest in the world), displays the gentler side of life in Tombstone. *Toughnut and 4th Sts., tel. 602/457–3326. Admission: $1.50 adults, $1.25 senior citizens with Golden Age Pass, children under 14 accompanied by adult free. Open daily 9–5. Closed Christmas.*

You'll get a more dramatic version of the town's history, narrated by Vincent Price, in the **Historama** on Allen Street, a block to the north. At the adjoining **OK Corral,** a recorded voice-over details the town's most famous event, while life-size figures of the gunfight's participants stand poised to shoot. Photographer C.S. Fly, whose studio was next door to the corral, didn't record this bit of history, but Geronimo and his pursuers were among the historical figures he did capture with his camera. Many of his fascinating Old West images may be viewed at the **Fly Exhibition Gallery.** *Allen St. bet. 3rd and 4th Sts., tel. 602/ 457–3456. Admission: Historama $2, OK Corral and Fly Exhibition Gallery $2; children under 6 free. Open daily 8:30–5; Historama shows every hour on the hour 9–4.*

Allen Street, the town's main drag, is lined with restaurants and curio shops. Many of the street's buildings still bear bullet holes from their livelier days, and some of the remaining artifacts are interesting—including the **original printing presses** for the town's newspaper, the *Tombstone Epitaph* (9 S. 5th St., tel. 602/ 457–2211), founded in 1880 and still publishing. (If the town's other newspaper, *The Nugget,* had survived instead, the Clanton boys might be mourned as martyrs today, but it was the Earp-supporting *Epitaph* and its version of history that endured.)

Two dollars will admit you to **The Bird Cage Theater** (6th and Allen Sts., tel. 602/457–3421). The displays in this former music hall, where Caruso, Sarah Bernhardt, and Lillian Russell— among others—performed, are dusty and chaotic. If you poke around, however, you can find such treasures as the 1881 Black Maria hearse that brought all the victims of the OK Corral shoot-out—and everyone else who died in Tombstone—to the Boot Hill cemetery.

Time Out Sightseeing is thirsty work, and what better place to wet your whistle than one of Tombstone's saloons? The **Crystal Palace** (Allen and 5th Sts., tel. 602/457–3611) sports a beautiful mirrored mahogany bar, wrought-iron chandeliers, and tinwork ceilings; locals come here to dance to the live country-and-western music. Those seeking solid refreshment in a historic setting might stop in for a burger at **Nellie Cashman's** (5th and Toughnut Sts., tel. 602/457–2212), a restored 1879 building.

From Tombstone, take U.S. 80 for 24 miles south to Bisbee. The drive here is a scenic one, climbing another 1,000 feet to a final elevation of more than a mile.

❸ Like Tombstone, **Bisbee** was a mining boomtown, but its wealth was in copper, not silver, and its success much longer-lived. It wasn't until 1975 that the last mine closed and the city went into decline. However, it was rediscovered in the early 1980s by burned-out city dwellers and revived as a kind of Woodstock West. The permanent population is a mix of retired miners and their families, aging hippie jewelry-makers, and enterprising young restaurateurs and antiques dealers. The three rather disparate groups seem to get along fine—Bisbee is that kind of place.

When you drive through Mule Mountain Tunnel on U.S. 80, you'll be getting close. You'll see the pretty, compact town hugging the steep mountainside on your left. If you want to head straight into town, get off at Brewery Gulch interchange. You can park here and cross under the highway, taking Main or Commerce or Brewery Gulch streets, all of which meet here.

Another option is to continue driving on U.S. 80 about a quarter of a mile to where it intersects with AZ 92. Pull off the highway on the right into a gravel parking lot, where a short, typewritten history of the **Lavender Pit Mine** can be found attached to the hurricane fence surrounding the area (Bisbee isn't big on formal exhibits). The hole left by the copper miners is huge, with piles of lavender-hued "tailings," or waste, creating mountains around it. Arizona's largest pit mine yielded some 94 million tons of copper ore out of more than 280 million tons of raw materials before the town's mining activity came to a halt. If you're interested in buying jewelry made from Bisbee Blue, the pretty turquoise stone still extracted from Lavender Pit, walk across the parking area toward the mountains to the right of the **Bisbee Blue shop.**

For a real lesson in mining history, however, you need to take the **Copper Queen mine tour.** The mine is less than ½-mile to the east of the Lavender Pit, across U.S. 80 from downtown at the Brewery Gulch interchange. Tours are led by one of Bisbee's several retired copper miners, who are wont to embellish their official spiel with tales from their mining days. They're also very capable, safety-minded people (any miner who survives to lead tours in his older years would have to be), so don't be concerned about the precautionary dog tags (literally—they're donated by a local veterinarian) issued to each person on the tour.

The tours, which depart daily at 9, 10:30, noon, 2, and 3:30 (you can't enter the mine at any other time), last anywhere from 1 to 1½ hours, and visitors go into the shaft via a little open train, like those the miners rode when the mine was active. Before you climb aboard, you're outfitted in miner's garb—a yellow slicker and a hard hat that runs off a battery pack strapped to your waist. You may want to wear a sweater or light coat under your slicker because the temperature in the mine is a brisk 47°F on the average. You'll travel by train thousands of feet into the mine, up a grade of 30 feet (not down, as many visitors expect). Those who are a bit claustrophobic might consider taking one of the surface tours that depart from the building at the same times as the mine tours (excluding 9 AM); they cover Old Bisbee and the perimeter of the Lavender Pit mine, as well as the old leaching plant. *478 N. Dart Rd., tel. 602/432–2071. Admission to mine tour $8 adults, $3.50 children 7–11, $2 children 3–6; the surface tour is $7 for everyone more than 3 years old. Open daily. Closed Thanksgiving and Christmas.*

Right across the street from the mine, in Copper Queen Plaza, is the **Mining and Historical Museum,** housed in the old redbrick Phelps Dodge general office (Phelps Dodge was the operator of the town's copper mines). The museum is filled with old photographs and artifacts from the town's mining days, and explores other aspects of the first 40 years of Bisbee's history, from 1887 to 1920. It's fun to walk out of the museum and view the same buildings you've just seen depicted inside. *No. 5 Copper Queen Plaza, tel. 602/432–7071. Admission: $3 adults, $2.50 senior citizens, children under 18 free. Open daily 10–4. Closed Christmas and New Year's Day.*

Behind the museum is the venerable old **Copper Queen Hotel** (*see* Lodging, *below*), built a century ago. It has housed the famous as well as the infamous: "Black Jack" Pershing, John Wayne, Teddy Roosevelt, and mining executives from all over the world made this their home away from home.

The Copper Queen is adjacent to **Brewery Gulch,** today a short street running north and south (walk out the front door of the Copper Queen, make a left, and you'll be there in about 20 paces) that's largely abandoned and lined with boarded-up storefronts. In the old days, the brewery housed there allowed the dregs of the beer that was being brewed to flow down the street and into the gutter.

Time Out | Café Maxie (tel. 602/432–7063), in No. 2 Copper Queen Plaza, once the Phelps Dodge General Mercantile Store and now the town's convention center, is a good place for homemade soups and sandwiches. Brightly colored parachutes are suspended from the ceiling, creating a festive, airy atmosphere. Take a trip upstairs to the rest rooms for a view of the lobby down below, with its rich copper (what else?) light fixtures and handrails.

There are no boarded-up storefronts on Bisbee's **Main Street,** which is very much alive and retailing. This hilly commercial thoroughfare is lined with appealing crafts shops, boutiques, and restaurants, many of them in well-preserved turn-of-the-century brick buildings.

From Bisbee, continue southeast on U.S. 80 until you reach **❹ Douglas,** on the U.S.–Mexico border. The town was founded in 1902 by James Douglas to serve as the copper-smelting center for the mines in Bisbee. Douglas's house, now owned by the Arizona Historical Society, is open to the public as the **Douglas/Williams House Museum** (1001 D Ave., tel. 602/364–7370). There's not much to see here and hours are limited, but there are some interesting old photographs and mementos.

The must-see historic landmark in town and still the center of much of Douglas's activity is the **Gadsden Hotel** (*see* Lodging, *below*), built in 1907. The lobby boasts a solid white Italian-marble staircase, two authentic Tiffany vaulted skylights, and a 42-foot stained-glass mural; 1,000 ounces of 14-karat gold leaf were used to decorate the capitals. When you leave the hotel and walk out onto G Street, Douglas's main thoroughfare, you'll be taking a stroll back through time; a film company shooting here recently had to do very little to make the restaurants and shop fronts fit its 1940s plot line.

Before Douglas became the smelter for Bisbee, the site was the annual roundup ground for local ranchers, Mexican and American—among them John Slaughter, who was the sheriff of Cochise County after Wyatt Earp. The 300-acre **John Slaughter Ranch/San Bernardino Land Grant** offers a glimpse of life near the border in the late 19th and early 20th centuries. This National Historic Landmark includes the Slaughter family ranch house, filled with period furnishings and old photographs, as well as a number of the ranch's original outbuildings; a car shed holds a 1915 Model T Ford identical to the one owned by John Slaughter. You can also visit ruins of a military outpost established here in 1911 during the Mexican civil unrest and maintained by the U.S. Army until 1923. Much of the ride out to the ranch is via a graded dirt road that traverses a strikingly Western landscape of rolling hills and desert scrub. *17 mi east of Douglas (from town, go east on 15th St., which turns into Geronimo Trail, and leads to the ranch), tel. 602/558-2474. Admission: $3 adults, 14 and under free. Open Wed.–Sun 10–3.*

Neither Douglas nor Agua Prieta across the way in Mexico fits the stereotype of a border town—both are clean, pleasant places. **Agua Prieta** offers well-priced Mexican goods, and shopping here involves neither haggling nor hassling. But it's easy to imagine you're far from the States when you sit in the leafy plaza at the center of town.

After touring Douglas, get back on U.S. 80 in the direction of Bisbee. It's less than ½ mile to the turnoff for U.S. 191; go north on this road for about 41 miles until you reach the intersection with AZ 181, where signs will direct you to Chiricahua National Monument, approximately 10 miles away. En route, just past the town of Elfrida on U.S. 191, you'll see a turnoff for the ghost towns of **Gleeson** and **Courtland;** there's little to see here now except a few adobe ruins, but it's an interesting side trip if you've got time—and good shocks; as you approach Gleeson, the paved road becomes rutted dirt.

The vast fields of desert grass you've passed during most of the drive are suddenly transformed into a landscape of forest, mountains, and striking rock formations as you enter the ❺ 12,000-acre **Chiricahua National Monument.** Dubbed the "Land of the Standing-Up Rocks" by the Chiricahua Apache, who lived in the mountains for centuries—and, led by Cochise and Geronimo, tried for 25 years to prevent white pioneers from settling here—this is an unusual site for a variety of reasons. The vast outcroppings of volcanic rock worn by erosion into strange pinnacles and spires are set in a forest where autumn and spring occur at the same time; because of the particular balance of sunshine and rain in the area, in April and May visitors will see brown, yellow, and red leaves coexisting with new green foliage.

Summer in Chiricahua National Monument is exceptionally wet: From July through September, there are thunderstorms nearly every afternoon. In addition, few other areas in the United States have such a variety of plant, bird, and animal life; along with the plants and animals of the Southwest, the Chiracahua Mountains also host a number of Mexican species. Deer, coatimundis, peccaries, and lizards live among the aspen, ponderosa pine, Douglas fir, oak, and cypress trees—to name just a few. This is a natural mecca for bird-watchers, and hikers have more than 17 miles of scenic trails, ranging from ½-mile to 13 miles long. At the visitor center, you can purchase a brochure describing the trails for 10¢; lists of the mammals, snakes, and birds in the region are also available, and in spring and summer rangers give interpretive talks at the visitor center or at the campground amphitheater. *Chiricahua National Monument, Dos Cabezas Route, Box 6500, Willcox 85643, tel. 602/824–3560. Entry fee: $4 per car. Visitor center open daily 8–5.*

In Chiricahua National Monument, AZ 181 turns into AZ 186. Continue north on this road for about 5 miles; you'll see signs directing you to the well-maintained gravel road leading to Bowie and the **Fort Bowie National Historical Site,** in the Dos Cabezas (Two-Headed) Mountains. A ranger station here (tel. 602/847–2500) is open daily 8–5. Admission to the site is free.

The fort and the nearby **Butterfield stage stop** played important parts in Arizona's history. The stage stop, in the heart of Chiricahua Apache land, was a crucial link in the journey from East to West in the mid-19th century. Chief Cochise and the stagecoach operators ignored one another until sometime in 1861, when hostilities broke out between U.S. Cavalry troops and the Apache. After an ambush by the chief's warriors at Apache Pass in 1862, U.S. troops decided a fort was desperately needed in the area, and Fort Bowie was built within weeks. There were skirmishes for the next 10 years, followed by a peaceful decade; then renewed fighting broke out in 1881. Geronimo, the new leader of the Indian warriors, finally surrendered in 1886. The fort was abandoned eight years later and fell into disrepair.

In order to get to the fort from the ranger station, you must take a 1½-mile unpaved footpath. The site is virtually in ruins now, but there's a small visitor center with a book-sale area, some historical displays, and rest rooms. Bring along lunch if you want to picnic at the spot where the last of Arizona's battles between Native Americans and U.S. troops was fought.

When you get back to the gravel road, take it another 6 miles north until you reach Bowie, where you'll pick up I–10. If you head west for 15 miles, you'll arrive at the turnoff for the town of **Willcox.** With fewer than 4,000 residents, Willcox is a major cattle-shipping center; its downtown looks like an Old West movie set. An elevation of 4,167 feet renders the climate here moderate in summer and a bit chilly in winter. Apple-pie fans from all over Arizona know this little town, located in an apple-growing area, as headquarters; enterprising Willcox cooks bake pies for customers as far away as Phoenix. If you visit in winter, you can see some of the more than 10,000 sandhill cranes that roost at the Willcox Playa, a 37,000-acre area resembling a dry lake bed some 12 miles south of Willcox; they come down in late fall and head north to various nesting sites in February. Also near Willcox is the headquarters for the **Muleshoe Ranch Cooperative Management Area** (tel. 602/586–7072), nearly 49,000 acres of riparian desert land in the foothills of the Galiuro Mountains that are jointly owned and managed by the Nature Conservancy, the U.S. Forest Service, and the U.S. Bureau of Land Management. You can hike out or drive out if you have a rough-terrain vehicle (the dirt road is bumpy and not well-maintained), or take one of the Jeep tours or horseback rides that can be arranged by the ranch; a variety of overnight accommodations are also available (*see* Lodging, *below*).

Stay on the I–10 frontage road and follow the signs to Willcox's historic district. Here you'll find the **Rex Allen Arizona Cowboy Museum,** set up as a tribute to Willcox's most famous native son, cowboy singer Rex Allen. He starred in several rather average cowboy movies during the '40s and '50s for Republic Pictures, but he's probably most famous as the friendly voice that narrated Walt Disney nature films. *155 N. Railroad Ave., tel. 602/ 384–4583. Suggested donation: $2 single, $3 couple, $5 family. Open daily 10–4. Closed major holidays.*

Less than a block down the street is the **Willcox Commercial Store.** Established in 1881, it's the oldest retail establishment in Arizona that's still operating in its original location; locals like to boast that Geronimo used to shop here. Today it's a clothing store, with a large selection of Western wear.

As you leave town, stop at **Stout's Cider Mill** (it's on the frontage road to I–10—roll down your windows and follow the aroma of apples and nutmeg). Across the parking lot from Stout's, the Chamber of Commerce hosts the **Museum of the Southwest,** which focuses on the life of the cowboy and the Native American in the late 1800s and early 1900s; the Cowboy Hall of Fame salutes the Arizona cattlemen. *1500 N. Circle I Rd., tel. 602/384– 2272 or 800/200–2272. Admission free. Open Mon.–Sat. 9–5, Sun. 1–5.*

To return to Tucson from Willcox, take I–10 west for 78 miles. It's an easy drive, unless you're doing it in the summertime toward the end of the day. It's best to wait until the sun has gone down and is out of your eyes.

Dining and Lodging

Bisbee **Stenzel's.** Although this small, attractive restaurant, set in a
Dining wooden cabin off the side of the road, is touted by locals for its seafood specialties, they're not really Stenzel's strongest suit. The barbecued ribs and grilled chicken breast are fine, however, and the fettuccine Alfredo is outstanding. There's a decent wine

list. *207 Tombstone Canyon, tel. 602/432–7611. Reservations advised for dinner. Dress: casual. MC, V. Closed Wed., weekend lunch. $$–$$$*

★ **Roka.** Opened in early 1993, Roka is the deserved darling of the hip Bisbee crowd. The constantly changing northern Italian-style evening menu is small, but you can count on whatever you order—chicken with ricotta and basil cannelloni, sea scallops with spinach pasta—to be wonderful. Portions are generous, and the entrée price ($8.50–$15.50) includes soup, salad, and a pasta-based main course preceded by a sorbet. The dining room, with exposed brick walls and the original 1906 tinwork ceiling, looks onto a central bar, which offers a nice selection of wines and cognacs. *35 Main St., tel. 602/432–5153. Reservations advised. Dress: casual but neat. No smoking. MC, V. Closed lunch Tues.–Sat., Sun. and Mon. $$*

Lodging **Copper Queen Hotel.** Built by the Copper Queen Mining Compa-
★ ny (which later became the Phelps Dodge Corporation) at a time when Bisbee was the biggest copper-mining town in the world, this hotel in the heart of downtown Bisbee has been operating since 1902; the upstairs halls are lined with photos of its early days. Some of the accommodations are small or oddly laid out and the walls between them are thin, but all have a Victorian charm. Ask for a room that's been renovated. Guests over the years have included a host of wild and crazy prospectors as well as more respectable types. Today's visitors are also a varied lot, as likely to include a film producer scouting locations as a retired snowbird from Minnesota. *11 Howell Ave., Drawer CQ, 85603, tel. 602/432–2216 or 800/247–5829, fax 602/432–4298. 43 rooms with bath. Facilities: pool, dining room, saloon, gift shop. AE, MC, V. $$*

The Bisbee Grand Hotel. Restored to Victorian excess in 1986, this 1906 structure on Main Street has 11 elaborately decorated accommodations. Some feature huge brass beds, others beds with lush red-velvet canopies; one suite even has a fountain with running water in its sitting room. The lodging section is adjoined by a Western saloon and "ladies parlor." In keeping with the general melodrama of the place, the Bisbee Grand runs themed murder-mystery weekends. *61 Main St., Box 825, 85603, tel. 602/432–5900 or 800/421–1909. 4 rooms and 3 suites with bath, 4 rooms share 3 baths. Facilities: bar, meeting rooms, complimentary breakfast. AE, D, MC, V. $–$$*

The Clawson House. Terrific views of the town from the sun porch, a light-filled kitchen, and generous but health-conscious breakfasts are among the reasons to seek out this B&B on Old Bisbee's Castle Rock. The owners' art and antiques collections grace a beautifully restored former residence, built in 1895 for the superintendent of the Copper Queen Mine. *116 Clawson Ave., Box 454, 85603, tel. 602/432–5237 or 800/467–5237. 1 room with bath, 2 rooms share bath. MC, V. $–$$*

Douglas **The Gadsden Hotel.** Although recently refurbished, the rooms
Lodging at this hotel—declared a National Historic Monument in 1976—
★ are rather strangely decorated: Some fine antique pieces are

thrown in among mismatched rugs, bedspreads, and drapes; the shower curtains are discordantly modern. But the accommodations, which include suites and apartments with kitchenettes, are clean, comfortable, and very reasonably priced, and the art deco public areas are beautifully maintained. The hotel bar, with its array of local brands and local characters, looks as if it's straight out of *The Life and Times of Judge Roy Bean*, which was filmed here. *1046 G Ave., 85607, tel. 602/364-4481, fax 602/364-4005. 160 rooms with bath. Facilities: restaurant, coffee shop, bar, dress shop, beauty salon. AE, DC, MC, V. $*

Pearce
Dining and Lodging
★

Grapevine Canyon Ranch. This guest ranch in the Dragoon Mountains, approximately 80 miles southeast of Tucson, adjoins a working cattle ranch. Visitors get the chance to watch—and, in some cases, participate in—real day-to-day cowboy activities. Horses for all levels of experience are on hand, and there are lots of trails for hiking this quintessentially Western terrain. Grapevine is also a good base from which to explore towns such as Douglas, Tombstone, and Bisbee, and nearby Chiricahua National Monument. Accommodations, either in adjacent cabins or private casitas, vary—some are rather plain, while others have striking Southwestern-style furnishings—but all have spacious decks and porches. There's a four-night minimum stay during peak season, two-night minimum off-season. *Box 302, 85625, tel. 602/826-3185, fax 602/826-3636. 12 rooms with bath. Facilities: pool, hot tub, riding, game room, TV/video room, gift shop. AE, D, MC, V. $$$$*

Tombstone
Dining

Bella Union. A good spot for a leisurely dinner—service is none too swift here—the Bella Union offers well-priced American standards such as steaks and chops in a nice setting. The 1881 building, off the main commercial drag, has a tastefully restored front saloon with a piano and low-key dining-room decor. An old gazette-style menu highlights breakfast combinations, blue-plate lunch specials, and a wide range of dinner entrées. Live honky-tonk revues are presented here occasionally. *401 E. Fremont St., tel. 602/457-3656. Reservations accepted but not necessary. Dress: casual. AE, D, MC, V. $$*

Longhorn Restaurant. Like most of the places in town, this one has been rigged up for the city slickers, so they'll get an idea of what it was like to grab some grub about 100 years ago in these here parts. Done in dark woods, the Longhorn is decorated with posters and artifacts from Tombstone's wilder days. Burgers, sandwiches, steaks, and Mexican dishes are available here. Service is very efficient. *Allen and 5th Sts., tel. 602/457-3405. No reservations. Dress: casual. MC, V. $*

Lodging

The Best Western Look-Out Lodge. Set off U.S. 80 on the way into town, this motel has a lot of character. The rooms feature Western-print bedspreads, Victorian-style lamps, and locally made wood-hewn clocks; all have views of the Dragoon Mountains and desert valley. A Continental breakfast is included in the rate. The front desk and switchboard close at 10 PM, so you'll need to check in and receive any phone calls before then. *U.S. 80 West, Box 787, 85638, tel. 602/457-2223 or 800/528-1234, fax*

602/457–3870. 40 rooms with bath. AE, D, DC, MC, V. Facilities: heated outdoor pool. $–$$

Tombstone Boarding House. Two meticulously restored 1880s adobes sit side by side in a quiet residential neighborhood; guests of this friendly B&B sleep in one house and go next door to have a hearty country breakfast and evening wine and cheese in the other. It's ideal for those who like the intimacy of a B&B but feel a bit odd about staying in someone's house. *108 N. 4th St., Box 905, 85638, tel. 602/457–3716. 5 rooms with bath, 2 rooms share bath. Facilities: piano and TV in living room. No credit cards. $*

Willcox   **Muleshoe Ranch.** A former late-19th-century health spa is now a
Lodging   uniquely appealing property run by the Arizona chapter of the Nature Conservancy. Accommodations vary—four furnished housekeeping casitas have kitchens or kitchenettes, baths, and linens, while one is more rustic—but all are in a beautiful natural setting on a dirt road. There's a camping area ($6 per night per vehicle; water and cold showers provided) as well as a visitor center, a nature trail, natural hot springs (for use by casita guests only), and a common room. The Conservancy runs natural-history workshops and, occasionally, guided hikes. Overnight horseback riding packages are available in fall and spring. *30 miles northwest of Willcox, R.R. 1, Box 1542, 85643, tel. 602/ 586–7072. 5 cabins, camping area. 2-night minimum stay Sept.–May and holiday weekends. No credit cards. $–$$*

Southwestern Arizona

Many folks just speed through southwestern Arizona on their way to California, but the area has much to offer travelers willing to slow down for a closer look. The turbulent history of the West is writ large in this now-sleepy part of the state. It's home to the Tohonó O'odham Indian reservation (largest in the country after the Navajo Nation's) and site of such towns as Ajo, created—and almost undone—by the copper-mining industry. Yuma, abutting the California border, was a major crossing point of the Colorado River as far back as the time of the conquistadors.

Natural history is also a lure in this starkly scenic region: Organ Pipe Cactus National Monument provides a number of trails for desert hikers, while birders and other nature-watchers will revel in the many unusual species to be observed at the little-visited Imperial National Wildlife Refuge on the lower Colorado.

Essential Information

Tourist   **Ajo Chamber of Commerce** (Hwy. 85, just south of the plaza, 321
Information   Taladro, Ajo 85321, tel. 602/387–7742). Open Mon.–Sat. 9–4:30.

Yuma Convention and Visitors Bureau (377 S. Main St., Yuma 85364, tel. 602/783–0071). Open weekdays 9–5.

Getting **There** *By Car*	Running north–south, AZ 85 to **Ajo** connects with the east–west I–8 at Gila Bend and with I–10 at Buckeye. For a scenic route west from Tucson, take AZ 86, which hooks up with AZ 85 at Why.

From the east, I–10 intersects with I–8 to **Yuma** near the town of Casa Grande; it's then a direct drive along I–8 west to San Diego. U.S. 95 is the route to take south from Las Vegas; it continues past Yuma into Mexico.

By Bus You can get to Yuma from a variety of directions via **Greyhound Lines** (tel. 800/231–2222). The **Ajo Stage Line** (tel. 800/242–9483) has bus service from Tucson and Phoenix to Ajo three times a week.

By Train **Amtrak** (tel. 800/872–7245) runs trains to Yuma from Tucson and Los Angeles three times a week.

By Plane Both **Delta Airlines** (tel. 800/453–9417) and **America West** (tel. 800/235–9292) have frequent direct flights to Yuma from Phoenix. Delta also flies nonstop from Los Angeles, and America West offers nonstops from Las Vegas.

Guided Tours **Ajo Stage Line** (410 N. Malacate St., No. 4, Ajo 85321, tel. 800/ 942–1981) runs naturalist-guided van tours to Rocky Point, the Pinacate volcanic field, the Kino missions, and other sites in northern Mexico and western Arizona.

Exploring

Numbers in the margin correspond to points of interest on the Southwestern Arizona map.

On warm weekends and especially during semester breaks, the 130-mile route from Tucson to Ajo is well traveled by cars headed southwest to Puerto Penasco (Rocky Point), Mexico, the closest outlet to the sea for Arizonans. Much of the time, however, one can go for long stretches west on AZ 86 without seeing another vehicle. A great part of the way the landscape is flat, abundant with low-lying scrub and cactus as well as mesquite, ironwood, paloverde, and other desert trees.

About 36 miles out of Tucson, you'll come to the turnoff for Kitt Peak (*see* Off the Beaten Track, *above*); to the south is the 7,730-foot Baboquivari Peak, considered sacred by the Tohonó O'odham as the home of their deity, I'itoi or "elder brother." Baboquivari sits on the eastern boundary of the Tohonó O'odham reservation, which covers some 4,400 square miles between Tucson and Ajo, stretching south to the Mexican border and north almost to the city of Casa Grande.

A little less than halfway between Tucson and Ajo, **Sells,** the tribal capital of the Tohonó O'odham, is a good place to stop for gas or a soft drink. Much of the time there's little to see or do here, but in March an annual rodeo and fair attract thousands of visitors; for details, call 602/383–2978.

At **Why,** approximately 60 miles from Sells, AZ 86 forks off into the north and south sections of AZ 85. Originally the name of the community at this Y-shaped intersection was spelled, simply and descriptively, "Y," but in 1950 the town was told that it had to have a three-letter name in order to be assigned a postal code. Hence the querying appellation that has kept travelers wondering ever since.

● Take AZ 85 north for 10 miles to reach **Ajo,** another town with a curious name. "Ajo" (AH-ho) is Spanish for garlic, and some say the town got its name from the wild garlic that grows in the area. Others claim the word is a bastardization of the Indian word "au-auho," referring to red paint derived from a local pigment.

For many years Ajo, like Bisbee to the east, was a thriving Phelps Dodge company town. Copper mining had been attempted in the area in the late-19th century, but it wasn't until the 1911 arrival of John Greenway, general manager of the Calumet & Arizona Mining Company, that the region began to be developed profitably. Calumet and Phelps Dodge merged in 1935, and the huge New Cornelia pit mine produced millions of tons of copper until the mine finally closed in 1985. With the town's main source of revenue gone, Ajo looked for a time as though it might shut down, but many retirees are now being lured here by the warm climate and low-cost housing.

Set in a desert valley flanked by low mountain ranges to the north, south, and west, Ajo is indeed a very pretty place in which to live. At the center of town and of community activities is a sparkling white Spanish-style **plaza,** designed in 1917 by Isabella Greenway, wife of the Calumet mine manager and an important figure in her own right: In the 1930s she opened the Arizona Inn in Tucson, and she was friends with such dignitaries as Eleanor Roosevelt. The shops and restaurants that line the plaza's covered arcade today are rather modest; unlike Bisbee, Ajo hasn't yet drawn an artistic crowd—or the upscale boutiques and eateries that tend to follow.

On Indian Village Road at the outskirts of town, the **New Cornelia Open Pit Mine Lookout Point** provides a panoramic view of the town's huge open pit mine, almost 2 miles wide. Some of the abandoned equipment remains in the pit, and various stages of mining operations are diagrammed at the visitors' ramada, which doubles as a real estate office. The number of buildings listed for sale—including the town hospital—comment poignantly on the gaping hole that was once the town's source of revenue.

Nearby, the **Ajo Historical Society Museum** has collected a mélange of articles related to Ajo's past from local townspeople. The displays are rather disorganized, but some of the historical photographs and artifacts are fascinating, and the museum is inside the Territorial-style St. Catherine's Indian Mission, built around 1916. *160 Mission St., tel. 602/387-7105. Admission free. Open daily 1-4.*

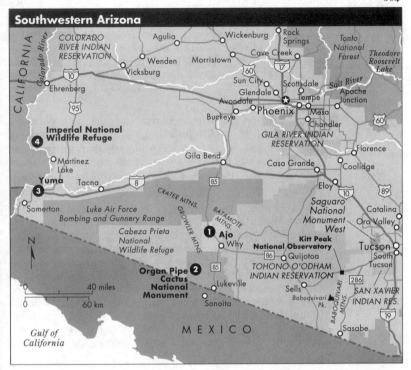

Twenty minutes from Ajo, the 860,000-acre **Cabeza Prieta National Wildlife Refuge** was established in 1939 as a preserve for endangered bighorn sheep and other Sonoran Desert wildlife. A permit is required to enter, and only those with four-wheel-drive vehicles, needed to traverse the rugged terrain, can obtain one. For additional information or for an entry permit, contact the refuge office (1611 N. 2nd Ave., Ajo 85321, tel. 602/387–6483).

Anyone interested in exploring the flora and fauna of the Sonoran Desert should head for **Organ Pipe Cactus National Monument,** abutting Cabeza Prieta but much more accessible to visitors; from Ajo, backtrack to Why and take AZ 85 south for 22 miles to reach the visitor center. The monument is the largest gathering spot north of the border for organ pipe cacti. These multiarmed cousins of the saguaro are fairly common in Mexico but rare in the States. Because they tend to grow on south-facing slopes, you won't be able to see many of them unless you take one of the two scenic loop drives, the 21-mile Ajo Mountain Drive or the 53-mile Puerto Blanco Drive, both on winding, graded dirt roads. The latter trail, which takes half a day to traverse, brings you to Quitobaquito, a desert oasis with a flowing spring. *Rte. 1, Box 100, Ajo 85321, tel. 602/387–6849. Admission: $4 per vehicle. Visitor center open daily 8–5.*

The drive from Ajo to Yuma is quick if not very picturesque: Take AZ 85 north for 40 miles to Gila Bend to pick up I–8 west. You'll come to three freeway exits for Yuma just before the California border.

❸ Many people tend to think of **Yuma** as a convenient en-route stop—these days, between San Diego and Phoenix or Tucson—and this was equally true in the past. It's difficult to imagine the lower Colorado River, now dammed and bridged, as either a barrier or a means of transportation, but up until the early part of the century, this section of the great waterway was a force to contend with. Records show that since at least 1540 the Spanish were using Yuma (then the site of a Quechan Indian village) as a ford across a relatively shallow juncture of the Colorado.

Some three centuries later, the advent of the shallow-draft steamboat made the settlement a point of entry for fortune seekers heading up through the Gulf of California for mining sites in eastern Arizona. Fort Yuma was established in 1850 to guard against Indian attacks, and by 1873 the town was a county seat, a U.S. port of entry, and an army quartermaster depot. The building of the Yuma Territorial Prison in 1876 helped stabilize the economy.

The steamboat shipping business, undermined by the completion of the Southern Pacific Railroad line in 1877, was finished off by the building of Laguna Dam in 1909, which controlled the overflow of the Colorado River and made agricultural development in the area possible. In World War II, Yuma Proving Ground was used to train bomber pilots, and General Patton readied some of his desert war forces for battle at a number of classified areas near the city. Many people who served here during the war returned to Yuma to retire, and the city's economy now relies largely on tourism. According to weather statistics, the sun shines more on Yuma than on any other U.S. city.

Most of the interesting sights in Yuma are at the north end of town. Stop in at the Convention and Visitors Bureau (*see* Tourist Information, *above*) and pick up a walking tour guide to the **historic downtown area.** Highlights include the Century House, which now hosts the **Arizona Historical Society Museum.** This adobe structure, built around 1870 and once owned by prominent businessman E. F. Sanguinetti, exhibits artifacts from Yuma's territorial days and details the military presence in the area. It's in a pretty complex with rose gardens, an aviary, small shops, and a restaurant. *240 S. Madison Ave., tel. 602/782–1841. Admission free. Open Tues.–Sat. 10–4, closed Sun., Mon., national holidays.*

If you cross the railroad tracks at the northernmost part of town, you'll come to **Yuma Crossing National Historic Landmark,** which consists of the Quartermaster Depot, the Territorial Prison, and Fort Yuma to the north. The mess hall of the former fort, later used as a school for Indian children, now serves as the **Fort Yuma Quechan Indian Museum.** Historical photographs, archaeological items, and Quechan arts and crafts, including beautiful beadwork, are on display here. *On CA 24, 1 mi north of town, tel. 619/572–0661. Admission: $1 adults, children under 12 free. Open weekdays 8–5, Sat. 10–4. Closed holidays.*

On the other side of the river from Fort Yuma, the **Quartermaster Depot,** created toward the end of the Civil War period, was responsible for resupplying army posts to the north and east. Freight brought upriver by steamboat was unloaded here and distributed by wagon overland to Arizona forts; the depot's earliest building (1853) originally served as the home of riverboat captain G. A. Johnson. Dubbed "the Williamsburg of the West" by *Arizona Highways* magazine, the site has costumed interpreters who adopt the roles of people who might have made the crossing; on the weekend, historical events are reenacted. There's a museum in the quartermaster's office, which is furnished in period pieces, as is his former residence; five covered wagons dating from the 1850s stand outside. *Off 4th Ave. between 1st St. and the Colorado River Bridge, tel. 602/329–0404. Admission: $3 adults, $2.50 senior citizens 55 and over, $2 children 6–15, $8 per family (2 adults and up to 5 children). Open daily 10–5. Closed Christmas Day.*

Head a few blocks east under the I–8 overpass to get to the most notorious—and fascinating—tourist sight in town, **Yuma Territorial Prison.** Built largely by the convicts themselves, the prison operated from 1876 until 1909, when it outgrew its usefulness. The hilly site on the Colorado River, chosen for security purposes, precluded further expansion.

Visitors gazing today at the tiny cells that held six inmates each, often in 115°F heat, are likely to be appalled, but the prison was once considered a model of enlightenment: In an era when beatings were common, the only punishments meted out were solitary confinement and assignment to a dark cell. The complex housed a hospital as well as the only library in Yuma, open to the public; the 25¢ fee charged townspeople for a prison tour financed the acquisition of new books. The inmates' food was sufficiently varied and plentiful to inspire locals to dub the place the "Country Club of the Colorado."

The 3,069 people who served time at this penal institution, the only one in Arizona territory during its tenure, included men and women from 21 different countries. They came from all social classes and were sent up for everything from armed robbery and murder to violation of the Mexican Neutrality Act and polygamy. R. L. McDonald, incarcerated for forgery, had been the superintendent of the Phoenix public school system; chosen as the prison bookkeeper, he absconded with $130 of the inmates' money when he left. Pearl Hart, convicted of stagecoach robbery, gained such notoriety for her crime that she attempted a career in vaudeville after her release.

Different groups continued to come, more or less voluntarily, after the prison closed. When the local high school burned down, classes were held for four years (1910–14) in the former hospital.

In the 1920s rail-riders took a break from the freights to sleep in the unsupervised buildings, and during the Depression the abandoned cells provided shelter for many homeless people. A number of films, including *Red River Valley*, were shot here in the 1930s and '40s. The site of the former mess hall opened as a museum in 1940, and the entire prison complex was designated a State Historic Park in 1961. *Near Exit 1 off I–8, Box 10792, Yuma 85366, tel. 602/783–4771. Admission: $3 adults, $2 juniors 12–17. Free interpretive programs at 11, 2, and 3:30. Open daily 8–5.*

A drive to the far southern end of town will take you past citrus orchards and ranches to the 40-acre **Saihati Camel Farm.** The landscape near Yuma inspired Saudi Arabia native Abdul-Wahed Saihati to raise and breed his favorite animals here, along with Arabian horses and more exotic desert-loving breeds such as oryx (antelope) and wildcats. It's fun to help feed the well-groomed, friendly dromedaries—not a biter or spitter among 'em—and to see some rare animal species, many of them purchased from the San Diego Zoo, at close range. *15672 S. Ave. 1 E (between County 15th and County 16th Sts.), tel. 602/627–2553. Guided tours $3, daily at 10 and 2. Reservations advised. Closed Thanksgiving and Christmas.*

Although shallow river steamers are no longer in operation, you can still take a boat ride up the Colorado with **Yuma River Tours** (1920 Arizona Ave., Yuma 85364, tel. 602/783–4400). Twelve-person jet-boat excursions run by Smokey Knowlton, who has been exploring the area for more than 35 years, offer a unique look at the formerly active life of the river; you glide past Indian petroglyphs as well as abandoned steamboat landings and mining camps. Tours range from one-hour trips ($12.50 per person) to full-day excursions ($49, including lunch), all departing from Fisher's Landing at Martinez Lake, 23 miles north of Yuma.

These full-day tours are the best way to visit the 25,765-acre ❹ **Imperial National Wildlife Refuge,** created by backwaters formed when the Imperial Dam was built. Something of an anomaly, the refuge is home both to species indigenous to marshy rivers and to creatures that inhabit the Sonoran Desert, which lines its banks here—desert tortoises, coyotes, bobcats, and bighorn sheep. Most of all, though, this is bird-lovers' heaven. Thousands of waterfowl and shorebirds live here year-round, and migrating flocks of swallows pass through in the spring and fall. Expect to see everything from pelicans and cormorants to Canadian geese, snowy egrets, and a variety of rarer species. Canoes can be rented at Martinez Lake Marina, 3½ miles southeast of the refuge headquarters. It's best to visit from mid-October through May, when temperatures are lowest and the ever-present mosquitoes least active. *40 mi north of Yuma off U.S. 95, tel. 602/783–3371. Admission free. Visitor center open mid-Apr.–mid-Oct. Mon.–Fri. 8–4:30; mid-Oct.–mid-Apr. Mon.–Fri. 8–4:30, Sat.–Sun. 10–4.*

Dining and Lodging

Ajo **The Mine Manager's House Inn.** Another remnant of the town's
Lodging Phelps Dodge heyday, this 5,000-square-foot, 1919 mansion
overlooks the entire town from its site atop the highest hill in
Ajo. The high-ceilinged guest rooms have period furnishings
and artwork. Full breakfasts are served on linens and fine china
in the former mine superintendent's light-filled formal dining
room. *1 Greenway Dr., Ajo, AZ 85321, tel. 602/387–6505. 5
rooms with bath. Facilities: TV and VCR in living room; coin
laundry; outdoor hot tub, evening snacks. MC, V. $–$$*
Guest House Inn. Built in 1925 to accommodate visiting Phelps
Dodge VIPs, this lodging is one of six Southwest "Bird 'n'
Breakfast Fly-Inns": Guests can head out early to nearby Organ
Pipe National Monument or just sit on the patio and watch the
quail, cactus wrens, and other warblers that visit the Sonoran
Desert. Rooms are furnished in a range of Southwestern styles,
from light Santa Fe to rich Spanish colonial. *3 Guest House Rd.,
85321, tel. 602/387–6133. 4 rooms with bath. DC, MC, V. $*

Yuma **Chretin's Mexican Food.** A Yuma institution, Chretin's opened
Dining as a dance hall in the 1930s before it became one of the first Mexican restaurants in town in 1946. Customers enter through the
back, passing the kitchen and cashier's stand, into three large
dining areas. The food is all made on the premises, right down to
the chips and tortillas. Try anything that features *machaca*
(shredded spiced beef or chicken); if you're really hungry, go for
the enchilada-style burritos, smothered with cheese and sauce.
*485 S. 15th Ave., tel. 602/782–1291. Reservations accepted ex-
cept Jan.–Mar. Dress: casual. MC, V. $*
Lutes Casino. Almost always packed with locals at lunchtime,
this large, funky restaurant and bar, at the historic North End
of town, claims to be the oldest pool hall and domino parlor in
Arizona. Decorated with photos of the bad old days, this is the
place for a brew and a burger; try the potato tacos or the "Especial" hot dog/cheeseburger combo, which tastes a lot better than
it sounds. *221 S. Main St., tel. 602/782–2192. No reservations.
Dress: casual. No credit cards. $*

Lodging **Best Western Coronado Motor Hotel.** This Spanish tile-roofed
  ★ lodging, convenient to both the freeway and downtown historical sights, was built in 1938 and is run by the son of the original
owner. Bob Hope used to stay here during World War II, when
he entertained the gunnery troops training in Yuma. Photos of
Yuma's territorial days line the walls of the hotel's restaurant,
where guests enjoy a free Continental breakfast. The rooms
have such extras as VCRs (with two free films each night), refrigerators, hair dryers, and modem phone jacks; some have
Jacuzzis and microwaves. Family suites with full kitchens are
available. *233 4th Ave., 85364, tel. 602/783–4453 or 800/528–
1234, fax 602/782–7487. 49 rooms, including 20 family suites.
Facilities: restaurant, lounge, pool, Jacuzzi, laundromat, video library, 3 gift shops. AE, D, DC, MC, V. $–$$*
Holiday Inn Express. Rooms in this motel, located near a large

shopping center, are generic but comfortable. Many complimentary extras are included in the rate: breakfast, cocktail hour, airport shuttle, newspaper, and passes to a nearby health club. All rooms have coffeemakers and refrigerators, and a number offer microwaves. *3181 4th Ave., 85364, tel. 602/344–1420 or 800/ HOLIDAY, fax 602/341–0158. 120 rooms. Facilities: pool, Jacuzzi, barbecue area, no-smoking rooms. AE, D, DC, MC, V. $*

Index

Personal Itinerary

Departure *Date*

Time

Transportation

Arrival *Date* *Time*

Departure *Date* *Time*

Transportation

Accommodations

Arrival *Date* *Time*

Departure *Date* *Time*

Transportation

Accommodations

Arrival *Date* *Time*

Departure *Date* *Time*

Transportation

Accommodations

Personal Itinerary

Arrival *Date*   *Time*

Departure *Date*   *Time*

Transportation

Accommodations

Arrival *Date*   *Time*

Departure *Date*   *Time*

Transportation

Accommodations

Arrival *Date*   *Time*

Departure *Date*   *Time*

Transportation

Accommodations

Arrival *Date*   *Time*

Departure *Date*   *Time*

Transportation

Accommodations

Personal Itinerary

Arrival	*Date*	*Time*
Departure	*Date*	*Time*
Transportation		
Accommodations		

Arrival	*Date*	*Time*
Departure	*Date*	*Time*
Transportation		
Accommodations		

Arrival	*Date*	*Time*
Departure	*Date*	*Time*
Transportation		
Accommodations		

Arrival	*Date*	*Time*
Departure	*Date*	*Time*
Transportation		
Accommodations		

Personal Itinerary

Arrival   *Date*   *Time*

Departure   *Date*   *Time*

Transportation

Accommodations

Arrival   *Date*   *Time*

Departure   *Date*   *Time*

Transportation

Accommodations

Arrival   *Date*   *Time*

Departure   *Date*   *Time*

Transportation

Accommodations

Arrival   *Date*   *Time*

Departure   *Date*   *Time*

Transportation

Accommodations

Addresses

Name	*Name*
Address	*Address*
Telephone	*Telephone*
Name	*Name*
Address	*Address*
Telephone	*Telephone*
Name	*Name*
Address	*Address*
Telephone	*Telephone*
Name	*Name*
Address	*Address*
Telephone	*Telephone*
Name	*Name*
Address	*Address*
Telephone	*Telephone*
Name	*Name*
Address	*Address*
Telephone	*Telephone*
Name	*Name*
Address	*Address*
Telephone	*Telephone*
Name	*Name*
Address	*Address*
Telephone	*Telephone*

Addresses

Name	*Name*
Address	*Address*
Telephone	*Telephone*
Name	*Name*
Address	*Address*
Telephone	*Telephone*
Name	*Name*
Address	*Address*
Telephone	*Telephone*
Name	*Name*
Address	*Address*
Telephone	*Telephone*
Name	*Name*
Address	*Address*
Telephone	*Telephone*
Name	*Name*
Address	*Address*
Telephone	*Telephone*
Name	*Name*
Address	*Address*
Telephone	*Telephone*
Name	*Name*
Address	*Address*
Telephone	*Telephone*

Addresses

Name

Name

Address

Address

Telephone

Telephone

Name

Name

Address

Address

Telephone

Telephone

Name

Name

Address

Address

Telephone

Telephone

Name

Name

Address

Address

Telephone

Telephone

Name

Name

Address

Address

Telephone

Telephone

Name

Name

Address

Address

Telephone

Telephone

Name

Name

Address

Address

Telephone

Telephone

Name

Name

Address

Address

Telephone

Telephone

Escape to ancient cities and exotic

islands  *with CNN Travel Guide, a*

wealth of valuable advice. Host Valerie Voss will take you

to all of your favorite destinations,

including those off the beaten path.

Tune into your passport to the world.

CNN TRAVEL GUIDE
SATURDAY 10:00 PMᴘᴛ   SUNDAY 8:30 AMᴇᴛ

Notes

At last — a guide for Americans with disabilities that makes traveling a delight

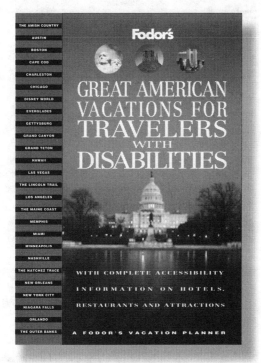

0-679-02591-X $18.00 ($24.00 Can)

This is the first and only complete guide to great American vacations for the 35 million North Americans with disabilities, as well as for those who care for them or for aging parents and relatives. Provides:

- Essential trip-planning information for travelers with mobility, vision, and hearing impairments
- Specific details on a huge array of facilities, along with solid descriptions of attractions, hotels, restaurants, and other destinations
- Up-to-date information on ISA-designated parking, level entranceways, and accessibility to pools, lounges, and bathrooms

Fodor's Travel Guides

Available at bookstores everywhere, or call 1–800–533–6478, 24 hours a day.

U.S. Guides

Alaska

Arizona

Boston

California

Cape Cod, Martha's Vineyard, Nantucket

The Carolinas & the Georgia Coast

Chicago

Colorado

Florida

Hawaii

Las Vegas, Reno, Tahoe

Los Angeles

Maine, Vermont, New Hampshire

Maui

Miami & the Keys

New England

New Orleans

New York City

Pacific North Coast

Philadelphia & the Pennsylvania Dutch Country

The Rockies

San Diego

San Francisco

Santa Fe, Taos, Albuquerque

Seattle & Vancouver

The South

The U.S. & British Virgin Islands

USA

The Upper Great Lakes Region

Virginia & Maryland

Waikiki

Walt Disney World and the Orlando Area

Washington, D.C.

Foreign Guides

Acapulco, Ixtapa, Zihuatanejo

Australia & New Zealand

Austria

The Bahamas

Baja & Mexico's Pacific Coast Resorts

Barbados

Berlin

Bermuda

Brittany & Normandy

Budapest

Canada

Cancún, Cozumel, Yucatán Peninsula

Caribbean

China

Costa Rica, Belize, Guatemala

The Czech Republic & Slovakia

Eastern Europe

Egypt

Euro Disney

Europe

Florence, Tuscany & Umbria

France

Germany

Great Britain

Greece

Hong Kong

India

Ireland

Israel

Italy

Japan

Kenya & Tanzania

Korea

London

Madrid & Barcelona

Mexico

Montréal & Québec City

Morocco

Moscow & St. Petersburg

The Netherlands, Belgium & Luxembourg

New Zealand

Norway

Nova Scotia, Prince Edward Island & New Brunswick

Paris

Portugal

Provence & the Riviera

Rome

Russia & the Baltic Countries

Scandinavia

Scotland

Singapore

South America

Southeast Asia

Spain

Sweden

Switzerland

Thailand

Tokyo

Toronto

Turkey

Vienna & the Danube Valley

Special Series

Fodor's Affordables

Caribbean

Europe

Florida

France

Germany

Great Britain

Italy

London

Paris

Fodor's Bed & Breakfast and Country Inns Guides

America's Best B&Bs

California

Canada's Great Country Inns

Cottages, B&Bs and Country Inns of England and Wales

Mid-Atlantic Region

New England

The Pacific Northwest

The South

The Southwest

The Upper Great Lakes Region

The Berkeley Guides

California

Central America

Eastern Europe

Europe

France

Germany & Austria

Great Britain & Ireland

Italy

London

Mexico

Pacific Northwest & Alaska

Paris

San Francisco

Fodor's Exploring Guides

Australia

Boston & New England

Britain

California

The Caribbean

Florence & Tuscany

Florida

France

Germany

Ireland

Italy

London

Mexico

New York City

Paris

Prague

Rome

Scotland

Singapore & Malaysia

Spain

Thailand

Turkey

Fodor's Flashmaps

Boston

New York

Washington, D.C.

Fodor's Pocket Guides

Acapulco

Bahamas

Barbados

Jamaica

London

New York City

Paris

Puerto Rico

San Francisco

Washington, D.C.

Fodor's Sports

Cycling

Golf Digest's Best Places to Play

Hiking

The Insider's Guide to the Best Canadian Skiing

Running

Sailing

Skiing in the USA & Canada

USA Today's Complete Four Sports Stadium Guide

Fodor's Three-In-Ones (guidebook, language cassette, and phrase book)

France

Germany

Italy

Mexico

Spain

Fodor's Special-Interest Guides

Complete Guide to America's National Parks

Condé Nast Traveler Caribbean Resort and Cruise Ship Finder

Cruises and Ports of Call

Euro Disney

France by Train

Halliday's New England Food Explorer

Healthy Escapes

Italy by Train

London Companion

Shadow Traffic's New York Shortcuts and Traffic Tips

Sunday in New York

Sunday in San Francisco

Touring Europe

Touring USA: Eastern Edition

Walt Disney World and the Orlando Area

Walt Disney World for Adults

Fodor's Vacation Planners

Great American Learning Vacations

Great American Sports & Adventure Vacations

Great American Vacations

Great American Vacations for Travelers with Disabilities

National Parks and Seashores of the East

National Parks of the West

The Wall Street Journal Guides to Business Travel

The only guide to explore a Disney World® you've never seen before:

The one for grown-ups.

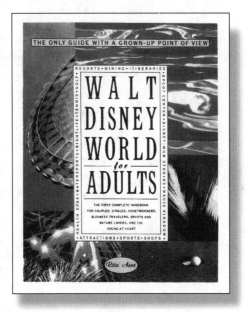

0-679-02490-5 $14.00 ($18.50 Can)

This is the only guide written specifically for the millions of adults who visit Walt Disney World® each year <u>without</u> kids. Upscale, sophisticated, packed full of facts and maps, *Walt Disney World® for Adults* provides up-to-date information on hotels, restaurants, sports facilities, and health clubs, as well as unique itineraries for adults. With *Walt Disney World® for Adults* in hand, you'll get the most out of one of the world's most fascinating, most complex playgrounds.

At bookstores everywhere, or call **1-800-533-6478**.

AT LAST

YOUR OWN PERSONALIZED LIST
OF WHAT'S GOING ON IN THE
CITIES YOU'RE VISITING.

KEYED TO THE DAYS WHEN
YOU'LL BE THERE, CUSTOMIZED
FOR YOUR INTERESTS,
AND SENT TO YOU BEFORE YOU
LEAVE HOME.

Fodor's WORLDVIEW
TRAVEL UPDATE

GET THE INSIDER'S
PERSPECTIVE. . .

UP-TO-THE-MINUTE
ACCURATE
EASY TO ORDER
DELIVERED WHEN YOU NEED IT

Fodor's
WORLDVIEW
TRAVEL UPDATE

Now there is a revolutionary way to get customized, time-sensitive travel information just before your trip.

Now you can obtain detailed information about what's going on in each city you'll be visiting <u>before</u> you leave home—up-to-the-minute, objective information about the events and activities that interest you most.

Your Itinerary:
Customized reports available for 160 destinations

Travel Updates contain the kind of time-sensitive insider information you can get only from local contacts – or from city magazines and newspapers once you arrive. But now you can have the same information before you leave for your trip.

The choice is yours: current art exhibits, theater, music festivals and special concerts, sporting events, antiques and flower shows, shopping, fitness, and more.

The information comes from hundreds of correspondents and thousands of sources worldwide. Updated continuously, it's like having your own personal concierge or friend in the city.

You specify the cities and when you'll be there. We'll do the rest — personalizing the information for you the way no guidebook can.

It's the perfect extension to your Fodor's guide and the best way to make the most of your valuable travel time.

Use Order Form on back or call 1-800-799-9609

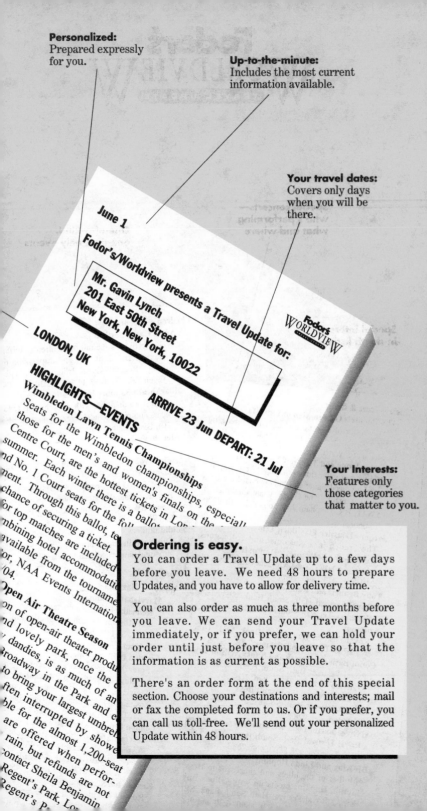

Personalized:
Prepared expressly
for you.

Up-to-the-minute:
Includes the most current
information available.

June 1

Fodor's/Worldview presents a Travel Update for:

Mr. Gavin Lynch
201 East 50th Street
New York, New York, 10022

Fodors
WORLDVIEW

Your travel dates:
Covers only days
when you will be
there.

LONDON, UK

ARRIVE 23 Jun DEPART: 21 Jul

HIGHLIGHTS—EVENTS

Wimbledon Lawn Tennis Championships

Seats for the Wimbledon championships, especiall
those for the men's and women's finals on the
Centre Court, are the hottest tickets in Lon
summer. Each winter there is a ballot
nd No. 1 Court seats for the foll
nent. Through this ballot, te
chance of securing a ticket.
for top matches are included
mbining hotel accommodatio
available from the tourname
or, NAA Events Internation
04.

Open Air Theatre Season
on of open-air theater produ
nd lovely park, once the
y dandies, is as much of an
roadway in the Park and e
to bring your largest umbrel
ften interrupted by showe
ble for the almost 1,200-seat
are offered when perfor-
rain, but refunds are not
contact Sheila Benjamin
Regent's Park, Lo
Regent's P

Your Interests:
Features only
those categories
that matter to you.

Ordering is easy.

You can order a Travel Update up to a few days
before you leave. We need 48 hours to prepare
Updates, and you have to allow for delivery time.

You can also order as much as three months before
you leave. We can send your Travel Update
immediately, or if you prefer, we can hold your
order until just before you leave so that the
information is as current as possible.

There's an order form at the end of this special
section. Choose your destinations and interests; mail
or fax the completed form to us. Or if you prefer, you
can call us toll-free. We'll send out your personalized
Update within 48 hours.

Fodor's WORLDVIEW
TRAVEL UPDATE

Special concerts—who's performing what and where

One-of-a-kind, one-time-only events

Special interest, in-depth listings

Children — Events

Angel Canal Festival
The festivities include a children's funfair, entertainers, a boat rally and displays on the water. Regent's Canal. Islington. N1. Tube: Angel. Tel: 267 9100. 11:30am-5:30pm. 7/04.

Blackheath Summer Kite Festival
Stunt kite displays with parachuting teddy bears and trade stands. Free admission. SE3. BR: Blackheath. 10am. 6/27.

Megabugs
Children will delight in this infestation of giant robotic insects, including a praying mantis 60 times life size. Mon-Sat 10am-6pm; Sun 11am-6pm. Admission 4.50 pounds. Natural History Museum, Cromwell Road. SW7. Tube: South Kensington. Tel: 938 9123. Ends 10/01.

Childminders
This establishment employs only women, providing nurses and qualified nannies to

Music — Jazz & Blues

Tito Puente's Golden Men of Latin Jazz
The father of mambo and Cuban rumba king comes to town. Royal Festival Hall. South Bank. SE1. Tube: Waterloo. Tel: 928 8800. 8pm. 7/15.

Georgie Fame and The New York Band
Riding a popular tide with his latest album, the smoky-voiced Fame and his keyboard are on a tour yet again. The Grand. Clapham Junction. SW11. BR: Clapham Junction. Tel: 738 9000. 7:30pm. 7/07.

Jacques Loussier Play Bach Trio
The French jazz classicist and colleagues. Kenwood Lakeside. Hampstead Lane. Kenwood. NW3. Tube: Golders Green, then bus 210. Tel: 413 1443. 7pm. 7/10.

Tony Bennett and Ronnie Scott
Royal Festival Hall. South Bank. SE1. Tube: Waterloo. Tel: 928 8800. 8pm. 7/11.

Santana
Royal Festival Hall. South Bank. SE1. Tube: Waterloo. Tel: 928 8800. 8pm. 7/12.

Count Basie Orchestra and Nancy Wilson Trio
Royal Festival Hall. South Bank. SE1. Tube: Waterloo. Tel: 928 8800. 8pm. 7/14.

King Pleasure and the Biscuit Boys
Royal Festival Hall. South Bank. SE1. Tube: Waterloo. Tel: 928 8800. 6:30 and 9pm. 7/16.

Al Green and the London Community Gospel Choir
Royal Festival Hall. South Bank. SE1. Tube: Waterloo. Tel: 928 8800. 8pm. 7/13.

BB King and Linda Hopkins
Mother of the blues and successor to Bessie Smith, Hopkins meets up with "Blues Boy" King. Royal Festival Hall. South Bank. SE1. Tel: 928 8800. 6:30 and 9pm

Music — Classical

Marylebone Sinfonia
Kenneth Gowen conducts music by Puccini and Rossini. Queen Elizabeth Hall. South Bank. SE1. Tube: Waterloo. Tel: 928 8800. 7:45pm. 7/16.

London Philharmonic
Franz Welser-Moest and George Benjamin conduct selections by Alexander Goehr, Messiaen, and some of Benjamin's own compositions. Queen Elizabeth Hall. South Bank. SE1. Tube: Waterloo. Tel: 928 8800. 8pm

London Pro Arte Orchestra and Forest Choir
Murray Stewart conducts selections by Rossini, Haydn and Jonathan Willcocks. Queen Elizabeth Hall. South Bank. SE1. Tube: Waterloo. Tel: 928 8800. 7:45pm

Kensington Symphony Orchestra
Russell Keable conducts Dvorak's Queen Elizabeth Hall. South Bank

Here's what you get . . .

Detailed information about what's going on — precisely when you'll be there.

Show openings during your visit

Handy pocket-size booklet

Reviews by local critics

Exhibitions & Shows—Antique & Flower

Westminster Antiques Fair

Over 50 stands with pre-1830 furniture and other Victorian and earlier items. Thu-Fri 11am-8pm; Sat-Sun 11am-6pm. Admission 4 pounds, children free. Old Royal Horticultural Hall. Vincent Square. SW1. Tel: 0444/48 25 14. 6-24 thru 6/27.

Royal Horticultural Society Flower Show

The show includes displays of carnations, summer fruit and vegetables. Tue 11am-7pm; Wed 10am-5pm. Admission Tue 4 pounds, Wed 2 pounds. Royal Horticultural Halls. Greycoat Street and Vincent Square. SW1. Tube: Victoria. 7/20 thru 7/21.

Hampton Court Palace International Flower Show

Major international garden and flower show taking place in conjunction with

Theater — Musical

Sunset Boulevard

In June, the four Andrew Lloyd Webber musicals which dominated London's stages in the 1980s (Cats, Starlight Express, Phantom of the Opera and Aspects of Love) are joined by the composer's latest work, a show rumored to have his best music to date. The 1950 Billy Wilder film about a helpless young writer who is drawn into the world of a possessive, aging silent screen star offers rich opportunities for Webber's evolving style. Soaring, aching melodies, lush technical effects and psychological thrills are all expected. Patti Lupone stars. Mon-Sat at 8pm; matinee Thu-Sat at 3pm. In-person sales only at the box office; credit card bookings, Tel: 344 0055. Admission 15-32.50 pounds. Adelphi Theatre. The Strand. WC2. Tube: Charing Cross. Tel: 836 7611. Starts: 6/21.

Leonardo A Portrait of Love

A new musical about the great Renaissance artist and inventor comes in for a London pre-_____ tested by a brief run at Oxford's Old _____ The work explores _____

Fodor's WORLDVIEW
TRAVEL UPDATE

London, England
Arriving: June 23
Departing: July 21

Spectator Sports — Other Sports

Greyhound Racing: Wembley Stadium

This dog track offers good views of greyhound racing held on Mon, Wed and Fri. No credit cards. Stadium Way. Wembley. HA9. Tube: Wembley Park. Tel: 902 8833.

Benson & Hedges Cricket Cup Final

Lord's Cricket Ground. St. John's Wood Road. NW8. Tube: St. John's Wood. Tel: 289 1611. 11am. 7/10.

Business-Fax & Overnight Mail

Post Office, Trafalgar Square Branch

Offers a network of fax services, the Intelpost system, throughout the country and abroad. Mon-Sat 8am-8pm, Sun 9am-5pm. William IV Street. WC2. Tube: Charing Cross. Tel: 930 9580.

Transworld

Interest Categories

For your personalized Travel Update, choose the categories you're most interested in from this list. Every Travel Update automatically provides you with *Event Highlights* - the best of what's happening during the dates of your trip.

1.	**Business Services**	Fax & Overnight Mail, Computer Rentals, Photocopying, Protocol, Secretarial, Messenger, Translation Services

Dining

2.	**All Day Dining**	Breakfast & Brunch, Cafes & Tea Rooms, Late-Night Dining
3.	**Local Cuisine**	In Every Price Range—from Budget Restaurants to the Special Splurge
4.	**European Cuisine**	Continental, French, Italian
5.	**Asian Cuisine**	Chinese, Far Eastern, Japanese, Other
6.	**Americas Cuisine**	American, Mexican & Latin
7.	**Nightlife**	Bars, Dance Clubs, Casinos, Comedy Clubs, Ethnic, Pubs & Beer Halls
8.	**Entertainment**	Theater—Comedy, Drama, English Language, Musicals, Dance, Ticket Agencies
9.	**Music**	Country/Western/Folk, Classical, Traditional & Ethnic, Opera, Jazz & Blues, Pop, Rock
10.	**Children's Activities**	Events, Attractions
11.	**Tours**	Local Tours, Day Trips, Overnight Excursions, Cruises
12.	**Exhibitions, Festivals & Shows**	Antiques & Flower, History & Cultural, Art Exhibitions, Fairs & Craft Shows, Music & Art Festivals
13.	**Shopping**	Districts & Malls, Markets, Regional Specialities
14.	**Fitness**	Bicycling, Health Clubs, Hiking, Jogging
15.	**Recreational Sports**	Boating/Sailing, Fishing, Golf, Ice Skating, Skiing, Snorkeling/Scuba, Swimming, Tennis & Racquet
16.	**Spectator Sports**	Auto Racing, Baseball, Basketball, Boating & Sailing, Football, Golf, Horse Racing, Ice Hockey, Rugby, Soccer, Tennis, Track & Field, Other Sports

Please note that interest category content will vary by season, destination, and length of stay.

Destinations

The Fodor's/Worldview Travel Update covers more than 160 destinations worldwide. Choose the destinations that match your itinerary from this list. (Choose bulleted destinations only.)

Europe
- Amsterdam
- Athens
- Barcelona
- Berlin
- Brussels
- Budapest
- Copenhagen
- Dublin
- Edinburgh
- Florence
- Frankfurt
- French Riviera
- Geneva
- Glasgow
- Istanbul
- Lausanne
- Lisbon
- London
- Madrid
- Milan
- Moscow
- Munich
- Oslo
- Paris
- Prague
- Provence
- Rome
- Salzburg
- * Seville
- St. Petersburg
- Stockholm
- Venice
- Vienna
- Zurich

United States (Mainland)
- Albuquerque
- Atlanta
- Atlantic City
- Baltimore
- Boston
- * Branson, MO
- * Charleston, SC
- Chicago
- Cincinnati
- Cleveland
- Dallas/Ft. Worth
- Denver
- Detroit
- Houston
- * Indianapolis
- Kansas City
- Las Vegas
- Los Angeles
- Memphis

- Miami
- Milwaukee
- Minneapolis/ St. Paul
- * Nashville
- New Orleans
- New York City
- Orlando
- Palm Springs
- Philadelphia
- Phoenix
- Pittsburgh
- Portland
- * Reno/ Lake Tahoe
- St. Louis
- Salt Lake City
- San Antonio
- San Diego
- San Francisco
- * Santa Fe
- Seattle
- Tampa
- Washington, DC

Alaska
- Alaskan Destinations

Hawaii
- Honolulu
- Island of Hawaii
- Kauai
- Maui

Canada
- Quebec City
- Montreal
- Ottawa
- Toronto
- Vancouver

Bahamas
- Abaco
- Eleuthera/ Harbour Island
- Exuma
- Freeport
- Nassau & Paradise Island

Bermuda
- Bermuda Countryside
- Hamilton

British Leeward Islands
- Anguilla

- Antigua & Barbuda
- St. Kitts & Nevis

British Virgin Islands
- Tortola & Virgin Gorda

British Windward Islands
- Barbados
- Dominica
- Grenada
- St. Lucia
- St. Vincent
- Trinidad & Tobago

Cayman Islands
- The Caymans

Dominican Republic
- Santo Domingo

Dutch Leeward Islands
- Aruba
- Bonaire
- Curacao

Dutch Windward Island
- St. Maarten/ St. Martin

French West Indies
- Guadeloupe
- Martinique
- St. Barthelemy

Jamaica
- Kingston
- Montego Bay
- Negril
- Ocho Rios

Puerto Rico
- Ponce
- San Juan

Turks & Caicos
- Grand Turk/ Providenciales

U.S. Virgin Islands
- St. Croix
- St. John
- St. Thomas

Mexico
- Acapulco
- Cancun & Isla Mujeres
- Cozumel
- Guadalajara
- Ixtapa & Zihuatanejo
- Los Cabos
- Mazatlan
- Mexico City
- Monterrey
- Oaxaca
- Puerto Vallarta

South/Central America
- * Buenos Aires
- * Caracas
- * Rio de Janeiro
- * San Jose, Costa Rica
- * Sao Paulo

Middle East
- * Jerusalem

Australia & New Zealand
- Auckland
- Melbourne
- * South Island
- Sydney

China
- Beijing
- Guangzhou
- Shanghai

Japan
- Kyoto
- Nagoya
- Osaka
- Tokyo
- Yokohama

Pacific Rim/Other
- * Bali
- Bangkok
- Hong Kong & Macau
- Manila
- Seoul
- Singapore
- Taipei

* Destinations available by 1/1/95

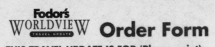
Order Form

THIS TRAVEL UPDATE IS FOR (Please print):

Name

Address

City _____ State _____ Country _____ ZIP _____

Tel # ( ) - Fax # ( ) -

Title of this Fodor's guide:

Store and location where guide was purchased:

INDICATE YOUR DESTINATIONS/DATES: You can order up to three (3) destinations from the previous page. Fill in your arrival and departure dates for each destination. <u>Your Travel Update itinerary (all destinations selected) cannot exceed 30 days from beginning to end.</u>

		Month	Day		Month	Day
(Sample) *LONDON*	From:	6	21	To:	6	30
1	From:	/		To:	/	
2	From:	/		To:	/	
3	From:	/		To:	/	

CHOOSE YOUR INTERESTS: Select up to eight (8) categories from the list of interest categories shown on the previous page and circle the numbers below:

1   2   3   4   5   6   7   8   9   10   11   12   13   14   15   16

CHOOSE WHEN YOU WANT YOUR TRAVEL UPDATE DELIVERED (Check one):
❏ Please send my Travel Update immediately.
❏ Please hold my order until a few weeks before my trip to include the most up-to-date information.
  Completed orders will be sent within 48 hours. Allow 7-10 days for U.S. mail delivery.

ADD UP YOUR ORDER HERE. *SPECIAL OFFER FOR FODOR'S PURCHASERS ONLY!*

	Suggested Retail Price	Your Price	This Order
First destination ordered	$ 9.95	$ 7.95	$ 7.95
Second destination (if applicable)	$ 6.95	$ 4.95	+
Third destination (if applicable)	$ 6.95	$ 4.95	+

DELIVERY CHARGE (Check one and enter amount below)

	Within U.S. & Canada	Outside U.S. & Canada
First Class Mail	❏ $2.50	❏ $5.00
FAX	❏ $5.00	❏ $10.00
Priority Delivery	❏ $15.00	❏ $27.00

ENTER DELIVERY CHARGE FROM ABOVE: + _____

TOTAL: $ _____

METHOD OF PAYMENT IN U.S. FUNDS ONLY (Check one):
❏ AmEx ❏ MC ❏ Visa ❏ Discover ❏ Personal Check (U. S. & Canada only)
❏ Money Order/ International Money Order
  Make check or money order payable to: Fodor's Worldview Travel Update

Credit Card —/—/—/—/—/—/—/—/—/—/—/—/—/—/—/ Expiration Date:___/___

Authorized Signature

SEND THIS COMPLETED FORM WITH PAYMENT TO:
Fodor's Worldview Travel Update, 114 Sansome Street, Suite 700, San Francisco, CA 94104

OR CALL OR FAX US 24-HOURS A DAY
Telephone **1-800-799-9609** • Fax **1-800-799-9619** (From within the U.S. & Canada)
(Outside the U.S. & Canada: Telephone 415-616-9988 • Fax 415-616-9989)

(Please have this guide in front of you when you call so we can verify purchase.)
Code: FTG   Offer valid until 12/31/95.